COMMEMORATIONS
AND THE SHAPING
OF MODERN POLAND

Commemorations and the Shaping of Modern Poland

PATRICE M. DABROWSKI

Indiana University Press
Bloomington and Indianapolis

This book is a publication of

Indiana University Press
601 North Morton Street
Bloomington, IN 47404-3797 USA

http://iupress.indiana.edu

Telephone orders   800-842-6796
Fax orders   812-855-7931
Orders by e-mail   iuporder@indiana.edu

The paper used in this publication meets the minimum requirements of
American National Standard for Information Sciences—Permanence of
Paper for Printed Library Materials, ANSI Z39.48-1984.

MANUFACTURED IN THE UNITED STATES OF AMERICA

Library of Congress Cataloging-in-Publication Data

Dabrowski, Patrice M., date
Commemorations and the shaping of modern Poland / Patrice M.
Dabrowski.
p. cm.
Includes bibliographical references and index.
ISBN 0-253-34429-8 (cloth : alk. paper)
1. Poland—History—1864–1918. I. Title.
DK4380.D33 2004
320.54'09438'09034—dc22

2004004359

1 2 3 4 5 09 08 07 06 05 04

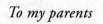
To my parents

Seize the opportunity afforded by the events of the present moment, and raise souls to the pitch of the souls of the ancients.

—Jean-Jacques Rousseau

For it rightly has been said that the stream of national life cannot constantly flow only in tiny, individual channels. If it is to survive and not get lost in the sands of wretched ordinariness, it must unite in certain solemn moments into one great majestic whole. Under such conditions, the strength of feeling intensifies in mutual excitement and clearly awakens a conviction of general solidarity, through which, of course, the internal element of the nation gains immensely.

—Bolesław Marczewski

The people will make itself by fêtes . . .

—Jules Michelet

CONTENTS

ILLUSTRATIONS

ACKNOWLEDGMENTS

That Poland was an entity that could be invented, much less reinvented, was something I began to fathom as a graduate student at Harvard University. It was there, under the tutelage of Roman Szporluk, that I first encountered the notion that nations were not immutable. This opened new vistas for historical investigation: how did people come to see themselves as Poles, and what did they understand by the term "Pole"? What repercussions did this process have for the larger East-Central European space? That I refracted these questions through the prism of historical commemorations and celebrations was in part due to the intellectual stimulation I received early on not only from Roman Szporluk, but from so many faculty members and colleagues. This book, thus, represents the fruit of my labors in the Department of History at Harvard University, first as student, then as teacher—a period that now has been relegated to the past.

While the writing of history is generally a solitary pursuit, I have profited immensely from the comments of numerous colleagues. Further necessary refinements to the manuscript were suggested by David Blackbourn, Keely Stauter-Halsted, Charles Maier, and Larry Wolff, all of whom read various drafts of the whole and offered their insights. Many others (too many to be listed here) commented on different chapters or the overall project (or both) presented in the form of papers at a number of conferences (AAASS, ASN, and PIASA), workshops (the Ukrainian Crucible series at the Harvard Ukrainian Research Institute and the Russian and East European History Workshop at Harvard), and lectures (at various universities in the United States as well as at Jagiellonian University in Poland). Parts of chapter 3 will also be familiar to readers of "Folk, Faith, and Fatherland: Defining the Polish Nation in 1883," *Nationalities Papers* 28, no. 3 (September 2000): 397–416; my thanks to Nancy Wingfield and the other editors of *Nationalities Papers* for permission to include these sections in the book. While working on the project, the Center for European Studies, the Davis Center for Russian and Eurasian Studies, the Ukrainian Research Institute, and Widener Library (all of Harvard University) provided me with space for research and interaction. Warm thanks to Mark Baker, Brian Boeck, David Brandenberger, Maria Bucur, Audrey Budding, John Czaplicka, Alex Dillon, Ben Frommer, Padraic Kenney, Jarmo Kotilaine, Robert Krikorian, Eric Lohr, Sean Martin, Terry Martin, Marshall Poe, Sean Pollock,

Tim Snyder, Corinna Treitel, and Ted Weeks for their insightful criticism and comments as well as camaraderie. John Connelly and John LeDonne helped me think through important issues, and Jagoda Hernik-Spalińska, Victor Hugo Lane, Brian Porter, and Jeff Rossman provided pertinent references and citations. Stanisław Barańczak, Bob Blobaum, John-Paul Himka, Paul Knoll, Antony Polonsky, and Piotr Wandycz have inspired and encouraged. Not least, the bright and engaged students who took my conference course, History 1523, forced me to reconsider the phenomenon of commemorations as seen throughout Europe over the past two centuries.

Research for this project was supported in part by a grant from the International Research and Exchanges Board (IREX), with funds provided by the National Endowment for the Humanities, and the United States Department of State, which administers the Title VIII Program. The Kosciuszko Foundation and Harvard University (the latter in the form of Graduate Society Fellowships, a Frederick Sheldon Traveling Fellowship, and a Whiting finishing grant) have been most supportive. None of these organizations is responsible for the views expressed.

I am also grateful to the many people and organizations abroad that took an interest in my work and provided me with advice as well as access to materials. These include the helpful staffs and scholars of the Jagiellonian Library, the State Archive in Cracow, the Jagiellonian University Archive, the Archives of the Polish Academy of Sciences (PAN) in Cracow, and the Library of the Polish Academy of Arts and Letters (PAU), the Archive of New Acts and the Main Archive of Old Acts in Warsaw, the State Archive in Łódź, and the Tatra Museum in Zakopane. Józef Buszko, Andrzej Chlipalski, Jerzy Jedlicki, Elżbieta Kaczyńska, Magdalena Micińska, Paweł Sierżęga, and Franciszek Ziejka were generous with their own materials and advice and pointed me toward useful sources. Many other scholars, in particular members of the history faculty of Jagiellonian University, offered useful comments. The Cracow Historical Museum and the various branches of the National Museum in Cracow graciously allowed me to examine artifacts from the period; they, as well as the National Museum in Wrocław and the Jagiellonian Library, provided photographs. Many thanks likewise to Roman Chmelyk of the Museum of Ethnography and Artistic Industry in L'viv, Ukraine, who showed me the lovely albums of photographs from the 1894 Exposition and provided reproductions. I am particularly indebted to Halina Florkowska-Frančić, Tadeusz Krawczak, and Grażyna Lichończak-Nurek for their unstinting support and invaluable assistance at various stages of the project.

The completion of the book would not have been possible without the help of yet others. Janet Rabinowitch and her staff at Indiana University Press have provided an ideal mixture of instruction, editing, and encouragement. The Camera Place of Wellesley, Massachusetts, reproduced a number of images for the illustrations. Bonnie Burns and Patrick Florance of the Harvard Map Collection provided invaluable assistance with the map. And the Watson Institute for International Studies at Brown University, my new academic home, has proven to be a congenial and supportive work environment as I tie up the remaining loose ends of this project.

Beyond the academic world remains a group of individuals to whom I owe much; they have provided the necessary balance in my life. My family has encouraged me in all my endeavors. My parents not only were among the first to read through the entire dissertation but provided extensive—and much-appreciated—editorial comments; my siblings have provided moral support. Closer to home, my husband and daughter put up with years of graduate study (which I began when my daughter entered kindergarten), countless conferences, and (somewhat fewer) research trips abroad without complaint. Natalie suffered through fifth grade in Poland so as to accompany me during my dissertation research, gaining unique insight—and Polish fluency—in the process. Despite the absences and the challenges posed by a wife whose work never seems to end (for such is academe), Janusz has been a solid rock of support. I owe them both more than I can say.

I also wish to acknowledge a special debt to my earliest mentors. I have been lucky to have had three sets of "parents," one natural and two "adoptive," all of whom gave me the confidence to set high goals for myself. With profound gratitude, thus, I dedicate *Reinventing Poland* to George and Mary Dabrowski, Richard and Regina Spurgeon, and Jerzy and Maria Kruczała.

Providence, R.I.
August 2003

COMMEMORATIONS
AND THE SHAPING
OF MODERN POLAND

Introduction

A crown, a scepter, a pair of spurs, a pile of bones—a treasure, chanced upon on June 14, 1869. The royal remains of Casimir the Great (1333–70), the only Polish monarch awarded that designation, had been discovered in Wawel Cathedral. At the time, minor repairs were being made to what had long been thought to be only a cenotaph, or monument, to the Polish king. While inspecting the foundation, a workman dislodged a stone, revealing an unexpected interior. Here lay what remained of King Casimir the Great, the last member of the Piast dynasty that had founded the Polish state.

Were he alive to meet the generation of Poles that peered into his tomb, King Casimir would have been surprised at the state of his kingdom. Political conditions had changed enormously in the space of five hundred years. The Polish state enlarged and strengthened by Casimir had been expanded further under the Jagiellonian dynasty to embrace the Grand Duchy of Lithuania, with its East Slav and Lithuanian populations, resulting in a country that stretched from the Baltic nearly to the Black Sea. Yet, by the mid-nineteenth century, this large East-Central European state—the Polish-Lithuanian Commonwealth—no longer existed, having been partitioned by Russia, Prussia, and Austria nearly a century before the discovery of King Casimir's final resting place.

Still, to say that no Poland existed in 1869 would in a sense be incorrect. References to this entity—to Poland—proliferated among those for whom the name had significance: the Poles themselves. Absent from the political map of Europe, Poland continued to exist in the minds of those who considered themselves Poles. And, although divided among three empires, with brethren in emigration elsewhere in Europe as well as across the Atlantic Ocean, nationally conscious Poles strove to maintain and foster a sense of national identity.

Signs of this can be seen in the reaction to the discovery of the royal remains. It was decided that these relics of the past deserved a solemn and public reburial. The ceremony was turned into a national event, as Poles from all over came to pay their respects to the renowned king. Following church services in the center of Cracow (Kraków, Krakau), representatives of Poles from local and regional organizations processed in silence to Wawel Cathedral, after which the remains of the Polish king were placed once again in their tomb. Still, the peaceful celebration had its detractors.[1] Polish commemorations were a touchy business. The last anniversaries celebrated publicly in the Polish lands, in 1860 and 1861, had emboldened Poles to rise up against Russian rule. The memory of the failed January Insurrection of 1863–64 was fresh enough to cause some Poles to hope in 1869 that no more royal remains would be discovered. Others feared a worsening of conditions for Poles elsewhere. These fears were not without foundation. The Cracow commemoration caused the Russian government to retaliate by announcing an imperial decree that turned the Warsaw university, the so-called Main School (*Szkoła Główna*), into a Russian university—this despite the fact that subjects of the tsar kept their distance from the festivities, so as not to be noted by the army of tsarist informers that did attend.[2] Celebrations that reminded the world that a strong and independent Polish state had once existed could prove costly.

This encounter of nineteenth-century Poles with a direct, tangible, and glorious past nonetheless proved stimulating. The impact of the reburial extended far beyond the confines of Cracow to those who were unable to attend the event, inspiring a number of publications and leading to the popularization of Wawel Cathedral as a site of a new kind of pilgrimage. It was as though these ancient remnants possessed a magical power to inspire and mobilize the nation. In the words of one writer, "The appearance of the great king among the living . . . had in it something mystical, summoning, as it were, faith in the future by recalling the past. . . ."[3] Could public recollections of the nation's past help Poles to transcend their partitioned present—and perhaps improve their chances for a united future?

The spontaneous commemoration of Casimir the Great in 1869 was simply the first of many public festivities in this period prepared by and for the Polish nation. Their Janus-like nature—one face looking toward the past, the other toward the future—made such celebrations quite attractive to a number of activists eager to foster a sense of identity for the partitioned nation. With anniversaries of influential individuals and important historical events to celebrate, late-nineteenth-century Poles found numerous occasions for similarly public commemorations of their interpretations of the nation's past.

THE AGE OF COMMEMORATIONS

The Poles were by no means the only people celebrating their past at this time, as the literature on commemorations makes clear. The final decades

of the "long nineteenth century"—to borrow Eric Hobsbawm's term—
might well be termed the commemorative age. Across Europe, much attention was being paid to national rituals and traditions, many of which, according to Hobsbawm and Terence Ranger, were being invented or shaped
in this period. For the British, this heyday of commemorations began when
Queen Victoria was proclaimed empress of India in 1877; elsewhere in the
West it was coterminous with, for example, the Third Republic in France
and the rule of William II in the new German Empire. This period coin-
cides with the development of "official nationalisms" in Europe, which
rode on the backs of earlier popular national movements. It marked not
only the height of imperialism, as the subdivision of Africa attests. New
trends of democratization and nationalism, the seeds of which had been
planted during the French Revolution, were pushing the boundaries of allegiance from the dynasty in the direction of the more problematic concept
of nation.[4]

Other advances of an increasingly modern age propelled the commemorations of this period into a genuine public sphere. Improved transporta-
tion and the wider reach of mass media enabled more people to view and
participate in the festivities. The technological advancements of the late
nineteenth century, combined with a degree of competitiveness among
states, lent these demonstrations a greater currency than ever before. Political developments during recent years and decades—the creation of Italy,
the unification of Germany, and the wars that made these possible—had
undermined any sense of stability regarding state borders and challenged
multinational empires to justify their existence. These are the types of conditions, according to Hobsbawm, that facilitate the "invention of tradition":

> We should expect it to occur more frequently when a rapid transformation
> of society weakens or destroys the social patterns for which "old" traditions
> had been designed, producing new ones to which they were not applicable,
> or when such old traditions and their institutional carriers and promulgators
> no longer prove sufficiently adaptable and flexible, or are otherwise elimi-
> nated: in short when there are sufficiently large and rapid changes on the de-
> mand or the supply side.[5]

When successful, state celebrations lent an air of stability, strength, and permanence, their carefully scripted rituals designed for international as well as
domestic consumption.

A mix of new and old, celebrations need not have furthered any progressive cause. In many cases, large multinational states such as Great
Britain, Austria-Hungary, and Russia continued to celebrate the birthdays,
coronations, and anniversaries of their monarchs, more or less as they al-

ways had. For example, practically every Sunday, churches in the Russian Empire were obliged to remind the faithful of greater or lesser anniversaries connected with the Romanov dynasty.[6] These were designed to keep the Russian rulers in the minds of the broader public. In Austria-Hungary, Emperor Francis Joseph ruled long enough to celebrate a half-century at the helm, and the name days, birthdays, and anniversaries of him and his family members were regular fixtures on the imperial calendar. Such celebrations tended to be more traditional.[7]

Rituals and symbols connected with other anniversaries had a more contemporary ring. In the case of British ceremonials, for example, coronations (the now-familiar ritual that was "invented" at this time) were transformed from "remote and inaccessible events" to publicly appreciated signs of empire—this despite the growing political (not symbolic) irrelevance of the monarch.[8] The way such events were celebrated in late imperial Russia, however, signaled something different. For example, the commemorative impulses of the last Romanovs, Alexander III and Nicholas II, belied a desire to return to the seemingly less complicated Muscovite past. This, they imagined, had been the heyday of Russian absolutism, entirely free of the plots and revolts that plagued their sprawling empire. Garish onion domes reminiscent of the Muscovite architecture of Saint Basil's Cathedral were imported into neoclassical Saint Petersburg, where they adorned the Temple of the Resurrection of Christ on the Blood, erected on the place where Tsar Alexander II had been assassinated. This idealized view of the pre-Petrine, pre-Westernizing Russian past also affected the architecture of the chapel dedicated on the anniversary of the tercentenary of Romanov rule in 1914.[9] These commemorative memorabilia were architectural anachronisms full of nostalgia for a distant past and out of place in the imperial capital.

The examples cited above involved official celebrations of more traditional anniversaries: coronations, anniversaries, and funerals. During the same period, various governments and activists also staged anniversary celebrations of a more "national" character. No longer a monarchy, Republican France exchanged dynastic celebrations for the annual holiday of July 14, Bastille Day (although the political opposition continued to rally around the figure of Joan of Arc). In the newly united Germany, the victory at Sedan in 1870 that had led to the unification of a new and powerful state gained currency in the public sphere. Beyond Europe, regular celebrations of the Fourth of July and Memorial Day became part of the American commemorative landscape in the years following the Civil War.[10]

While these fetes often sought to fuse the dynasty, state, or empire with the nation, national interpretations not sanctioned or organized by the respective authorities also gained public attention. The celebratory public sphere proved no government monopoly. Many commemorations were initiated and supported by members of the general public, who proclaimed individuals such as Pushkin in Russia, Michelet in France, or Schiller and Bismarck in Germany worthy of national celebration.[11] The respective governments found themselves reacting to these initiatives. In the minds of many activists, such nonroyal figures personified important qualities of the collective hero celebrating them: the nation. It is this type of celebration, of potential interest to the nation as a whole, that concerns us here.

For commemorations could potentially play an important role in the making of nations. This was significant in a period where the peasants of even a relatively advanced country such as France, as Eugen Weber has made clear, were still being turned into Frenchmen. The visual and communal nature of many of these events was of particular value in this regard. Commemorations incorporated a wide range of activities representing a number of genres, the fact of which has the added boon for the historian of requiring forays into a variety of disciplines. Celebrations involved—among other things—the unveiling of great historical canvases and bronze monuments, the public reading and dissemination of historical novels, plays, and anthems in forms that reached a broad swath of society. In this way, they were more accessible to the illiterate than the printed word. They also served as miniature history lessons—perhaps no surprise, as the academic study of the historical past (if one is to date this phenomenon, as does Benedict Anderson, from the establishment of chairs in history) was barely half a century old in the most advanced parts of Europe.[12] The historical content of the commemorations could be a revelation for others besides uneducated peasants. This was particularly true in regions where the history that was taught was that of the triumphant empires and not of the ethnic minorities within. For example, most Poles were not taught "Polish" history at all during this period. In addition, Polish historiography was in its infancy, with the first historical journal founded only in 1887.[13] This meant that knowledge about the Polish past tended to come from legends and historical novels, such as those written by Józef Ignacy Kraszewski (the subject of chapter 1). Commemorations, thus, served as a means of conveying an interpretation (or multiple interpretations) of the historical record via a variety of media to a broad and diverse constituency.

Commemorations were also highly politicized, even contested, events. As John Gillis has asserted in his introduction to a collected volume dealing with commemorations, "commemorative activity is by definition social and political, for it involves the coordination of individual and group memories, whose results may appear consensual when they are in fact the product of processes of intense contest, struggle, and, in some cases, annihilation."[14] This raises the question of the usefulness of commemorations for nation-building. It turns out that much of the recent literature on the nineteenth century suggests that, instead of unifying disparate constituencies, celebrations often exacerbated divisions within societies. Writing about the celebrations of 1848 in the German lands, Jonathan Sperber declared that "the one thing that the symbolic discourse of national unity could not express was the unity of the nation"; Charles Rearick noted the fears of French officialdom that spontaneous "celebration" would metamorphose into "contestation."[15] The thesis of Alon Confino's monograph on the Sedan Day celebrations in Württemberg likewise highlights their divisive nature. If one of the main goals of organized celebrations is, according to Peter Carrier, the "diffus[ion] and implant[ation of] a specific interpretation of the past," to what extent were such commemorations successful?[16] Could public opinion really be "coerced" (Carrier's term) or manipulated in this way? Indeed, were public celebrations worth the investment of time, talent, and treasure they diverted from other nation-building endeavors?

Polish historical commemorations of the late nineteenth and early twentieth centuries suggest that they were. That self-conscious recollections of the past contributed to the construction of a modern Polish nation is the thesis of the present work. Historical commemorations of illustrious Poles and famous events were part of a process of rediscovering the past and finding its usefulness for the present. Public celebrations became a venue for Polish national activism, replacing less attractive alternatives: armed insurrection and peaceful yet apolitical organic work. While anniversaries publicly celebrated by the Poles during this period were often "accidental" (that is, they reflected the occurrence of round anniversaries rather than any particular Polish predilection for an event or person), many nonetheless became part of a canon of anniversaries that would be featured in the decades to come as quintessential embodiments of Polish national identity. New interpretations of the past helped to expand the target public to include those who historically would not have been considered members of the nation. This in turn reinforced the notion that the Polish nation was being updated in keeping with the demands of an increasingly modern age, while popular and well-attended festivities gave rise to a more palpable sense of national unity and strength. In short, commemorations helped to make Poles "national"—an outcome that was hardly inevitable or predetermined.

In order to understand the particular significance of commemorations for the Poles, we must turn to the specific conditions—political, social, and ideological—that helped shape late-nineteenth-century East-Central Europe and affected the course of Polish commemorations. What follows is a review of the state of the nation, beginning with its unique partitioned and "stateless" predicament and ending with what may almost be termed a "nationless" predicament. Two important facets of the historical legacy—the fact of Polish partition and the century of foreign rule—hindered Polish nation-making. The process was further complicated by the need to make the transition from what remained of a relatively inflexible, premodern, caste identity to a more elastic, modern, national one. The story of how the Polish nation was able to make that transition is in part a story of how Polish activists were able to build upon past traditions while finding more creative ways to further the national cause.

POLISH PREDICAMENTS

The conditions for commemorating that existed for the Poles were hardly those enjoyed by Britons, Germans, or Russians. That the "short, tight, skin of the nation" was being stretched "over the giant body" of each of Europe's multinational empires did not bode well for those subjects who did not identify with the ruling nationality.[17] Indeed, during this same period, many smaller nationalities were trying to turn themselves into full-fledged nations. Czechs, Slovaks, Finns, Estonians, Lithuanians, and others were engaged in a process of identity formation, generally beginning with an emphasis upon cultural characteristics—native literature and folklore—and moving in the direction of a mass-based national and political identity. This process has been analyzed most notably by Miroslav Hroch, who produced a typology of national movements of such small nations.[18]

Yet do the Poles belong in this category of small nations? Seeing the Poles as a more hybrid entity, Hroch labeled them a "transitional" nation.[19] Sharing qualities of both large and small nations, the Poles were in a unique situation. Despite the fact that their country had ceased to exist, they were not a nation without a past but rather, in Marxist terms, a "historic" nation. Prior to the partitions, the Polish state had numbered among the larger political entities of Europe and boasted a population that was multi-ethnic and multi-denominational; it was home to Jews, Ukrainians, Belarusians, Lithuanians, and Germans (not to mention Tatars and Armenians) as well as to Poles. Nineteenth-century Polish activists, thus, grappled with a uniquely Polish predicament: that of having the mind of a large nation in a stateless body.

They also had to deal with the effects of nearly a century of partition, which could not help but work against the development of a pan-Polish consciousness. Each of the three partitioned territories—which, for brevity's sake, I will call Russian Poland, Prussian Poland, and Austrian Poland —gradually became integrated into the economy and life of its respective empire. By the last third of the nineteenth century, the distinctiveness of these regions was unmistakable.

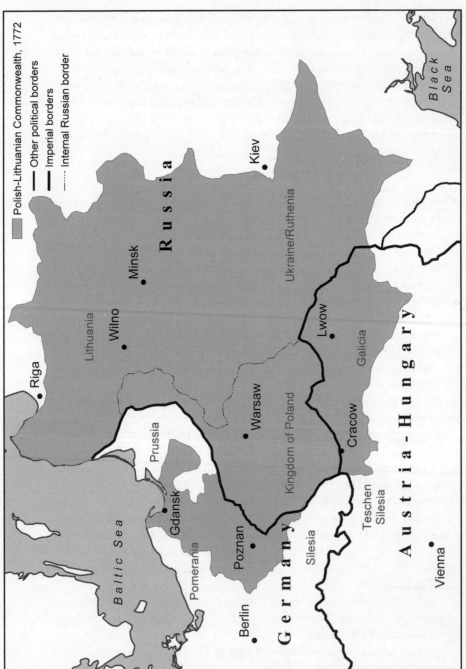

Map of the partitioned lands, ca. 1880. The dark borders reflect the imperial reality; the shaded area approximates the "Poland of the mind," the pre-partition (ca. 1772) borders of the Polish-Lithuanian Commonwealth. *Prepared by Patrice Dabrowski.*

The largest piece of the former Polish-Lithuanian Commonwealth, controlled by Russia, consisted of two parts. The first was the Kingdom of Poland—also known as the Congress Kingdom, as a result of its creation at the Congress of Vienna in 1815. It had begun as an independent kingdom, with its own constitution, parliament, citizenship, borders, even army—albeit under the rule of Alexander I of Russia. That the Russian tsar was only King of Poland led to tensions between the two polities, which had different understandings of how states were to be governed. Two major insurrections in the kingdom during the nineteenth century ultimately resulted in its demotion to the status of a Russian province after 1863. These central Polish territories represented the most industrially advanced of the partitioned lands as well as of the Russian Empire proper.

The rest of the territories seized by Russia in the eighteenth century lay further to the east. Poles referred to this region as the eastern borderlands (*kresy*), while the Russian authorities called it the Western Region or Recovered Territories. Instead of the predominantly Polish population of the Congress Kingdom, the borderlands were ethnically, linguistically, and denominationally diverse: there one found islands of Polish and Jewish urban populations in a vast sea of Lithuanian, Belarusian, and Ukrainian peasants.[20] Despite this diversity, Polishness had made deep inroads in this territory. Polish language and culture had actually gained a stronger foothold in the eastern borderlands in the early part of the nineteenth century through the efforts of Adam Czartoryski, the curator of the Wilno (Vilnius) educational district. Many of Poland's most ardent patriots—including the Romantic poet Adam Mickiewicz (discussed in chapters 3 and 5)—came from precisely this region. After the Insurrection of 1863–64, the tsarist government strove to strengthen the "Russian" element in these lands.[21] The peasantry of both the Kingdom of Poland and the Western Provinces was finally emancipated as well.

The people and lands associated with Prussian Poland (part of the German Empire after 1871) looked rather different. Poles with the strongest ties to the old Polish-Lithuanian Commonwealth resided in West Prussia (which became part of a unified province of Prussia/Preussen) and Poznania (Provinz Posen), the latter being the part of Prussian Poland most identified as Polish. The territories under German rule were the most agriculturally advanced part of the former Polish lands. On the whole, they also had the most nationally conscious population. This, paradoxically, was the contribution of the *Kulturkampf* unleashed against the Catholics—and Poles—of Prussia by Bismarck in the 1870s. The unification of Germany led many Poles, who earlier might have considered themselves "Prussian Poles" (that is, loyal subjects of the Prussian king), to reconsider their relationship to the state.

That this multinational state increasingly sought to define itself in national terms eventually prompted the rediscovery of "ethnic" Poles (or, perhaps more accurately, non-Germans) within the empire: the peoples of the Baltic regions of Pomerania and East Prussia and the industrial stronghold of Silesia to the south. As the century progressed and national consciousness increased, these peoples and territories—which had not been part of a Polish state since medieval times—would become a bone of contention: Germans as well as Poles strove to transform these minorities into members of their respective national groups.

Despite (or perhaps because of) this preoccupation with the national in the new Germany, Austrian Poland proved to be the part of the former Polish-Lithuanian Commonwealth where most public celebrations took place. The Habsburgs labeled their territorial gains Galicia (more precisely, the Kingdom of Galicia and Lodomeria), after an ancient Slavic province to which the Habsburgs laid a rather feeble historical claim. Separated from much of the rest of Austria-Hungary by the Carpathian Mountains, Galicia was undeniably the most economically backward part of the former Polish lands and the most "premodern" in its social structure. However, Galician Poles had gained the most propitious conditions for national and political development, having managed to win a degree of autonomy within the Austrian half of the empire after the *Ausgleich,* or Compromise, of 1867. Essentially in charge of their own crown land, the Polish gentry (*szlachta*) continued to dominate the impoverished and numerous peasantry, emancipated in 1848 but only just beginning to see itself as free. By ethno-linguistic standards, the peasants of western Galicia would be considered primarily Polish, while those of eastern Galicia were mostly Ruthenes (today's Ukrainians); at the beginning of my story, neither had any real sense of national identity.

Three partitions, with disparate levels of social, economic, and political development in three very different empires, presented a very real challenge to those who imagined one united nation. Still, Poles had two traditions upon which to build: their memory of political independence and the nation's military heritage. The experience of statehood was never so distant for Poles during the one hundred–plus years of partition when ties to the past had been severed. A degree of continuity in political autonomy was maintained by a series of smaller states—the Duchy of Warsaw, the Congress Kingdom/Kingdom of Poland, the Free City of Cracow—and only really became circumscribed in the 1860s. Nor had Poles forgotten how to fight for their freedom: regular outbursts of armed insurrection—the Kościuszko Insurrection of 1794, the November Insurrection of 1830, smaller movements in 1846 and 1848, the January Insurrection of 1863—punctuated the Poles' "long nineteenth century" of bondage. The national idea was

+ third tradition of positive work by the beginning of the 20th century

being championed by practically every generation of Poles, each involved in some armed attempt at regaining genuine Polish statehood.

Paradoxically, the final third of the nineteenth century represented the first lull in post-partition history. No insurrections sent further generations of Polish activists to emigration abroad or banished them to Siberia.[22] Did this mean that Poles had lost interest in working toward political independence? This book argues that they did not. While the failure of the 1863 uprising clearly placed a damper upon insurrectionary initiatives, it likewise provided the nation with a chance to develop new strategies, even to re-shape itself. Not as quick to rise up in arms, Polish patriots now opted for a different approach.

POLISH HEARTS, POLISH HISTORY

Already in 1772, on the eve of the partitions, the Polish nation had received prescient advice from Jean-Jacques Rousseau. Anticipating Russian oppression of the Poles, he urged the latter to do whatever was necessary to "establish the republic in the Poles' own hearts."[23] Rousseau recommended that the Poles maintain their ancient customs and introduce new, purely Polish ones. His advice calls to mind more recent scholarship on national development concerned with the "invention of tradition" and "imagined communities."[24] Rousseau encouraged Poles to celebrate past deeds to ensure that "the stor[ies] of their glorious episode[s]" would be "carved in sacred characters upon each Polish heart" and foster national institutions that would inspire ardent love for the fatherland.[25] Some of this advice seemed to have been followed not long after Rousseau gave it: witness the eighteenth-century celebrations of the centennial of the Relief of Vienna and the creation of a National Education Commission, the first such organization in Europe.[26]

The need for such forms of nation-building was even more pressing in the late nineteenth century. Poles confronted the long-standing division of the nation into three parts, each ruled by a different empire, as well as the rampant transformations of the modern age, with increasing urbanization, industrialization, and mass migrations. Various initiatives within Polish society sought to cope with these challenges. New approaches gave priority to building up the strength of the nation, economically and socially, instead of seeking political gains through insurrectionism. First taking hold in the lands under German control, these approaches—known as organic work and positivism—were developed further in the lands under Russian control by Poles such as Aleksander Świętochowski and garnered support in Galicia. The failure of the 1863 insurrection led many Poles to emphasize the strengthening of the national organism over military prowess. Without such grassroots work, they believed, even a successful Polish insurrection would likely bring the Poles only a temporary victory, as they would have no basis upon which to consolidate their political gains.

Organic work and positivism had one great drawback, however: like all doctrines emphasizing material well-being, they could be used to espouse an apolitical stance. Extrapolating from these doctrines, Poles might be exhorted to resign themselves to a subnational or ethnographic existence and cooperate fully with the partitioning powers. This essentially seemed to be the program of influential conservatives in each of the three empires. Such cooperation, referred to as tri-loyalism, was supposed to provide the Poles in each partition with material advantages in exchange for their being loyal subjects of their respective emperors. Indeed, society's increasing acceptance of the reality of partition and imperial rule was one of the greatest hurdles facing those who sought to promote national identity. Were Poles to privilege regional or imperial allegiances, the nation would be reduced to mere historical status—a remnant of a premodern past with no relevance for the present.

Polish national activists, thus, were challenged to find a means of overcoming the inertia of tri-loyalism while avoiding both the Scylla of insurrectionism and the Charybdis of organic work. Yet another major hurdle faced the nation—insofar as there was one. For most of those whom today we would call Poles hardly felt themselves as such. It is all too easy for us to project national identity into the past, to assume that those who later became citizens of the Second Polish Republic after World War I thought of themselves as Poles when there was no Polish state. This was hardly the case. Relatively few "Poles" thought of themselves in national terms. Those who did were likely to fall into the nationally conscious category that Hroch would term "patriots."[27] These patriots were a small, if significant, subset of the body of Polish speakers in East-Central Europe: Łepkowski estimates—some believe rather optimistically—that around 1870, approximately 30–35 percent of the Polish-speaking population (speaking limited Polish, in some cases) was conscious of being Polish.[28] Such was the situation after nearly one hundred years of partitioned existence. Descendants of the old Polish nation, peasantry, or burghers had had ample time to opt for different identities. They could choose to assimilate into the dominant imperial group, speak German or Russian—or instead call themselves Ukrainians, Belarusians, Lithuanians, and the like. Or—and this, as Jeremy King has shown, is even more likely—they could have amassed quite a collection of equally interchangeable identities (local, regional, confessional, linguistic, cultural, imperial, perhaps even national) from among which they could pick and choose, as the situation required.[29] Based upon a conscious decision to privilege national over other allegiances, the modern national view was the exception, not the rule. Patriots were Poles by choice, people for whom the fate of the nation rated high on the list of priorities.

Who, then, were the patriots? Those whose identities were most tightly intertwined with the former Polish state were descendants of the nobility. This is true in particular for the masses of petty noblemen whose claim to distinction lay in their political membership in the nation—the "noble nation." (The premodern state had been based upon the "noble nation," consisting entirely of a relatively broad—9 to 10 percent of the population—ethnically heterogeneous stratum, descended from the chivalric estate.[30]) Many of their less well-to-do descendants lost their status after the partitions, the imperial powers reluctant to give privileges to those who lived like the peasants around them but professed a chivalric heritage. Others lost their land holdings on account of revolutionary activities. Disenfranchised, they formed the core of what came to be known in the mid-nineteenth century as the intelligentsia. Having the most to gain from the reestablishment of a Polish state, these Poles were the most natural activists. The déclassé nobility was joined by members of what elsewhere would become a full-fledged bourgeoisie, of native as well as foreign descent: a number of Czechs, Germans, Hungarians, and others who settled in these lands chose to identify themselves with the Polish nation and cause.

While the natural basis of the nation was the intelligentsia, the greatest potential force for the nation was the peasantry. The most numerous element within the old Polish-Lithuanian Commonwealth, peasants were perceived as Poles in the making. Their emancipation, completed in the mid-1860s, gave villagers an opportunity to see themselves in a new light. Would they become Poles, though? After all, the developments underscored by Eugen Weber—the establishment of a network of roads and railroads, conscription into the army, and universal schooling—within the various empires exerted a different pull on the folk.[31] If Norman or Breton peasants could be turned into Frenchmen, why could not Silesian or Galician peasants assimilate to an imperial identity, with their primary allegiance to the emperor?

This was a genuine threat. The Polish peasant as yet had little consciousness of his Polishness.[32] I call him Polish, for his dialect was closest to that literary language; but, for the most part, he did not identify with those he called Poles: the lords, the nobility, the gentry. A social chasm separated villagers, political nonentities, from their lords, and the emancipation of the peasantry in the nineteenth century hardly narrowed that divide. Even the right to participate in the political process, bestowed upon Galician villagers in 1848, failed to engage the peasantry in the affairs of the nation. With only an indirect vote, easily enough manipulated by the lord or his henchmen or purchased with sausage and vodka, the Galician peasant remained essentially indifferent to the entire process. He remained, in his own words, a "Mazurian," distinct from the "Poles" in the manor or town, and he was more likely to profess allegiance to the good emperor in Vienna than desire the restoration of a Polish state. Indeed, many peasants found the thought of Poland most frightening, for more than anything else they feared the return of serfdom, which they associated with Polish rule. Winning over the peasant to the national cause, thus, was not going to be an easy task.

Not only the peasantry had to be won over to Polish nation-building. The aristocracy, having the most to lose in case of rebellion against the partitioners, often preferred to adjust to the new conditions and reinforce its privileged status. Its concept of Polishness, heavily influenced by its Latin education and cosmopolitan perspective, distinguished it from the rest of society. This is seen by its peculiar understanding of what actually constituted the Polish past, as described by the writer Stefan Żeromski. For many aristocrats, the "Polish, holy, inviolable tradition" consisted of family relations: they treated Polish history as a glorified family tree, reveling in marriages, alliances, and the like among the "historic" (noble) families of the Polish state—often with the non-Polish nobility of other European states, including those perceived as enemies of the Polish state.[33] Members of the aristocracy were most likely to be adherents of the doctrine of tri-loyalism, which allowed them to maintain their historic ties to the highest imperial spheres while still claiming a leading role within their respective partition.

This attitude as well as this interpretation of history were incomprehensible to many nineteenth-century Polish activists. In their view, the hallmark of Polishness was the desire for freedom from tyranny. Emphasizing deeds and accomplishments to which a broader swath of society could relate, they recalled names, places, and symbols connected with the oppressed but heroic Poles' fight for freedom. These Polish "realms of memory" consisted of names such as Kościuszko and Mickiewicz or shorthands for the failed insurrections such as manacles, the "smokes of fires" (*dymy pożarów* —an image from a revolutionary song), and the Warsaw citadel (where so many insurrectionists had been imprisoned).[34] According to these activists, not bloodlines but ideological lineages were important: those who fought for Poland were the true makers of history.

This recasting of the very definition of history stood at the heart of the Polish commemorative impulse. National heroes and past experiences (in particular, significant battles and other manifestations of national independence) formed the slogans behind which the nation was to rally. Yet the immediate goal had changed. Armed uprising was no longer an option. Had the insurrections succeeded, Poles might have found themselves in a situation not unlike that of Italy, where the state was created before the nation, according to the famous dictum, "We have made Italy: now we must make Italians."[35] Their failure encouraged Poles to try something new: to give priority to nation-building from within. Thus, despite this focus on the military and insurrectionary legacy, Poles were exhorted not to rise up in arms but rather to use their energies in a new way. To foster a sense of nationhood that transcended the partitions, Polish activists needed to attract the nationally indifferent, those who ranked other allegiances ahead of the nation, to the national cause.

In this task, history could help. The past, it could be argued, was extremely pertinent to a stateless nation. Polish history provided a sense of national continuity, linked present generations with their forefathers, and helped them to identify with past deeds and goals. Furthermore, it could be used to connect the descendants of all residents of the Polish-Lithuanian Commonwealth, noble and plebeian, and unite across the artificial divides —social and political as well as physical—that separated them. Nineteenth-century Poles, thus, had a chance to turn what had formerly been the province of the nobility into a concept embracing the full range of a modern, socially differentiated nation. The creation of a stronger nation, many hoped, would eventually lead to the re-creation of a Polish state.

This new nation-building strategy of historical commemorations combined the best of two former Polish approaches: it availed itself of the pragmatic, constructive potential of organic work while engaging the heart and emotions as well. This new potent hybrid belies the simplistic categorization of all Polish politics as falling into either the "idealist" or "realist" camp.[36] Indeed, new scholarship views organic work not as a political program or alternative to armed insurrection but as something more fundamental: as a means of mobilizing society in the direction of creating a genuine civil society—a hallmark of a modern society.[37] What these commemorations show is that Polish "idealism" and "realism" both were very much alive in the commemorative endeavor—indeed, as they were, to varying degrees, in the various political programs of the late nineteenth century. One might even venture to say that it was the combining of both "idealist" and "realist" trends, and thus increasing the attraction of this new means of bringing the nation to the fore, that made commemorations so powerful. This new brand of Polish "defiance" was tempered by concrete deeds that were designed to bring the nation up to the level of other nations. In this way, one can think of commemorations as a constructive, creative, yet intensely national variant of organic work—an attempt at national modernization, Polish style.

COMMEMORATIONS
AND NATION-BUILDING

This study of Polish nation-building under conditions of national partition is informed by a number of approaches, theoretical and empirical, to the study of nations and nationalism,[38] festivals and celebrations,[39] monuments and symbols,[40] concepts of collective memory,[41] myths and national mythologies,[42] and the like. Looking at national commemorations also offers a means of transcending traditional approaches to Polish history that offer a partition-by-partition look at the events of the nineteenth century. Such regionalizations of the Polish past cannot answer a crucial question: if the Poles' experiences of partition were so different, how did they manage to come together so easily to form a united state after World War I? An examination of the nation's evolution during the crucial decades preceding the outbreak of war, seen through the prism of a shared and commemorated past, sheds more light on this subject.

The construction of the modern Polish nation has been a topic of interest to intellectual historians, as demonstrated by the recent work of Brian Porter, Tomasz Kizwalter, and others. Works that focus solely on the musings of intellectuals, however, cannot account for the emergence of nationalism as a mass movement.[43] Polish nation-making was not a monopoly of philosopher-kings but rather a pursuit conditioned by the opinions, actions, and reactions of the general public. Certainly this was true as of the last decade of the nineteenth century, when Polish activists were confronted with a new reality: the emergence of mass politics. What moved the masses was rarely—if ever—the logic of ideas. Seeking to win converts for their cause, the activists involved needed to make their conceptions of the nation *popular*. Polish nation-making was not a top-down phenomenon, in which a narrow group of elites dictated to the masses the shape of the nation, but a two-way street. By considering the actual political situation in the three partitions as well as taking into account a broader range of voices in the public sphere, this book represents an attempt to present the phenomenon in all its messy reality.

This investigation of Polish nation-making through the study of historical commemorations fills a gap in Polish historiography. Despite a number of essays and articles dealing with aspects of individual commemorations, there is no monograph treating the broader phenomenon of historical celebrations in Poland.[44] While the present work does not pretend to be comprehensive, it contextualizes the commemorations in a way that chronicles of individual celebrations cannot. This method allows me to ascertain why some anniversaries became great public events, while others—ostensibly of equal importance to Polish history—garnered less attention or had less impact on the nation as a whole. For not all anniversaries were created equal. The subject matter of some was considered more valuable at the time by the organizers, keen on promoting their own agendas. Other anniversaries were conveniently "forgotten," thus demonstrating Renan's statement that being a nation required some kind of collective forgetting.[45]

Casting a wider net across the commemorative impulse of the age also reveals the way in which these occasions to celebrate were variously used or manipulated over time.

The political usefulness of commemorations reminds us of the historical significance of celebrations as part of the fabric of the past, of a given time and place. Certain events or people had a special resonance for nineteenth-century Poles, which is what makes this examination so different from sociological or ethnographic studies of festivals. The way the festivities took place tells us much about the existing constellation of power, both within the internal social and political structure as well as within the various empires. The historical context is extremely important: who organized and/ or controlled the events, who attended them, how symbols were interpreted, and—in the case of the Poles—to what extent the nation was permitted to celebrate at all.

This broader look at the commemorative impulse among the Poles likewise highlights the changing fortunes of various political players in the last decades before World War I. My investigation calls into question some assumptions about the impetus for these celebrations, particularly as concerns those celebrated within Galicia. Recent literature on the province continues to credit the group I would identify as tri-loyalists—the so-called Cracow conservatives—with initiating the great national anniversary celebrations.[46] A closer investigation of the celebrations, however, paints a more subtle and interesting picture. Commemorations proved to be a natural field for political contestation: the liberal democratic opposition—the true initiators of the celebrations—tilted with the conservatives, who sought to control, even limit, the celebrations. The political fortunes of both groups changed over the course of these decades, however: both were increasingly marginalized by those who sought most vigorously to create a pan-Polish politics that could resist the centripetal pull of Vienna, Berlin, and Saint Petersburg. Commemorations, thus, both reflected and contributed to the decline (or increased irrelevance) of notable politics and the rise of this new mass politics, a phenomenon seen in other parts of Central and Eastern Europe at this time.[47]

While the Poles' use of commemorations may conjure up images of "inventing" identities or "imagining" nations, it also demonstrates the limits of invention. Notions of what it meant to be a Pole did not emerge out of nowhere: the Polish elites involved availed themselves of preexisting building blocks—episodes, images, symbols from the past—that suited their conception of the nation. For, although there was no "master plan" for Polish nation-making, over the course of these decades the contours of a new phenomenon emerge: Poles were becoming more "national." Ultimately, commemorations contributed to the nation's reconfiguration, or "reinvention": this new, modern entity would be augmented by peasants, workers, and others newly conscious of their Polishness. Yet, paradoxically, this broadening of the nation was accompanied by a narrowing. Other descendants of the inhabitants of the Polish-Lithuanian Commonwealth—Lithuanians, Ukrainians, Belarusians, Jews—would find themselves increasingly marginalized. The multi-ethnic, multi-denominational "noble nation" —the "Poland" of the pre-partition period—was transformed into a more homogeneous ethnic community, and the old "Polish" history became the purview of the new, ethnically Polish nation.

This nation-building process had other ramifications for the Polish community. Through public celebrations of historic events and illustrious individuals, Poles were able to transcend borders, interact with compatriots from other regions, establish a national discourse, turn growing numbers of peasants into nationally conscious citizens, and raise the visibility of the nation. The commemorations highlighted important aspects of the life of the partitioned nation, illuminating nineteenth-century perceptions of the state of the Polish community and its place in Europe. Furthermore, these celebrations were one of few means by which the political divide between the three empires could be traversed collectively. Thanks in part to these celebrations, Poles were better prepared for the outcome of World War I: a state of their own.

Indeed, the process of remembering the past contributed significantly to Polish nation-building in the last decades before the reconstitution of a Polish state after the war. Was it really a coincidence that Poles such as pianist Ignacy Jan Paderewski, novelist and Nobel laureate Henryk Sienkiewicz, and politicians Roman Dmowski and Józef Piłsudski—all of whom, as we shall see, figured prominently in the celebrations of this period— played key roles in raising the Poles' international profile during World War I? With the organizational skills, national outreach, and networking honed during the celebrations, the Polish nation was better prepared to seize the moment during the war and fight—both in the realm of diplomacy as well as on the battlefield—for its independence.

THE AGE OF POLISH COMMEMORATIONS

A decade after the reburial of Casimir the Great, the nation had recovered sufficiently from the failed insurrection to take a renewed, active interest in its future. My study begins precisely then, with a pathbreaking commemoration that in turn emboldened Poles to find other persons and events worthy of honoring. That the year 1879, and not 1869, has been selected as a starting point reflects important changes in conditions for the Poles. The creation, under Prussian aegis, of the German Empire in 1871 was one of them. The Russo-Turkish War of 1877—a conflict that threatened to undermine the alliance between the partitioning empires of Germany, Austria, and Russia that guaranteed the continued partitioned status of the Poles—was another. While the war did not result in an international conflagration, it did thrust a sharp wedge into the alliance that held the German, Austrian, and Russian Empires together. Bismarck's redistributive work as an "honest broker" at the Congress of Berlin hardly pleased the victors: Tsar Alexander II was disillusioned by the lack of German support for his endeavors and wrote a sharp letter to his uncle, the German emperor William I. War seemed imminent in the summer of 1879, and Bismarck sought an alliance with Austria-Hungary.[48] That the signing of the Dual Alliance between these two states on October 7 coincided with the first of our celebrations, the Kraszewski jubilee in Cracow, adds to the sense of the dawning of a new era.

Other conjunctures held promise for the Poles. The same decade witnessed the rise of destabilizing threats to one of the partitioning empires from within. Like the tsar himself, Russian liberals and Pan-Slavs were discontented with the outcome of the Russo-Turkish War, and they were increasingly disenchanted with the state of Russia. The final years of the 1870s witnessed the growth of internal opposition to the tsarist regime. From the nihilism of the 1860s, extremism among the intelligentsia led to the Russian populist movement, which spun off an even more radical organization called the People's Will. This launching of the "socialist-revolutionary terror" in 1878 would plague the Russian government for the next three years, culminating in the assassination of Alexander II in 1881.[49] The vulnerability of the Russian government must have been sensed by the Poles living both inside and outside of the empire: April 1879 saw an attack on the life of the tsar.

While all gatherings of Poles remained suspect in Russia and the newly united Germany, conditions in Galicia became more favorable for celebrations. Since the end of the 1860s, the winds of change had been blowing in the Galician Poles' favor. After the Compromise of 1867 divided the Habsburg lands into a Dual Austro-Hungarian Monarchy, the Poles won concessions that gave them a degree of self-rule within their own province. Polish replaced German as the official language of administration and in the schools (1869), allowing for the repolonization of the universities in Cracow and Lwów (Lemberg/L'viv/Leopolis), and the Poles were allowed to establish an Academy of Arts and Letters (Akademia Umiejętności) in Cracow as well. More closely allied with and supportive of the monarchy, Poles increasingly found positions within the imperial government. All of these changes vastly improved the relative situation of Galicia vis-à-vis the other partitions, where denationalization policies (part of the reaction to the 1863 insurrection in the Kingdom of Poland and connected to the *Kulturkampf* in Bismarck's Germany) constantly threatened the Poles.

Other developments within the Austrian half of the empire also had an impact. Less than two months before the first commemoration, a major change took place in Vienna. After a decade of rule, the German liberals lost control of the government. Under the new government of Count Eduard Taaffe, conservatives and clericals moved again to the fore, with Czechs entering the cabinet for the first time since the compromise.[50] Liberalism and centralism were increasingly eclipsed by decentralization and the acknowledgment of national differences.

The commemorations I study, thus, took place in an age in which Polishness was suspect in Germany and Russia while given some latitude in Austria-Hungary. Not surprisingly, Galicia proved to be the most conducive site for Polish celebrations; commemorations helped to revitalize the ancient capital of Poland, Cracow, where the largest public commemorations were held.

A select number of commemorations form the background for this study of Polish nation-building. I have chosen to focus on notable public celebrations with a broad reach and impact, events more likely to involve a wide variety of Poles, both socially and geographically. The three parts of the book reflect three distinct periods: the 1870s and 1880s, the 1890s, and the decades of the twentieth century preceding the outbreak of World War I. Each chapter presents a commemoration or cluster of commemorations.

Part 1 consists of two chapters in which the parameters of large public commemorations are established. I begin with the jubilee of Polish historical novelist Józef Ignacy Kraszewski in 1879. Attracting Poles from all over the globe, the writer's jubilee helped to elevate the city of Cracow, Austrian Poland's "second metropolis" (behind the provincial capital of Lwów), to the status of spiritual capital of the nation.[51] The next major event (the subject of chapter 2) was the 1883 commemoration of the Relief of Vienna, the rescue of the capital of the Holy Roman Empire by the Polish king John Sobieski. This celebration essentially resulted in foreign policy initiatives—if one can speak of a nation without its own state having such powers—designed to remind the world of Polish contributions to Catholicism and the West. In both sets of commemorations, the contributions of artists brought the festivities to another level. The Sobieski anniversary likewise sheds light on the organizers' attitudes toward the peasantry as a whole and Ruthenian peasants in particular.

The celebrations discussed in part 2 represent the "mature" stage of commemorating—coinciding with, and affected by, the advent of mass politics in the region. The 1890s witnessed a string of commemorations that involved an increasingly large spectrum of Polish society. Celebrations of the Polish Romantic poet Adam Mickiewicz both began and ended that decade: the translation of his remains to Wawel Castle in Cracow took place in 1890 (the subject of chapter 3), and the one hundredth anniversary of his birth was celebrated in 1898 (chapter 5). The same decade witnessed a series of centennial celebrations connected with the disappearance of the Polish state from the map of Europe: the anniversary of the Constitution of May 3, 1791, the Targowica betrayal and the partitions of Poland, as well as the Kościuszko Insurrection of 1794. These are discussed in chapter 4. In these chapters, the dramatis personae of the earlier commemorations (comprised primarily of Galician political, intellectual, and cultural elites) encountered new forces: Poles abroad, an increasingly conscious and organized peasantry, as well as Polish politicians and activists from both German and Russian Poland. Reflecting different political agendas, all involved parties strove to shape the commemorations to suit their own visions of the nation.

Part 3 comprises the commemorations of the first decades of the twentieth century. They bring to light important national perceptions of the Poles' relationships with their neighbors, such as the Germans, visible in the renewed celebrations of the anniversary of the Battle of Grunwald in 1902 and 1910 (the latter represented the largest of all celebrations of the partition period). These commemorations are the subject of chapter 6. Chapter 7 deals with manifestations of renewed interest in the Poles' military legacy in the years preceding the outbreak of World War I: in 1913, anniversaries of both the 1863 insurrection and the death of the heroic Napoleonic officer Prince Józef Poniatowski were celebrated. These events were marked by the participation of Polish paramilitary organizations, whose swelling ranks were to provide active recruits for the conduct of the war that would lead to the reestablishment of a Polish state in 1918.

Various themes transcend chapter boundaries. Given the historical connection of commemorations with religious celebrations, attitudes of the Catholic Church—always of interest where "Polish" matters are concerned—are discussed repeatedly. The celebrations themselves are laden with symbolic meaning, represented through ritual, rhetoric, and artistic expression; we will see the varying role played by contemporary artists and novelists. Of particular note are signs of the relationships between and attitudes toward neighboring peoples (such as Ukrainians and Jews) as well as the nations associated with the ruling dynasties. In an age of increasing modernization, the participation of various segments of society would prove significant, as would the emergence of the new political forces that would come to shape the Brave New (national) World of Polish independence, just around the corner as I finish my narrative but already very much in the minds of Polish activists.

Part One

THE EARLY PERIOD

ONE

Polish Phoenix:
The Kraszewski Jubilee of 1879

The 1879 celebration of the writer Józef Ignacy Kraszewski in Cracow has been called the "first pan-Polish manifestation of the national spirit."[1] It brought about what some considered a miracle: a coming together of Poles that showed no signs of turning into revolution. This gathering countered stereotypes of the nation still in currency after the Insurrection of 1863–64. Even the foreign press expressed its wonder: "In what . . . lay the attraction that caused this unprecedented unity among all estates, all parties of the nation; what was the magnet that attracted guests from all corners of former Poland and even from America and Australia to this half-forgotten capital of kings; and what kind of talisman saved this holiday . . . from dangerous incitements of misfortune?"[2] Political and social unity in celebration; Poles arriving from all over the globe; and disaster averted—all these were accomplishments of the Kraszewski jubilee. The means by which Poles came together to commemorate one of their own illustrate the way such festivities were perceived by many members of the nation: as a new form of nation-building. Those who traveled to Cracow for the festivities had not armed rebellion but more constructive aims in mind.

First, however, they needed to overcome several obstacles. The Austrian garrison town of Cracow seemed an unlikely host city for a major national event, particularly when the city's influential conservatives liked neither Kraszewski nor the idea of public celebrations. Likewise, was there any reason to believe that the partitioning powers—Russia, Germany, and Austria-Hungary—would allow Poles a *national* celebration? A Polish celebration of "mere" cultural significance—the honoring of a writer—could not be written off as an inconsequential event by any of Poland's partitioners:

The reason for a congress could be completely literary, but its character could not be exclusively so. Poland is . . . a question so completely political and thorny that in everything that concerns it . . . there must be a political element; and where we . . . saw Kraszewski's literary jubilee, the Russian and Prussian government had to see a congress of Poles from all three zones.[3]

Do what they might, Poles, by their very status as national minorities within the three empires, could not put on a show of national unity without turning heads. In many ways, thus, the celebration does seem miraculous: for the degree of national unity that was attained; for the fact that the partitioning powers allowed Poles from their lands to participate in the festivities; and for the impact this commemoration had on a sleepy corner of Habsburg Austria, now roused from its lethargy and renewed in its commitment to its Polish heritage. The Kraszewski jubilee attests to the emergence of new forces and strategies within the Polish community that cast the honorand, city, and nation in a different light.

WHY KRASZEWSKI?

The idea of commemorating Kraszewski's fifty-year career as a writer first occurred to a group of writers and publishers congregating at the residence of Adam Pług (the pen name of Antoni Pietkiewicz), the editor of *Kłosy* (Sheaves), a popular illustrated weekly, in 1877.[4] That the impetus came from Warsaw writers reflects their relative strength as well as their admiration of Kraszewski. Despite the perennial problems of Russian censorship, Warsaw was the publishing metropolis of the Polish nation. The intelligentsia flocked to the last capital of Poland, where numerous journals, newspapers, and publishing houses afforded the chance of gainful employment. Educated Poles associated themselves with different periodicals, the editorial bureaus of which often served as centers of social and cultural life.

Kraszewski was no stranger to the Warsaw intelligentsia. Although in exile since the January Insurrection, he continued to play an active role in the intellectual life of the nation. Remembered today mainly for his historical novels, Kraszewski was a cultural jack-of-all-trades. A sometime editor of papers and journals, he also wrote articles for numerous periodicals, exhibited competence in the fields of art history and Polish history, tried his hand at painting, as well as illustrated some of his own books. Kraszewski was a tremendously prolific writer, averaging over five volumes a year; many of his novels were translated into foreign languages, including German, French, Italian, Dutch, Russian, Czech, and Slovak.[5] Polish editors constantly sought the right to publish his writings, which, given his émigré status, were often published anonymously or under pseudonyms (the most famous of which was B. Bolesławita).

The idea of feting Kraszewski soon caught on in various circles. A string of celebrations in 1878 served as an "overture" to the main festivities in Cracow and gives some indication of the breadth of Kraszewski's popularity. From Dresden to Bydgoszcz (Bromberg), Inowrocław (Inowrazlaw), Pleszew (Pleschen), Poznań (Posen), and Toruń (Thorn) in the German Empire; the cities of Kielce, Łódź, and Płock in the Kingdom of Poland; the Siberian town of Irkutsk, the Russian capital of Petersburg in the north, and Kharkov (Kharkiv) and Odessa in the southwest of the Russian Empire proper; the east Galician towns of Brody, Przemyśl, Stanisławów (Ivano-Frankivs'k), and the region's capital, Lwów—all these localities saw fit to honor the Polish writer.[6] One commemoration involving (unofficial) representatives from all three empires took place in the Tatra Mountains: the Tatra Association (Towarzystwo Tatrzańskie) renamed the entrance to the picturesque Kościeliska Valley "Kraszewski's Gate" and unveiled an inscription to that effect in August 1879.[7]

Why so much interest in celebrating the writer? Other accomplished Poles also celebrated jubilees, which were plentiful during this period. Furthermore, most national commemorations—as we shall see—did not fete living Poles but rather focused on personages and events of the past. What made Kraszewski so special as to warrant this far-reaching public display of respect, turning his jubilee into an event of national, even international, importance?

The Kraszewski jubilee represented more than a tribute to an illustrious career. The way the writer was presented to the general public attests to the organizers' sense of the special nature of this celebration. Kraszewski was turned into a symbol of the nation as a whole. A Pole from German Poland noted, "Kraszewski is popular, venerated and admired by the nation because he is its truest and most faithful reflection, because he is a writer exclusively and thoroughly national."[8] Indeed, Kraszewski's life had reflected its turbulence and shared its woes. His knowledge of the formerly Polish lands of the *kresy* (the easternmost part of the former Commonwealth incorporated into Russia proper after the partitions), his experience of Warsaw and the January Insurrection, and his familiarity with the fate of Poles in all three empires (having lived in Austria as well as Germany) enabled him to be seen as the embodiment of the nation.

In addition, there were lessons to be learned from the writer—lessons that reflected the desire of the honorand to emphasize values he hoped fellow Poles would cherish. This Kraszewski made clear at the festivities in Dresden, where he stated that he accepted the honor "only as proof of your love for the language, for the past, for education."[9] Reflecting the needs of a modern Polish society, these elements were highlighted by commemoration organizers. A modern language, capable of expressing every modern thought, was the first. Here Kraszewski's ability to wean the nation off French novels was crucial. As one contemporary put it: "Kraszewski taught us to read Polish, and . . . he also gave us something to read in Polish."[10] Kraszewski's historical novels provided Poles with a sense of their own history at a time when they were not being taught their own history in schools.

Kraszewski's popular works helped to bring history to an increasingly broad spectrum of society. As one unabashed fan declared, "There is no more popular writer in Poland than Kraszewski; whoever knows how to read knows his name."[11] There is a degree of truth in this hyperbole, for Kraszewski provided a type of literature that interested not only the educated nobility and intelligentsia but also newly literate peasants. The fact that Kraszewski's works were read across the whole of the old Poland also provided a crucial bond for Poles, separated by political boundaries imposed by the partitioning powers.

The writer's advocacy of organic work was also presented as worthy of emulation. It was hoped that Kraszewski's diligence and prodigious output might inspire other Poles to similarly productive lives. Kraszewski agreed with this interpretation: his task, he said, had always been to awaken and strengthen the spiritual life of the nation, to encourage persistent, peaceful work in all areas.[12] By singling this writer out for praise, the nation could be shown to be more levelheaded than the stereotype of rebellious Poles would admit. Linking Kraszewski with organic work also made the jubilee more palatable to tri-loyalists—to those Poles who stressed the need to remain loyal subjects of the three partitioning states. By focusing on organic work, they could remain faithful to their respective sovereigns, as self-improvement was a desirable aim for residents of any state. Thus, before the main festivities began, interpretations of Kraszewski and his jubilee were being consciously shaped to make both of them palatable to the nation at large.

CELEBRATING KRASZEWSKI IN CRACOW

The regional celebrations mentioned above were limited and private, even when, as in the case of the Zakopane festivities, Poles from other empires took part. Polish activists sought a more accessible physical locus that would allow for a public celebration of the Polish writer on Polish soil. For the reasons advanced earlier, Galicia—and Cracow in particular—held the most promise as a site for national festivities.

That the city was reinvigorated by the celebration can best be shown by reviewing its sad state prior to 1879. Cracow was hardly a modern metropolis. Situated neatly between the three empires, it had been a lively center of regional interaction and trade in the early nineteenth century when it was a tiny but independent entity, the Free City of Cracow. A failed attempt at insurrection on the part of a small group of Polish noblemen in 1846 drastically altered its fate. Incorporated into the Austrian Empire, Cracow was demoted to the status of borderland outpost and subordinated to Lwów, the capital of Galicia and the seat of provincial government. The former capital of the medieval Polish state had become marginalized; in the vast Austrian Empire, it was just another provincial town.

Lacking economic and political significance, Cracow's attraction was limited to the members of the partitioned Polish nation, for whom it still had sentimental value. The city's sole claim to distinction lay in the surviving monuments of the medieval Polish state, for the most part unrenovated. The heart of the town, the large main market square (Rynek Główny), was defined by its border of storied residences, home to burghers and aristocrats. Its centerpiece was the dilapidated Old Cloth Hall (Sukiennice), its crumbling Renaissance facade obscured by a blight of market stalls and shops in the adjacent square. From the marketplace, a narrow road led to Wawel Hill, where both castle and cathedral overlooked the meandering Vistula River at their feet. The ancient cathedral, enlarged by the addition of royal chapels over the centuries, boasted a national pantheon of sorts: its crypts contained the tombs of Polish royalty, clergymen, and military leaders (the last from the early nineteenth century). Most of the crypts, however, were inaccessible to the public.

These national monuments seemed irrelevant to the Austrian garrison town that Cracow had become. Far from being a tourist site, the royal castle housed Austrian troops and was encased by modern military fortifications. These and other changes made to the city's appearance under foreign occupation had destroyed or blighted some of the Poles' remaining cultural inheritance. Cracow's fifty thousand inhabitants seemed suspended in time; the city held little relevance for the modern world. But not for long. Soon it would be said that the choice of Cracow as a site for a national celebration was apt, "for Cracow is a royal town, the . . . heart and soul of each Pole; Cracow is the Polish Rome."[13]

By the end of 1877, plans to celebrate Kraszewski in Cracow were already being formulated.[14] The early preparations, led by the poet Adam Asnyk, gave no signs that the celebration might be any larger than those being readied in the other two empires. The scope of involvement increased during the next year, as the Cracow committee engaged in correspondence with Kraszewski committees in Poznań, Warsaw, and Lwów. By the end of 1878, cross-partition consensus building characterized the workings of the Cracow committee, which sought solidarity with the other groups, particularly with Warsaw.[15]

The laconic minutes of these early meetings suggest that the preparations for a public celebration in the ancient capital of the Poles proceeded

coalition building

smoothly. Nothing could be further from the truth. Mutiny simmered within Cracow, with the most influential group of citizens—the Cracow conservatives—threatening to absent themselves from the celebration. The most powerful Galician cohort of the period, the Cracow conservatives ruled supreme in Cracow and controlled its one Polish daily, *Czas* (Time). They were often referred to as the Stańczyks, after the court jester to King Sigismund, whose name had been invoked in the title of their programmatic statement of 1869. The leaders of this political orientation—Stanisław Koźmian, Józef Szujski, Stanisław Tarnowski, and Ludwik Wodzicki—presented themselves as political realists with a Catholic, conservative value system. Historical pessimism served as the backbone of their ideology as well as the foundation of the so-called Cracow school of history, which claimed that the nation needed to be ruled by a strong hand in order to avoid the anarchy of the past. The Stańczyks were suspicious of popular opinion. Their Galicia was an etatist one, run by the elites: the magnate class, the wealthy landed nobility, and the upper spheres of the intelligentsia. They feared anything that might incline the nation to indulge itself emotionally and jeopardize the relative well-being that Austria-Hungary afforded Poles. In their view, any signs of Polishness that overstepped the bounds of quaint ethnic custom or linguistic prerogative allowed the Galicians by their emperor were to be avoided.

This being the case, it should come as no surprise that the very thought of publicly celebrating Kraszewski troubled the Stańczyks.[16] Kraszewski was on the other side of the ideological fence. As an apologist for the insurrections, he was anathema; nor did they approve of his more positive view of the Polish past. They criticized the portrayal of Polish history in his novels: for while he was negative about the nobility, apparently he was not negative enough about the elements of the past of which the conservatives disapproved. The enmity between Kraszewski and the Cracow conservatives was visible well before the 1879 celebration.[17]

News of the impending festivities dislocated the noses of several notable conservatives. Father Walerian Kalinka's extreme reaction gives a sense of the animosity the conservatives harbored toward Kraszewski. The priest advised Tarnowski to abscond to Paris so as to avoid being in Cracow during the celebration. Although even some conservatives maintained that, as a celebration of the Polish language, the jubilee would have particular significance for Poles living in areas of linguistic oppression, Kalinka demurred: "Why is Kraszewski to be the symbol of the Polish language? If Polish children are to learn from him, they will learn pretty things besides language."[18] Kalinka also feared—not incorrectly—that this "Kraszewscade" (*Kraszewskada*) would give rise to further national demonstrations in Cracow.[19]

A means of softening conservative opposition to the jubilee celebration was contrived by one of the most fascinating politicians of the period: the mayor of Cracow, Mikołaj Zyblikiewicz. By any measure, the Galician career of Zyblikiewicz was incredible. In a period of still relatively weak upward mobility, he conquered two immense barriers: ethnic and social. Of Ruthenian descent, Zyblikiewicz had not shown any signs of considering himself Polish until into his school years; with time, however, he came to see himself as a Pole of Ruthenian stock (*gente Ruthenus, natione Polonus*). Against all odds, this son of a Ruthenian furrier from a provincial backwater managed to attain high posts in the municipality of Cracow and later rose to control the Galician provincial government. Indeed, he became very much a part of the conservative establishment, with the Stańczyks his closest political allies and supporters.[20]

Zyblikiewicz had attended meetings of the Cracow committee since its inception and monitored its progress. As mayor, he had much to gain from a successful celebration. He also was in a position to make a proposal that the committee, and all its contacts in the other empires, could hardly refuse: to hold the celebration in a renovated Old Cloth Hall, the centerpiece of the market square—the very heart of Cracow. (While the idea of renovating the building came in the first years of Galician autonomy, the actual restoration did not begin until plans for the Kraszewski jubilee were being hatched.[21]) Zyblikiewicz's proposal appealed to the committee and its contacts in the other empires. They doubtless recalled the building's glorious past as a hall worthy of kings and princes and where, in more recent times, Poland's last great military leader, Prince Józef Poniatowski, had been feted. Zyblikiewicz suggested as well that the Kraszewski jubilee be scheduled to coincide with the unveiling of the renovated Old Cloth Hall. This constituted a seemingly ideal compromise for his own constituency. The fact of a double celebration allowed for a degree of ambiguity that alleviated the discomfort of the Cracow conservatives and the ultramontanes, who found the Kraszewski jubilee difficult to stomach, while allowing more liberal and democratic participants to revel in the historical connection and featured location of their celebration.

Zyblikiewicz's proposals did not raise suspicions at the outset. The mayor mediated between two camps, the patriotic urban intelligentsia and their well-heeled conservative-clerical opponents. Both had reasons to support Zyblikiewicz—undoubtedly one of the reasons why his career was so successful. While enjoying the patronage of the conservatives and sympathizing with many of their views, Zyblikiewicz betrayed an independent streak, as seen in his recent opposition to plans to erect a monument to Pope Pius IX in the Wawel. Zyblikiewicz had undercut both conservative and clerical supporters of this plan by suggesting that foreigners should not be honored in the "Polish national pantheon." This defense of Polish control over the interior of the cathedral enhanced the mayor's standing in the eyes of many Poles at home and abroad.[22]

With time, however, those more closely connected to the preparations wondered whether the commemoration was being used to advance conservative aims. Official meetings of the Cracow committee throughout 1879 showed signs of tension. Already in January, Asnyk voiced fears that the jubilee would take a backseat to the unveiling of Old Cloth Hall. Beginning the festivities with the unveiling of Old Cloth Hall would give a more prominent role to the municipal and even the provincial government (for by now Alfred Potocki, the viceroy of Galicia, was involved).[23] As late as September, Zyblikiewicz tried to reassure a skeptical Kraszewski that he remained at the center of the celebration.[24] It remained to be seen whether those with "historic surnames" (that is, the nobility) would come, and what kind of welcome conservative-controlled Cracow would provide for those who wished to celebrate Kraszewski.

THE KRASZEWSKI JUBILEE,
OCTOBER 3–7, 1879

The first days of October brought trainloads of visitors to Cracow from Galicia and beyond.[25] Prussian Poles streamed into the town, as did Poles from the Russian Empire, the latter amazingly not having been denied passports by the authorities. Over eleven thousand guests attended. As one commentator boasted, whatever Poland possessed that was eminent—people, institutions, artists—was represented at the seven-day celebration.[26]

The influx of guests invigorated Cracow in interesting ways. Unaccustomed to such popularity, Cracow lacked the hotels necessary to house all the guests. People, even strangers, were put up in homes wherever possible: shoemakers took in shoemakers, typesetters made room for typesetters, lawyers housed lawyers, making this a prime opportunity for expanding contacts and networking.[27] As many guests had not managed to obtain tickets to the various events prior to their arrival, Cracow residents offered them their theater and dinner tickets. Cracow also showed signs of economic life. A new *Guidebook to Cracow* directed pilgrims around the sites of the city. Masses of commemorative souvenirs awaited pilgrims wishing to take tangible signs of the jubilee back home: silver medals with Kraszewski's portrait, commemorative rings, bronze medals, portraits, even jubilee hats. Asnyk composed a verse that was set to music by the director of the Warsaw Conservatory, Władysław Żeleński, five thousand copies of which were purchased by the city council for the festivities. Signs of national life after dark included slide illuminations: paper transparencies were placed in windows and lit from behind, making the images visible to passersby on the street. Most of the available displays and souvenirs commemorated Kraszewski; evidently the enterprising locals knew which of the two festivities was bringing in the visitors. . . . Still, the local daily, *Czas,* made no mention of Kraszewski's jubilee prior to his arrival, which so irritated one guest that he burned an issue of the paper in front of the bookseller.[28]

The whole city was abuzz with rumors of a special award awaiting Kraszewski. The Austrian emperor had decided to bestow upon Kraszewski the Great Commander Cross of the Order of Francis Joseph. This unexpected distinction—for Kraszewski was not an Austrian subject—altered the tenor of what thus far had appeared to be solely a Polish (national) celebration. This seal of approval from the host country was likely inspired either by the Galician authorities, concerned that the festivities not get out of hand, or by Poles involved in Viennese politics.[29] It was interpreted to signify the emperor's continued patronage of Polish arts and sciences as well as the desirable qualities of hard work and perseverance exemplified by the honorand. It also was a reminder that the jubilee was to be a peaceful event, one that did not threaten the status quo.[30] The order added a loyalistic note to the festivities: pro-Austrian conservatives could now attend in good conscience.

This news preceded Kraszewski's arrival at the train station on the afternoon of October 2. Enthusiastically received by city delegates, the jubilee committee, city councilors, writers, and friends, he made a triumphal entrance into the city. Although posters freshly plastered about town gave the guests only an hour's notice of Kraszewski's impending arrival, they turned out in large numbers to welcome the honorand.[31] The municipal fire brigade escorted Kraszewski in a carriage that a local burgher placed at his disposal. Accompanied by Mayor Zyblikiewicz, he traveled down Lubicz and Floriańska Streets, flanked by an honor guard of students and well-wishers, to his hotel.[32]

Despite his reception, Kraszewski arrived with a heavy heart. The writer had dreaded his Cracow jubilee, anticipating trouble on the part of the Stańczyks. Knowing their antipathy, he anticipated something akin to "civil war."[33] Why, then, had Kraszewski agreed to participate in this celebration? At his age (sixty-seven), the writer might have pleaded illness and contented himself with attending the local Dresden festivities, thus avoiding the stress of a confrontation with old enemies in Cracow. Yet—as discussed earlier— the commemoration stood for more than just fifty years of writing. Words written to his friend Agaton Giller in the days before the celebration make clear Kraszewski's real views of its significance: "I am all too convinced that basically nothing is happening for me, but rather for the Polish idea that stands above all of this. . . . I myself disappear entirely and do not credit myself with anything, but I am happy that I served as a pretext and, at least, a pretense for this great gathering."[34] Kraszewski saw his commemoration as transcending his own person and rallying the nation as a whole, which amazingly was being allowed to celebrate him collectively. It was the "Polish idea," not his accomplishments—simply a convenient pretext—that was being celebrated. Kraszewski, thus, chose to play the role assigned to him, despite the mental and physical anguish it would bring.[35]

The writer also feared the repercussions his jubilee might have for the Poles in the various empires. Paradoxically, he shared the concerns of the Stańczyks that his fellow Poles might be moved to utterances that the nation would later regret. Kraszewski stipulated that all speakers at the ceremonies must keep their comments in line: "It must be taken as a rule that each person wishing to speak must confer ahead of time with the committee and give his *word of honor* that he will not say anything beyond that to which he had committed himself."[36] As we shall see, this was not a groundless concern.

Kraszewski likewise attempted to mend fences so as to allow the jubilee to fulfill its mission of uniting and strengthening the Polish nation. Instead of resting after his journey, the elderly honorand immediately set off for a meeting with the two most notable Cracovians: the mayor and the newly consecrated bishop of Cracow, Albin Dunajewski. The seventy-year-old Dunajewski filled an office that had been left vacant for forty-four years.[37] As bishop, Dunajewski was well placed to influence the outcome of the jubilee, as the fact of his meeting with Kraszewski and Zyblikiewicz attests. In an unlikely setting—the closed tavern of a brewery, if police records are to be believed[38]—the parties seemed to reach some sort of agreement.

The results of the secret meeting were visible the next day, the official beginning of the festivities. The celebration began with a mass in Saint Mary's Church. Choirs sang old Polish church songs as well as a new mass by Rychling, the music director at Wawel Cathedral. One needed a ticket to attend, for even this large Gothic church could house only a small fraction of Cracow's visitors. Kraszewski sat next to the two ranking dignitaries: the mayor and the Galician provincial marshal, Ludwik Wodzicki, the latter dressed in traditional Polish noble garb. Following the church service, the assembled guests filed out of the church in the direction of the restored Old Cloth Hall.[39] Bishop Dunajewski solemnly blessed the knob, containing commemorative documents, to be placed atop the building.

Dunajewski's benediction made clear his position vis-à-vis the festivities and Kraszewski. The bishop had come to bless "this work, . . . this building only just finished." The crowds had come too because "memories, tradition . . . connects us to those walls."[40] Nary an acknowledgment of the Kraszewski jubilee about to begin within the walls being blessed. The bishop cautioned those present that it was not enough to come from one land: they "must be connected by one Church."[41] His job completed, Dunajewski retreated to the church. The significance of this benediction of building, not jubilee, was not lost on the guests.[42] While Dunajewski avoided the Kraszewski jubilee, the writer absented himself from the blessing of Old Cloth Hall. A convenient excuse had been offered him: the writer needed to pick up his Austrian order from the fully uniformed deputy viceroy, Kazimierz Badeni, in a nearby building.[43]

As the description above indicates, a curious separation of Church and state characterized the celebration. The liberal Kraszewski could not allow himself to be seen as a pawn of the ultramontanes. Already earlier that year, the writer had been given an ultimatum by this camp: if he did not go to confession (to confess his anticlerical past) and receive communion publicly in Saint Mary's Church in Cracow during his jubilee, the clergy would boycott the event.[44] His decision not to comply with their demands forced Dunajewski, who owed his position to the efforts of both Rome and the Cracow conservatives, to shun Kraszewski and his jubilee.[45] Not even the decoration of the writer by Emperor Francis Joseph could sway the new bishop of Cracow, whose first allegiance had to be to Rome.[46] The bishop's caution paid off: the following year, Dunajewski's diocese became the only one in the Austrian Empire to be directly subordinated to the Apostolic See.[47] Still, the relationship of the Church to the Polish nation would prove problematic for many Poles. Were they to be (or appear) Catholics first, Poles second (like Dunajewski) or Poles first, Catholics second (like Kraszewski)?

While many guests seemed to side with the honorand in this matter, the Kraszewski camp lost on one important front: few peasants were in attendance. Kraszewski's intransigence kept villagers from being led en masse to the Cracow celebration by Father Stanisław Stojałowski. A parish priest from the Lwów region in east Galicia and editor of several folk weeklies, Stojałowski had led pilgrimages of villagers for the last several years as well as organized the first folk rallies in Lwów and Cracow. As recently as May 1879, he had brought nearly three thousand peasants to Cracow for the anniversary of Saint Stanislas, Poland's patron saint.[48] That even Stojałowski, who was viewed with increasing suspicion by the conservative nobility, found it imperative to side with the ultramontanes in this matter demonstrates the influential role played by the Church among Poles in Galicia.

One peasant did make an appearance, however: a fifty-three-year-old peasant from the nearby village of Brzegi nad Wisłą. Maciej Szarek had met Kraszewski while working as a raftsman along the Vistula in the early 1860s, when the writer still resided in Warsaw. Kraszewski had endeared himself to Szarek by presenting the self-educated peasant with a much-appreciated gift of books, and the two corresponded over the years. In turn, Szarek helped to publicize Kraszewski's jubilee among the peasantry by composing a poem to Kraszewski, which was published in the folk paper *Włościanin* (The villager).[49]

Szarek had hoped to attend the jubilee celebration. Producing a letter from Kraszewski, the villager convinced Zyblikiewicz to write him down for a ticket gratis. Ultimately, though, he was not given one, as the event was oversubscribed.[50] Even the pleas of Kraszewski fell on deaf ears. A peasant was not going to be admitted when so many dignitaries had to be refused. To circumvent this dilemma, Kraszewski devised a plan. The main jubilee event was scheduled to take place in Old Cloth Hall after Dunajewski's benediction. Kraszewski told Szarek to meet him at the entranceway, whence he would escort him to the dais. Let everyone see, he said, that "the guest in the *sukmana* [the russet coat worn by peasants] is for me the nicest guest."[51] This particular peasant might well have impressed those gathered, as Szarek was prepared to recite his poem. On the day of the celebration, however, Kraszewski cast his eyes about in vain for his peasant friend. Szarek lost his nerve and did not show up. Kraszewski later voiced his displeasure: "I intended to take you onto the dais in order to teach several of our magnates that they should not scorn the villager and isolate him from provincial and national matters, for the strength of the nation rests on unification."[52]

It is a pity that this lesson was not taught to the three thousand guests assembled for the main celebration.[53] His wait having proved futile, the honorand entered Old Cloth Hall, escorted by the jubilee committee, the city council, and the mayor (who had changed into national dress).[54] A fifty-piece orchestra, with a choir one hundred strong, performed a cantata written especially for the occasion.[55] A lengthy formal presentation of gifts and addresses followed. Delegation after delegation presented gifts and sentiments to the writer.[56] First came the academic organizations of Lwów, Cracow, Toruń, Poznań, and Paris; Kraszewski's Warsaw friends and their committee; representatives from the town of Lwów and its committee. They were followed by a series of delegates who underscored the continued Polish presence in more distant lands, some beyond the boundaries of the old Commonwealth: these included the Polish colonies in France, Australia, Italy, Sweden, Chicago, and Rapperswil (Switzerland).[57]

Dedicated to Kraszewski were 71 books, 14 brochures, 26 musical compositions, 12 drawings and paintings. He was awarded 20 honorary diplomas, given 130 addresses, sent 509 telegrams.[58] (The numbers do not include those that for reasons of security could not be acknowledged publicly.) Unique gifts included a bronze copy of the Golden Gate of Kiev; a buffalo horn in a silver mounting from the Bielsko (Bielitz) lands; a silver cup with gilded decorations on an ebony base, with the coat-of-arms of the Commonwealth, from the Brody district; and a fancy cane sent by Poles in California. News came likewise of a commemorative runic stone honoring Kraszewski, which had been placed in a park by Poles in Sweden. Most unusual, perhaps, was the "pyramid of cabbage" that accompanied a poem from the village commune of Krowodrza near Cracow, testifying that at least some peasants recognized the writer.

At some point the organizers interrupted the proceedings so that the honorand could take the floor himself. Kraszewski had agonized over his speech, which he saw as a "great responsibility in his own conscience and in face of the future."[59] While he would speak about the Polish language and literature, Kraszewski felt compelled to "weave in the entire national question as it stands today."[60] This he had to do without references to "Poland" or anything that might not pass Russian censorship. Only then could his speech be reprinted in papers and publications throughout the Polish lands, thus allowing his message to reach an audience much larger than the several thousand who strained to hear his voice in Old Cloth Hall.

In his speech, Kraszewski emphasized the continuing love of the fatherland, linked with a deep belief "that nations under Christ's law do not perish and do not die, that our nation denied independence, having disappeared as a state, has the right, the duty to exist as a nation, and will exist until it itself does not renounce life or commit suicide."[61] He summarized the last century of Polish history, which—in contrast to the historians of the Cracow School—he saw as confirming his faith in the vitality of the nation.[62] Even calamities, according to Kraszewski, helped to raise the nation further; and dreams, such as those inspired by Napoleon, gave birth to people in whose breasts were preserved "a spark of the former hearth fire." He cited Polish achievements of the period, adding that they should inspire the nation to remain steadfast: the hearth fire, carried from one Polish zone to another, burned continuously and would not be extinguished. Turning briefly to his own accomplishments, Kraszewski spoke of the easily digestible nourishment of the novelistic form, which he had baked daily for half a century. He affirmed that he refused to jettison ideals, although he added that Poles should climb toward them "along the wooden rungs of reality." The writer concluded his speech with the sentiment of biblical Simeon, who, having seen the infant Jesus, said: "Let your servant go, Lord, for my eyes have seen the most beautiful day of life!"[63] This clearly was Kraszewski's own reaction to the sight of Poles assembled in commemoration, which he took as a sign of the nation's vitality and promise.

In the next days, a variety of occasions, both prearranged and spontaneous, underscored the coming together of Poles from all over and the sharing of common experiences and history. Leading Polish actors, including Jan Walery Królikowski from Warsaw, Bolesław Ładnowski from Lwów, and the famous Helena Modrzejewska (known in the United States as Modjeska), entertained theater audiences. Outings for guests by the thousands were arranged to the Wieliczka salt mines, the Kościuszko Mound, and other places of historic interest.[64] Other dinners and events were also organized. On Saturday, October 4, Kraszewski attended a reception held in his honor at Saint Anne's Gymnasium, the preeminent secondary school in Cracow. In his speech to the students, the writer addressed two dangers threatening Polish youth: denationalization and cosmopolitanism. Those two terms euphemistically referred to a political orientation gaining more and more Polish adherents: socialism.

Kraszewski chose an apt topic. The presence of socialism was increasingly felt even in conservative Cracow.[65] Ludwik Waryński, organizer of the first Polish socialist circles, had been arrested there earlier that year. Socialists apparently comprised a good part of the Cracow teachers' college and were viewed as a radicalizing—and dangerous—force.[66] They gave a warm welcome to the honorand, whom they saw as an ally against the conservatives. Socialists had plastered their greetings across the city, while their brethren in prison went so far as to send Kraszewski a letter and poem.[67]

Kraszewski, thus, had to dispel any suspicions that he might be associated with this radical movement. This he set out to do in his speech to the youth at Saint Anne's. "One must not know me at all to suspect me of any kind of relations with revolutionaries," he asserted, "being fundamentally against all revolution, all violence, which always wrests society from the correct march on the road to progress and brings more harm than good."[68] Kraszewski warned those present against expecting that genuine progress could be gained through violent means or by cutting ties to the past. The past held special value for them, according to Kraszewski; the "strength of a relic" could be found in the Polish heritage. Without renouncing progress or accepting the nation's vices, Poles needed to retain the faith, customs, language, and other characteristics that made them what they were; they were not to shed their "Polish skin" or let their "Polish blood."[69] Polishness was not to be cast aside for attractive yet deceptive theories, according to the writer who had brought to life the Polish past for so many readers. These, thus, were the messages that the honorand wished to impress upon his compatriots.

THE BANQUET IN OLD CLOTH HALL

A larger event on the calendar of festivities illustrates other aspects of the commemoration. An official gathering, it not only sheds light on the com-

Fig. 1.1 Souvenir napkin, 1879. Only in words (upper-left-hand corner) did the Kraszewski jubilee get acknowledged: "The Jubilee of J. I. Kraszewski in Cracow, 3 October 1879." *By M. Salba; photo courtesy of the National Museum, Kraków.*

memorative process but gives a sense of the different agendas being advocated by various members of the dispersed Polish family in this public, and highly publicized, setting.

On Saturday evening, the ground floor of Old Cloth Hall was transformed into a banquet hall. Three rows of tables were arranged to accommodate over eight hundred guests. The city council, sponsor of this affair, strove to make a good impression; perhaps Mayor Zyblikiewicz aspired to replicate the legendary feat of another Mikołaj from Cracow, Mikołaj Wierzynek, who provided a lavish feast to European heads of state in 1364. The space was illuminated by hundreds of candelabras, and an orchestra was placed at each end of the long hall. An elegant meal was served, the dishes and beverages including 150 kilograms of fish shipped in from Vienna, 366 bottles of Môet et Chandon imperial champagne, 244 bottles of Ofner wine, and 200 bottles of white Hungarian wine.[70] The iconography of the Cracow city council's contributions bespoke conservative influence as well as a desire for self-promotion: paper napkins designed by the artist Juliusz Kossak featured a lovely print of Old Cloth Hall, with the Cracow coat-of-arms at the bottom for good measure (figure 1.1).[71] Patriotic Varsovians contributed to this "family reunion" ten thousand cigarettes as well as a cake that could feed a thousand people, decorated with a life-sized sugar bust of Kraszewski.[72]

Old Cloth Hall that evening resembled an enormous heaving anthill, with guests moving about to meet and visit with friends old and new. The raising of toasts occasioned pilgrimages to the center table, where Kraszewski was seated. The ranking Galician, Provincial Marshal Ludwik Wodzicki, began the series of pre-prepared toasts over dessert by reminding those present of the debt they owed to Emperor Francis Joseph. Wodzicki commended the renovation of Old Cloth Hall, then praised Kraszewski's industry and perseverance while admitting that he could not agree with all of the writer's views and opinions. With a nod to the Czech dignitaries present, Wodzicki emphasized the improved situation of the Poles under Francis Joseph and implied that other nationalities deserved the same.[73] The toast was followed by the playing of the Austrian anthem. A pro-Austrian tone had been set.

Given Kraszewski's insistence on prepared (and vetted) speeches, no surprises were expected. A Pan-Slavic note was nonetheless sounded by an influential attorney and literary critic from St. Petersburg, Włodzimierz Spasowicz. The son of a Russian Orthodox father and Roman Catholic mother, Spasowicz was equally comfortable in Russian and Polish circles and contributed to the intellectual life of both. For this occasion, Spasowicz had been asked by Ivan Turgenev to raise a toast to Kraszewski.[74] The famous writer was not the only Russian making conciliatory noises at this time. As its relations with Austria-Hungary and Germany worsened, the Russian government was inclined to play the Pan-Slavic card.[75] Various press organs in Russia found positive things to say about Kraszewski and the Poles. During the period leading up to the commemoration, they expressed hopes that the celebration would be a demonstration of Slavic solidarity. This explains why the government issued its subjects passports for travel to Cracow, permitted addresses to Kraszewski to be signed, and allowed for souvenirs of the writer to be exhibited back home. Thus, "for the first time since 1863, Poles from Warsaw and Wilno, from Ukraine, Podolia and Volhynia ha[d] the opportunity to profess to be Poles loudly, openly and without hindrance."[76]

As regards Spasowicz's toast, the attorney cited Turgenev's assertion that the majority of the Russian intelligentsia extended its hand to Kraszewski in a brotherly fashion, a sign of a "new and fruitful era of free, peaceful and friendly development."[77] Spasowicz, however, may have paraphrased Turgenev, and he added commentary of his own. Despite the desire to keep the Kraszewski jubilee within the realm of "national exclusivity," the Petersburg attorney asserted that this had not happened: instead, "the steel band snap[ped]," and the Polish song was joined by "the quieter but audible Slavic notes."[78] This unfortunate mixture of metaphors may have been inspired by the presence of the Czechs, but those present for the toast did not interpret the attorney's words this way. Spasowicz's contextualization of the ideas expressed by the Russian writer raised hackles, and the crowd hissed.[79]

The person next in line to speak, Ksawery Liske, responded to Spasowicz's comments. President of the University of Lwów, Liske interpreted Spasowicz's musical metaphor to be a political allusion to the Russians, not the Czechs. Small nations needed to ally themselves with larger states, according to the professor; yet Poles should ally themselves only with genuine friends. An alliance of all Slavs would harm the Poles—indeed, be "more than harmful," according to Liske.[80] While the university president was used to taking on powerful enemies (in 1867 he had refuted Bismarck's claims that the lands taken from the Poles belonged to the Germans on historical grounds), his response was nonetheless safely pro-Habsburg—*schwarz-gelb* (black and yellow, the Habsburg colors), as some of the Prussian Poles noted.[81] It underscored the anti-Russian position of the Galician Poles, who had kinder words for the Czechs, the Poles' coalition partner in Vienna.

If conservative Galician Poles proved *kaisertreu* (loyal to the emperor) and at least one Russian Pole more conciliatory toward the Russians, the Prussian Poles present in Cracow had their own agenda. At this same dinner, Prussian parliamentarian Józef Męciński brought up the subject of the so-called Kraszewski Fund, one of many initiatives inspired by the jubilee. This fund was to provide financial support for the Polish Theater in Poznań. Not just a local issue, Męciński claimed, the fund would contribute to the general battle against German oppression, especially Germanization. Put the Polish language onto the stage of the Polish theater, he said, and let the Germans hear it. Just in case those present still remained unconvinced of the needs of Poles within the united Germany, the parliamentarian touted the accomplishments of his region, in particular its success in turning peasants into patriotic and Catholic Poles who voted together with the intelligentsia—something that had not been accomplished by the Galician Poles.[82] This initiative was looked at with favor by those who chose to emphasize the linguistic end of the jubilee.[83] One hopes that they paid more than lip service to the cause.

SIEMIRADZKI'S SURPRISE— AND OTHER PATRIOTIC ENDEAVORS

The Kraszewski jubilee provided Poles with an opportunity to raise other issues of mutual importance. It introduced other nation-building efforts that galvanized those present and sparked further initiatives, thus leading to a continuous atmosphere of patriotic engagement. Witness the banquet organized by "all the Polish journalists present at the time in Cracow."[84] Not part of the official celebration, this was a gathering of the Polish intelligentsia, inspired by those who first thought of celebrating Kraszewski's jubilee. A more spontaneous and modest event, the banquet was held at the Victoria Hotel and attended by over one hundred writers and artists, the cream of the Polish intellectual elite. Even the Russian press remarked that "never, perhaps, in such a tight space had such a mass of Polish intelligentsia gathered, such color and selection."[85] These were the people who would communicate the events of the festivities far beyond the borders of the old medieval capital. One can imagine the reunion of those who depended upon the Polish language for their living. At the banquet, they could relate experiences, share anecdotes, reconnect with old friends, and make new contacts. Still, there appears to have been some underlying tension as well among the guests—perhaps no surprise, as Cracow's conservative daily *Czas* was well represented; while newspaper accounts tended to downplay differences, these were significant enough to warrant a ban on references to political parties during the banquet.[86]

The big surprise of the event—indeed, of the commemoration as a whole—followed the arrival of Zyblikiewicz. Reportedly word had reached the mayor of Cracow that he had been toasted by the journalists. Never one to let an occasion for self-promotion pass, Zyblikiewicz hurried over to the hotel to offer a toast of his own. The mayor raised his glass to the artist Henryk Siemiradzki. Although a subject of the Russian tsar (from the region of Kharkov[87]), Siemiradzki had resided in Italy since 1872, and his paintings of classical and early Christian themes were enjoying international renown. The artist's most recent major work, *Nero's Torches,* depicting the persecution of the Christians in Rome, had toured the capitals of all major European states in 1876–77 as well as Warsaw, Lwów, and Poznań.[88] Thanking the mayor for his acknowledgment, Siemiradzki proceeded to make an announcement of his own: he was donating *Nero's Torches* to the homeland to be hung on one of the walls of the newly renovated Old Cloth Hall.

The news of Siemiradzki's generous gift stunned the banqueters, who jumped up to shake the artist's hand. In the flurry of so many patriotic words, someone had done something concrete. That *Nero's Torches* would remain accessible to Polish viewers pleased those present. The canvas (figure 1.2) is dominated by a scene of decadent splendor of Nero and his court, present at the immolation of a number of Christians—Nero's "torches"— bound to stakes. While the painting may be viewed as just another competently rendered picture of antiquity, it had greater purchase with Poles, who suspected that a parallel was being drawn between that distant past and the present age. They saw not a classical scene but their own lives: they identified with the persecuted Christians, who, despite their martyrdom and

Fig. 1.2 Henryk Siemiradzki, *Nero's Torches*. The opulent decadence of the imperial scene, which Siemiradzki painted so well, nearly overshadows the horror of Christians being set afire at the far right. *Painting; photo courtesy of the National Museum, Kraków.*

sacrifice, would give rise to a Church that would inherit the mantle of the empire. While the subversive nature of the painting (for any of the partitioning empires persecuting the Poles might be seen as the Romans) received no mention in the press, speeches at a later dinner, one too radical to receive in-depth newspaper coverage, reported the Poles' correct interpretation of Siemiradzki's intent.[89] The content of the painting spoke directly to the Poles and would now continue to do so.

One Pole present at the banquet that Sunday remained unmoved by Siemiradzki's announcement. Cracow historian Józef Szujski proceeded to give a speech that could be considered a paean to the "firefighters' brigade," that is, to those who threw cold water on Polish patriotic initiatives. Szujski depicted the national spirit as immortal, which meant there was no reason to doubt its existence or fear that it might wither. The intelligentsia should not stir or shape it: "Writers, poets, artists—not we are the creators of the nature [of the national spirit], not we that lute, which predisposes it so—it itself is the lute. We extract songs and tones from the sea of feelings which lurk in its depths." These feelings, Szujski seemed to imply, would bubble up by themselves at the appropriate moment. While the historian's comments and multiple metaphors failed to impress many guests, his view echoed those expressed in the conservative organ *Czas,* which discouraged further celebrations.[90]

The timing of the announcement of Siemiradzki's gift seemed to serve the local conservatives. One wonders whether the news was intended to distract from the celebration at hand, for that same day the mayor had posters plastered about town informing the public of the artist's donation.[91] Given the delay in posting the time of Kraszewski's arrival the previous Thursday, one senses more enthusiasm on the part of the mayor for this new contribution to the nation than for Kraszewski's accomplishments.

The feting of Siemiradzki the following evening suggests this is true. Two thousand torches were lit, and a river of light wound its way down the narrow streets of the city to the hotel where the artist was staying.[92] Siemiradzki was praised in a number of speeches, his donation termed a "royal gift [*królewski dar*]."[93] Yet, while pleased that his deed had been appreciated, Siemiradzki attempted to redirect the crowd's attention: he led the crowd to Kraszewski's hotel, where he exclaimed that what he did was under the inspiration of the spirit with which the Kraszewski jubilee had enlivened everyone.[94]

Siemiradzki's "royal gift" for the king-less nation inspired others. The next day, a number of other Polish artists promised works to Old Cloth Hall, which they hoped would give impetus to the establishment of a museum. Convening in response to the gifts, the Cracow city council committed itself to dedicate part of the second floor of Old Cloth Hall for a museum of Polish painting—a National Museum.[95] The donation of an internationally renowned painting and a host of lesser known works, thus, became the cornerstone of a national museum for the Poles. While renovated under Austrian auspices (although with the initiative of the essentially autonomous Poles), Old Cloth Hall was guaranteed a degree of Polishness. Polish art would leave a permanent mark within the building and become a destination for pilgrimages in its own right. At the same time, the actions of Siemiradzki and the others point toward a new role for Polish artists. Whereas Cracow traditionally had been the national Mecca, it recently had begun to resemble more a Polish Munich or Düsseldorf: "thanks to Siemiradzki, it is becoming a Polish Florence. But with what a difference! There . . . artists had Medicis; . . . *here the artists are Medicis for the Fatherland.*"[96]

Another important endeavor was begun at the same time. Kraszewski learned that an anonymous donor planned to give him 27,500 rubles. Impressed by the successes of the Czech Matica and German Schulverein, he decided to create an institution designed to educate the broad masses of Polish society, Macierz Polska (Polish Motherland). According to the foundation act, the interest on the fund was to be used for folk publications, with the first 500 guldens earmarked for educational allowances for children of impoverished parents. Profits from sales of the publications were to be used for other goals of the fund.[97] While the act is vague about the scope of the foundation's work, Kraszewski thought in broad terms. The allowances were to be earmarked for children of impoverished refugees from the other empires, and the publications were to educate and strengthen the national spirit of a broadly defined "folk,"[98] without regard for religious denomination.[99] This organization was to play an important role in the ensuing years: by 1900 it would publish 127 books on Polish history, amounting to nearly a million (958,000) copies.[100]

Kraszewski's plans could not have been realized without the assistance of highly placed Poles within Galicia. The writer thus resolved to entrust the organization to Zyblikiewicz, who would be the deputy curator (the curator being Kraszewski). Although Kraszewski thought the mayor "rather questionably disposed" toward the jubilee, he availed himself of Zyblikiewicz's assistance.[101] Rightly so: by the time the organization was officially approved, Zyblikiewicz had become provincial marshal for all Galicia. Zyblikiewicz helped to make the proposal for Macierz Polska palatable to the Austrian authorities, who gave their permission in April of 1882.[102]

The official part of the festivities ended with a great ball given by the city of Cracow to celebrate both Old Cloth Hall and Kraszewski (figure 1.3). Much music and merriment accompanied the approximately two thousand guests who danced away the night.[103] The whirling figures inspired images of other magnificent celebrations of the past: the time of Wierzynek's feast or the ball in honor of Prince Józef Poniatowski. Were the conservatives to have their wish, however, this would be the last fling before the nation returned to its productive endeavors, to "uninterrupted work."[104] The viceroy, Alfred Potocki, also attended this event, after which he traveled to Vienna—presumably to report on the jubilee.[105]

More patriotic notes sounded at a farewell dinner given for Kraszewski at the Sharpshooters' Hall (Sala Strzelecka) organized by the townspeople. Poles from the other empires and abroad indulged in the type of speeches that had been frowned upon elsewhere.[106] The fact that Siemiradzki had painted *Nero's Torches* for the Poles, who would understand the significance of the painting, was confirmed. A parliamentarian from Germany toasting both Kraszewski and Siemiradzki exclaimed that his country must now reckon with the Poles, for clearly "we are not a decaying corpse but a nation that knows how to live and that strives for something."[107] Another delegate—this one from the Historical Society in Paris—broached a subject more inflammatory than his lecture earlier that day (on cuneiform writing). He said, "gentlemen, let us work *together,* learn together . . . let us not give in and we will resurrect Poland."[108] The singing of the mazurka "Jeszcze Polska nie zginęła" (Poland has not yet perished) was also noted by the Cracow policeman in attendance. Not controlled by the Cracow conservatives,

Fig. 1.3 "The Celebration of the Jubilee of 50 Years' of Literary Activity of J. I. Kraszewski," woodcut by Ksawery Pillati, published in *Tygodnik Powszechny* no. 45 (5 November 1879). A medley of images from the festivities. On the left (top), Kraszewski's entrance into Cracow, (bottom) dinner in the Sukiennice in honor of the honorand; in the center, the procession out of Saint Mary's Church (note the figure of the bishop at the front) into the Sukiennice; and on the right, the ball in the Sukiennice. *Photo courtesy of the Jagiellonian Library.*

this event at the Sharpshooters' Hall showed signs of a more spontaneous Polish life, a desire for mutual understanding and cooperation, and surging national sentiments.

The Kraszewski jubilee continued to have positive repercussions for the nation. After the festivities ended, Kraszewski paid a visit to Emperor Francis Joseph to thank him personally for the order. Apparently this encounter inclined the emperor to plan a trip to Galicia in the summer of 1880, during which he was enthusiastically received.[109] During his stay, Galician officialdom availed itself of yet another opportunity to reclaim Polish buildings for the nation. Zyblikiewicz initiated the first steps toward the removal of Austrian troops garrisoned in Wawel Castle. The Cracow mayor tendered an urgent motion to the provincial marshal, asking that Wawel Castle be restored to its former status of royal residence. A committee was formed, the emperor was approached, and the matter ultimately was agreed upon.[110] The royal castle was on its way to being restored to the Polish nation.[111]

FESTIVITIES TO THE FORE

The jubilee festivities in honor of Kraszewski were viewed as successful by all sides. The Kraszewski jubilee raised the profile of local dignitaries such as Mayor Zyblikiewicz and Bishop Dunajewski. The painter Siemiradzki gained fame as a patriot; his later works, such as the curtains, decorated with allegorical scenes, for both the Cracow and Lwów municipal theaters, would be revered by generations of Poles.

While Cracow conservatives bemoaned the fact that Kraszewski received the recognition that had not been given other, greater writers such as Mickiewicz, they acknowledged that such festivities had become necessary for the nation: "For the nation is not presently concerned with even the most magnificent past, it is concerned with the present; it wants life."[112] The Polish commemoration was an open, legal celebration that posed a threat to no one, they claimed, as seen by the emperor's praise for the writer, which as we know compelled many of Kraszewski's opponents to participate.[113] His approval of plans to reclaim Wawel Castle as a royal residence likewise contributed to an increasingly favorable portrait of the Habsburg ruler and buttressed the notion of Francis Joseph as the "good emperor." Apparently, one could be a Pole and still be a loyal subject of the Habsburg emperor.

One might ask whether nation-building was taking place in spite of the Cracow conservatives, or whether conservatives were generally more concerned with the external trappings of the nation. Was the Kraszewski commemoration, as one scholar concludes, just another "Galician pageant" (*szopka galicyjska*) demonstrating national freedoms under Austrian rule?[114] While a *schwarz-gelb* veneer was daubed on the festivities, courtesy of the emperor's inspired acknowledgment of the writer, it could not obliterate the patriotic, national content that imbued the celebrations. The Kraszewski commemoration was an enabling device for the Poles, who engaged in nation-building despite some limitations, backpedaling, and cleverness. The conservatives did not emerge entirely victorious; the creative intelligentsia in particular found ways of pushing the authorities farther than perhaps they had intended.

This is evident in the transformation of Old Cloth Hall. The conservatives' attempt to put the unveiling of the building first had not succeeded in detracting from the larger issues. Henceforth, the site would be associated with patriotic accomplishments: the celebration of Kraszewski, which took place within its walls, as well as a more permanent memento, the National Museum. Polish artists strove to renationalize that space with their donations of artworks and were supported in their endeavor by the Cracow city council. Old Cloth Hall stood for more than Poland's ancient and august past. It was now a mix of old and new: essentially traditional in form but with a reinvigorated national content.

Could the bounds envisaged by the conservatives, who otherwise tried to discourage further commemorations, hold back the nation? The tide seemed to be flowing in the opposite direction. A group of jubilee guests published their wish that Cracow experience more such times "in which such an atmosphere of hearts and minds, such splendor and celebration, such a . . . joyful and sublime life . . . should be no longer only an exceptional, extraordinary occurrence, but might enter into the common mode, having become the natural and necessary result of the situation and the need of the nation."[115] Even peasant papers praised Kraszewski for having "pulled out decrepit Cracow" from its "tight casket."[116]

In these celebrations, an interesting symbiosis between the supporters and detractors of commemorations allowed both to forward their own agendas. The Kraszewski celebration—specifically, Zyblikiewicz's skillful control over the event—boosted the mayor in the eyes of Cracow citizens as well as others in the empire. The establishment of Macierz Polska clearly involved two important personages rendering each other favors. By supporting Kraszewski's causes, Zyblikiewicz guaranteed himself control over funds and their disposal as well as greater personal status. At the same time, Kraszewski gained the ear of an influential Galician who could make his wishes come true. The conservative Zyblikiewicz would also support another of the writer's pet projects: the erection of a monument in Cracow to Adam Mickiewicz, which will be discussed in chapter 5. In some circumstances, thus, conservatives and liberals could work hand in hand.

While the Kraszewski jubilee was considered a "truce of God" (*treuga Dei*) for Polish society, Czech and Russian interest in the anniversary lent an international dimension to the festivities.[117] One Russian paper called the jubilee "a historic event, more serious than perhaps the Poles themselves think."[118] But there was no Pan-Slavic meeting of the minds here: the local Poles clearly favored their Austrian Slavic brethren over subjects of the Russian tsar.

The commemoration of 1879 contributed toward the rebuilding of the nation, both literally and figuratively. As site of the festivities, Cracow was becoming a national destination of significance. In the words of one observer, it was the Polish "Mecca" to which pilgrims had traveled for the commemoration.[119] The celebration emphasized some of the trappings of nationhood: the value of the vernacular and of a shared past. It led to the creation of national institutions—a renovated and reclaimed Old Cloth Hall, a National Museum, Macierz Polska, and the first stirrings of the reclamation of Wawel Castle—that would gain in importance over the next decades. Nor did its impact end there. The success of the Kraszewski jubilee inspired Poles to celebrate other anniversaries publicly.

TWO

The Relief of Vienna, 1683–1883: Celebrating Victory

Not long after the Kraszewski jubilee, the idea of celebrating a major Polish national anniversary was raised by a group of young Poles in Vienna.[1] That the impetus for the celebration should come from this quarter is apt, for the anniversary highlighted an intersection of Polish and Habsburg history. The bicentennial of the Relief of Vienna commemorated the rescue of Vienna from Turkish onslaught. The battle on September 12, 1683, with the Polish king, John III Sobieski, commanding imperial as well as Polish troops, marked the turning point in the relation of Islam and Christianity in East-Central Europe. Called by Lord d'Abernon one of the eighteen decisive battles of the world, the Relief of Vienna proved to Europe that the mighty Ottoman Empire could be defeated.[2]

The year 1883 was hardly the first time that the Relief of Vienna was feted or its merits championed by the Poles. The last king of Poland, Stanisław August Poniatowski, had a marble sarcophagus fashioned for Sobieski during the centennial year; he also honored John III with a monument as well as a painting commissioned from the artist Bacciarelli, which was hung in Knights' Hall (Sala Rycerska) in the Warsaw castle. Interest in the Relief of Vienna had already been demonstrated by the Commission of National Education (Komisja Edukacji Narodowej), the first such institution in Europe; it had advocated school celebrations of the anniversary and sought to use the heroic virtues of the Polish knights as examples for young Poles.[3] Since these initiatives followed the first partition of Poland, one suspects that Sobieski's example was touted for its chivalric qualities, necessary if Poles were to regain control over their destiny—and their lost territories.

References to the valiant king did not cease with the disappearance of the Polish state. Echoes of Sobieski surfaced in various revolutionary periods. Before leading his troops to battle in 1794, Tadeusz Kościuszko requested that his sabers be blessed by a clergyman, just as Sobieski had done a century earlier. In 1830, Poniatowski's monument to Sobieski served as a meeting place for insurrectionists, thus compounding the symbolism of 1683.[4] Images of the Relief of Vienna, thus, were superimposed on the struggle for national liberation, and the Poles' military efforts were redirected from the enemies of Christianity to the enemies of the nation.

The commemoration in 1883 shaped perceptions of the Sobieski legacy in different ways. The reversal of fate that had befallen the Poles since that last splendid military victory, the subsequent rise of the Habsburgs, and changed conditions within Austrian Poland lent a unique resonance to the festivities. The downtrodden Polish nation might take pride in, or consolation from, its recollection of a greater age or—conversely—beat its collective breast in anguish over its decline. The descendants of the besieged Viennese, however, were long since masters of their own fate; they viewed their past predicament in a completely different light, as reflected by the fact that their ancestors saw fit to discontinue annual celebrations of the city's liberation after Poland was partitioned.[5] The 1883 celebration, then, illuminates attitudes of these two groups toward their past as well as the relationship of nineteenth-century Poles and Austrians.

It also had implications that transcended the borders of the Habsburg Empire. Key to an understanding of Sobieski's role in 1883 as well as in 1683 was the Poles' image of themselves as defenders of Christendom—defenders of the very capital of the Holy Roman Empire—against the infidels. The Relief of Vienna was touted as one of the nation's greatest international achievements, even as the Poles' greatest deed for the good of humanity.[6] Intrinsic to the celebration, thus, were notions of the Poles' relationship to the West, to Western Europe, as well as to Catholicism. Poles likewise grappled with their relationship to that past: in the words of one contemporary, Poles were celebrating the Relief of Vienna "as a national holiday" in order to "get to know ourselves, what we were earlier, what we are today" as well as to figure out how to address the future.[7] In the course of redefining what it meant to be Polish in 1883, Poles also grappled with their relationship to the East and to Slavdom. In sum, the Poles' celebration of the bicentennial of the Relief of Vienna had important repercussions in three realms: imperial, national, and international.

THE IMPERIAL CONNECTION

Anyone familiar with the Kraszewski jubilee would be struck by the contrast: this time, support for festivities was forthcoming from the Cracow conservatives, who were among those initiating preparations for the anniversary of the Relief of Vienna. Perhaps, given the Austrian connection, this was perceived as a "safe" celebration, one that did not necessarily clash with loyalty to the empire. The relative weight of imperial and national elements in the Cracow commemoration, thus, is worth investigating.

There were reasons for the conservatives to wax enthusiastic about the anniversary. By 1883, the former Polish capital was becoming a favorite destination. If Cracow had become the "theater of national celebrations," someone had to write the script, hire the players, and publicize the play.[8] The conservatives as well as the municipal government could assume what other Poles might consider their logical role as organizers of national events and take pride in their ability to host Poles from other empires in Cracow, who could for a time breathe "Polish air and . . . take comfort (*pokrzepić się na duchu*)."[9] The conservatives' acknowledgment that "historical commemorations are a moral necessity of societies" reflected a broader consensus of conscious Polish society that transcended the partitions.[10] Many Poles wanted to celebrate their past, and the party in power could hardly disregard this desire without being criticized for being *schwarz-gelb*.

One might expect that the conservatives or the Cracow city council would choose to direct—and control—such initiatives, to dictate what could be celebrated and how. That there is no chapter on the fiftieth anniversary of the 1830 uprising attests to the fact that those in power deemed some anniversaries more worthy of public celebration than others. The bicentennial of the Relief of Vienna belonged to the former category. As the conservative paper *Czas* explained, "such celebrations can beneficially influence the health of the nation, [its] present life and its future if they concern facts [that are] indeed worthy of remembrance, illustrious, positive," and not "trivial" or "deplorable"—terms used to describe the insurrections.[11]

While the imperial connection allowed Galician Poles to embrace the commemoration without fears of reprisal—after all, the event was being feted officially in Vienna—the festivities in Cracow were nonetheless more than a *galówka,* an official Habsburg celebration. Typically "Polish" aspects abounded, as seen from the schedule of events. The stateless nation planned its associational life around the anniversary. The commemoration of the historic event (September 11–12) was immediately preceded by a ceremony of religious significance: the crowning of a miraculous image of Mary in a Cracow monastery church (September 10).[12] The Sobieski celebration included not only a special exhibition of objects from the seventeenth century, the unveilings of a bronze tablet and monument (similar events took place in Vienna); a special reception of peasant representatives from across Galicia was also planned. These were followed by other excuses for remaining in the city: the twenty-fifth jubilee of painter Jan Matejko (September 13) as well as the first congress of Polish writers and artists (September 14–15).[13]

CONTENDING VISIONS

One of the earliest projects for the celebration was advanced by Zuzanna Czartoryska in 1880. The wife of the president of the Society of Friends of the Fine Arts (Towarzystwo Przyjaciół Sztuk Pięknych) in Cracow suggested that the city organize an exhibition of objects from the period.[14] Czartoryska hoped that artists would take inspiration from the relics and create their own tributes to the age, thus producing more high-quality works of national content. Even conservatives such as the highly influential Stanisław Tarnowski, professor of the history of Polish literature at Jagiellonian University and general secretary of the Academy of Arts and Letters, admitted the need for something visible, something tangible, something that would act on "minds via the senses."[15] Art could have an impact not only on artists and historians interested in the seventeenth century, but on a broader public as well. Czartoryska hoped that the collection would travel to Vienna, where it would be seen by the Viennese citizenry, the imperial court and bureaucracy, thus exposing them to the history of the Polish nation, which once had come to their defense.[16]

Ultimately, 1883 witnessed the mounting of an exhibition in Old Cloth Hall that set the tone for the celebration. Approximately fifteen hundred items were lent by individuals in the various empires, with some shipped from Warsaw, Frombork (Frauenberg), Gdańsk (Danzig), and Rome as well as from aristocratic residences in Nieśwież (Niasvizh), Wilanów, Łańcut, and Podhorce (Pidhirci).[17] Visitors to the exhibition found themselves transported to the age of John III Sobieski. The walls were hung with Turkish tents and rugs; Turkish trophies as well as Western arms and armor surrounded a bronze bust of the king as victor.[18] There was a little field altar, as well as a marble bas-relief of Pope Innocent XI, to whom the victorious Sobieski sent word of the rout of Islam with the phrase *Venimus, vidimus, Deus vicit* (We came, we saw, God triumphed). Mannequins of Polish winged hussars on horseback guarded a tent containing a "relic" of the relief: an image of the Mother of God found during the campaign. The over seventeen thousand visitors who communed with these national and religious mementos were to leave "revived in spirit, desiring to imitate what had made the nation great and famous in the past."[19]

This linkage of the religious and national was amplified further at the exhibition's opening by Mikołaj Zyblikiewicz, now provincial marshal. Zyblikiewicz claimed that, despite the vicissitudes of history, Poles remained faithful to what he termed Sobieski's central idea: Poland's "constant connection with the West." The Relief of Vienna stood out in Polish military history because "it [was] not an ordinary battle of great powers, it [was] the battle of two worlds: the barbarity of the East against the Christian civilization of the West." Zyblikiewicz underscored the lack of greed on the part of Poles, who "went to fight for faith and civilization."[20] Local conservatives seized upon the slogan of "the Poles with the West."[21] It also served the pro-Habsburg interests of the ruling Galician elites: Poles had fought with the Austrians against a common enemy then, and they would continue to do so. Subsidized by the Galician Diet (Sejm), the Cracow exhibition could thus be viewed as a properly official (Habsburg) as well as a national event.

That the opening of the Sobieski exhibition upstaged a purely national event contributes to that sense. The National Museum, whose collection was begun so handsomely by Siemiradzki in 1879, was not opened until September 11, 1883. It had taken four years for a statute to be drafted and passed and might have taken longer, had the plans to celebrate 1683 not surfaced.[22] The preparations for a commemorative exhibition within Old Cloth Hall afforded a welcome opportunity to make as little as possible of the actual museum collection, which in the opinion of the Galician elites consisted primarily of "undeniable mediocrities."[23] This view seems to have been shared by Zyblikiewicz, who insisted that the Sobieski exhibition be unveiled immediately before the opening of the National Museum on the same floor of Old Cloth Hall.[24] In this way, those in control of the celebration managed to dispatch with an event that, in the eyes of many, did not warrant a celebration of its own.

That the Sobieski anniversary preoccupied Galicians at this time is related to the Poles' political irrelevance since the partitions, which allowed many non-Poles, such as the Austrian liberals, conveniently to "forget" elements of the past. A noted adversary of the Poles in this regard was the historian Onno Klopp.[25] Klopp awarded the victory at Vienna to Charles V, Duke of Lorraine, the progenitor of the Austrian dynasty.[26] Charles V was made out to be the real leader of the combined armies; Sobieski became involved in the city's defense only out of pride and in seeking personal gain, and the Polish forces hardly figured in the battle. According to Józef Szujski, Klopp's interpretation was an "attack on the reputation of John III, . . . one of our dearest national treasures."[27] The Polish historian defended Sobieski's role as the commander of the battle of September 12, 1683—and thus the liberator of Vienna. Austrians and Germans may choose to honor others who fought, he acknowledged, but they could not relegate John III Sobieski to a lesser position: "one may erect monuments to the Duke of Lorraine and Count Starhemberg, but one cannot give *second* place to him who had *first*."[28]

This battle for historical interpretation resonated far beyond the halls of academe. According to a bibliography of publications—a sign of how seriously the anniversary was taken by Poles—well over a thousand commemorative works of various kinds were produced.[29] These ranged from the scholarly publication of historical documents through journalistic treatments, theatrical, and literary works. Also included was an avalanche of souvenirs—photographs and drawings, medals, and medallions—that brought the celebration into the homes of countless Poles while emphasizing the primacy of Sobieski. A commemorative medal designed by the artist Juliusz Kossak, for example, presented the entrance of the king into Vienna surrounded by welcoming Austrian archdukes, with the text "Ach —unser brave Koenig" (Ah—our brave king) and the date 12 September 1683. Other medals praised the king as the "defender of Christianity." Yet another one that must have been relished by the Prussian Poles boasted that Sobieski "saved Germany, made Poland famous" (figure 2.1).[30]

Although it is hard to say what the demand for such items was, the identification of nineteenth-century Poles, Austrians, and Germans with their seventeenth-century forebears proved remarkable. The descendants of the various parties to the battle took the depiction of their respective roles seriously, as if their own reputations and positions within the empire depended on it. Poles accused the Austrian commemorative committee that produced the monument at Saint Stephen's in Vienna of slighting Sobieski and his forces. Even Viennese burghers were so outraged at Klopp's portrayal of the (less-than-admirable) behavior of the city's leaders during the siege that the city's mayor, Edward Uhl, felt obliged to lobby for a recasting of that history. And the committee responsible for the Saint Stephen's monument reportedly was besieged by calls for the inclusion of a representative of the Czechs so that the monument might reflect the empire's multinationalism.[31]

This rewriting of history to suit the needs of the present irked Galician Poles, who felt that their historic contributions were being discounted: the victor nations that remained powerful in the nineteenth century had forgotten that Poland was a political nation with a history.[32] Prussian Poles complained of a similar bias in the German press, which was "treat[ing] John III and Poles as if [they were] subjects of their own country, as if they were perhaps some Fifth Posen Corps" in the Austro-Prussian or Franco-Prussian War, "which in the name of military discipline was to share its contribution to the victory at Sadowa or Sedan with the German corps of the Prussian army."[33] When Uhl spoke of the "defense" but not the "relief" of his city in his invitation to the Viennese celebration of 1683, the Polish commemoration committee objected. If the contributions of the Polish king and Polish forces that liberated Vienna were not recognized by the descendants of the very burghers he rescued, then Poles would not attend the Viennese celebration. The nation would celebrate by itself, with Cracow to be the "center of gravity."[34]

Fig. 2.1 Medal with the inscription "Niemcy zbawił, Polskę wsławił" (he saved Germany, made Poland famous). The inscription encircling Sobieski's bust reads "John III Sobieski, King of Poland; he saved Germany, made Poland famous"; on the obverse, "The Folk Celebration of the Jubilee of John Sobieski in Cracow, 12 September 1883."

Photo courtesy of the National Museum, Numismatic Bureau, Kraków.

CELEBRATING POLISH LEADERSHIP

While this decision was made at the provincial level, Cracow had long planned for festivities to take place in the former royal city, whence Sobieski had set off for the fateful battle. By late 1882, a Cracow committee was established by city councilors, who set about organizing the festivities and gaining support for the earmarking of funds.[35] In addition to a loan made to the exhibition committee, the large municipal expenditure of over seventeen thousand Austrian crowns (guldens) was in part justified by the strong conviction that Cracow had a "moral obligation" to lead the celebration. Likewise, the city council wished to show itself "the worthy representative of the capital of Polish kings [which] knows how to realize its significance and its position."[36] Such sentiments reflected the pride Cracow burghers took in their role as tenders of the national hearth.

Two themes dominated the city's plans for the commemoration. First, local Poles chose to emphasize the leadership role of the Polish king, John III Sobieski, in the victory. This was in part the legacy of Józef Szujski, who did not live to see the celebration. Second, the commemorators underscored the religious, crusading, even moral impulse behind the Polish involvement—an approach supported by the Catholic Church as well as the political elites. The celebration was to underscore what had been great and noble in the king and nation, to show that it had not been extinguished and "that what was good and beautiful in the Polish soul centuries past still smolders today under the rubble and ash, and, if need be, could begin again to smolder anew and ignite."[37]

To convey the importance of Sobieski's leadership for the victory and the Poles' underlying religiosity to the general public, the organizers of the commemoration focused on visual strategies. The main contribution of the city council to the 1883 celebration was a bronze tablet commissioned from Pius Weloński, a Polish sculptor residing in Rome. Weloński created an enormous bas-relief of a triumphant Sobieski on horseback. Saber in his right hand, flag with Polish eagle unfurled in his left, the Polish king trampled a bare-chested Turk under the hooves of his mount. The inscription on the frame included the phrase "relief of Vienna," although its statement "in honor of King John III" was not enough for at least one reporter, who added the phrase "king of Poland"—perhaps wishfully—in his article.[38]

By far the most expensive item in the commemoration budget, the bronze tablet represented the best permanent memorial that could be had under the circumstances. Neither the constraints of time nor the city's insistence on funding the monument itself (that is, without gathering donations from the public) would have allowed for, say, a free-standing monument of the type to be featured in the coming decades. Most important, however, it was accessible to the general public. The tablet was mounted on the outer wall of Saint Mary's Church, across from Old Cloth Hall. Saint Mary's Church occupied one of the corners of the market square, the best location for outdoor gatherings since the renovation of that space in 1879.

The unveiling of the commemorative tablet was envisaged as the highlight of the celebration. It was scheduled for five o'clock in the afternoon of September 12, the hour when the Polish cavalry had made their charging frontal attack on Kara Mustafa two hundred years earlier. On the day of the celebration, all of Cracow took to the streets. The rains of previous days finally abated, and the sun shone upon the procession to Wawel Castle for a high mass of thanksgiving for the victory. An eight-hundred-strong honor guard of Cracovians lined the route to Wawel Castle from the Carmelite church in Piaski, where an early morning service had been held.[39] To the accompaniment of church bells, all imaginable organizations processed, their members decked out in traditional costume. Visitors to Cracow might have thought that the pages of history had been turned back to the Middle Ages. Religious brotherhoods bearing banners led the procession, followed by the ancient guilds and artisanal associations. The elected "king" of the Sharpshooters' Society carried a silver cock, gift of King Sigismund Augustus; he was accompanied by colorfully dressed sharpshooters from Cracow, Poznań, and elsewhere.

All imaginable local societies, trade and professional associations, and clubs joined the procession: musicians and merchants, lawyers and notaries, teachers and scientists. The professors of Jagiellonian University treaded stately in their caps and gowns, the president of the university wearing a crimson gown with an ermine collar. Also processing were the scholars of the Academy of Arts and Letters, the School of Fine Arts, students from the universities of Cracow and Lwów, and representatives of local and regional governments from Cracow, Lwów, and Poznań, as well as members of the Galician Diet and both chambers of the Council of State. Local musicians in peasant dress serenaded the visitors lining the market square and street leading to the castle.

Toward the end of the procession came the numerous clergy with Bishop Dunajewski, shaded by a canopy and attired in a two-hundred-year-old bejeweled cope embroidered with a silver Polish eagle. He was followed by three political heavyweights: Provincial Marshal Zyblikiewicz, Prelate Stablewski (representing the Polish caucus in the Berlin Parliament), and Cracow mayor Ferdynand Weigel, who were accompanied by members of the Galician Provincial Executive Council (Wydział Krajowy). Several platoons of volunteer firemen closed the procession, after which the rest of the city and visitors joined in the hike up Wawel Hill as well.

The sight of so many Poles winding their way along the Cracow streets in celebration of a Polish accomplishment made an impression upon participants as well as spectators. A word frequently used to describe this first large national procession was "majestic," as if Poles were reliving the days when they had a king of their own in the castle. Also underscored was the fact that "this procession [was] not official"; it was "not commanded . . . but originat[ed] from religious motives and from a national consciousness."[40] The overflowing cathedral witnessed a thanksgiving mass, which was also attended by the imperial military authorities stationed in Cracow, a fact noted—for did it not reflect a degree of appreciation for Sobieski's contribution?—in Polish accounts of the event.[41]

Crowds returned that afternoon for the unveiling of the commemorative tablet. Grandstands to seat two thousand paying guests had been constructed for the occasion. Many more onlookers crowded the terraces of Old Cloth Hall, hung out of the windows of the surrounding buildings, even peered down from the rooftops upon the proceedings. Two platforms held the members of the city council and the choir of the Cracow Music Society, fortified with members from cognate clubs. Upon the arrival of Bishop Dunajewski, the combined choirs broke into song. After a speech by Mayor Weigel, the monument was unveiled to prolonged applause. The bishop blessed the tablet, and a peasant also addressed the crowds. The event concluded with a cantata for male choir and brass band composed for the occasion (lyrics by Anczyc, music by Żeleński).[42]

The white eagle, Poland's emblem, appeared as a leitmotif of the celebration. It dominated the embroidery on Dunajewski's ancient cope, embellished the red cloth that covered the commemorative tablet prior to the unveiling, and appeared, together with Sobieski's coat-of-arms, on the frame of the tablet.[43] Mayor Weigel made much of this patriotic symbol, also found (newly restored) on the Florian Gate at the medieval entrance to the city. Addressing the assembled crowd, he recalled avian omens in Sobieski's life: a white dove upon the election building that would not fly away until Sobieski had been elected king, and yet another seen at the height of the battle for Vienna over the monarch's head. Noting several birds flying over the Cracow market square, Weigel wondered aloud "whether among this whiteness of doves a *white eagle* is able to push its way out (*wylegnąć*)."[44]

Did such patriotic comments suffice to make this a Polish celebration? It was clear that the central authorities wished for symbols of imperial rule to be present. Prime Minister Taaffe reportedly decreed that, as Austrian officials, the viceroy and provincial marshal were to appear in uniform, if invited to church services. It is not clear that these orders were followed, however. Contemporary sources maintain that Provincial Marshal Zyblikiewicz was seen in magnificent Polish costume during the procession. Other highly placed Poles also chose to emphasize their Polishness. Konstanty Czartoryski, vice president of the House of Lords in Vienna, attended neither the celebration at the Kahlenberg nor the opening of the new Rathaus in the imperial capital. Instead, he joined a thirty-person delegation of Poles from Vienna in the solemn parade in Cracow on September 12. If the Cracow festivities were only an extension of the official imperial celebration, it is odd that, at least for some highly placed individuals, national allegiances apparently outweighed imperial loyalties.[45]

There was yet another way to underscore the Polish interpretation of the Relief of Vienna. One Cracow resident came up with his own plan for reaching a broader audience. Jan Matejko was the preeminent painter of large canvases depicting scenes of Polish history and rector of the School of Fine Arts in Cracow. A year earlier Matejko gained public renown by donating to the nation his painting *The Prussian Homage,* depicting the swearing of an oath of allegiance to the king of Poland by the Prussian prince Albert Hohenzollern in 1525. Praise poured in from Poles from all parts of the globe, and the historical canvas was exhibited elsewhere in Europe, most notably in Vienna and Rome.

After that triumph, Matejko undertook to paint something appropriately festive for the 1883 anniversary. At 4.6 meters high by 9 meters wide, *Sobieski at Vienna* (figure 2.2) was Matejko's biggest work to date.[46] Despite the king's reputation as a warrior, the scene depicted is not of the battle itself. Sobieski is shown handing a letter with news of the victory to the monk Denhof, who was to deliver it to the pope. The Polish king sits triumphantly on the Grand Vizier's horse, with signs of the battle—captured banners and horsetail ensigns, a dead Turk, and a dead German woman— in the foreground. At Sobieski's side is his son Jakub; behind the pair are a host of Polish hussars, their red-and-white banners filling the sky. Above the troops and over the distant tower of Saint Stephen's in Vienna a rainbow brightens the heavens, and a white dove can be seen hovering over Sobieski's head. On either side of the canvas other knights (including Charles of Lorraine) acknowledge Sobieski as the victor. In an unusual step, the artist signed his work "Jan Matejko rp. 1883 Polonus," reportedly so that he would not be mistaken for an Austrian.[47]

Although *Sobieski at Vienna* was completed not long before for the celebration, it did not remain in Cracow. Instead, Matejko sent it to be exhibited at the Gartenbau-Gesellschaft in Vienna. The Polish painter set out to correct Austrian perceptions of this episode in history. That the central figure in the painting was a victorious Sobieski must have surprised the Viennese visitors, who expected to see their own princes featured. To make sure the message penetrated far into Viennese society, Matejko ordered his secretary to announce at the opening of the exhibition that there would be no

Fig. 2.2. Jan Matejko, *Sobieski at Vienna*. Even this tiny reproduction of a huge canvas conveys the centrality of the Polish king. *Sketch, Matejko House; photo courtesy of the National Museum, Kraków.*

entrance fee. Anyone could view the Polish version of the famous relief. The Viennese public was amazed at Matejko's generosity and, accordingly, showed up in large numbers. As intended, "guards, cooks, Viennese vendors and even villagers from the region of Vienna viewed the painting."[48] In addition, a booklet explaining the work was translated into German and made available to visitors. While the crowds thinned after the first week, Matejko's deed certainly caused a stir. Nineteenth-century society was not used to free exhibitions of major works of art. Such actions underscore the opportunities that these commemorations afforded to men of the brush— and of action.

FOLK, FAITH,
AND THE FATHERLAND

Visual images of the 1683 battle proved powerful in presenting the Polish view of the past. Most images from the Cracow celebration, however, were created with the domestic populace in mind. The commemoration was expected to have an important impact on the Polish nation itself, as seen from comments made by elites of varied political persuasion. For example, the citizens' committee declared it was "indispensably necessary that . . . as wide as possible a circle of the population take part" in the commemoration so that "a national consciousness would awaken more strongly in the folk" and "would immortalize in [their] memory its recollection of national praise."[49]

The efforts of the citizens' committee and the local conservatives (who also sought to impress the folk) were met with success: peasants flocked to the celebration. Over twelve thousand peasants came, saw, and brought their experiences from their trip back home with them, as did the father of Stanisław Pigoń, whose trip to Cracow in 1883 was the farthest he ever traveled from his village and about which he reminisced with pleasure for years.[50] Smaller celebrations were attended by peasants in over 140 Galician cities, towns, and villages. While these festivities paled by comparison with those in Cracow, with their church ceremonies, commemorative sermons, lectures, perhaps even theatrical performances and songs, a tablet or other commemorative deed had an impact. It has been said that "the celebrations of 1883, like none previously, exerted a strong influence on the national consciousness of the Galician villagers."[51]

How did so many peasants come to celebrate an anniversary from the Polish past, a past that doubtless had more relevance for the descendants of the noblemen who fought the Turks in 1683? Recall that peasants had long thought that only nobles were Poles; they considered themselves Mazurians, distinct from the nobles. Yet peasants also considered themselves Christians. Religion proved to be what the peasants and the nobility had in common. Catholicism could bring them closer together than could tales of a distant past. It might also lead them to accept the notion that they too might be Poles. Indeed, the equation of Polishness with Catholicism became tremendously important for Polish nation-builders precisely because of peasant piety. Religious language and imagery spoke to a peasantry raised almost exclusively on sermons—something that no Polish activist could afford to ignore.

A unique and powerful aspect of the 1883 celebration was the clever juxtaposition of the religious and the national. As noted earlier, the coronation of a miraculous image of the Virgin Mary at the Carmelite church at Piaski preceded the official Sobieski celebration. The connection between the two events is interesting, if not immediately apparent. The crowning of the fresco of the Virgin and child ostensibly represented the fulfillment of plans laid over a hundred years earlier, when Pope Clement XIII approved permission to crown the miraculous Piaski Madonna.[52] This delay in action would turn what in the eighteenth century might have been viewed as just another coronation into a more uncommon, and thus noteworthy, nineteenth-century event. It also raises questions as to what prompted this renewed interest in such displays of popular piety as would necessarily accompany the solemn fixing of gold crowns to a venerated image. That three coronations in Galicia were scheduled in the space of six years (1877–83) suggests that something was afoot. Was this part of a general Galician strategy to provide opportunities for a popular religious revival?

This new spate of coronations turns out to be related to a crisis affecting the Uniate Church, also known as the Greek Catholic Church.[53] Established at the end of the seventeenth century, this new branch of Catholicism was designed to bring closer the two main peoples of the Polish-Lithuanian Commonwealth: the (primarily Catholic) Poles and the (Orthodox) Ruthenes. As a result, many Ruthenes came under the jurisdiction of the pope while being allowed to retain their eastern rite (including language and the right of priests to marry). Primarily of peasant stock, the Ruthenes could be considered the east Galician counterpart to the Polish-speaking "Mazurians" of the western Galician lands.

Ruthenes also populated parts of Russian Poland. The crisis alluded to above began in the region of Chełm (Kholm), the site of the last remaining Uniate eparchy of the Kingdom of Poland. It was abolished in 1875, and its Uniate inhabitants were converted to Orthodoxy, many against their will. Paradoxically, the forcible conversion was carried out in part by disaffected Uniate clergymen from Galicia.[54] This "defection" of Uniates both brought the Ruthenian Catholic clergy and faithful in Galicia under closer observation and led to attempts to strengthen the ties between the various Catholics of the crown land. As a sign of Catholic unity, the leading clergymen of all three Catholic rites in Galicia—the Roman, Greek, and Armenian Catholic Churches—took part in the festivities connected with the Piaski Madonna. Their bishops took turns celebrating masses in the Carmelite church during the week preceding the coronation, at which the charismatic Armenian archbishop Izaak Mikołaj Issakowicz delivered the sermon.[55]

Yet the coronation of the Piaski Madonna proved to be a national as well as a religious or Galician event. The figure of Mary, after all, was shared property. The Queen of Heaven and Earth had been identified as Poland's Queen since the sixteenth century, when King John Casimir made an oath to that effect. The Galician clergy often reminded the populace of this royal oath, and the connection was not unfamiliar to the peasantry.[56] In the case of the Piaski Madonna, national elements were incorporated into the very design of the crowns. Historical motifs as well as the initials "R. P." embroidered on the crimson velvet lining of the crown announced unequivocally that Mary was *Regina Poloniae*—Queen of Poland. Nor was the coronation simply an all-Galician celebration. Polish bishops in exile from the other two empires (one a former exile to Siberia) also attended. Their presence reminded Galicians of the sacrifices Poles had made over the ages as a consequence of their fidelity to their Catholic faith. History, too, facilitated the merging of the national and the religious: Sobieski had prayed before the miraculous image before setting off for Vienna.[57]

This last connection allowed for a unique amplification and adjustment of both events. The coronation gained a new resonance, while the Sobieski celebration gained a new audience: peasants, some of whom remained for the festivities. Father Stanisław Stojałowski single-handedly led the vast majority of the peasants to the celebration. By the end of August, nearly eight thousand had signed up for special trains departing for Cracow on September 6 and 7. Stojałowski's villagers hailed from all of Galicia, but also from Bukovina, Podlasie, Hungary, and Silesia—a tribute to the reach of his folk papers, *Wieniec* (The wreath) and *Pszczółka* (The bee). Ruthenes also joined the pilgrimage, as the inscription on a laurel wreath—"Polish and Ruthenian folk on the 200th anniversary"—placed on Sobieski's tomb attests.[58]

While some peasants left on September 10, before the actual Sobieski anniversary got under way, this does not mean that they were exposed only to the religious aspects of the celebration. They had visited Wawel Castle, attended special lectures on Sobieski, and otherwise were exhorted by both Cracow Canon Ignacy Polkowski and Stojałowski to imitate the "living faith that led our knights at Vienna" as well as consider the responsibilities that follow from love for the fatherland.[59] That they had traveled to Cracow under the banner "For faith and the fatherland" was also underscored by the red and white cockades they wore, inscribed with the words "Folk pilgrimage—Cracow 1883. The celebration of the coronation of the miraculous image of the Blessed Virgin Mary.—The jubilee of the victory of John III."[60]

The stimulation provided by Father Stojałowski and the organizers likely had a greater impact on the pilgrims than did the actual coronation on September 8. Only a lucky few, let in through the side door of the church by Father Stojałowski, had a view of the proceedings. The church was not large enough to hold the peasant throngs, being filled instead by delegates. The vast majority of pilgrims in attendance stood outside in the rain, where a mass was being celebrated for the crowds (the celebrant sheltered by a canopy). Furthermore, inclement weather deprived all present of what was generally the high point of any popular religious celebration: the colorful procession of peasants in their Sunday best accompanying the clergy. Twice it was scheduled, and twice rained out.[61] The loss of this "picturesque effect" was mourned by the conservatives, who longed to perpetuate the myth of docile and well-behaved "holiday" villagers devoted to traditional ways of life and satisfied with the status quo.[62]

The lack of a procession deprived the peasantry of its only role, albeit a secondary one, in the ceremony. During the coronation, other estates were given a more active part in the coronation. Burghers representing the urban political and economic leadership carried the crowns to be placed on the image. Several noblemen assisted Bishop Dunajewski.[63] Not included in the coronation ceremonial, peasants were simply window dressing for the event, in the celebration but not of it. In some ways their fate at the Piaski coronation seems an apt metaphor for their status within society: welcome as colorful repositories of national tradition but kept from participating in any meaningful way.

THE "POLISH FOLK" CELEBRATES SOBIESKI

Another dimension of the festivities, the Sobieski anniversary proper, witnessed some new approaches to the peasantry. A folk celebration was proposed by an independent citizens' committee (*komitet obywatelski*). It had a different vision of peasant participation, one that emphasized *uobywatelnienie*—literally, the turning of the peasant into a citizen (*obywatel*).[64] Not satisfied with mere religious allegiance, the citizens' committee underscored the villagers' status as political beings and organized its celebration around that principle. Peasant delegates from Galicia were to come from all of Galicia: in the final version of the project, each of the sixty-two districts was permitted to send three delegates.[65]

The plans of the citizens' committee were designed to ease the entry of peasants into the larger Polish community.[66] By organizing a meal and other events that would bring delegates into contact with each other and with peasants from the Cracow region, the committee sought to provide the peasant delegates with the same opportunities for networking that commemorations generally afforded the traveling middle and upper classes. Funded by donations, in cash or in kind, the meal for the delegates also emphasized the ties across the estates; the Cracow liberal-democratic daily *Nowa Reforma* (New reform) faithfully recorded the donation of each bucket of beer or bottle of alcohol—a good way to encourage support for the cause from individuals and firms. Like other Poles, villagers would make a symbolic procession along the former Royal Road, place wreaths at Sobieski's tomb, and generally be a visible presence in Cracow. Several would even be given the opportunity to speak to the crowds.[67] A commemorative stone trumpeting the presence of the peasantry at the celebration was to be placed at the foot of a Sobieski monument being erected by the Cracow Sharpshooters' Society; its unveiling would doubtless result in the intermingling of the urban middle classes with the villagers. In sum, peasants would be treated more like rank-and-file Poles of the middle and upper classes, making this truly an uplifting experience for them.

The ambitious plans of the citizens' committee came under fire, however.[68] Complaints were motivated by various concerns, as seen from a letter—published and endorsed by *Czas*—written to the mayor by Paweł

Popiel. The old conservative claimed that the emotions that might manifest themselves at the planned banquet in dance and cavorting would "lessen the celebration" and leave the folk with rather frivolous memories of the event. Claiming to know peasants well, Popiel asserted that they were moved only by the spiritual and added, "Appearances notwithstanding, our folk is serious, and it really is not our business to act on its senses."[69] In addition to these concerns, Popiel's letter also hints at other fears shared by the conservatives—including the fear that the conservatives' political rivals, the weaker democratic forces congregating around the daily *Nowa Reforma,* would gain influence among the peasantry at the former's expense.

Popiel's letter resulted in a compromise between the various parties. The conservatives, together with the official Cracow committee, remained in charge of the celebration as a whole but made room for some of the popular initiatives: several leaders of the citizens' committee were co-opted into the ranks of the city committee, the folk festivities were added to the official program, and a peasant would be allowed to speak at the unveiling of the commemorative tablet.[70] At the same time, the Cracow Sharpshooters' Society denied permission for part of the folk celebration to be held there. This decision had repercussions for the tenor of the folk celebration. The folk banquet was transferred to the grounds of the Carmelite church, and the planned tablet attesting to the presence of the peasantry at the Sobieski celebration was mounted on the outer wall of the church.[71] This ironically brought the peasants full circle: even those delegates who had not traveled to Cracow for the coronation of the Piaski Madonna found themselves directed to the site. One might think of the new arrangement as a sort of "ghettoization" of the peasant: he was returned to his traditional place, near the church . . .

The Carmelite church also came to be the site of the commemorative tablet prepared by the citizens' committee. Not simply another independent initiative, it speaks volumes about the ways the peasants, Polish and Ruthenian speakers alike, were perceived relative to the Polish nation. After all, a large Polish nation could hardly exclude the over two-million-strong Ruthenian population. But strength in numbers was not as important as the nature of the nation. The inclusion of Ruthenes reinforced Polish perceptions of a national mission: to "carry the banner of Catholic faith, liberty and civilization to the East."[72] Russia had sought to establish its own place as the central and hegemonic Slavic power; a strong Polish nation called this entire concept into question.

This aspect of the Sobieski festivities was noticed by the power to the east. The Russian rulers of the former Kingdom of Poland forbade even mention of the festivities in the press: cross-border solidarity would undermine Russian rule of the partitioned territories.[73] The conceptions of Polish national identity that girded the celebration help explain Russian fears. Thoughts of Poland as a great nation were inimical to Russia, for reasons of geography as well as ideology. Any larger Polish presence would require Russian territorial losses in the western guberniias (provinces), which had been ruled by the Poles until the late eighteenth century. But Russians had another reason to worry: for any large Slavic nation must be considered as a potential leader of the little Slavic nations or nationalities. Russia had sought to exert influence among the Slavs, but a strong Polish nation could undermine its influence. However paradoxical it may seem, given the fact of partition, Poles were seen as challenging Russians for hegemony over the Slavs.[74]

Indeed, many Poles thought that the ultimate advantage lay on their side. They saw Poles and Russians as representing two trends in Slavdom. Each was an archetype of a different type of civilization. In the words of one activist, Russians had been corrupted by Mongol influence—that is, by "elements foreign to Slavdom," which led them to use brute force and hampered free national and individual development. In contrast, Poles were a genuinely Slavic nation, which would like to erect, "on the domestic foundation of national individualisms, a building of common freedom under the influence of education and genuine progress."[75] One option, thus, was characterized by domination, coercion, and stagnation; the other stood for freedom, individuality, and progress.[76] Poles clearly believed that their option would be more attractive to other Slav populations. Thus the situation looked—in theory. If Poles were to challenge Russia for Slavic hegemony, it was crucial that they win over their own domestic Slav minority. In other words, they needed to impress the vast masses of peasants in the eastern part of Galicia, whence so many delegates had come.

In order to do this, those behind the commemoration had to convince Ruthenes that their interests lay with the Poles. History played an important role in this argument. The ancestors of the Ruthenes—the people who had lived in the easternmost part of the Polish-Lithuanian Commonwealth —had served as the bulwark against invasion by Turks and Tatars. Furthermore, some twenty thousand Cossacks had fought under Sobieski.[77] It was hoped that Ruthenes might see themselves as part of that same heritage, connected to the Polish past. The figure of Sobieski proved an important unifying symbol: the Polish king was descended from the Ruthenian princes of Halich (Halicz). In order to spread this message, Galician officialdom printed announcements and published brochures and broadsides in both Polish and Ruthenian.[78] Visual images, such as one broadside showing the duke of Lorraine doffing his hat to Sobieski, were designed to convey the leadership role of the Polish/Ruthenian king (figure 2.3).[79] This left a potent message: working together, Poles and Ruthenes had proved superior to their German allies.

[II   Na pamiątkę
**dwóchsetnej rocznicy odsieczy
Wiednia.**
 	
    Turcy oblegli Wiedeń w r. 1683. Ce-
sarz Leopold I. uprosił króla polskiego na
pomoc. Król Jan III. Sobieski przybył pod
Wiedeń. Dnia 12. września pobił Turków
i oswobodził stolicę cesarstwa. Obrazek
przedstawia początek bitwy. Król Jan III.
na czele wojska polskiego, mając przy boku
swoim królewicza Jakóba, wydaje rozkazy
wodzowi cesarskiemu, księciu Karolowi
Lotaryńskiemu.
	**Въ память
	двусотпои рôчницѣ освободженя
	Вѣдня.**
	
	    Турки осадили Вѣдень въ ропѣ 1683.
	Цѣсарь Леопольдъ I. упросивъ короля поль-
	ского на помôчь. Король Иванъ III. Собѣскій
	прибувъ пôдъ Вѣдень. Дня 12. Вересня побивъ
	Туркôвъ и освободивъ столицю цѣсарства.
	Образокъ представляе початокъ битвы. Король
	Иванъ III. на чолѣ войска польского, маючи
	при собѣ королевича Якова, выдае приказы
	вождови цѣсарскому, князю Каролеви Лота-
	риньскому.

Fig. 2.3 Color postcard, souvenir of the two hundredth anniversary of the Relief of Vienna, with text in Polish and Ruthenian; drawing by Juliusz Kossak. "In memory of the two-hundredth anniversary of the Relief of Vienna. Turks besieged Vienna in the year 1683. Emperor Leopold I asked the Polish king for help. King John III Sobieski came to Vienna. On September 12 he beat the Turks and freed the capital of the empire. This picture depicts the beginning of the battle. King John III, at the head of the Polish army, having by his side his princeling [son] Jakób, gives orders to the imperial leader, Charles, Duke of Lorraine." *Photo courtesy of the Jagiellonian Library.*

The organizers of the folk celebration also strove to unify the peasantry under the Polish banner. Speakers underscored the role of Sobieski and the Ruthenes in defending the faith and in defending Poland. "One faith and one God" was "over all Poland."[80] Addressing the folk delegates, Weigel reminded them that their brethren under Russian rule were taking part in a bloody and holy war. Like Sobieski and the knights, Uniate villagers were risking their lives for their faith.[81] The mayor's address concluded with the words, "We are children of one land, and we understand each other."[82]

Some present clearly hoped that all these "children of one land" would consider themselves Polish. This is seen in the wording of the commemorative tablet on the Carmelite church. Unlike the wreaths deposited under Stojałowski's care that mentioned Polish and Ruthenian folk, the tablet stated: "On September 11, 1883, Polish villagers gathered in Cracow solemnly celebrated the two hundredth anniversary of the relief of Vienna by John Sobieski, in remembrance of which this stone has been funded." "Polish villagers" (*włościanie polscy*)—was this a slight to the Ruthenes present? One villager attempted to justify the wording to his compatriots:

> By this phrase: Polish folk, I understand the old Polish folk from sea to sea. I too, as a Mazurian, could demand the phrase on the tablet: Mazurians, but . . . that would be superfluous, for by this phrase I understand Mazurian and Red Ruthenian and Belarusian and Silesian, Pomeranian, . . . that is, all the provinces, thus I consider the inscription as fair. Is this right?—you decide.[83]

Jan Czesak (or whoever inspired him to speak in this way) treated the term "Polish folk" as encompassing the peasantry of the former Commonwealth, that country that once stretched from the Baltic to the Black Sea. The map of the old state warranted a statist approach to Polishness; no villager at that time, whether of Mazurian or Ruthenian descent, had identified himself with the nation of noble Poles. But this too was changing. Addressing the crowds after the blessing of Sobieski tablet, another villager exhorted: "Following the example of that great king . . . let us stand persevering where God placed us, with our holy faith, on the native plot, and we will be worthy sons of those Poles who near Vienna saved the Christian nation from annihilation."[84] Peasants were exhorted to embrace this broader definition of Polishness and become sons of the victorious troops at Vienna. They were to transcend parochial allegiances and political borders and become part of a historic nation—a political, not ethnic nation.[85] They all shared a common past; might they not come to share a common future?

This may have been wishful thinking. Ruthenes had many options: they could identify themselves as Russians, Ukrainians, or Poles. Those Ruthenes who considered themselves Ukrainians saw no reason to celebrate a Polish anniversary, as seen in the reaction to the celebration of certain Ukrainian-language journals.[86] Still, some Ruthenian literati more well disposed toward Poles—the type often referred to as *gente Ruthenus, natione Polonus*—published poems on the occasion of the bicentennial.[87] The Basilian monasteries reportedly also decided to celebrate the anniversary, calling Sobieski the "solicitous protector and benefactor of the Ruthenian clergy and folk."[88] Present in Cracow to observe the celebration, a Prussian agent concluded that the anniversary might lead to better relations between Poles and Ruthenes.[89]

POLISH "FOREIGN POLICY"

That the Polish celebration also had an international dimension should surprise no one. These discussions of both the imperial and domestic scenes have raised issues that transcended parochial borders—much as Poles from the German and Russian lands crossed over into Galicia to participate in various aspects of the festivities, such as the unveiling of the Sobieski monument in Sharpshooters' Park (September 13) or the first pan-Polish Congress of Writers and Artists (September 14–15).[90] Neither empire was pleased with this manifestation of Polish nation-building. None too fond of the Poles' claim to have rescued the Germans and the German emperor, some feared that the folk would confuse this mention of the Holy Roman Emperor with the emperor of the still relatively new Second Reich. On the whole, however, limited celebrations (not extending beyond church walls or private buildings) were allowed by the Prussian authorities, and Prussian Poles took advantage of the opportunity by mounting commemorative tablets on the walls of their churches and holding their own celebrations. These endeavors, although not outlawed, were frowned upon by the authorities, who thought that Poles should be proud to be subjects of the German emperor, whose "praise and magnificence surpasses in its brilliance all recollections of an irretrievably bygone past."[91]

Beyond their ability to hold the kinds of anniversary celebrations discussed above, Poles within the three empires had little recourse to forums for expression outside of the Catholic Church. An important aspect of the anniversary festivities was the way Poles sought to utilize their connection to Rome to make statements about who they were—present as well as past. Their reliance on the goodwill of the Church became visible in the historiographical debate in Austria-Hungary during this period. Pope Leo XIII contacted the archbishop of Vienna at the end of August regarding an indulgence for the faithful on the occasion of the anniversary. Imitating the tone of the pope's letter, which underscored Sobieski's leadership and contributions, Archbishop Ganglbauer composed a pastoral letter in which he gave Sobieski his due, calling him the leader of the combined forces.[92] Read from pulpits all over Austria, the words of the archbishop reached even more people than did Matejko's painting, making it a powerful counterweight to historical revisionism. The Church Universal, thus, could exert pressure on the Church Imperial.

One other by-product of the 1883 commemoration resulted in what might be termed a Polish foreign policy initiative, were it not for the lack of a Polish state. It was the work of Jan Matejko, the Polish artist who exhibited his painting of 1683 to the Viennese public. This year also happened to be the twenty-fifth year of Matejko's career as a painter. Dignitaries from major Polish cities—Lwów, Warsaw, Poznań, Toruń, and Cracow—formed a jubilee committee to honor him.[93] As a convenience to those attending the 1683 festivities, Matejko's jubilee was scheduled for the day after the Sobieski anniversary. The jubilee committee used its influence to gain access to the Wawel for this occasion; its other accomplishment was to be the purchase of Matejko's *Sobieski at Vienna* with funds collected from the nation at large. It was thought that the painting—described earlier—could compensate for the nation's inability to present itself to the world: "our celebrations in Sobieski's honor are good for us, but they cannot speak well enough for us. In this situation the most splendid thing that the nation . . . can afford is Matejko's painting. It will speak to everyone in a language understood by all; it will speak well for our honor and our memory; it will prove that among us there are great hearts and great abilities."[94] The painting, which the Polish public had not yet had occasion to view, was valued for its pedagogical as well as its symbolic value.

Matejko's depiction could convey more than mere words could—but only to those who saw the painting. At the time of the artist's jubilee, *Sobieski at Vienna* was still being exhibited in Vienna. Few Poles had seen the new canvas, displayed in Cracow for less than a week in August, a time when many Cracovians were vacationing elsewhere. Given the collection of donations for the painting's purchase, doubtless they and many others expected to have the occasion to view the work in the National Museum before long. But this was not to be the case.

Those who attended the Matejko jubilee on September 13 learned of the artist's intent for his painting. When publicly asked whether the nation would be allowed the honor of purchasing *Sobieski at Vienna* for posterity—a question that seemed more rhetorical than real—Matejko surprised those gathered by not answering, simply, "Yes." Instead, the honorand suggested, in a rather cryptic manner, that the nation should send the painting to the same destination as Sobieski's royal letter: Rome.[95] It turned out that *Sobieski at Vienna* was intended to be a gift for the Vatican. Instead of permitting the painting to enrich the collection of the National Museum, the artist bestowed the canvas on the nation on the condition that it be given to the Holy Father, Pope Leo XIII, in the name of the Polish nation.[96] Poles would profess their faith, much as Sobieski had two centuries earlier, by sending a work of art that gave proof of their long-standing devotion to the Roman Church.

Matejko's gift echoed Sobieski's own interest in reaching the spiritual authorities. Although times had changed, the idea of serving a higher cause (the integrity of the Catholic Church on earth) remained paramount in both instances. Both Poles went over the heads of the temporal authorities—the Holy Roman Emperor, Leopold I, or Habsburg monarch Francis Joseph, both influential Catholic rulers of their age—and dealt directly with the Vicar of Christ. While by this act the seventeenth-century Polish king could raise his visibility, improve the reputation of his country, and reinforce diplomatic ties with Rome, Poles in the nineteenth century had no country of their own and thus could not engage in traditional diplomacy with the Vatican (or with any other state). Matejko nonetheless appealed, over the head of his Habsburg monarch, to the pope to support the Poles' good name, their unswerving Catholicism and defense of the faith. A permanent reminder of the Poles' defense of Christianity, his gift could raise the Poles' profile in Rome among Church authorities, thus enhancing the status of the Polish nation. Were the work to be hung in view of the public in this prime destination of pilgrims from around the world, Matejko's depiction of the Polish-led victory could have an even greater impact.

Indeed, later that year, the painting and Matejko were warmly received by the pope in Rome. Matejko had hoped that a delegation of Poles from all three empires (and from the émigré community) and representing all estates would be present at the presentation of the painting. While the delegation did not meet his expectations, an important symbolic statement was made by Cardinal Mieczysław Ledóchowski, the Polish primate in exile, who did attend. Occupying Poland's most ancient metropolitan seat (in Gniezno—under German rule at the time), the Polish primate played the same role as did the archbishop of Canterbury for the English. He was the recognized leader of the Polish faithful. Even in exile, Ledóchowski's role was greater than that of mere spiritual leader. Under Poland's elective monarchy, the Polish primate had served as interrex—that is, as temporary ruler until a new monarch was chosen. This doubtless explains why Cardinal Ledóchowski was considered by the delegation to be the only person who could give the painting in the name of the Polish nation.[97] With the artist Matejko and Polish delegation in the background, the Polish primate, spiritual and temporal head of a Polish state that still existed in the hearts of the nation, bestowed this new trophy on the head of the Universal Church.

The extent to which this symbolism was recognized by Poles back home is hard to say. Coverage of the event was understated, for obvious political reasons. A troubled Matejko conferred with Father Henryk Jackowski, provincial of the Jesuits in Cracow, to determine how best to convey Leo XIII's blessing for the entire Polish nation to the people.[98]

Matejko's gift nonetheless made an impression in Rome. Pope Leo XIII accepted the painting "as proof that the long-standing obedience and faith . . . of the Polish nation for this Apostolic See have survived in all fullness . . . , and at the same time will attest to how artists find wondrous and creative inspiration in the Catholic religion."[99] Matejko and his delegation inspired another work, a fresco depicting the presentation of the painting, which can be found in one of the lunettes of the Gallery of Chandeliers in the Vatican Museum to this day. As regards the painting itself, *Sobieski at Vienna* came to grace the hall (now known as Sobieski Hall) near the Raphael Stanze, next to the hall of the Immaculate Conception. All visitors to the Raphael rooms pass *Sobieski at Vienna* along the way. Thus, one goal—increased visibility of the Polish nation—was attained.

VICTORIOUS VISIONS

For a nation without a state, the Poles accomplished a good deal in 1883. The accomplishments were based upon a new approach to the events of 1683, in which Polish piety—past and present—took precedence over (past) knightly valor. This reflected the changed conditions of the Poles, whose faith in their military ability had waned since the partitions of Poland and a number of unsuccessful insurrections. When examining the contribution made by their forefathers at Vienna, what spoke loudest to many late-nineteenth-century Poles was the significance of the victory over the Islamic forces. While the political wisdom of the Poles' defense of the Habsburg capital may be questioned, the Poles did save the West from Turkish conquest. The nation had a clear conscience insofar as Christianity and civilization were concerned: that contribution had not lost its seventeenth-century luster.[100]

The refocusing of the celebration toward the religious underpinnings of the event reflected contemporary needs. More than just a "spectacle," the festivities were intended to "collect and raise the falling spirit and in the name of eternal national ideals become a turning point on the way to internal rebirth."[101] One of those ideals was the Catholicism of the Poles, the nation's loyalty to Rome. Conservatives and clergy were happy to underscore the religiosity of the peasants and encourage the rest of Polish (or should one say Galician) society not to stray from the Catholic Church. This message was directed toward Ruthenes as well: as the conservative Father Walerian Kalinka remarked, if Ruthenia would remain faithful to the Church, it would go with the West and with the Poles and spurn Eastern temptations.[102] Liberals saw religion as a means of reaching a new national constituency and hoped that the commemoration would bring the devout peasantry into communion with the nation. Yet others, such as Father Stanisław Stojałowski, united the various threads. Religious language and imagery permeated the entire celebration, and all sides claimed Catholicism as a pillar of national identity.

Added to the religious dimension was the Poles' concept of themselves as a large, historic, even influential nation. The inclusion of Ruthenes in both the celebration and its imagery made a statement regarding this minority's identity within the old Poland as well as within Galicia. Did this mark a return to the old notion of the political nation, according to which not nationality but political allegiance (once contingent upon noble patent, now more a function of citizenship) determined membership? Or were the Catholic Ruthenes expected to Polonize, as had their noble forebears? This issue remained unresolved, as did the still uneasy relationship of Poles and Ruthenes in Galicia.

The third element underscored in the 1883 festivities was the sense of national mission. The Poles saw themselves as bearers of Western Christianity to the East as well as model Christians for the West. Connected to both previously mentioned components of Polish national identity, the mission was the glue that held it all together. The Poles' role in defending the West and expanding Catholicism in the East could be construed as justification for the nation's continued existence. Those who identified with this mission—it was hoped, peasants and Ruthenes—would augment the nation's numbers and strengthen its position within Galicia and beyond. In sum, the Poles of 1883 saw themselves as a large nation of Catholics from all estates and classes with a mission vis-à-vis both East and West.

At the same time, the degree of interaction among "Poles" was unprecedented. The Cracow festivities afforded an occasion for the inhabitants of all the Polish lands—this time, including the peasantry—to grow closer to each other. Those who attended saw all kinds of people, noted "their differences, but no less their close kinship, their unity of blood and faith."[103] Conservative assessments anticipated positive results on both religious and national fronts.

The celebration also sheds light on the Poles' position within Austria-Hungary. This particular intersection of Polish and Habsburg history ended by emphasizing what was common to both: their Catholicism. The bad blood between Viennese liberals and Poles had no impact on the status of the latter within the empire. Galician Poles continued to stand by the emperor. The conservatives remained positively inclined toward Habsburg rule, given its relatively generous treatment of the Poles and allowances made for Polish governance of the province. Of course, in Galicia such a pro-West, pro-Catholic emphasis hardly rocked the political boat.

The commemoration of the Relief of Vienna was not only for domestic consumption. Another Polish artist proved to be a man of action. Jan Matejko bypassed both the conservatives and committees to appeal first to the Viennese, then to the pope. As an influential painter and generous patriot, Matejko effected a type of foreign policy in the name of his nation. Here we see the diplomacy of art as well as the politics—national and international—of religion. With no state of their own, the Polish nation relied upon artists to an unprecedented degree. It also saw the Church as a defender of the Catholic nation's interests. The Poles' membership in the Universal Church provided them with one of their only opportunities for international expression—or so it seemed.

Part Two

THE 1890s

THREE

Eloquent Ashes: The Translation of Adam Mickiewicz's Remains

The celebrations of the 1870s and 1880s belonged to the initial phase of commemorating the Polish past. Many were events of a somewhat elitist nature, dominated by local and provincial notables, and their demonstrations of Polishness were in keeping with the Austrian regime's allowances for the preservation of nationality and local traditions within the multinational empire. The commemorations of 1890 and beyond were qualitatively different from those that followed—in part attributable to the changing circumstances in which Poles found themselves, as well as to their response to new stimuli.

A new trend toward national activity—a discussion of which follows—also explains why initiatives begun earlier came to fruition in the last decade of the nineteenth century. Poland's preeminent Romantic poet, Adam Mickiewicz, was honored in a special way: his remains were brought from Paris to Cracow, where they were interred in the same cathedral crypts that housed Polish royalty and the nation's greatest military figures. The return of Mickiewicz's ashes to Polish territory marked the beginning of this more active period of national commemoration.

NEW CHALLENGES, NEW INITIATIVES

Despite various opportunities for commemorating the past, Polish activists had little reason for optimism in the 1880s. While conservative loyalism dominated in Galicia, the doctrines of positivism and organic work kept the Poles in the Russian partition in a state of political quietude. Former insurrectionists, some of whom were returning from Siberian exile at this time, were pained to see the inroads made by Russification and political passivity.

The Saint Petersburg weekly *Kraj* (Homeland), founded by Włodzimierz Spasowicz and Erazm Piltz in 1882, adopted a conciliatory stance toward the Russians; members of a nascent Polish middle class in the Kingdom of Poland were migrating elsewhere in the empire in search of employment, often losing any sense of Polishness they might have had in the process. The tsarist regime sought to hoodwink the pious masses into believing that it, not the gentry and clergy, was its ally: witness the monument to Tsar Alexander II erected at the central Polish religious shrine of Częstochowa in 1889. The new united Germany introduced measures designed to weaken the Polish element within. In 1883, a new campaign against "foreigners"— Poles and Jews who were citizens of the Russian or Austrian Empires—residing in the Reich was begun: within the space of two years, thirty-two thousand had been expelled from Berlin and the eastern provinces of the state.[1] This was followed by the creation of a Colonization Commission to purchase estates held by the Polish gentry and distribute them to German peasants.

What could Polish patriots do to inject some life into Polish society, grown lethargic under these conditions? In late 1886, an answer was found: a pamphlet suggesting new options to counter the effects of oppression and organic work. Written by the émigré Zygmunt Miłkowski, *On Active Resistance and a National Treasury* (Rzecz o obronie czynnej i skarbie narodowym) became the handbook for a new generation of Polish activists. Miłkowski advocated that Poles take a more active stance as well as amass financial means—the so-called National Treasury—to finance this new engagement in national life. The brochure led to the creation of a secret patriotic association, the Polish League (Liga Polska), which would coordinate such activity. The league was a clandestine organization run from Switzerland by former insurrectionists. Its goal was to train and assemble national forces in all the Polish lands so that independence might eventually be regained within the borders of 1772 as well as collect the necessary funds to accomplish this goal. The Polish League also had a youth branch, the Union of Polish Youth (Zjednoczenie Młodzieży Polskiej, or Zet), founded the same year by Zygmunt Balicki. Over time, Zet became active in all university centers where Poles studied, both at home and abroad, and trickled down to the secondary schools. The new trend represented by the Polish League was likewise reflected in the Warsaw weekly *Głos* (The voice), founded in 1886.[2]

The new move from passivity to activism may have found another source of inspiration: a new set of historical novels written in the 1880s and likely inspired by the first honorand, Kraszewski.[3] Already at the time of the 1883 commemoration, readers of the Warsaw newspaper *Słowo* (The word) and Cracow's *Czas* were devouring installments of *With Fire and*

Sword (Ogniem i mieczem) by the writer Henryk Sienkiewicz. Sienkiewicz's tale of Polish exploits during the Cossack uprising of 1648 was the first part of a trilogy of novels on challenging episodes of seventeenth-century Polish history. Depicting a swashbuckling and heroic Polish nobility, Sienkiewicz's Trilogy was designed to "uplift hearts" and remind the nation of its great past. Readers in all three empires—for the Poznanian paper *Dziennik Poznański* (Poznań daily news) soon began to serialize his works as well—were exposed to the stirring prose of the Polish novelist.

Sienkiewicz did for Polish history in literature what Matejko did in art. He gave Poles more reasons to be proud of their heritage. In the words of one activist, these novels were "a great song of our past, a collection of the content of our political existence, a photograph of the national spirit not in a given epoch but in the course of its entire existence."[4] Sienkiewicz was also involved in activities intended to strengthen the Polish nation. In 1882 he initiated a public collection to purchase Matejko's *Prussian Homage* for a future Warsaw museum. After the artist donated the painting to Cracow, Sienkiewicz proposed that the funds be designated for a monument to the great nineteenth-century Romantic poet Adam Mickiewicz in Warsaw.[5]

Sienkiewicz's idea of a monument to Mickiewicz (1798–1855) was another sign of the growing desire to commemorate illustrious Poles. It was not the first move in this direction of this most famous of Polish poets, however. By 1883, various plans to honor Mickiewicz had been percolating in Galicia for well over a decade. The fact that no monument had yet been erected hints at the complexity of the undertaking. It was one thing to celebrate a dead king, and quite another to deal with the more recently dead—especially those whose deeds and exploits took place after the partitions. Poets proved even more controversial. Their writings were more malleable than the deeds of military men. Poetic works could be decontextualized, touted for their beauty of form, praised for their descriptions of Polish traditions and scenery. At the same time, their depths could be probed for their political significance, for evidence of new approaches to different social groups, for definitions of what it meant to be a Pole. This kind of "poetic license" was practiced by subsequent generations to shore up their own views of the Polish nation, its characteristics, and its goals.

ADAM MICKIEWICZ: THE FIRST BARD

This treatment was certainly applied to the works and deeds of the poet Adam Mickiewicz. By the 1840s, he had been singled out for a particular Polish honor: the title of *wieszcz*.[6] The full sense of this word, often translated as inspired poet or bard, is hard to render into English.[7] Although master of the poetic arts, the Polish bard possessed powers far above those of a talented composer of verses or singer of songs. Attributed to him were heightened sensibilities, a sort of seeing with the heart that was privy to a special kind of revelation. This power supposedly came from "the spirit of the collectivity, from auguries and inspirations of primitive-childlike humanity, untouched by civilization, close to nature and capable of making spontaneous contact with the higher world."[8] The bard spoke for the nation in one voice, expressed what was in his heart, even suffered in the name of the nation.[9] As Konrad, one of Mickiewicz's characters, exclaimed, "The fatherland and I are one; / My name is million: because for the millions / I love and suffer torment" (*Dziady*, part 3).

The *wieszcz's* elevated status reflected the needs of the nation during this period. Had there been no partitions of Poland, poets—even divinely inspired ones—could not have played such an important role. However, in the nineteenth century such poets filled a void in the Polish community. When the Poles lacked leaders or when their leaders did not satisfy the people's expectations—as, for example, during the November Insurrection of 1830—poets filled the vacuum. They espoused a Polish messianism, a millenarian religious consciousness predicting that the Poles had a role to play in the salvation of mankind here on earth.[10] Still, theirs was a spiritual power: instead of creating political programs and ideologies, they sketched their own visions of the nation, explaining its past suffering and predicting a return to independent statehood.[11] The governance of souls (*rząd dusz*), not partisan temporal politics, absorbed them. This did not mean that the bards paid no attention to the actual status of the Polish nation. It has been said that the great Romantic poets "wrote the scripts of the Polish conspiracies, patriotic demonstrations and . . . insurrections."[12] Stirred by the predicament of lost independence and unsuccessful insurrections, they took to heart the Romantic credo of concern for the rights of peoples, their own and others. Mickiewicz—like Byron—was very much a part of early-nineteenth-century Romanticism; he, too, fought for subjected nations (for the Italians, not Byron's Greeks).

Mickiewicz's biography, with its recurrent strains of poetry and revolution, suggests the problems and promise that might accompany any celebration of his life and work. While Kraszewski had lived in all the partitioned lands, Mickiewicz's horizons were at once narrower and broader. "A Ruthene by birth, a Lithuanian in heart and thought, a Pole in word and deed," he united many of the disparate elements comprising the Polish nation.[13] A scion of an impoverished noble family in the eastern borderlands of Poland, the young Mickiewicz was a conspirator as well as a poet. For his participation in a secret youth society in Wilno, he was sentenced to exile and spent the years 1823–28 in Russia—fortunately for him, not in Siberia but in Petersburg, Odessa, and Moscow, where his poetic talent opened the doors to the salons of Russian aristocrats and literary figures and gained him recognition. During this period he wrote not only evocative sonnets but also the allegorical *Konrad Wallenrod,* in which a small nation (Lithuania) rises to defeat a much larger one (the Teutonic Knights). Although set in medieval times, *Konrad Wallenrod* was perceived as a political manifesto by the Poles and enhanced Mickiewicz's reputation among his compatriots.[14]

Departing the Russian Empire for the West in 1829, Mickiewicz spent the rest of his life in emigration, primarily in France. There he furthered Western knowledge of Slavic culture through his lectures at the Collège de France (1840–44): he was the first occupant of the newly created chair of Slavic languages and literatures. While many of his most famous works were completed by the early 1830s, Mickiewicz soon cast aside poetry, instead becoming involved in the revolutions of the day: he formed a legion to fight for Italian freedom during 1848, edited the revolutionary journal *Le Tribune des Peuples* (Tribune of the people) in 1849, and traveled to Constantinople during the Crimean War to organize further military actions until his death there in 1855.

Given Mickiewicz's varied experiences, Poles of all stripes could find something to admire, whether his rhymes or deeds, his opposition to tsardom, or his professorship at the Collège de France. As in the fable of the blind men and the elephant, each champion of Mickiewicz described what he felt—or chose to feel, as seemed to be the case here. In the second half of the nineteenth century, nearly everyone seemed to be proclaiming a connection to Mickiewicz, claiming descent from him. Although it referred to the indebtedness felt by Mickiewicz's contemporaries, Krasiński's famous phrase "We all stem from him" (*My z niego wszyscy*) could be reinterpreted for this later age as "We all took advantage of him."[15] Poets such as Mickiewicz presented endless possibilities to those who sought a bard's imprimatur for their own political, social, and national aims. The Poles who celebrated the Polish poet made use of varied aspects of Mickiewicz's legacy. They attached themselves to those works and deeds that spoke most eloquently to them.

In the final third of the nineteenth century, numerous celebrations honored Mickiewicz. Small, local, or private initiatives, these events were most often prompted by the annual anniversaries of the poet's birth and death. I will focus here on the first of two major public celebrations of Mickiewicz, the return of the émigré poet to Polish territory via the translation of his remains to Cracow in 1890. (The second—the centennial of Mickiewicz's birth in 1898—is the subject of chapter 5.) These events provide insight into the complicated nature of the relationship between this noted poet and late-nineteenth-century Poles, a relationship that persists to this day.

"A TOMB FOR
OUR BONES IN OUR LAND"

In his "Pilgrim Litany," Mickiewicz prayed for "a tomb for our bones in our land." He could not know at the time that this prayer would find an echo in the desire of the generations that followed him: to bring the poet's remains back to Poland. For, after his sudden death in Constantinople in 1855, Mickiewicz's body was shipped not to his homeland, but to France. The great Polish poet was buried at the cemetery in Montmorency near Paris, where so many Polish émigrés were laid to rest.

While there had been some interest in relocating Mickiewicz's remains to a site on Polish ground soon after his death, not until 1866, the beginning of Austria's constitutional era, was such a move considered possible. It was in conjunction with another anniversary, the three hundredth anniversary of the Union of Lublin in 1869, that the idea of bringing Mickiewicz home entered into the public discourse.[16] The Wawel crypts beneath the cathedral were the historic burial site of the Polish kings, the Polish Acropolis, the "holiest shrine of the Polish nation."[17] Would it not be of benefit to the nation, it was thought, if the remains of illustrious Poles, such as Mickiewicz, were transferred there?

After all, the Wawel crypts were not reserved for the long-deceased Polish royalty. Precedent for new burials had been set in the early nineteenth century. In 1817 and 1818 two military heroes were laid to rest in the Wawel crypts: Prince Józef Poniatowski and Tadeusz Kościuszko. Both men had filled the king-less void during the partition period, Poniatowski liberating part of Galicia from the Austrians and fighting under Napoleon, Kościuszko as the *wódz naczelny*, or main leader, of the 1794 insurrection. The importance of these figures during the short-lived independence of the Free City of Cracow was reflected in the relative accessibility of their tombs. Prior to the mid-nineteenth century, only one of the Wawel crypts was open to the public: Saint Leonard's crypt, the original Romanesque crypt containing the tombs of Kościuszko, Poniatowski, and—the sole royal figure—Sobieski. Only after the reburial of Casimir the Great were the royal crypts linked with Saint Leonard's and made accessible to the public, thus expanding the "national catacombs."[18]

This desire for proximity to the physical remains of the illustrious dead should hardly be surprising in a predominantly Catholic nation. For centuries, relics had been featured in churches and in rituals of the faith. The remains of Saint Stanislas, bishop and martyr, were found in the same Wawel Cathedral as the royal tombs. Parallel to the ancient translation of relics by the Church, the idea of repatriating, or translating, Mickiewicz's remains was saturated with religious symbolism. His remains were referred to as "relics" and their translation as "elevation" or "exaltation."[19] These patriotic Polish relics of the Polish emigration—for this is how they were viewed abroad—were supposed to serve as a "testimony, as a stimulus, and as instructions."[20] The relics found in the Wawel were to hearten, even embolden, the nation back home.

Cracow's unique status meant that repatriating Mickiewicz to Cracow would be seen as his return to the fatherland. Given the unfavorable conditions in Mickiewicz's "little homeland"[21]—the "Lithuania" of the Polish-Lithuanian Commonwealth, now incorporated into Russia proper—Cracow seemed the best of possible alternatives. The former capital was the spiritual homeland of late-nineteenth-century Poles, a Poland in the minds of the masses. The crypts in particular appeared to be one place where foreign domination could not penetrate. As one contemporary noted, "from under the sepulchral shroud a different reality spoke than that which surrounded society."[22] There Poland could be envisaged by those who spent their lives as subjects of Habsburg, Hohenzollern, or Romanov monarchs. Visitors to Cracow "drew in that Polish atmosphere, from the stones, from the houses, from the towers redolent of antiquity" and for a moment "lost all other thoughts besides the delight of breathing in this city of the spirit, this 'center of Polishness.' "[23] This Polish center would be home for the Russian subject Mickiewicz, even though he had never set foot in Cracow.

Even a spiritual capital required real physical markers to jolt the nation's imagination to life. The translation of Mickiewicz's remains can be viewed as part of the movement from a Poland of the mind to one with some physical basis. This and other pieces of "Polish" territory would be marked in special, symbolic ways by national burials and monuments as the Poles reclaimed both physical and temporal space for their nation. Many Poles were convinced that the nation's continued existence had been furthered by the inspiration of the great Romantic poets, who understood the pain of statelessness, of separation from the homeland, and fought in their own way for Poland's independence. As leader of the nation—not to mention a "ruler of souls"—Mickiewicz deserved to join other such leaders in the Wawel. Here, thus, should be his final resting place.

OVERCOMING OBSTACLES— CONSERVATIVE AND OTHER

While the idea of celebrating Mickiewicz within Galicia was first raised in the late 1860s, interest in the project surged at the end of 1879, after the Kraszewski jubilee—revitalized by a donation by Kraszewski.[24] Responsibility for the preparations was transferred by the Cracow city council to the new Committee for the Construction of a Monument (Komitet Budowy Pomnika) to Mickiewicz.[25] The committee needed a good deal of prodding, however, for the idea of burying Mickiewicz in the Wawel crypts worried many local notables. While the Cracow conservatives may have thought the burial of military or political leaders of the nation in the Wawel crypts to be fitting, the émigré poet-turned-revolutionary was harder for them to stomach. Part of the problem seemed to be Mickiewicz's connection to the émigré community. Many Poles abroad tendered more radical views of a future Poland, views that were anathema to the empires of the East. The émigrés' vision of what was needed back home contrasted sharply with that of the Cracow conservatives, content with the status quo that permitted them to control Galician affairs.

The Cracow conservatives did not want Mickiewicz to be buried alongside Poland's kings and warriors. "Your father did not foresee the Wawel [as his final resting place]," they told Mickiewicz's son Władysław in Paris.[26] Instead, they proposed a different destination for his remains: the crypt at the Pauline Church of Saint Stanislas at Skałka. Renovated in 1880, the crypt had been transformed into a pantheon for meritorious Poles and, within the space of several years, contained the remains of Jan Długosz and several other "persons of merit in the nation."[27] Its establishment nonetheless seemed to be a qualified victory for the nation at large. While it provided a place to honor national figures, it could also serve as a convenient pretext to exclude them from the most prestigious national catacomb: the Wawel.

Already in 1879 Kraszewski warned Mickiewicz's son of the conservatives' plans. The "ultramontane leadership and clergy," he claimed, would not allow for the poet's burial in the Wawel: instead, they were preparing the Skałka crypt, "where they want to segregate all writers, poets, etc., so that they might not rub shoulders with the kings and military commanders [z hetmanami], although more than one of them, like your Father, commanded [hetmanił] the nation."[28] Taking the warning to heart, the poet's son settled the matter by declaring that the family would reject all propositions except for "the Wawel, near Kościuszko and Poniatowski."[29]

Given this ultimatum, the committee slowly undertook preparations for the move. Approval for the use of the Wawel crypt was gained from the Cathedral Chapter in 1884, after which the committee balked at making further arrangements.[30] This foot-dragging irritated a large group of Cracovians, primarily members of the local liberal- and democratic-minded intelligentsia. They formed their own citizens' committee, collected funds, and resolved to complete the preparations by the end of 1884, if possible. The translation soon became a bone of contention between the local liberal-democratic opposition and the Cracow conservatives. The initiative to bring Mickiewicz's remains to the Wawel was blamed on the press organ of the democrats, *Nowa Reforma* (New reform), and its editor Tadeusz Romanowicz. The debate even colored regional electoral politics. For example, one local notable accused *Nowa Reforma* of using the Mickiewicz translation for its own aims in the 1884 elections. The democrats had a ready response. Citing the difficulties encountered by those who had fought for the public reburial of Casimir the Great, the beginnings of fund-raising for a Mickiewicz monument, the Kraszewski jubilee, and the folk celebrations in honor of Sobieski, the editors of *Nowa Reforma* retorted: "The 'decision-making circles' have always opposed this kind of demonstration until public sentiment forced them to be silent and even to participate, until [public] opinion 'became impatient,' until other people took matters into their own hands. And then the opponents became converted, came, took part and even . . . even sometimes collected laurels for what others had done."[31] This was not just a battle between those who thought Mickiewicz a poet of genius but an inferior politician and those who considered his ideas, not his rhymes, to be of primary importance. It was a political battle. Claiming better to sense the mood of the public, which wanted to commemorate great Poles, the democrats sought to make inroads in local and regional government, to displace some of the conservative voices dominating Galician affairs.

A regular ally of the democrats in their commemorative endeavors was Polish youth. Young Poles had long been enamored of Mickiewicz, whom they saw as their "spiritual leader on the way to liberty and social justice."[32] Evenings to celebrate the bard were first organized by the student body of Jagiellonian University in 1870. Beginning in 1873, the Student Union (Czytelnia Akademicka, a student society that organized a library for members) actively collected donations for the Mickiewicz monument.[33] Perhaps inspired by Kraszewski, the more senior students of Saint Anne's Gymnasium in Cracow began a tradition of annual Mickiewicz evenings in December 1879, in which scenes from his plays were presented. The local student body, thus, was ready to take action, and in 1887 the Student Union formed a committee of its own. Two years later, the new committee gained permission from the Provincial Executive Council to collect donations; it made arrangements for the rest of the formalities, including the preparation of the crypt, in the beginning of 1890.[34]

Given the imminence of Mickiewicz's translation, Cracow conservatives made their move. What followed was a veritable seizure of power by the Galician authorities from this independent group of students, democrats, and patriotic citizens that had managed to sidestep the official foot-dragging. Once the citizens' committee had conquered all the hurdles connected with the translation, various murmurs reverberated through the press and society that control over the celebration should be handed over to the elected Galician officials who could claim to represent the Polish nation. Doubtless many Galicians thought it appropriate that the translation be organized by the provincial authorities, the only autonomous Polish governmental institution in the world at the time. Nonetheless, some of the seemingly spontaneous calls for the Provincial Executive Council to take control of the festivities as well as other moves connected with the events were actually stage-managed by the influential Tarnowski brothers. At the time, Jan was the provincial marshal (the second highest post in the land, behind the viceroy), Stanisław still a figure to be reckoned with in Cracow.[35] As neither were genuine fans of Mickiewicz (Stanisław reportedly had once told an audience that "the poetry of Mickiewicz did Poland more harm than good"), their active campaigning would have left contemporaries suspicious.[36]

Why go to all this trouble? The official hijacking of the festivities served the authorities' interests. As seen in other, earlier commemorations, these unwilling tooters of the national horn could not risk being excluded from or letting others lead a national event. Now, by taking over the reins, they were able to ensure that only the older members of the citizens' committee would be included in the new, government-controlled one. The coup allowed them to get rid of the students who had been the mainstay of the committee and replace them with students of their own choosing. This was the coup over which the brothers gloated in their private correspondence.[37]

In setting the agenda as well as the tone of the event, the new official committee allowed for little spontaneity, thus making sure "that the nation would not be overly enthusiastic" during the translation.[38] The official committee also limited foreign participation: no invitations were sent to institutions abroad, which learned of the celebration only through newspaper announcements.[39] This turned out to be in keeping with orders from the Austrian Ministry of the Interior: after being informed that Poznanians intended to march in the procession, it secretly forbade the Cracow organizing committee to allow foreign associations and institutions to participate.[40] The authorities also nipped in the bud a student initiative for a congress of Polish and Slavic academic youth. (The increasingly radical student body of Jagiellonian University had sought to resurrect the insurrectionary slogan of 1830—"for our freedom and yours" (za naszą i waszą wolność)—and unite Slavic youth against absolutism and reaction.[41])

The Galician authorities found themselves fighting not only the local democrats and students. Despite their much-touted provincial autonomy, they still had to obtain Vienna's permission for the translation. This proved more difficult than one might imagine. Emperor Francis Joseph ostensibly held a grudge against Mickiewicz for his unflattering comments on the emperor's ancestor, Maria Theresa. In his *Books of the Polish Nation,* Mickie-wicz had called the Habsburg empress, one of the three royal leaders who partitioned Poland, part of the "satanic trinity."[42] (Apparently one of the emperor's ministers put the offending text into his hands.) Of course, Fran-cis Joseph hardly needed such an excuse to refuse to allow the remains of a Russian subject, and a rebel to boot, to be buried in a castle belonging to the King of Galicia and Grand Duke of Cracow . . . !

The emperor's opposition to the translation (never made public) re-sulted in a paradoxical situation: men personally unenthusiastic about Mickiewicz had to persuade their monarch to allow the Poles their celebra-tion. According to the poet's son, in a personal audience with the emperor, the two most highly ranked Poles in Galicia, Viceroy Kazimierz Badeni and Provincial Marshal Jan Tarnowski, tendered their resignations: for how could they hold their heads up back home again if they were unable to de-liver what the people demanded? The surprised emperor relented.[43] At any rate, official permission came from the Austrian minister of interior with the stipulation that the celebration "not take on the character of a political demonstration." In reporting this to the Cracow police, Badeni added that he counted on them to put a stop to any attempts by persons or institutions outside of the committee to give the celebration a political character.[44]

THE TRANSLATION

The Mickiewicz translation was of necessity an international affair. Travel-ing from France to Austria-Hungary, the remains of the dead Polish poet had to cross several borders and several hurdles en route to their destina-tion, the Wawel. First, however, the Polish community in France had to re-linquish control over the remains of its illustrious countryman. On June 27, Mickiewicz's remains were exhumed before a small group of family and dignitaries, then placed in a new metal coffin. The public celebration was slated for the following morning, with a special discount on tickets to Montmorency from the Gare du Nord. Delegations of French, Polish, Hungarian, and Czech organizations, individual Poles, and representatives of the French press poured into the cemetery at Montmorency to pay homage to the Polish poet.

At the Montmorency celebration, the Polish nation seemed to be repre-sented in nearly all its diversity. Official Polish representatives from Galicia and other Poles traveling the distance from back home encountered mem-bers of the Polish émigré community, many of whom lived in Republican France and were accustomed to speaking their minds with a greater degree of freedom. All these groups tried to take advantage of this rare occasion to broadcast their views to the larger Polish and European community. Inspired by different political agendas and views of the nation, speeches ranged from the fawning to the feisty. (Not all talks given at Montmorency would be deemed publishable in Austria-Hungary, let alone in the other empires.) Perhaps the one thing that all participants could agree upon was the existence of decidedly different visions of the Polish poet and varied agendas for the celebration. In the words of one scholar, "Here, over the open tomb of Mickiewicz, the debate over the ideological legacy of the great Polish poet flared up."[45]

Even the participation of a genuine Frenchman was not without controversy. Given Mickiewicz's connection to the Collège de France, it was expected that someone from that august institution would speak at the ceremony. But who? Mickiewicz's son (and the Polish community) objected to the most obvious person, the occupant of the chair of Slavic literature and successor to Mickiewicz, the Russophile Louis Léger.[46] Władysław Mickiewicz, thus, approached a former professor at the Collège de France: Ernest Renan. In the eyes of the Galician ultramontanes, Renan was hardly a palatable choice: with their usual circumspection, they considered the "atheist Renan" to be "the most notable enemy and destructor of Christianity today in the world."[47]

While Renan was not universally endorsed, it was nonetheless appropriate that he spoke at the Mickiewicz celebration in France. Both he and Mickiewicz, after all, had lost their chairs at the Collège de France on account of their controversial views. Renan found kind and encouraging things to say about both Mickiewicz and the Polish nation: "You give a great lesson of idealism here; you proclaim that a nation is a spiritual thing, that it has a soul which one does not crush as one crushes bodies."[48] This sentiment echoed those of Renan's famous lecture at the Sorbonne, "What Is a Nation?" (1882), in which he declared that a nation was "a soul, a spiritual principle" and its existence was a "daily plebiscite."[49] In moving Mickiewicz's remains to the Polish "Saint Denis," according to Renan, Poles were voting for their nation.[50] They also appeared conscious of the "social capital" their "heroic past, great men, glory" provided. As Renan explained, "To have shared glories in the past, a shared will in the present; to have performed great deeds together, to wish to perform still more—these are the essential conditions for the making of a people."[51]

The controversy concerning Renan, however, was nothing compared to the reaction to other aspects of the celebration. It was said by some that the Montmorency ceremony had been organized by "some nameless and shapeless group of people without a past, without any contributions in any field."[52] The culprits were a group of young socialists surrounding Stanisław Kraków, the man who published the invitations. The backbone of the local committee, which wanted to be recognized as representing the Polish emigration, this group was blamed for confusing the time the ceremony was scheduled to begin, with the result that some participants arrived after Renan had begun his speech.

The socialists present did not endear themselves to other Poles at Montmorency, where they were given the opportunity to express their views—an opportunity that would be denied them in Cracow, where socialism was anathema. Yet, despite the politicization of their speeches, Władysław Mickiewicz paid them an interesting compliment: "Despite this, they, better than their opponents, understood his [father's] views on the future of our society. . . ."[53] This observation hints at the uniqueness of Polish democratic and socialist thought, quite distinct from both Western and Russian socialism yet more like the revisionism of Eduard Bernstein and Jean Jaurès. Socialists such as Bolesław Limanowski were national patriots and considered the restoration of Polish independence their first priority. Indeed, all the socialist speakers at the Montmorency celebration underscored their desire for the rebirth of the Commonwealth, for the rebirth of a Polish state—a stance that helped to blur the lines between Polish "democrats" and "socialists" at the time.[54] Many Poles shared Limanowski's concerns with social justice, with the fate of the peasantry; even more valued his work as a historian of Poland, particularly of the 1863 insurrection. These shared interests may explain why the Polish socialist was asked to give two speeches at Montmorency: one in the name of the National-Socialist Commune, the other as spokesman for the Union of Polish Exiles, as well as why he might think Mickiewicz better understood the aims of socialism than did many contemporaries.[55]

Students at Montmorency also found themselves under a cloud of controversy. Although a representative of Polish youth abroad was given the opportunity to speak at Montmorency, he managed to alienate members of the audience by criticizing the treatment of Cracow students (one of the Jagiellonian University students had been denied permission to speak and replaced with an official student delegate chosen by the Galician authorities).[56] Stanisław Bouffał had harsh words for the self-serving "clique" that cooperated with the partitioning powers while, in the name of "reason," trying to stifle all manifestations of national life. The same young man—a mathematician (*kandydat nauk matematycznych*) at the university in Dorpat (Tartu)—had challenged a critic of the Parisian committee to a duel.[57] (Even socialist sympathizers could resort to old-fashioned [chivalric?] methods of dealing with enemies.)

Polish student delegates present for the translation also availed themselves of more modern forms of interaction. Cracow student Franciszek Siedlecki presided at a banquet in Zurich en route to France.[58] This suggests that young Poles were developing their own networks.[59] One supposes that they conversed with their counterparts in France as well. Comments made at the celebration suggest that the traditional French sympathy for the Poles was reinforced, at least symbolically: Mickiewicz's former secretary, the now aged Armand Lévy, charged Siedlecki with conveying to his comrades back home a "fraternal kiss" as a sign of French friendship for Poland.[60]

Such signs of Franco-Polish friendship could not have pleased the Austrian authorities. Official Austrian antipathy toward the celebration was visible in the reaction of officials in Vienna, through which the train transporting Mickiewicz's remains had to pass. Whereas the French train had been met with fanfare, flowers, and speeches (in six languages) in Zurich, demonstrations were forbidden at the Viennese train station. Polish requests to speak and deposit wreaths were thwarted by bureaucratic technicalities, and railroad officials transferred the coffin from the French to the Austrian wagon without Mickiewicz's family being present.[61] So much for the reception onto Habsburg territory of the remains of a man who had never been a Habsburg subject.

BURYING THE BARD IN CRACOW:
JULY 4, 1890

Compensating for this lack of consideration on the part of Austrian officialdom was the enthusiasm for the bard visible in Cracow, his final resting place. The Cracow reception of Mickiewicz's remains proved to be the public event of the decade, if not the century: Poles arrived in record numbers to witness the procession and entombment in the crypt of Wawel Cathedral. No larger manifestation of national unity had taken place since the January Insurrection of 1863.[62] At eight o'clock on July 4, 1890, the remains of Adam Mickiewicz began the last and most festive leg of their long journey. That fourth of July was for Władysław Mickiewicz the "radiant day of [his] life." After a long struggle with the partitioning powers, the Polish nation gave signs of life, like a long-dormant volcano that suddenly begins to erupt, and "the nation showed others and itself what streams of lava boil beneath its ash."[63]

This impression of the poet's son clashed with the desire of the Galician officials to contain the celebration. The latter were helped in part by the circumstances of the reburial. The Mickiewicz translation was not an anniversary celebration: it was a reburial, a funeral. They would treat the event like a regular state-sponsored funeral: the same order of procession—approved by the bishop—would apply as during the translation of the remains of Kraszewski and the funeral of Zyblikiewicz in 1887.[64] The presence of human remains en route to their final burial would set a solemn tone of mourning, as would the use of black flags in city decoration.

Fig. 3.1 Catafalque, Wawel Cathedral. *Drawing by Michał Pociecha, from* Świat *no. 14 (15 July 1890). Note the prominent display of the image of the Mother of God, Queen of Poland.*

Setting the right tone for the reburial was particularly crucial in the case of Mickiewicz, whose religious orthodoxy was questionable. (While abroad, the Polish poet had come under the influence of Andrzej Towiański, the leader of a millenarian religious sect; his influence, felt in Mickiewicz's lectures, led the French authorities to dismiss the Polish poet from his chair at the Collège de France.[65]) Nonetheless, there were ways to fill the celebration with religious symbolism. The conservatives associated the bard with Polish images of the Mother of God: the Częstochowa Madonna as well as Our Lady of Ostra Brama, the Madonna of Wilno. Both had been mentioned in the opening verses of Mickiewicz's epic poem *Pan Tadeusz:* longing for his homeland, the émigré narrator asks the Virgin to bring his soul back home and expects that someday, miraculously, she would return him to the Fatherland.

These religious images were featured in the Mickiewicz celebration in Cracow. Pictures of the two Madonnas were affixed to two gold spears supporting the front of the canopy over the horse-drawn hearse. Across the street from where the procession began, the Tarnowski palace on Szlak Street displayed a large image of the Wilno Madonna. The catafalque in the central nave of the cathedral, on which the coffin lay during the funeral mass, was also crowned with the two Marian images.[66] Ultimately, the Wilno Madonna came to grace the mosaic for the Mickiewicz crypt; it was the only decoration in the space.[67] The bard, thus, continued to foster the cult of the Wilno Madonna even after his death, and the Madonna of his childhood cast a sanctifying shadow upon Mickiewicz.

Something else contributed to the religious fervor of the assembled crowds. Cracow bishop Albin Dunajewski had been elevated to the rank of cardinal. He was the first Polish cardinal of the partitioned nation to be actively involved in pastoral duties (the other two Polish cardinals of that century, Ledóchowski and Czacki, had been made cardinals in Rome). Emperor Francis Joseph was to present the cardinal's biretta to Dunajewski on June 30, the day that the Mickiewicz translation had originally been scheduled to take place. The committee, naturally, moved its event to July 4 so that the new cardinal could participate.[68] While the solemn presentation of the biretta to Dunajewski did not upstage the Mickiewicz translation, it did ensure that, as in 1883, the national celebration would be preceded by an event of significance for the Polish Church.

For the vast crowds present on July 4, the Mickiewicz translation in Cracow was a visual, sensual, and emotional experience. Summer resorts reportedly had emptied out for that day: Poles able to travel seemed intent upon witnessing the return of Mickiewicz to the Fatherland. While Cracow was decorated in solemn tones, the poet was greeted with showers of petals as the procession made its way from the train station to the Wawel. The beauty of the procession on a sunny day in Cracow was striking. The rich draperies on the hearse, canopy, and catafalque were not solemn black but royal purple, that deep crimson color once the prerogative of crowned heads and princes of the Church. The procession itself was a patchwork of colors as representatives of over one hundred different organizations proudly bore wreaths; many onlookers also paraded in distinctive Polish national dress.

The celebration was full of music and speeches. Władysław Mickiewicz officially entrusted the remains of his father to Provincial Marshal Jan Tarnowski, who took pains to thank the "magnanimous Monarch."[69] An hour after the procession had begun, the hearse, led by the clergy and followed by the Mickiewicz family and Galician and local governmental officials, finally was able to begin its journey. To the strains of Chopin's Funeral March, the coffin was transported down Warszawska Street, past Matejko Square (plac Matejki). It entered the town center via Sławkowska Street, passed the decorated seat of the Academy of Arts and Letters, and headed along the northern and eastern sides of the market square, where another

Fig. 3.2 "In Front of the Doors of the Wawel Cathedral (Adam Asnyk speaking)."
Drawing by Michał Pociecha, from Świat *no. 14 (15 July 1890). This drawing by Michał Pociecha conveys a sense of the crowds. Note the students bearing the coffin.*

concert was heard near Saint Mary's Church. A mark of the times: at Saint John's Street (*ulica św. Jana*), the canopy had to be lowered to pass under the telephone wires without incident.

At Saint Mary's Church, the place of Armenian Catholic bishop Issako-wicz was taken by the Roman Catholic bishop of Lwów, Seweryn Moraw-ski. Pallbearers, representing a curious pan-Polish mix of artists, politicians, and noblemen, were also exchanged several times along the route.[70] The procession filed down a flower-strewn Grodzka Street, past the Bernardine church, to the base of Wawel Hill. The steep last leg of the journey led to the cathedral, the coffin transferred to the shoulders of university youth—fittingly, for they and their predecessors had worked for so many years toward the translation. A university student, Włodzimierz Lewicki, addressed the crowds.

Students were the only social group to be allowed to have its representative speak at the ceremony.[71] From the point of view of the authorities, this concession to the students backfired. Selected from a handful of candidates proposed by the university authorities, Lewicki, a Ruthene who had switched from the Eastern to the Roman Catholic rite five years earlier, was asked to submit a copy of his speech to the provincial marshal.[72] Even the few omissions suggested by Tarnowski proved unpalatable to the student, who delivered his text as it had been written. This perceived disobedience brought the wrath of Tarnowski upon him. Lewicki further ingratiated himself with the authorities by publishing the uncensored text in *Kurier Lwowski* (Lwów courier) as well as in brochure form instead of making a public apology. Although the publications were confiscated, the student succeeded in making waves that were felt around Galicia.[73]

Once the coffin was delivered to the entrance of the cathedral, Adam Asnyk and Stanisław Tarnowski gave speeches. Their words, doubtless, were better remembered for their being reprinted in the press and commemorative publications than for their delivery. Nor were they what more radically inclined Poles wished to hear: a friend of Stefan Żeromski complained that such lukewarm sentiments were not what should be said at Mickiewicz's tomb.[74] Father Władysław Chotkowski gave a lengthy yet stirring sermon in Wawel Cathedral. (Although the funeral mass was celebrated by the new cardinal, generally sermons at such gatherings were assigned to more dynamic preachers like Chotkowski.) As befit a man of the cloth, he chose to emphasize Mickiewicz's Catholicism, to demonstrate to what extent Mickiewicz "contributed . . . to the salvation of souls in our nation." Mickiewicz was responsible for the nation turning away from apostasy as well as realizing that it could not count on the help of others. While praising Mickiewicz's piety and use of religious themes, the preacher extended a warning to poets who saw other uses for their poems. Poetry was to serve the Lord, according to Chotkowski: it was "God's gift for the strengthening [*pokrzepienie*] of human hearts and bread for the soul only insofar as it is true to God's spirit," otherwise the bread would not be worth eating.[75]

Chotkowski's words rained down upon those delegates fortunate to have gained entrance to the cathedral. Given the great crowds at the celebration, only those carrying wreaths from institutions were allowed inside. Even fewer were allowed into the crypt, where the celebration's workhorses —the university youth who had carried the coffin up Wawel Hill—headed with their precious burden after the funeral mass.

NATIONAL RELICS, NATIONAL TRIBUTES

In some respects, the remains of Adam Mickiewicz were and continued to be treated like relics—if not religious then national ones. Interestingly, the translation, as well as the earlier journeys of his remains, followed procedures echoing those prescribed by canon law to ensure a relic's authenticity and keep it from harm.[76] Still, clergymen involved in the translation made clear their view of the bard. Addressing the deceased, Chotkowski stated: "We know that you were a mortal and sinful man, but you died with God; the clergy has offered prayers and bloodless offerings for your soul to God all these years because we all learned to love the Fatherland and our brothers from you, because you spread love and strengthened hope with your songs."[77] Despite his sinfulness, Mickiewicz's national contributions could not be overlooked, even by the most faithful sons of the Church, who likewise had been touched by the bard. His transfer to the Wawel crypt was more than a funeral; yet if he were a saint, he was one only in the eyes of the nation at large.

Poles, nonetheless, did revere him to an unusual degree. An example of their veneration is seen in an event that took place during the transfer of Mickiewicz's remains at Montmorency to a new coffin. The old metal coffin, no longer necessary, was cut into pieces, which then circulated among those present. Accounts disagree on whether this was done by Poles or the French gravediggers.[78] Still, some decried the profanation of the national relics as well as their haphazard privatization. As Maria Szeliga wrote, these pieces "were a great keepsake and genuine relics. . . . I believe that numerous compatriots would have wanted to receive a piece similar to that which now rests next to my dearest keepsakes." She added that the pieces should have been distributed by "Polish hands" and distributed to the people like the Holy Eucharist (*opłatek,* or host).[79] That the committee organizing the event did not think to take care of such matters may reflect its socialistic bent; perhaps it was simply a lack of forethought. Still, it is clear that many Poles would have cherished a piece of the past that had touched their great bard. Mickiewicz relics were part of a treasured heritage, mementos of which were multiplying in the course of the commemoration.

INTO "THATCHED HUTS". . .

Other artifacts from the translation shed light on the way Mickiewicz was used as a mirror by those who honored him. Witness the inscriptions on wreaths prepared for the translation, which groups of Poles laid at the feet of the bard.[80] They not only demonstrate how, and that, Mickiewicz was being remembered, but also convey a sense of their bearers' overt identification with the Polish nation. As seen in figure 3.3, Varsovians advertised their difficult circumstances by identifying themselves as "born in bondage" (the phrase, taken from Mickiewicz's *Pan Tadeusz,* was used by Warsaw youth); yet others placed a chain on their wreath (as did the editors of the periodical *Głos*). A wreath sent from Podolia, Volhynia, and Ukraine (that is, from the former Polish provinces lost to Russia in 1793–95) came with a

Fig. 3.3 Silver laurel wreath. The inscription reads: "To Mickiewicz: from the Warsaw youth, born in bondage . . ." *Photo courtesy of the National Museum, Kraków.*

verse declaring that they too were "the children / of one fatherland, of our Poland—of one mother." Silesians also linked themselves to the Polish past. Never part of the Polish Commonwealth, the common folk of that region advertised its past association with Polish history with the inscription "The Silesian Folk of the ancient Polish province of the Piasts." Even Jews demonstrated their identification with Mickiewicz's nation. A group of assimilated Jews cited a verse about the Jewish innkeeper Jankiel from *Pan Tadeusz.* The poet stated that Jankiel "loved the fatherland like a Pole"—the implication being that "Poles of the Mosaic persuasion" were also faithful sons of the same fatherland.

One large set of wreaths is worth discussing at greater length. They were a tribute to the poet of the Polish landscape, to one who fought for the freedom of all people—those parts of Mickiewicz's oeuvre with which a predominantly illiterate peasantry could identify.

That villagers joined in the celebration is largely due to the efforts of Father Stojałowski. A committee of peasants from all of Galicia gathered in Wadowice, the seat of some of Stojałowski's initiatives, to determine how peasants might celebrate Mickiewicz's Wawel burial. The committee noted the relevance of Mickiewicz to their own lives, emphasizing his love for the common people and desire that they gain their freedom. From the fruits of their beloved land, about which he wrote so eloquently, it proposed to make "a gigantic wreath, as great, long and wide as our land, and cover the mortal remains of this immortal father of the nation in the royal tombs in the Wawel."[81]

This announcement led to a flood of packages from all regions of Poland, from which not one but forty-four wreaths of grain, branches, and grasses were braided by hundreds of local volunteers. Never before had peasants been directly involved in the preparations for a national celebration. The peasant effort was all the more impressive, as it came from all parts of the former Commonwealth. Not only peasants from Galicia, where patriotic activities of this type were tolerated, responded to the committee's announcement. Palpable pieces of numerous regions were sent to Cracow to be woven into wreaths, each representing a different segment of the nation. For example, the wreath carrying the letter "A," for Adam, contained materials from Lithuania, Mickiewicz's homeland. Another wreath was made of grasses from the Gopło area, the letter "U" from the Kingdom of Poland (the "U" of *lud,* the folk, supposedly standing for *utrapienie,* or the affliction of tsarist rule). Returning to the subject of relics: reportedly the wreath from Nowogródek (Novogrodok, Navahrudak), the hometown of Mickiewicz, was later torn into shreds by the public, its branches and ears of grain taken as souvenirs of the celebration.[82]

The forty-four wreaths had their own significance. Forty-three wreaths spelled out, one letter at a time, the peasant committee's message: "TO ADAM MICKIEWICZ FROM THE FOLK OF ALL THE LANDS OF POLAND."[83] Given that those involved in the committee were readers of Stojałowski's papers, it seems appropriate that the peasants' contribution to the procession should attest to their literacy. This was a sign that perhaps Mickiewicz's works were beginning to "wander into thatched huts," a wish of the bard's often noted during this period.[84] Those familiar with Polish Romantic poetry saw a more profound significance here. The number forty-four was Mickiewicz's mystical name for the one who would save the Polish nation. Could forty-four be the Polish peasantry?

Such thoughts failed to cheer Galician officialdom. This new popular movement—for the folk committee advertised itself on the first wreath as the Wadowice Society of the Defense of the Land and the Folk[85]—struck terror into the hearts of the authorities, who distrusted Stojałowski.[86] They feared that a peasant rally being planned for July 5 or 6 would become a demonstration and were determined to stop it from taking place. To do so, they arrested Stojałowski on July 3, holding him for over a week.[87] For the first time, the priest was physically unable to lead a pilgrimage to Cracow. Permission for the peasant rally was denied; the usual reduction in train fares was announced too late for news of it to reach potential pilgrims; and the authorities limited the number of villagers allowed to carry those immense wreaths in the procession.[88] Police likewise were instructed to confiscate two publications of the peasant committee. These and other moves testify to the apprehensions of both Galician and Austrian authorities.[89]

In contrast, news of peasant engagement comforted many in the émigré community who had been opposed to the bard's precious remains being moved. They had hoped that Mickiewicz's final resting place would be a free Poland, not an Austrian garrison (which is what Cracow was during this period). News of the formation of the Wadowice committee in the late spring of 1890 convinced some of them that the translation made sense. Zygmunt Miłkowski concluded that Mickiewicz's ashes were far from mute: they were speaking to and awakening the masses. Would these eloquent ashes be able to bring about the miracle "on which depends the salvation of Poland": the Polish folk joining the Polish nation?[90]

Krasiński's "miracle" of the village folk uniting with the nobility was not understood by Miłkowski and others abroad as it might have been back home. When they made use of the verse, Galician conservatives referred to the premodern status quo that suited them so well: peasants content with their lot, and all estates living together in harmony. Miłkowski's was a different view of the relationship, one in which equal status and equal rights were to be granted to the peasant. The dream of an active, independent peasantry that considered itself an integral part of the nation motivated these émigrés. If the relics of the great Romantic poet were not enough to awaken villagers to their identity, heritage, and fate, there were more where these came from, claimed Miłkowski. The bones of numerous émigré Poles, "a host of skeletons crying out from their tombs for the defense of the rights of Poland," could also speak to the folk.[91]

THE ELOQUENCE OF ASHES

The translation of more émigré bones was hardly what the official organizers of the Cracow celebration sought at this time. Once the peals of the royal Sigismund Bell marked the end of the ceremony, the conservatives could sigh with relief. An anonymous report on the celebration in the conservative monthly *Przegląd Polski* (Polish review) suggested that a plethora of new commemorations would cheapen those that had taken place: "Let us not . . . make posthumous homage common now, when we have given [homage] to the best and most beloved of our dear and great ones."[92] The bard's remains were now in the Wawel crypt: what more could the nation want? One émigré poet should suffice. It was time to cease with celebrations and get back to work. This attitude calls to mind Władysław Mickiewicz's comment on the pusillanimity of those who could not see beyond the limitations of the present: those "who never foresee another solution to problems than compromises with evil would like to celebrate a great man on the condition that it would not have the consequence of obliging them to imitate him in anything."[93]

Other Poles present at the celebration not only chose to imitate Mickiewicz: they were inspired by their experience to persist in a different kind of work than that which captivated the Stańczyks. One student visiting Cracow resolved to get rid of the foreign soldier standing guard outside the castle complex and remove the two-headed imperial eagle from Polish buildings, and thus he returned to conspiratorial work.[94] Other students also continued to defy the conservatives: reportedly some kind of Slavic congress did take place. Ruthenes/Ukrainians had mixed views regarding the celebration. The national populists Yuliian Romanchuk, Natali Vakhnianyn, and Ivan Belei had declared that Ruthenes would not participate in the translation. That they dared to speak for the entire nation angered a group of Ukrainian progressives, who gathered to protest—and ended up founding the Ukrainian socialist party, the Radical Party. In a way, thus, Ukrainians have Mickiewicz to thank for this new political organization.[95]

Activists continued to strive to enlighten Polish villagers and demonstrate the important role they could play in the history of the nation. The Association for Folk Education (Towarzystwo oświaty ludowej) in Lwów initiated a competition for a short popular work to be distributed among its 120 reading rooms and libraries. Directions for what the booklet should contain were quite specific: the author was to mention the accomplishments of the end of the eighteenth century—the 3 May Constitution's recognition of the common folk, their fight under Kościuszko, and the emancipation of the villagers, as well as show how "Adam Mickiewicz, with his works, in which he embraced the village people as the vital part of the nation called to action, contributed most strongly to the high idea of the Fatherland, which remains alive in the minds and hearts of Poles, despite the division of the Polish Lands."[96] The book was to emphasize the duty of the citizen to spread love for the Fatherland and awaken national consciousness in himself and others.

The general public appeared to have been moved by the translation, which offered an occasion for collective national mourning. Years later, one woman recalled her impressions as a seventh grader. Present near the doors of Wawel Cathedral when the students arrived with the coffin, she was overcome by a mixture of happiness and sadness, sensations unifying the crowd: "everyone, the rich and the poor, the old and the young, felt like brothers, children of a common mother, to whom with certainty they had never felt love so strongly as in that moment."[97] Mickiewicz had brought them together, and, as Adam Asnyk reminded the crowds near the cathedral, his thought was not the "property of one epoch, one generation, one party, one layer or part of the nation but is the property of the entire suffering Poland, striving for life."[98] The Poles gathered together that day shared one overwhelming feeling: with the arrival of Mickiewicz among them, "the moment of the deliverance of our Poland" must be closer.[99]

In 1890, the nation enthusiastically embraced its great poet. Perhaps imported ashes really had been necessary to give life to Poles back home. With the translation came more interaction, more intra- and inter-national intercourse. Poles from abroad came into contact with their brethren from the partitioned lands. Having played an important role in the preparations for Mickiewicz's translation, youth in particular moved into the public realm, both at home and abroad, and shared its ardor for the more politically engaged side of the bard. Even peasants were being introduced to "their" poet and encouraged to join in the national celebration.

The burial of Mickiewicz in the Wawel crypt established the bard as a national figure acceptable even to those less enamored of his work and life. His accession to the Polish pantheon turned him into a potent national symbol that each political party wished to claim. The battle for Mickiewicz was only beginning.

FOUR

"Poland Has Not Yet Perished":
From the Third of May
to the Kościuszko Insurrection

A string of important anniversaries followed the Mickiewicz translation in the first half of the 1890s. These dates included the centennials of the final years of the Polish-Lithuanian Commonwealth—dates of immense significance for the nation. The events began with initiatives produced by a four-year-long session of the Sejm (1788–92), the most important of which was the Constitution of May 3, 1791. This first European constitution abolished aspects of the political system that had caused so much grief—the *liberum veto,* the elective monarchy, and the like—while creating a constitutional monarchy more along Western lines, where citizenship was based upon land ownership, not birth.[1] This legislative initiative, which Karl Marx called "the only work of liberty which Eastern Europe has ever created independently," served as shorthand for the ability of the Polish nation to reform itself and marked the dawn of a new era.[2] At the same time, it was seen as a threat to the partitioning states, as the reaction of one influential Prussian suggests. He wrote: "The Poles have dealt a fatal blow to the Prussian monarchy, by bringing in a hereditary throne and a constitution better than England's. . . . Sooner or later, Poland will take West and perhaps even East Prussia from us. How can we, exposed from Teschen to Memel, defend ourselves against a populous and well-ruled nation?"[3] Such words belied the stereotypes of Polish anarchy emphasized by the partitioners and suggested that the nation was more than capable of reforming and governing itself. The prospect of a reinvigorated Polish community nonetheless prompted the partitioning powers to seize further territory in 1793. In this they were aided by an ad hoc assembly of nobles known as the Confederation of Targowica, which invited Catherine the Great of Russia to interfere in Polish internal matters. As a result, the word "Targowica" entered into Polish discourse as a synonym for treachery.

The indignity of the second partition prompted Poles who supported the Third of May Constitution to rebel in the spring of 1794. Their leader was the Polish officer and veteran of the American Revolutionary War Tadeusz Kościuszko. Despite a series of successful battles—including their first and most famous battle, at Racławice, during which scythe-bearing peasants helped to defeat the Russian army—and the spread of the insurrection to Warsaw, Wilno, and other cities, on October 10 the Polish campaign came to an end. The nation was unable to fend off the final blow: the third and final partition in 1795 that wiped the country off the map of Europe.

The events of the final years of independent statehood nonetheless became the cornerstone for late-nineteenth-century Polish optimism about the future. Despite accusations by the Cracow school of history that the Poles had been to blame for their downfall, others felt it was important to demonstrate that the nation had not taken partition lightly, that a broad cross section of the eighteenth-century population of the Commonwealth had contrived, politically and militarily, to change the nation's fate. The anniversaries of the Third of May Constitution and the Kościuszko Insurrection celebrated in 1891 and 1894 could potentially influence a broader swath of masses, including peasants. Both centennials were seen as opportunities for making progress with the goal of nationalizing the masses, of making villagers feel a part of the Polish nation; they also shed light on the changing face of Polish patriotism.

This series of commemorations promised to be more potentially explosive than those of writers or royalty discussed to date. The Constitution and other Polish initiatives of the 1790s, after all, had been designed to shore up the Polish state and fend off further partition. Memories of these accomplishments and events could lead members of the nation to reflect upon the injustice wrought by the partitioning powers. Such recollections were inherently destabilizing, as they challenged Poles worldwide to question their present condition and seek to change their state of affairs, at times through illegal means. Perhaps most important, the celebrations of the Constitution of the Third of May, the partitions, and the Kościuszko Insurrection emboldened Poles across the social spectrum to believe that they could work together toward a brighter future.

CELEBRATING THE 1791 CONSTITUTION

For nineteenth-century Poles, a particularly attractive aspect of the Constitution of May 3, 1791, was that it gave the lie to the view that the eighteenth-century Polish state was ungovernable and unreformable, which had been used to justify its elimination by the partitioning powers. It initiated important changes to the state's social system. In their view, this "first act of a new Poland" changed the composition of the nation by increasing the rights of two social groups hitherto excluded from the noble nation: "the folk and the townspeople."[4] Buttressed by the Law on the Towns of April 18, 1791, the Constitution of the Third of May ended noble hegemony and facilitated the rise of the townspeople and their union with the nobility. While it did less for the peasantry—article 4 merely recognized the serfs as subjects under the law—even such timid beginnings signaled a change in thinking about the most numerous segment of the population. Although one hundred years later many decried the incompleteness of this move, article 6 had foreseen the need to revise the Constitution periodically, stipulating that necessary changes be introduced every twenty-five years. Had the partitions not put an end to Polish reforms, further modifications would have been expected: Polish activists believed that, over time, the entire nation would become noble, not at the expense of the nobility, but by raising the masses up to their level.[5]

The centennial of the Constitution nonetheless found the population of the former Commonwealth still plagued by sharp social divisions. This is underscored by the juxtaposition of another May celebration: May Day, the socialist holiday. Established at the first congress of the Second International a year before the centennial of the Constitution, the first celebration of May Day "led the new movement out onto the street, gave it a public character."[6] May Day festivities in Lwów and Warsaw that first year each involved thousands of workers; and Galician celebrations encouraged the establishment of a workers' party, renamed the Polish Social-Democratic Party (Polska Partja Socjalno-demokratyczna, or PPSD) two years later.[7]

These first May Day demonstrations were seen as a challenge to Polish unity by nonsocialists. Much was at stake, given the potential for growth of a working class, even in economically backward Galicia. The Galician press exhorted workers to ignore May Day and celebrate the Third of May, to join the "all-national" celebration or move their workers' celebration to May 3 to coincide with the national celebration.[8] While they refused to abandon their own holiday, socialists in Lwów and Cracow did take part in the celebrations of the Third of May in 1891.

While the anniversary of the Polish Constitution could have been seen as an antidote to the socialist May Day, neither Austrian nor Galician officialdom was enthralled by the specter of more Polish national celebrations. The Cracow conservatives mistrusted all independent efforts to celebrate the Polish past. Fears that the Mickiewicz celebration would spawn such initiatives had not been unfounded, as peasants, artisans, and the democratic intelligentsia began to make plans for 1891 even before the dust had settled on Mickiewicz's tomb.[9]

The Galician authorities strove to keep anniversary events out of public sight. Without outlawing celebrations of the centennial outright, which would have been politically disastrous, they strove to ensure that initiatives were kept small and localized. The viceroy, Kazimierz Badeni, forbade the organizing of an all-Galician committee planned by an association of Lwów lawyers. Appeals to the Polish parliamentary club in Vienna did not lead to any easing of the "prohibitions of the k.k. [königliche-kaiserliche, or royal and imperial] political authorities."[10] Polish celebrators of the Third of May would have to act in isolation, for no all-Galician endeavor would be tolerated. No official or preexisting associations would be allowed to commemorate the anniversary. Witness the decree of the police directorate in Lwów forbidding the Jewish organization Covenant of Brothers from celebrating the Constitution: as an apolitical society it was not "authorized to organize a political celebration, which is what the granting of the political constitution of the Third of May is."[11] Only ad hoc citizens' committees—weak, poor, unaffiliated (at least directly) with any political party—could attempt to marshal their limited means to honor this document from the Polish past.

Many Poles thought the interference of the authorities in the celebration to be groundless. After all, article 19 of the Austrian Constitution of 1867 guaranteed the Poles the freedom to cultivate their "nationality, national tradition and national past."[12] Of course, the authorities may have wondered why Austrian citizens would wish to celebrate the Constitution of the Third of May: Galicians had not experienced the benefits of the Polish Constitution, as this territory had become a part of the Habsburg Empire in 1772 as a result of the first partition of Poland. Influential conservatives feared the anniversary would serve as a "pretext for agitation."[13] At any rate, Badeni ordered the local sheriffs (starostas) to discourage or limit the celebrations—"on no conditions permit any kind of demonstration," he charged—and insisted that permission for public performances and lectures would have to be obtained from himself.[14] Badeni stood firm in this regard, as deciphered telegrams of late April in the police records make clear.[15] The viceroy's hostility caused some quarters to accuse him of organizing a "Second Targowica against the living tradition of the Third of May."[16]

Yet, despite these official roadblocks, the Third of May did not pass by unnoticed. Festivities took place in well over one hundred towns and villages in Galicia.[17] Indeed, sources note that the first stirrings of patriotic activity in a given town or village often dated from this anniversary.[18] Most of these celebrations were on a small scale. They began with church services, sometimes preceded by the firing of salvos or the playing of patriotic tunes. Many included a topical sermon or lecture, after which souvenirs of the event—pictures, brochures, inexpensive medallions—were distributed. A booklet on the Third of May apparently was sent to all folk school teachers in Galicia, with the request that they read it to the folk on this occasion. The same booklet was also distributed in Prussian Poland and among Galician villagers.[19]

Cracow and Lwów had more elaborate celebrations, complete with street and window decorations; various soirées, theatricals, and scholarly presentations; church services; and parades.[20] Descriptions of the Lwów festivities alone cover nearly twenty pages in an important commemorative publication from which we learn that the celebrations transcended Galicia, the former Polish lands, even Europe.[21] Bartoszewicz's commemorative volume contributed a sense of belonging to something larger than a town or province for the readers, who themselves experienced only a small piece of the totality of Polish celebration. Readers of this and other publications learned that perhaps Maria Wysłouchowa was not far wrong in writing that "wherever Polish hearts beat, wherever Polish speech sounds, people are thinking and speaking about the . . . constitution."[22]

In the case of the 3 May anniversary, works of art once again figured prominently in the largest Galician celebrations. A still-unfinished canvas by Matejko on the subject of the Constitution of the Third of May was exhibited in Cracow; yet another present from the artist to the crown land, Matejko's *Third of May*, would eventually grace the provincial marshal's hall in Lwów.[23] In Lwów, Poles were treated to the sight of a large painting by another artist of mixed Polish-Czech descent, Jan Styka; entitled *Polonia*, this new canvas was purchased by the Lwów municipality—with public donations—in honor of the anniversary.[24]

Polonia (figure 4.1) encompassed more than the Third of May Constitution. Through the use of both historical and allegorical elements, Styka set out to tell the "history of the martyrology of Poland and the hope of its rebirth."[25] The leader of the Insurrection of 1794, Tadeusz Kościuszko, stands in the center of the canvas. He points toward the figure of Polonia, the allegory of the fatherland, surrounded by murdered civilians and dead soldiers. A group of peasants rally behind him and contemplate the sight, coming to understand—one imagines—the reason why Kościuszko had summoned them to fight. A crowd of people who had served the fatherland since the partitions stands to the side of Kościuszko: these include the framers of the Constitution, Mickiewicz, historians Szajnocha and Lelewel, painters Matejko and Grottger, and composers Ogiński, Chopin, and Moniuszko. The painting reads like a "Who's Who" of the Polish fight for independence. As the writer Kornel Ujejski observed:

> Everything that hurts and soothes, enlivens and brightens is there. A thick
> book, written by a masterly hand, would be needed to give a picture of what

Fig. 4.1 Jan Styka, *Polonia,* reproduction. *Photo by Arkadiusz Podstawka; courtesy of the National Museum, Wrocław.*

the painter conveyed in the one word of his canvas; one does not need to append to the painting any commentary. It itself will speak to the living Polish soul clearly and impressionably like no other word, and he who looks lifelessly at this painting can no longer be enlivened by anything.[26]

In keeping with the tenor of Ujejski's comment, the painting was used as a didactic tool. Groups of "innocents" (that is, those of the lower classes who were only gaining a sense of themselves as Poles) such as members of the artisanal association Skała were brought to view the painting; and, over the ensuing decades, numerous reproductions of the painting, perhaps in the hundreds of thousands, made their way to Poles in all three empires and even in America.[27] *Polonia,* thus, proved the artistic hit of the celebration. Assembled on this one large canvas, these positive role models (the Targowica confederates excepted) provided a lesson of hope for those who studied the nation's past.

The drawing of sharp lines between patriotic Poles and their nemeses, as seen in this publicly displayed canvas, had a basis in the reality of the times as well. We have seen how some Poles portrayed the viceroy as a traitor of the nation. Recalcitrant clergymen—that is, those who did not embrace the idea of national commemorations—were given similar treatment. Such a fate did not befall the Armenian Catholic archbishop Issakowicz, who proved to be a major supporter of the plan to purchase the painting.

His Roman Catholic counterpart, the Lwów archbishop Seweryn Moraw-ski, fared worse. In a way, this lack of clerical enthusiasm for the 3 May Constitution is paradoxical, given that its framers made the point of establishing Catholicism as the ruling religion in article 1. But the objections to this and other national celebrations went much deeper.

Morawski's attitude toward the commemoration and the subsequent conflict it generated is a case in point.[28] The archbishop considered the commemoration organizers "*sui generis* Catholics" who placed the father-land before the Church, and he asked them why they would celebrate an anniversary of a constitution in a region that had come under Austrian rule nearly two decades earlier. Morawski proved unable to celebrate the commemorative mass, as he suddenly became indisposed on the day of the anniversary, his place taken by the cathedral vicar. While the more mature "patriots" of Lwów responded to Morawski's slights by lavishing praise upon Issakowicz, who had celebrated an anniversary mass in his cathedral, local students began a campaign against his Roman Catholic counterpart that summer, throwing stones at Morawski's window and calling him names. Such actions were on one occasion timed to coincide with the anniversary of the execution of the members of the National Government from the January Insurrection—and, as such, were somehow kept out of the press. All through this, Morawski saw himself as defending the Church against the terrorism of the masses. He did not want commemoration organizers to think that they could exert control over their archbishop; rather, he thought it "improper for a bishop to be only one of many decorations of such a celebration."[29] This controversy illustrates the great divide that separated the patriotic extremism of the students, who treated those not sympathetic to their cause as their enemies, and conservative clericalism, which did not want the Church be used merely as a prop in the national drama. This was a serious problem for Polish society, one that would remain painful in the ensuing years.

While Morawski's views may discomfit those accustomed to looking at the past through a strictly "national" lens, in a way his reaction was not so different from those of other Poles who sought to participate in the commemorations on their own terms or shape the way these anniversaries were perceived. As far as the democrats were concerned, the celebration of the Third of May presented an opportunity to highlight the value of democratic principles and promote both the transformation of the masses into citizens and the transition from a noble nation to a more comprehensive body.[30] Up until this point, Father Stojałowski had played the biggest role to date in mobilizing the villages; now members of the Polish intelligentsia were to try to reach out to their brethren in the fields.

The Cracow citizens' committee concocted various proposals that would allow for contacts between the villagers and the Polish middle classes. Again, although critics characterized the democrats as all noise and no content, this group clearly perceived the need for actions, not just words. Włodzimierz Lewicki, whom we met in conjunction with the Mickiewicz translation, suggested they found a folk theater. Ludomir Benedyktowicz, a veteran of the January Insurrection, proposed a constitutional mound, along the lines of the existing Kościuszko Mound in Cracow and the Union of Lublin Mound in Lwów, as its construction would require the efforts of wide swaths of society. The proposal that gained the committee's approval, however, came from a young lawyer from Lwów employed as a journalist for *Nowa Reforma,* Michał Danielak. Danielak came up with the idea of a committee of friends of village folk schools.[31]

Danielak's idea inspired the establishment of a new organization, the People's School Society (Towarzystwo Szkoły Ludowej, or TSL).[32] The society's founders sought to make contact with village youth, "of whom *nearly 5 million* in Galicia can neither read nor write, and thus do not have a sense of national affiliation."[33] Education was seen as a necessary step on the road to turning villagers into full-fledged citizens of the Polish nation, as demonstrated by the TSL's slogan, "Through an enlightened folk to a free Poland." A patriotic education would help turn peasants into Poles, inoculate those in the border regions against the influence of the Czech Matica and the German Schulverein, and counter any other pressure that might convince them to consider themselves Czech, German, or even Ukrainian.[34]

The announcement of the founding of the People's School Society was wrapped in historical symbolism. The citizens' committee strove to get maximum publicity for its new endeavor and availed itself of a historical parallel. Thus, as the 3 May Constitution had been signed a century earlier, another signing took place at the Third of May commemoration in Cracow in 1891. A petition for permission to found a People's School Society was circulated among the participants, allowing those present to affirm their support. Just as their forefathers had done one hundred years before them, Poles were given the opportunity to commit themselves to strengthening the nation.[35]

The idea of the democratic opposition gaining influence among the peasantry was anathema to both conservative and clerical forces, both of which came up with their own alternatives to the People's School Society. A group of conservatives in Cracow founded a National Union (Związek Narodowy) to attract new blood into Galician conservatism. In turn, a Cracow clergyman advocated membership in the apolitical Brotherhood of the Immaculate Conception of Our Lady, Queen of the Polish Crown during his sermon on the Third of May. These three initiatives reflected different approaches to the challenges of the early 1890s: the conservatives hoped to augment their own ranks, the Church to raise the moral level of the nation, and the democrats to improve the lot of the peasantry.[36]

Approved by the Galician authorities in 1892, the People's School Society met with the greatest success. It flourished in the coming years, establishing schools and peasant reading rooms in villages where there were none. In 1893, its membership had mushroomed to 5,050, with 33 branches—to reach 53 in 1894 and a whopping 302 branches, with 42,000 members, in 1913. Concentrating its initial educational efforts on the neighboring (borderland) regions of Silesia and Bukovina, areas where support for Polishness was particularly needed, the People's School Society funded or constructed schools and libraries. It also ran schools for the illiterate in Cracow, Rzeszów, Stanisławów, and Kołomyja (Kolomyia); published and distributed various educational materials; and gave awards to the best village teachers. The society's work escalated in the decade preceding World War I; by the outbreak of the war, it had funded 4 real *gimnazja,* 3 teachers' seminaries, 242 folk schools, 480 primary schools, and numerous courses for the illiterate. The TSL likewise organized numerous national celebrations: 145 in 1903, 1,080 in 1908, and 1,159 in 1913.[37] As education and literacy helped shape the national identity of the region's villagers, the People's School Society—rightly called the "largest [*najliczniejszy*] and most versatile educational association" in Galicia before World War I—deserves much of the credit for peasants identifying with the Polish nation.[38]

WARSAW OBSERVANCES

In their criticism of others' plans for the anniversary, conservatives faulted a certain group of "nameless agitators" for "calling for solemn celebrations of the Third of May where such celebrations must engender harsh repression and bring the greatest misfortune upon the inhabitants"—that is, under tsarist rule.[39] With the 1891 commemoration of the Third of May in Warsaw, the Kingdom of Poland entered into the realm of national public demonstrations. A small but significant group of activists, primarily from Polish underground organizations, ventured into the public space controlled by the Russian authorities, producing "the first serious patriotic demonstration in Warsaw since the time of the [January] insurrection" of 1863.[40] This marked a turning point in the intellectual life of a region that had been dominated by positivism and organic work for the last several decades. These doctrines had not brought any respite, however, from Russification and repression, which is why, in the words of the commemoration's organizers, the "eternal spirit of protest against everything vile [had] beg[un] to awaken again."[41]

Fig. 4.2 "Muscovite tricks on the occasion of the Third of May." This cartoon in the satirical weekly *Djabeł* presents a dialogue between mother (Polonia) and son: "Mother! What does this bear mean? These dogs running with his pamphlets (*odezwy*)?—That is a Muscovite, son, who wants to give Warsaw new wounds, but we won't be deceived!" In other words, the agitation to celebrate the Third of May in Warsaw is being blamed on the Russians. Djabeł *23, no. 8 (21 April 1891).*

Warsaw was the most appropriate location for the celebration: this is where the Constitution of the Third of May had been born, voted, signed, and trumpeted. However, given the treatment of Poles in the Russian Empire, who would dare to organize a (necessarily illegal) commemoration? Those behind the demonstration included members of the conspiratorial Polish League and Zet. By 1891, the Polish League felt the need to go public—that is, to do more than work behind the scenes on behalf of the nation. Prior to the anniversary, it prepared and circulated an announcement about the upcoming centennial, including mention of local sites with a historical connection.[42]

The announcement prompted action on the part of both the Warsaw police and the conciliationists. The police increased its vigilance to discourage crowds and the mulling about of people on the streets. Fearing unpleasant repercussions, the conciliationists, through the local Polish press, decried the notion of public demonstrations. As seen in figure 4.2, the Galician press depicted the distributors of the leaflets as servile dogs of a

Russian bear in Polish clothing, intent on harming the Warsaw Poles.[43] None of this, however, discouraged a group of young people from making a pilgrimage to the ruins of the Church of Divine Providence in the Botanical Garden. During the first commemoration of the Third of May Constitution (in 1792—the only celebration of the event before the Poles lost their independence), the king had laid a cornerstone for this church, which was never built.[44] Seventy years later, the anniversary of the Constitution was celebrated in Warsaw during the period leading up to the January Insurrection, and the tradition of visiting the spot was recalled. Now it would figure for a third time in Warsaw's history.[45]

Following church services on the morning of May 3, a small group of Poles paid a short visit to the ruins. Emboldened by that first outing, about one hundred young people returned to the Botanical Garden later that afternoon with flowers. This time, the police appeared and asked those present to leave. The group set off in the direction of Castle Square (Plac Zamkowy), attracting the attention of a larger crowd of passersby. Police and cossacks dispersed the crowd, and several dozen were taken into custody. Only nine were kept longer, one of whom, the student Bolesław Bruliński, cut his own throat out of fear of what might come.[46] Arrest and imprisonment awaited a larger group, apprehended after incriminating materials were found at the home of one of the organizers. Among those arrested and given sentences, ranging from short prison stays to years in Siberia, were the future president of interwar Poland, Stanisław Wojciechowski; the former president of Zet in St. Petersburg, Tomasz Ruśkiewicz; the student activist Stanisław Bouffał, whom we last saw in Paris during the Mickiewicz translation; and the future leader of the National Democrats and, ultimately, the most important of the commemoration organizers, Roman Dmowski.[47] For Dmowski, this turning point in the life of Polish society marked his entry into the broader public sphere. Still a student in 1891, Dmowski was not arrested until his return from a post-graduation trip to France and Switzerland in August 1892. His imprisonment, then banishment to Mitawa (Jelgava) for three years influenced his decision to make his career in politics, not biology—a decision with important ramifications for Polish politics in the ensuing decades.[48] Thus, not only young activists but future Polish politicians cut their eyeteeth on this illegal centennial commemoration of the Third of May.

The illegal 1891 demonstration affected both partition politics and the commemorative process. It marked the first tear in the political fabric of the day: tri-loyalism. Whereas tri-loyalism posited a conciliatory attitude toward the empire, Dmowski and his colleagues underscored the incongruity of considering oneself a Pole while living in harmony with the gendarmes.[49] That commemorations were increasingly seen as a means of reaching the broader public becomes clear from the publications put forth by the Polish League and ancillary organizations. For example, the group Łączność (Liaison) produced a number of brochures and leaflets, the majority of which concerned anniversary commemorations.[50] The 3 May celebration was seen as a turning point in the life of Polish society. After thirty years of oppression by the police state, a return to illegal action was necessary. The intelligentsia was now turning to workers, artisans, and villagers, teaching them, distributing illegal literature, and organizing national celebrations. Celebrations, it was argued, had greater impact than leaflets, which reached only as many as could read them.[51] National celebrations were central to the vision of the Warsaw activists, who in turn breathed new life into public demonstrations. The Russian authorities responded by postponing the opening of the Botanical Garden each year until after the Third of May.[52]

HOW BEST TO COMMEMORATE THE PARTITIONS?

Warsaw now began to set the trends for national celebrations. This was most visible during the string of sad centennial anniversaries marking the end of the Polish state. Members of the Polish League and others in Warsaw chose to advocate a period of national mourning. Poles were asked to desist from holding lavish parties and invest the money in national consciousness-raising. Those in Warsaw began their mourning in 1892, the centennial of the Confederation of Targowica; instigated by a group of aristocrats, the confederation had led to the invasion of Russian troops in May of 1792 and subsequent (second) partition of Poland. Poles—generally aristocrats—who did not mourn publicly were mocked in verses that circulated about town or found their parties interrupted by protesters.[53]

The idea of national mourning was embraced by students in Galicia. Polish secondary school pupils had recently exhibited their national consciousness by wearing Polish-style caps (so-called *batorówki*), color-coded according to school. Many college students as well were members of a group known by names such as "White Eagle" or "Zouaves," the different names being adopted to keep the authorities from thinking that they were connected. After voting to support national mourning in November 1892, members of the secret youth group printed leaflets exhorting others to do likewise. Students also wore black mourning bands on their left shoulders to commemorate the anniversary of the second partition.[54]

Such actions were outlawed by the Galician authorities, who rejected national mourning and punished mourners.[55] This pan-Polish symbolic act undermined the modus vivendi they had reached with the regime; questioned the legitimacy of the noble domination of politics (for references to the noble traitors of Targowica were hardly subtle); and hinted that independence was preferable to subjugation, the relative lenience of Austrian rule notwithstanding. The authorities may have feared that national mourning would lead to armed insurrection; it had been proposed in 1846, 1848, 1861, and 1863—all years of upheaval. To that end, those in positions of power strove to control the impetus to commemorate in Galicia. They argued that commemorations of Targowica were best postponed until 1893, to coincide with the official promulgation of the second partition.[56] In the meantime, influential Galicians—including the mayor of Lwów, Edmund Mochnacki, democratic politician Tadeusz Romanowicz, and the conservative Wojciech Dzieduszycki—came up with an alternative means of commemoration. They proposed that Poles eschew symbolic mourning in favor of redoubled organic work. Believing the nation ought to celebrate its greatest misfortune "solely with deeds testifying to life, health and courageous deliberation insuring a better future," they proposed to establish a new fund, named after Tadeusz Kościuszko, the "first hero of the regenerating Poland."[57] Donations would be used (among other things) to construct a dormitory for those studying to be folk teachers.

Even well-intentioned, constructive deeds often appeared designed to distract the nation from national mourning and counter independent public initiatives. Was the Kościuszko Fund simply a poor imitation of the People's School Society, as one newspaper maintained?[58] Supporters of national mourning saw its avoidance in Galicia as a "great political mistake": the lack of cooperation across imperial borders demonstrated to the Poles' enemies that the nation was not united. It was important to celebrate the act of partition, to show that Poles were cognizant of its significance, that they had been wronged: "We cannot protest against the foreign state of affairs *actively,* because this is not the time for that; but we can make a passive protest through the united manifestation [*solidarne wystąpienie*] of the entire subjugated Nation—through the general celebration of mourning of the partition of Poland."[59] Such sentiments were repressed by the Galician government: leaflets inciting the Poles to national mourning, such as the one cited above, were confiscated and destroyed, thus denying the opposition a voice.[60]

Lwów's youth nonetheless found other ways of expressing their disgust at those who disregarded their calls for national mourning. Members of the city's secret organizations patrolled the streets in early 1893 to see where parties were being held, often breaking windows in those buildings. In some cases, youthful "undertakers" would deposit a coffin and serenade guests with properly funereal song. They occasionally resorted to the use of chemical agents in test tubes or catered food to upset the guests physically as well as psychologically. While these reactions dampened festivities, they also resulted in court cases being brought against individual students for their participation.[61]

Yet other Galicians managed to commemorate the more distressing moments from the Polish past, perhaps with greater success. In 1893, Father Stojałowski organized a peasant rally in Cracow on the occasion of the partitions. This was the first time peasant delegates of agricultural circles had gathered for a general meeting. No less important, however, was the impact that this trip had on the peasants' sense of belonging. The old medieval capital of Poland was an ideal destination for such excursions—an education in itself for visiting peasants, who were escorted about the town, shown its historic sites, and told of Poland's past. Wawel Cathedral overflowed with monuments of that past, reminders of what had been lost. We know that a lasting impression was made on a literate peasant, Franciszek Magryś from the village of Handzlówka (near Łańcut). At a church service in Wawel Cathedral, Magryś found himself under the spell of Wawel Castle and the Poles' tragic past:

> I saw before me the whole enormity of unhappiness that fell on the nation through the negligence of our nobility. Although I tried to restrain myself, tears streamed from my eyes. I muffled my face with a handkerchief, so that those standing next to me would not see that I was crying, for they might think that the church music had so moved me; but I was crying over the partition of Poland.[62]

Magryś later shared his impressions of this visit with other villagers through a poem, which was published in a peasant paper.[63]

That peasants were beginning to relate to relics of the old Polish state does not mean that many understood that past. Few peasants had any knowledge of Polish history in 1893. Maciej Szarek, whom we met in conjunction with the Kraszewski jubilee, complained that even literate peasants did not understand what they read. The concept of a constitution was foreign to them; they did not know who Kościuszko was.[64] Villagers needed a patriotic education. We have seen that the founders of the People's School Society shared this concern. The national education of the Polish peasant was aided by another anniversary: the centennial of the Kościuszko Insurrection, to which I now turn.

THE KOŚCIUSZKO ANNIVERSARY OF 1894

The centennial of the Kościuszko Insurrection of 1794 was the high point of the commemorations of the last years of the Polish state. The complexity of the insurrection, featuring other actors in addition to Kościuszko and fought in different locations, gave rise to a particularly multifaceted commemoration of the events of 1794, one that helped to transform large numbers of peasants into nationally conscious and politically engaged Poles.

Long before 1894, Tadeusz Kościuszko (1746–1817) had been recognized as a great national figure.[65] His remains had been transferred to the Wawel crypt in 1818, when Cracow was still a free city, and the military leader was soon honored with a large earthen mound bearing his name—the Kościuszko Mound—on the outskirts of Cracow. The Kościuszko Insurrection involved more than this famous Pole, however. The year 1794 marked what a centennial publication called the "bloody christening of the peasantry and townspeople."[66] The burghers and artisans of Warsaw, Wilno, and other towns defended their cities. The peasantry also took part in this struggle: the most famous fighting force under Kościuszko were the scythe-brandishing peasants who helped him win the Battle of Racławice in the spring of 1794. Kościuszko proceeded to ennoble several peasant scythemen and don the *sukmana,* the russet overcoat of the Cracow peasants, to express his respect for his fellow soldiers. This image of Kościuszko, the nobleman in the *sukmana,* predominates in the iconography: Kościuszko was a republican demanding the rights of man, fighting for both liberty and the folk.[67]

The commemorations of the Kościuszko Insurrection in 1894 had a tremendous impact on the development of Polish national consciousness, an impact that has not always been given full acknowledgment, as Franciszek Ziejka has noted.[68] Polish peasant engagement of this period reached a new height in these celebrations. To the cult of Kościuszko was added a new cult: that of the Battle of Racławice, marking the engagement of the peasantry in the defense of the nation. In Galicia, peasants, no longer passive participants in the commemorative process, helped to shape both the cult and the celebration. The tremendous symbolism of the peasantry defending the Polish nation in the Kościuszko Insurrection was both popularized and exploited by the peasants in 1894.

The events of 1794 provided Polish commemorators with a wide range of events to celebrate, as seen from the celebrations in Cracow, Warsaw, and Lwów.[69] Each city stressed a different part of the Kościuszko Insurrection, as reflected in the scheduling of the festivities.[70] Cracow, for example, emphasized a date with local resonance: the anniversary of the proclamation of the insurrection and the oath given by Kościuszko at the Cracow market square on March 24, 1791. It was the giving of the oath, not the proclamation of the insurrection, that the municipal officials behind the celebration strove to underscore, much to the chagrin of the local democrats.[71] The organizers likewise underscored religious motifs connected with the anniversary. According to legend, prior to the insurrection Kościuszko had his saber blessed in the Capuchin church, in this way "beginning with God," just like the Third of May Constitution, as Father Chromecki was quick to point out in his sermon.[72] The Cracow organizers commissioned a commemorative tablet to be placed on the outer wall of the Loreto chapel of the Capuchin church; only later did they contact Kościuszko's biographer, Tadeusz Korzon, to ask whether this blessing had really taken place. Korzon, amused by the Cracovians' rather tardy inquiry, replied that he had seen no evidence that it had. A temporary tablet commemorating the act was unveiled, all the same, on March 30.[73]

The official Cracow celebration downplayed or amended the image of armed peasants. The lone exception to this rule was the plaster monument commissioned for the anniversary, a provisional copy of a future bronze monument to Kościuszko. The artist Walery Eliasz Radzikowski modeled the main figure of Kościuszko on a pedestal, his arm raised to swear his oath; at his feet, with a scythe, was the peasant Bartosz Głowacki, whom Kościuszko had ennobled for his valor during the Battle of Racławice. Antagonism to this latter image perhaps explains why the monument, still at its temporary location on the market square, was destroyed—on orders of the police to Mayor Friedlein—even before the weekend of celebration was over.[74] Both the Catholic Church and the provincial authorities distanced themselves from the celebration, which otherwise seemed potentially to offer so much to the local peasantry (a peasant rally was scheduled to follow the Cracow celebration).[75] This antipathy was likely related to the fact that relations with Father Stanisław Stojałowski had soured. At the end of 1893, the popular priest had been attacked by the episcopal triumvirate of Ignacy Łobos of Tarnów, Seweryn Morawski of Lwów, and Łukasz Solecki of Przemyśl, who forbade the sacraments to readers of Stojałowski's popular papers and temporarily suspended the priest from religious duties.[76] Stojałowski responded by lashing out at his enemies, including the viceroy, in a brochure on the Kościuszko Insurrection, which the police confiscated. Badeni redoubled his efforts to hamper distribution of Stojałowski's publications, which by then were being mailed into Galicia from Teschen Silesia. All peasants not firmly under official or clerical control may have been suspect.[77]

In general, the Cracow festivities were plagued by social tensions. "Street excesses" had broken out the evening before the peasant rally, leading to the breaking of windows—including the windows of Austrian officers—that had not been illuminated during the festivities. The Viennese daily *Neue Freie Presse* noted that stones were thrown at the windows of the former Austrian finance minister, Julian Dunajewski, probably because "his brother the cardinal went to Rome instead of leading the church celebrations."[78] Other newspapers—such as *Czas* and *Gazeta Narodowa* (National gazette, published in Lwów)—saw a trace of anti-Semitism in the acts.[79] The editor of the monthly *Kościuszko,* Antoni Kostecki, accused forces opposed to the democrats of inciting the unrest.[80] Whatever its source, the violence played into the hands of the conservatives, who took advantage of the confusion to criticize public festivities; as an alternative, they advocated more innocuous forms of organic work, such as the establishment of institutions of social and cultural importance or the organization of exhibitions.[81]

The Warsaw celebration was organized by a nascent nationalist group that placed Polish independence and Polish interests above all other issues—the National League. Founded by Roman Dmowski, the National League was comprised of former members of Zet and Łączność who questioned the usefulness of the émigré-directed Polish League.[82] Acknowledging the different conditions within each empire, Dmowski nonetheless maintained that a general principle should apply: "each political deed of a Pole, without regard to where it is executed and against whom directed, must have in view the interests of the entire nation."[83] Class-based politics would be defeatist, as the energies of all Poles were needed to combat the Russian threat. Dmowski wrote: "National politics in its main principles cannot be either Poznanian, or Galician, or Varsovian—they must be pan-Polish."[84] Indeed, the Warsaw commemoration was "pan-Polish" in more than spirit. Although organized by members of the editorial board of *Głos* in Warsaw, leaflets had been printed in Silesia and were carried to Warsaw by a Jagiellonian University student of peasant extraction. These were handed out several days before the commemoration, especially to artisans. The organizers hoped that the lower classes of Polish society would take their historic place—as seen in the Kościuszko Insurrection—and join the active opposition to the Russians.

While Warsaw activists celebrated both the anniversary of the Battle of Racławice (April 4) and the Warsaw uprising (April 17), the latter date was given pride of place. The Warsaw uprising was also known as the Kiliński uprising, after the shoemaker Jan Kiliński, who led a regiment of urban soldiers. A radicalized force, they killed not only Russians but also traitors, including Bishop Józef Korwin Kossakowski. While what happened in Warsaw was decried by some as having harmed Kościuszko's insurrection, the organizers of the Warsaw celebration viewed the Kiliński uprising more instrumentally. Commemoration of that past was seen as a way to engage the descendants of the shoemakers and butchers who had participated in the insurrection—thus prompting the Russian paper *Varshavskii Dnievnik* to complain that Polish society was succumbing to the "old disease" of insurrectionism.[85]

The events of April 17 were notable only under the conditions of Russian Poland. A special mass, offered for a "sick child," was held at Saint John's Cathedral.[86] Several thousand attended, including several dozen shoemakers and butchers. After the church service, participants set out to visit places of note in 1794. They proceeded through Old Town (Stare Miasto), heading to the street where Kiliński had lived (ul. Szeroki Dunaj), and from there toward the palace of Josif A. Igelström, the main leader of the Russian forces in 1794. There a police cordon awaited them. Many were arrested. The artisans were released, as the authorities took great pains to assert that the demonstration was "organized by the Polish intelligentsia and not by the street crowd," perhaps fearing what might happen if the laboring classes started taking a direct interest in Poland's future.[87] In contrast, the government had no qualms about punishing members of the intelligentsia, particularly uniformed students. The police arrested 158 students from Warsaw University, three from the veterinary school, and an additional 46 men and 32 women. Over 160 languished in prison for up to four months before being exiled to Russian guberniias for two to three years. The nascent nationalist movement in Warsaw—not to mention the editorial board of *Głos*—was wiped out in one blow. Numerous participants, students as well as political activists, eventually would resurface—in Galicia.[88]

THE LWÓW EXPOSITION

Looking at the commemorations of the spring of 1894, one might conclude that, while a certain symbolic statement had been made in Warsaw, the anniversary of the Kościuszko Insurrection had had little impact on the masses. What, then, prompted the populist Jakub Bojko to comment, "When 1894 came, this tough, taciturn peasant gave signs of life, and here Lwów was the witness of his stirring"?[89] A new venue provided the best opportunity both for uniting the Poles and for bringing to life the events of 1794. In 1894, Lwów played host to a Provincial Universal Exposition (Wystawa krajowa powszechna). In just over four months, from June 5 to October 16, it was visited by over a million people—ten times the population of the city.[90]

The Lwów Exposition lacked the international stature of the London Exposition of 1851 or the Paris Exposition of 1889. Still, Galicia had already held two smaller fairs, one in Lwów in 1877, the other in Cracow ten years later. The largest by far, the exposition of 1894 could be compared to another Austro-Hungarian effort, the Czech exposition of 1891; indeed, some Poles maintained that the one had given impetus to the other.[91] While this may have been true, the Lwów Exposition, plans for which were announced on June 29, 1892, fit too perfectly the needs of the most influen-

Fig. 4.3 The Provincial Universal Exposition in Lwów. The "fairgrounds," with its variety of buildings. *Original photograph by E. Trzemeski of Lwów; courtesy of the Library of the Museum of Ethnography and Artistic Industry, L'viv.*

tial Galicians at that time to have been inspired by the Czechs.[92] The construction of this monument to local achievements provided a much-needed distraction from the less constructive national urge to mourn the partitions. The decision to hold an exposition three years ahead of schedule came at a peculiar moment, according to Prince Adam Sapieha, the exposition's president: "in the life of nations there come times when they cannot satisfy themselves with common daily life but feel . . . the necessity of stating, with an uncommon deed, that they feel in the prime of this life and look into the future with a healthy gaze."[93] This unusual national energy, perhaps associated with agitation for national mourning, needed to be channeled into productive veins.

To turn the nation's gaze from the past toward the future seems to have been at least part of the goal of the exposition. Costing as much as the annual budget of Cracow at the time, the exposition was an expensive endeavor for this poor region.[94] The exposition was in fact a small town, comprised of 129 pavilions, various restaurants, coffee shops, and bakeries, constructed on a fifty-hectare plateau adjoining Kiliński Park and towering over the Galician capital. The organizers needed to move fifty thousand cubic meters of earth and pipe water to the plateau—all costly undertakings.[95] The exposition would showcase what the inhabitants of the region had accomplished in thirty-four fields as varied as the fine arts, oil production, forestry, publishing, and animal husbandry. The pavilions themselves highlighted a Galician strength: architecture. Not only was the work of Poland's best architects in numerous architectural styles exhibited, but native regional peasant dwellings were constructed on the site by their traditional builders: highlanders from Podhale and eastern Galicia, villagers from the regions of Sokal and Podolia.[96] While wood was the predominant building material, several edifices were designed to stand there permanently. These included the Palace of Art as well as Matejko's mausoleum, the latter begun shortly after the artist's death in November 1893: it would house many of the artist's works during the exposition.

That Galicia was touting its progress in the exposition might seem paradoxical. After all, it was considered the most economically backward of the partitioned lands. An economic backwater even within Austria-Hungary, Galicia was hard-pressed to find a niche for itself that would take it into the twentieth century. Its proverbial "misery," already made famous by Stanisław Szczepanowski's book of 1888, contributed to its role as a source of emigrant labor. If the Galician peasantry could not make the transition from impoverished self-sufficiency (and, thus, indifference to the broader world) to domestic industry, villagers would continue to be lost to the region—and, perhaps, to the nation.

Anything that smacked of progress in the exposition, thus, might encourage peasants to stay put. One sign of technological advancement was the newly constructed electric tramline leading from the center of Lwów to the exposition site. Visitors could travel underground from the exposition square to the base of Kiliński Park through an eleven-meter shaft in the Paraffin Wax Mining Pavilion in Borysław. And sixteen persons at a time could ride in the two wagons of the cable railway linking the oil and ethnographic pavilions.[97] Praise was lavished upon another novelty: a luminous fountain (*fontaine lumineuse*), awash in colored lights. The anticipated appeal to the Galician folk was underscored in the poster by Piotr Stachiewicz advertising the exposition: a Ruthenian girl with a wreath and a "handsome Mazurian" holding a torch were featured alongside symbols of art, science, ethnography, agriculture, forestry, and industry.[98]

In the Lwów Exposition, the theme of work was paramount, with some even calling the exposition the "holiday of work."[99] This work, as the exposition's slogan dictated, was to be done for the "honor and profit of the country."[100] While the organizers did not intend to compete with more fortunate nations, they did hope to "demonstrate . . . that we do not remain behind others in general development and progress, that . . . among us rule unity and solidarity without limit [*bez granic*]."[101] The "we" of the quota-

Fig. 4.4 The Provincial Universal Exposition in Lwów. Among the technological innovations visible at the Exposition were the pneumatic chairs lining the walkways. Drop in three cents, and you could sit until you stood up again (which reportedly often happened when greeting friends). *Courtesy of the Library of the Museum of Ethnography and Artistic Industry, Lviv.*

tion, of course, could refer either to the nation or to the province. Indeed, the choice of Lwów over Cracow downplayed the exposition's Polishness, a perception reinforced by the participation of non-Poles, such as the Austrian archduke Albrecht, whose personal pavilion showcased the achievements of his holdings in Żywiec, or Archduke Charles Louis, who opened the exposition.[102] The unity about which Sapieha bragged apparently embraced Ruthenes as well. Many of the developments from eastern Galicia, certainly on the estates of large landowners, involved the participation of the Ruthenian masses. A member of the Provincial Executive Board, Damian Sawczak, spoke in Ukrainian at the opening and closing of the exposition as well as during the visit of Emperor Francis Joseph in September. Sawczak's presence enabled the emperor to speak of the "work produced by the concerted cooperation of both tribes [*obu szczepów*] of this crownland," which led him to hope that "the economic welfare of the population would grow more and more happily."[103]

The visit of the emperor, accompanied by his entire cabinet, on September 8 was hoped to reassure the Austrian government that provincial autonomy was beneficial to Galicia. More ambitiously, Wojciech Dzieduszycki stated that the "already mature" Poles contributed to the well-being of the empire as a whole: "the nations inhabiting the state . . . recognize more and more clearly that the Poles best understand the essence and limits of parliamentary freedoms, and that they best know how to reconcile the needs of the nations with the interest of the state," which is why the Poles should not be deprived "either of their own freedom or of participation in government."[104] Such sentiments assume greater significance when one reflects that, within the year, a Pole—Kazimierz Badeni—was appointed head of the Austrian government.

The loyalistic approach seemed to work. Emperor Francis Joseph was impressed that the "allowance for national peculiarities and the respect for national traditions ha[d] only tightened the knot between the state and the crown land."[105] That knot could still restrict, however, as the producer of a medal with the visage of Kościuszko and the words "God Save Poland" learned: his medals were confiscated for "disturbing the public peace."[106]

Yet, the exposition was not devoid of pan-Polish elements. While the vast majority of the over five thousand exhibitors hailed from Galicia, several hundred came from other Polish lands, and over fifty from abroad.[107] There was also a connection made to the Polish centennial. For example, the "illustrated organ" of the Lwów Exposition, the periodical *Świat,* contained a number of articles on Kościuszko. Weighing the scales even more heavily in favor of Polishness was the reason why the exposition is addressed here: the Racławice Panorama.

THE RACŁAWICE PANORAMA

World expositions have often been identified with a particular symbol. The Crystal Palace showcasing technological progress served as shorthand for the London Exposition of 1851; the Paris Exposition of 1889 provided the French capital with the Eiffel Tower. The Polish exposition of 1894 had its own great national souvenir.[108] The Racławice Panorama—a realistic painting-in-the-round depicting the one major battle in which Polish peasants had played a decisive role—is practically the only reason why the exposition is remembered by Poles today.

The Racławice Panorama was more than just another painting of the Battle of Racławice. This enormous painting-in-the-round represented the most advanced art experience available before cinematography. The panorama was to the nineteenth century what the moving picture was to the twentieth. This precursor of film sought to convey both realism and a sense of motion through space and time, even if that sensation was attained by the movement of the spectators inside the pavilion to view the painting that surrounded them. It was the mass medium par excellence of the day.[109]

Fig. 4.5 The Racławice Panorama: painters posing in front of the canvas.
A work-in-process: see the scythe-bearing peasants to the left, already marching
across the canvas. *Courtesy of the Jagiellonian Library.*

As such, any self-respecting international exposition had a panorama—or
more than one: the World Exposition of 1889 in Paris had seven.[110]

Like those earlier panoramas, the Racławice Panorama was art for the
masses. It spoke "to the soul of the people," who, in great numbers, were
awakening to intellectual and national life.[111] Of the many events and
venues connected with this anniversary, the Racławice Panorama was the
most significant for the development of national consciousness among the
peasantry; it also marked an important transformation in the nation's consideration of its past, present, and future.

After entering the building through a dark corridor leading to the view-
ing platform, visitors to the panorama literally found themselves in the center of the battle, and they were able to follow the course of events that led
to the Polish victory. The painting's naturalism was enhanced by the thorough research of the artists Jan Styka and Wojciech Kossak. Armed with a
detailed sketch of the battle plan, copied out of the Vienna military
archive, Styka surreptitiously visited the village of Racławice—within the
Russian border zone, and thus off-limits to visitors—in April 1893 in order
to see both the surroundings and the play of light at that time of year. The

artist also spirited back to Galicia a number of cannonballs and remnants of weapons. These authentic three-dimensional artifacts, placed in the earth-strewn space between the wall and the viewers, made the battle scene seem genuine. One peasant even jumped over the balustrade, only to learn to his amazement that there was nothing there but canvas.[112] Visitors felt transported to the battle scene, and the Polish insurrection—now real for them—took on a heightened immediacy.

Notwithstanding a degree of naturalism and Kossak's desire for historical accuracy, the painting contained various anachronisms and ahistorical moments.[113] Some of these involved symbolic details inseparable from the Kościuszko myth, which doubtless is why Styka insisted on their inclusion. The military banner featured in the panorama boasted the slogan "They feed and defend" (żywią i bronią), which was created only after the demonstration of the peasants' new talents at Racławice. The Polish peasant garb depicted was characteristic of the nineteenth, not eighteenth century—which may have made peasant viewers identify more closely with their armed forebears. And the commanding figure of Kościuszko was painted in his *sukmana,* or peasant russet overcoat. Kościuszko's wearing of peasant dress was emblematic of many Poles' desire that the peasantry should be raised to the level of the nobility, not the latter demoted to the level of the former.[114] One socially significant scene was fabricated: Styka painted a group of villagers praying together with a disabled noble veteran of the Confederacy of Bar.[115] Thus new and old elements of the myth of Kościuszko, the Polish insurrectionary tradition, and peasant strength were melded into one tantalizing moment, in which both independent statehood and social justice seemed within reach.

During the exposition, at least two hundred thousand persons viewed the Racławice Panorama.[116] It played a key role in shaping the way peasants viewed Kościuszko and the insurrection. This was particularly important for those who had little sense of national patriotism, who hardly even felt themselves Poles. The panorama technique amazed these new viewers, while its topic engaged and ennobled them. This was understood by noblemen like Wojciech Dzieduszycki: he already led a group of about three hundred peasants, Cracovians as well as Ruthenes, to see the work-in-progress on April 4, 1894, the hundredth anniversary of the Battle of Racławice.[117]

Dzieduszycki's peasants were only the first to visit the panorama. A large number of peasant excursions were arranged during the exposition, thanks to various individuals and organizations. Peasant initiatives, supported by other segments of society, brought visitors to the panorama in droves. The matter was discussed at a meeting of over one thousand villagers in Rzeszów on May 27, 1894, organized by the populist newspaper *Przyjaciel*

Ludu; those present voted to ask all villagers of the country to consider it their obligation to visit the exposition in Lwów.[118] This vote gave impetus to excursions for numerous peasants: three hundred from the Jarosław district, six hundred from Łańcut, one hundred from Gorlice, and five hundred from Dolina (Dolyna) and Bolechów (Bolekhiv).[119] On a local basis, some villages and towns strove to visit the exposition; yet others financed trips for representatives from their communes.[120] Many initiatives were inspired by the peasant Jakub Bojko, who came up with the idea to organize excursions of villagers, particularly of children, to the exposition.[121]

The People's School Society seized upon Bojko's idea. It had already planned to participate in the exhibition, providing statistics on illiteracy and schools. It now lent its support by organizing group excursions to the exposition. The executive board of the People's School Society called for local committees to arrange for group excursions of schoolchildren, especially from rural areas—at least several from each commune; its Lwów branch later created a committee to take care of trips of village schoolchildren to the exposition (and requested donations). For example, the organization funded the trip of Silesian children, and donations collected by members paid for forty-nine excursions of a total of 6,645 children to the Lwów Exposition.[122]

The ladies of Lwów predominated on the receiving end. Women and their children greeted and accompanied dozens of village excursions through the exposition. The populist activist Maria Wysłouchowa escorted an estimated three thousand peasants to the Racławice Panorama and lectured to them on the significance of the battle.[123] Members of the women's branch of the Society of Folk Education (Towarzystwo Oświaty Ludowej), headed by Maria Łomnicka, took care of the logistics for many groups of children and youth.[124]

Many of these arrangements required contacts in other cities. A network of women's branches took care of meals for groups such as school youth from Czernowitz (Chernivtsi) in northern Bukovina. After their train crossed the Galician border, members of the group, sponsored by members of the Society of Women's Work (Towarzystwo Pracy Kobiet), breakfasted in Kołomyja and were met there by the local mayor. Their next meal, arranged by the women's branch, was taken in Stanisławów. The following day they arrived very early in Lwów and heard mass at the cathedral. After breakfast, the young people of Czernowitz were taken to see the Racławice Panorama at seven o'clock in the morning (one hour before the regular opening of the building) with discounted tickets. They visited the industrial pavilion at eleven o'clock, met with the exposition's director, Marchwicki, and were fed several more times, including dinner in the Dreher restaurant, where they were serenaded by the band of Saint Anne's Elementary School in Lwów. After what must have been an exhausting visit—they did not leave the exposition until six o'clock in the evening—they returned home the next day.[125]

Numerous other groups—including two large excursions from Cracow—were similarly welcomed, treated to meals, given mementos, and shown around the exhibition site as well as local sites of interest. For the young villagers, this doubtless was the first train ride, not to mention the first exposure to the best in the way of advanced technology that fin de siècle Galicia could offer. Greeted at the station with patriotic songs, they were met by a variety of Poles, Jews, and Ruthenes, the exposition providing informal lessons in comparative folklore and regional dress. The Racławice Panorama seemed to be the one pavilion visited by them all, initiating what well might have been their first lessons in Polish history. These could be memories of a lifetime for any peasant.[126] For the even more impressionable children, this visit must have contributed greatly to their patriotic education. The exposure of rural youth not only to the attainments of the country but to a glorious moment in history assured that the younger generation would be gained for the Polish cause—a small investment that would pay off in later decades.[127]

CONGRESSES AND CONSCIOUSNESS-RAISING

The exposition made Lwów the primary destination for meetings of Poles from all over. One of the most noteworthy congresses involved Galician villagers. Several thousand attended the peasant rally in the last days of August to discuss the state of the populist movement and attempt to organize themselves politically before the impending elections to the Galician Sejm.[128] Escorted by Maria Wysłouchowa and Lwów students, the peasants visited the Racławice Panorama before their congress began—an encounter with the Polish past likely to give the villagers a better sense of their own capabilities. It certainly seemed to affect the ability of one peasant to respond, in historically conscious fashion, to the welcome speech of Prince Adam Sapieha: pointing at the building housing the Racławice Panorama, Jan Skwara of Krosno asserted, "when the right time comes, Racławice will repeat itself."[129] This new attitude is part of what made 1894 such a special year. The deeds of the past did more than move those who were exposed to them—they were used as a lesson for the future and shaped a program of action.[130]

Although the peasant rally was timed to coincide with the three hundredth anniversary of the canonization of Saint Hyacinth (św. Jacek), the full gamut of political views was offered the villagers during their stay in the city. The elderly poet Kornel Ujejski, whose letter to the participants was read aloud by Jakub Bojko, emphasized the inclusion of the peasants in the nation—"your cause is not the peasant cause, it is the national cause" (*sprawa Wasza, to nie sprawa chłopska, to sprawa narodowa*)—and the significance of the "nobleman in the peasant *sukmana.*"[131] Sapieha's assertions that "the exposition also reached back into the nation's past, since without remembering the past one cannot have a future" and his exhortation for those present to be like their ancestors were greeted with bravos.[132] The Ukrainian Ivan Franko lectured on the significance of the Lwów Exposition and spoke at the rally. Those present discussed electoral reform and sought to establish an electoral committee so that votes would no longer be bought—a motion not allowed by the police commissar present. The rally likewise conveyed the sentiment, expressed by Bolesław Wysłouch, that through the populist movement, which marked a return to Kościuszko's ideals, the nation would be reborn, raised up from its downfall by the folk.[133]

The presence of so many peasants in Lwów attracted attention. The vice president of the Lwów Exposition, Stanisław Badeni, reportedly commented to the Austrian finance minister that the notion of the Polish peasant as ignorant, uninterested, and not ready to participate in public life was no longer correct.[134] The following year would cement this conviction in the nation as a whole. The peasant rally of 1894 led to the founding of the Peasant Party (Stronnictwo Ludowe) at a rally in Rzeszów in July 1895. The previous year's discussions of electoral reform resulted in a concerted effort of populists as well as democrats sympathetic to the peasant cause, which led to the election of nine deputies, including Jakub Bojko, to the Galician Sejm. One wonders whether this empowerment of the peasant masses would have come so soon, had thousands not seen with their own eyes the peasant scythemen and Kościuszko in the peasant *sukmana* marching across the canvas of the Racławice Panorama. Increasingly aware of the services rendered the nation by their ancestors, peasants were becoming full-fledged citizens cognizant of the role they might play in the nation's future.

Many other organizations took advantage of the interest in the exposition to schedule their congresses for Lwów in 1894. The exposition thus afforded another occasion for meeting and mingling. Yet another Congress of Polish Writers and Journalists assembled the literati in step with the commemorative calendar. The Falcon Jamboree (Zlot Sokoła) marked the first gathering of Polish Falcons from both Prussian and Austrian Poland since the recent formation of the Union of Polish Falcons. A large field in the exposition complex housed demonstrations of fifteen hundred uniformed members performing exercises in unison. The popular gymnastics society conducted various races and contests and touted its achievements in its own pavilion.[135] These two events were among the exposition's largest. Other congresses or meetings are noteworthy for whom they brought to Lwów. Former Siberian exiles; highlanders, including the famous Sabała; alumni of Kiev University; as well as Polish technical specialists, teachers, doctors, scientists, and many more all gathered in the Galician capital during this period.[136]

The visit of a hundred Teschen Silesians on August 12 illustrates the degree to which Galician Poles strove to foster the Polishness of this minority from beyond Galicia. Led by Father Jan Michejda, the group was received by the mayors of both Cracow and Lwów en route to the exposition. There they were addressed by Director Marchwicki, who noted the common bond of religion uniting the Teschen Silesians and the Galician Poles: "And when today, at the train station at the moment of greeting, that song, dear to us all, which each mother hums over the child's cradle, sounded from your mouths, we were possessed by a strangely joyful sensation. It seemed to us as if that song of faith were a new junction of Polish hearts, for your hearts too are Polish through and through."[137] The piety of Teschen Silesians was highlighted outside the exposition as well; in addition to visiting numerous churches and attending mass in one of them, they were received by Archbishop Issakowicz in his cathedral. That the Armenian archbishop gave the Teschen Silesians copies of the image of Our Lady of Częstochowa attests not only to the reach of this pan-Polish symbol but to the centrality of the Catholic faith as a national marker.[138] Their trip to Lwów was punctuated with excursions underscoring the content and accomplishments of the Polish nation: the Silesians reflected upon Styka's *Polonia* in the town hall and were taken to the Dzieduszycki museum and to the industrial school and museum. The trip was designed to strengthen their Polishness and pride in being Polish. As if to prepare the Teschen Silesians for the long fight against Germanization and Czechification that awaited them, at the train station upon their departure the Harmonia Orchestra played "Jeszcze Polska nie zginęła"—"Poland Has Not Yet Perished."[139]

The exposition and the concomitant congresses afforded many opportunities for cross-partition interaction. Teschen Silesians were not the only visitors from outside Galicia. Some crossed the borders of the German Empire. A group from Upper Silesia, from the cities of Racibórz (Ratibor), Bytom (Beuthen), and Opole (Oppeln), among others, visited the exposition on August 26. Other trips of Poles from Germany provided more grist for the national mill. The exposition occasioned the first organized expedition of Poles from Poznania to Lwów since 1871, the founding the Second Reich. Three such trips took place that summer. During their stay, these visitors from the German Empire were praised for their work among their own peasants, who for the most part considered themselves Polish. Still, the Galician Poles were careful to note their own advantage: the relative freedom they had in Austria-Hungary. The exercise of this freedom of speech got a Poznanian Pole into a predicament.

This incident took place during the second excursion from those parts, which brought a group of landowners and lawyers to Lwów for the Congress of Polish Lawyers and Economists in mid-August. Tongues were loosened at a banquet held in the municipal casino—most notably, that of Józef Kościelski, the most famous of the Poznanian conciliationists. A friend of Emperor William II, he was nicknamed "Admiralski" for his unswerving support for the plans to finance new ships for the navy; for his support, he had been decorated by the emperor.[140] Nonetheless, attacks from Polish populists had caused the conciliationist to resign his seat in parliament earlier that year. In Lwów, while toasting the "political idea" of those who had fought for Galicia in its current position, Kościelski defended the unity of the Polish nation. In spite of the efforts of "some" (meaning the partitioning powers) who "drew certain lines on the body of the nation" and "painted it in certain colors," expecting to "wreck it and divide it into pieces," he claimed that the nation was "but one organism, has one heart, one idea."[141]

This unexpected expression of Polish national solidarity was duly noted in the Polish, German, and French press, and in turn seemed to spark new developments within the German Empire over the next two months: a pilgrimage of several thousand German nationalists to the home of Otto von Bismarck, the establishment of the anti-Polish Society for the Support of the Germans in the Eastern Marches (Verein zur Förderung des Deutschtums in den Ostmarken, more commonly known as the Eastern Marches Society or Hakata), and the firing of Chancellor Leo von Caprivi, whose "New Course" had included some concessions to Poles.[142] Although Kościelski tried to make amends in the Viennese *Neue Freie Presse* already on September 22, the damage was done, offense had been taken, and the loyalty of the Poles was once again questioned.[143]

But not all was bad news, certainly not in Galicia. Galician peasants were not only learning more about the Polish past: they were assuming an active role within the nation. Peasants organized their own tributes to Kościuszko and the heroes of 1794 during the anniversary year. In the town of Nowy Sącz, for example, a parade was held on April 4, a monument to Kościuszko was erected, and a park given his name. This was not, as the peasant organizers made clear, a celebration organized by someone for the common folk, but one which the folk itself observed in order to demonstrate its own national sentiment.[144] And, at the 1895 congress in Rzeszów, the populists resolved to celebrate the Battle of Racławice as a folk holiday.

The attraction of the Kościuszko Insurrection did not dim with time. Within the next few years, dramatic reenactments of the famous battle involving scythemen were organized—most notably by the peasant Wojciech Wiącek of Machów, near Tarnobrzeg, in 1898. The energetic peasant activist understood the usefulness of the reenactments: "The factors that acted best on peasant souls turned out to be those battles, for, like tableaux [żywe obrazy], they best found their way to peasants' hearts and recalled Poland."[145] The reenactment of larger battles such as that of Grochów (during the November Insurrection) as well as of Racławice attracted crowds in the thousands. In 1898, the Racławice reenactment was attended, according to Wiącek, by about twenty-five thousand people, with over two thousand participants playing Russian and Polish soldiers under the command of Wiącek's Kościuszko.[146] In 1904, forty peasants from Polesie stole across the Russian cordon to participate in a reenactment of the Racławice battle, after which several thousand participants had to be restrained from crossing the Vistula River to attack the real Russian army and begin a new insurrection.[147] Peasants were also circulating in the broader national realm. Bojko and Wiącek, among others, traveled to Rapperswil in 1897 for the opening of the Kościuszko mausoleum containing the one relic of Kościuszko that had not been buried in the Wawel crypt: his heart.[148] Nor did peasants hesitate to provide a more lasting monument to their growing national consciousness: on September 9, 1904, a peasant-funded statue not of Kościuszko, but of Bartosz Głowacki, the most famous of the peasants who fought under him, was unveiled in Tarnobrzeg.[149]

In addition to their use of the visual, peasant activists found other ways of wooing villagers for the nation. The educated son of a peasant from Borek (in the county of Krosno), Kasper Wojnar, published an inexpensive commemorative booklet of over forty patriotic songs entitled *National Songs, Published under the Aegis of Youth in Memory of the One Hundredth Anniversary of the Heroism of the Folk.* This four-cent edition was designed to reach the folk, if through the mediation of the educated classes such as school youth spending its summers in the villages. Wojnar and his friends knew the value of song for the peasantry and sought to enrich its repertoire with songs that would enhance its patriotism. Songs such as "Look at Us, Kościuszko, from Heaven" and "Bartosz, Bartosz" brought the heroes of 1794 back to life; others taught the peasantry Polish history. When millions of peasants would sing "Poland Has Not Yet Perished," claimed Wojnar, then "the chains of bondage would break and a newly free song would be heard from sea to sea."[150] This same "Dąbrowski's Mazurka" would later become the Polish national anthem. That Wojnar's booklet had thirty-two editions, amounting to a printed total of over eight hundred thousand, suggests that commemorative song continued to resound long after the large anniversary celebrations had taken place.[151]

PROGRESS: POLISH AND POPULIST

The celebration of the centennial of the Kościuszko Insurrection continued along the trajectory established three years earlier with the founding of
the People's School Society at the anniversary celebration of the Constitution. The focus on the Battle of Racławice in 1894 empowered increasing
numbers of enlightened villagers to contemplate the role they could play
within society. Celebrations of the Third of May broadcast the sentiment
of "Dąbrowski's Mazurka": Poland had not yet perished. With the celebrations of the Kościuszko Insurrection, one could see more clearly why.

The commemorations of the first years of the 1890s helped to augment
and strengthen the Polish nation. Poles saw hope in the Constitution of
May 3, 1791, which attested to the existence of a Polish past not set against
reform—indeed, one that made provisions for regular periodic adjust-
ments. Europe's first constitution gave the lie to tales of Polish anarchy and
unfitness for governance such as had become common in the century since
the partitions. As the historian Oswald Balzer wrote, the Constitution
"showed that 1795 [the final partition of Poland] came four years too late":
Poles had already learned that they could reform themselves, and this gave
them hope for the future.[152] This positive message was important to late-
nineteenth-century Poles, particularly in an age of tremendous economic,
social, and political change. In 1791, their nation had proven that it could
adjust to new circumstances and might have succeeded in doing so, had it
not been for the ensuing partitions.

The Constitution's broadening of the nation, through its treatment of
both urban dwellers and peasants, provided an example that many nineteenth-century Poles wished to emulate. No longer the exclusive domain of
the nobility, the nation needed to be augmented by newer social elements.
With the establishment of the People's School Society, the emphasis on
peasant education and nationalization was given institutional form. Even
those opposed to this particular endeavor strove to be more inclusive in
their own proposals, whether of a religious or political nature. Polishness
was becoming an active, not a passive, characteristic: genuine Poles were
not those born on Polish land or those whose mother tongue was Polish but
those who felt themselves Poles, "who, loving the language and the past,
work[ed] for the future of the nation."[153]

The entrance of Roman Dmowski and the Polish League into the public sphere marked the emergence of new, self-reliant national forces unwilling to settle for conciliation. It also signified a break in commemorative
practice: illegal means became an important aspect of celebrating the past.
This worried many Poles, in the Russian Empire and elsewhere, who feared
the consequences of unlawful behavior. Calls to commemorate the treach-

ery of Targowica and the second partition with national mourning raised more painful issues—painful enough to spur Galician elites to channel these energies into other spheres of activity. It also led them to stage an exposition showing the nation's progress during the Kościuszko Insurrection centennial year. Poles of various political stripes highlighted positive themes that showed what the nation could accomplish: the Constitution of the Third of May, the Battle of Racławice, the Kiliński uprising. Relatively little was said about the Połaniec Manifesto, in which Kościuszko tried to improve the lot of his peasant soldiers (the attempt being seen as ineffectual or radical), and the military leader's defeat at Maciejowice; these anniversaries passed without any public sign whatsoever.[154]

The Racławice Panorama presented the type of scene that nearly all Poles could appreciate. This depiction of the famous battle helped to convince peasants that there was more to the Polish past than serfdom. It also encouraged them to take responsibility for their political life, as the establishment of the Peasant Party attests. The success of the Racławice Panorama led to a series of new paintings-in-the-round, none of which, however, equaled the popularity of the first Polish panorama.[155] Its impact was felt even in the New World, where a committee proposed to purchase it. One New Yorker thought the panorama superior to a traditional monument: he claimed that Styka's work would engrave itself in the minds of the second generation of Polish émigrés a hundred times more powerfully than would dozens of traditional stone or bronze monuments.[156] Whether among the Poles in emigration or those back home, the Racławice Panorama helped to keep the idea of Poland alive. The commemorations of the early 1890s made it clear that Poland was not yet lost.

FIVE

Bronzing the Bard:
The Mickiewicz Monuments of 1898

While the Racławice Panorama served as a kind of national memorial, it was not, as we know, the only landmark in the Polish commemorative landscape. Preexisting locales, such as Old Cloth Hall, were being infused with national significance. The Wawel crypts had gained a new set of relics, the remains of Mickiewicz, whose bones—it was hoped—would speak to the people and inspire them in ways that would benefit the nation. But not everyone could gain access to the insides of these crypts or buildings. More concrete reminders of the past were needed that would be easily visible to passersby: traditional monuments of bronze or stone.

This is the tale of the erection of several bronze monuments to honor that newest inhabitant of the Wawel crypts, Adam Mickiewicz. In 1898, the centennial of the bard's birth, one bronze monument made an appearance in Cracow, another in Warsaw—both, incidentally, cities that Mickiewicz had never visited in his lifetime. While each celebration raises the question of how best to commemorate a great national poet, each likewise illuminates the conditions for Polish national activities within the two empires. The unveiling of a monument to Mickiewicz in Warsaw—a legal commemoration—marked a clear change in Russian policy. No Polish national monument had been erected in Warsaw since before the abortive insurrections. Its unveiling, thus, testifies to a new activism on the part of Poles in the Russian Empire. Plans for the Cracow monument had predated the translation of the bard's remains; this was a bit of unfinished business for the Poles of Galicia. This commemoration of Mickiewicz also gave rise to new controversies about the nature of Polish heroes; at the center of this was the Ukrainian literary critic Ivan Franko, whose revised assessment of the Polish bard jolted Polish society. Bronzed or tarnished, boasting a laurel wreath or enveloped by an overcoat, Mickiewicz would appear in many guises and carry varied messages during his anniversary year.

EXEGI MONUMENTUM . . .

There were few bronze statues in the Polish lands, which lacked a tradition of erecting public monuments. The first half of the nineteenth century had witnessed two such efforts in Warsaw: Poles commissioned monuments from the Danish sculptor Bertel Thorvaldsen honoring the astronomer Copernicus and Prince Józef Poniatowski, the Polish military leader of the Napoleonic era. Only the former was unveiled in Warsaw before Poles revolted in November 1830; after the insurrection, it was no longer possible for Poles to erect bronze monuments to heroes of their own choosing.[1]

As regards Mickiewicz, Prussian Poles decided to honor him with a monument of stone not long after his death in 1855. However, erecting it, even in the "only zone where this idea could be turned into action," at that time proved difficult.[2] Seeing the monument to Mickiewicz as a symbol of Polish rebellion, the Prussian authorities balked. It took the well-argued intervention of a Polish deputy in the Berlin Parliament to gain German support for its erection;[3] even then, approval was slow in coming. Finally unveiled in 1859, the Mickiewicz monument was situated not in a public square, as had originally been hoped, but in the cemetery of Saint Martin's Church in Poznań. Thus, while a move toward public commemoration, the Poznanian effort could not transcend the limitations imposed by the Prussian authorities.[4]

Conditions for honoring the Polish bard improved in Galicia after the Poles gained autonomy. Still, a bronze monument was not ready in time to be unveiled at the translation of Mickiewicz's remains, thirty-five years after his death. Not until the celebration of a Mickiewicz centennial in 1898—the anniversary of his birth—did Cracow witness the unveiling of the long-awaited bronze Mickiewicz. Plans for that monument had been in the works for over two decades.

Yet Cracow was not the only city to produce a Mickiewicz monument on the occasion of the centennial. A bronze Mickiewicz stood in Warsaw after less than two years of preparation. How did it happen that Varsovians managed to do, in the space of two years, what took Galician Poles over twenty? The reasons for this discrepancy shed light on the varying situations in which Poles found themselves at this time. Although the nation was generally united in its desire to honor the bard with a monument, the problem of whether diverse views could be accommodated in the actual decision-making process proved sticky indeed.

The permanence of such monuments meant that more was at stake than at more ephemeral celebrations. Among other issues, decisions regarding their design and location could be agonizingly painful. Further compli-

cated by the lack of territorial sovereignty, the means to arrive at such determinations were not well developed in a society that had erected few
monuments prior to the partitions. While Poles shared the goal of honoring the great Romantic poet, they differed in their views of how best to do
so. The joke "where there are two Poles, you will find three opinions" could
easily have dated from this period, so divided was the nation.

By 1898, the value of monuments was nevertheless clear to contemporaries, for whom bronze statues represented more than imposing sculptures.
They indicated the values and desiderata of a collectivity, according to one
commentator, who defined a monument as "a symbol of . . . powerful mental, social, religious, national, state, or . . . general humanitarian aspirations." These desires were associated with a more concrete form—generally,
a human one: "That which a given group . . . regards at a given moment as
the pinnacle of its dreams, as the ideal towards which one should aim in
spiritual or material life, becomes incarnate most often in some brilliant,
demonic, or simply lucky person, endowed with the talents of realizing in
word or deed the thoughts of his compatriots (*współbraci*)."[5] A select individual, thus, could be designated as the incarnation of the collectivity's aspirations. But how best to depict such a person so as to convey the essence
of his deeds and works in useful ways? This is where monuments could be
useful. Synthetic, laconic, and palpable, monuments have an appeal that is
directly linked to the senses, which makes them "the most reliable and at
the same time most accessible way" to reach broader strata of society.[6]

Several inferences can be drawn from these points. One of the problems of the Poles' statelessness was that national life rarely made it into the
public sphere beyond the printed page. Poles possessed few means for expression that would appeal to an audience less literate, less able to read between the lines of censored texts, less committed to a Polish identity. In an
age when students and intellectuals were reaching out to villagers in all the
partitioned lands, the lack of accessible visual aids must have been acutely
felt. The reality of foreign rule allowed for relatively few appeals to the
senses of the Polish national constituency.

The unveiling of a national monument could present such an opportunity. Gracing the urban landscape, the monument would be a concrete reminder of the value attached by the nation to the person or event being so
honored. (Of course, it would be accessible only to those who dwelled
nearby or made special efforts to visit it—something anniversary celebrations could encourage.) Monuments also provided physical evidence of the
dedication of the nation to the cause or person being honored, given that
scarce monetary resources had to be allocated for this purpose. They also
gave hope. If the poor Poles were able to amass the necessary funds to provide a concrete reminder of their fidelity to the national cause, could other,

more significant deeds not be far away? If the hero or genius being honored returned to the living, albeit in bronze, perhaps his spirit would inspire the nation to realize its aspirations.

MONUMENTALIZING THE BARD
IN CRACOW

Of plans to erect a monument to Mickiewicz in Cracow, Mikołaj Zyblikiewicz once boasted, "this is the first work since the partition of Poland that all zones are to raise by common effort."[7] If this is true, it paints a less than flattering picture of Poles' ability to organize on a national scale. Moving in fits and starts, tremendously wasteful of resources, its end result—the monument—of dubious artistic value, this pan-Polish endeavor perhaps best serves as an example of how *not* to erect a monument. It was hardly the fine artistic ornament for a reinvigorated Cracow sought early on by the conservatives.[8] Still, an understanding of the workings of the committees, panels, as well as the public's reaction can shed light on the difficulties such an ambitious project posed.

The beginnings of interest in honoring Mickiewicz in this way date from 1869, the dawn of the constitutional era in Galicia.[9] The idea of erecting a monument (actually, to the Three Bards: Słowacki and Krasiński as well as Mickiewicz) surfaced in Lwów at a banquet for the Poznanian philosopher and activist Karol Libelt. As with other such initiatives, the thought of celebrating the great Romantic poets in this way came not from the political right but from the left, from the Democratic Party (Stronnictwo Demokratyczne). Within a year, a competition was held, a model selected, and donations solicited. Yet early enthusiasm soon waned, as did donations. As often happened, international developments—this time, the Franco-Prussian War and the Paris Commune—diverted Polish attention.[10]

The next important steps were taken during the Kraszewski jubilee in 1879—an example of how one commemoration often facilitated another. Taking advantage of the influx of guests to the city, university youth organized fund-raisers to raise money for a Mickiewicz monument.[11] These events complemented their efforts, since 1873, to resurrect the initiative. Kraszewski encouraged the students in this direction and donated three thousand francs to the cause.[12] The proceeds from both the exhibition of Kraszewski's gifts in Old Cloth Hall and sales of a commemorative volume were likewise earmarked for the Mickiewicz monument.[13] These contributions were designed to raise as much money as possible, for Kraszewski was worried that something less than worthy of the poet might be erected.[14] That Kraszewski was able to gain Zyblikiewicz's support speeded up the process: the mayor gained the necessary permissions to collect donations, which soon came in droves from the Russian Empire (the Warsaw press serving as intermediaries), with particularly large contributions from the actress Helena Modrzejewska (Modjeska) and the writer Deotyma. By 1883, nearly one hundred thousand guldens had been collected.[15]

HURDLES: DESIGN AND LOCATION

Given the level of interest and commitment, how did it happen that this monument-building endeavor did not live up to expectations? There was no reason, one would have thought, why a monument could not be ready by the end of the decade. Yet, the process was fraught with controversy. Three highly contested competitions—in 1882, 1885, and 1888—produced no model considered worthy of being constructed as designed. Polish society also found it difficult to agree on a site for the monument. The outcome: bronze figures that made such a bad impression that they were rejected by the committee and recast by the sculptor, still to no one's satisfaction.

In comparing this effort with other commemorative endeavors, one contrast becomes apparent. As in the case of the desire to bring the poet's remains to Cracow, this project was not bound to any particular timetable nor (originally) linked with any major anniversary of the poet. Simply, favorable changes in Galicia in the late 1860s had emboldened Poles to contemplate such undertakings. This lack of focus allowed for a lengthy and uneven germination period. It also enabled those in no hurry to see a monument to Mickiewicz erected to dawdle without being pushed by organized public opinion, which might have coalesced had some perception of a deadline existed. Indeed, the monument might never have been erected, had not the approaching centennial of Mickiewicz's birth renewed interest in its fate.

The matter of the design of the Mickiewicz monument proved problematic from the outset. Once it was apparent that the collected funds would be sufficient to cover the necessary costs, decisions had to be made as to the shape the monument would take. A competition was announced in 1881. Its flawed organization not only set a negative tone but introduced elements into the preparations that boded ill for the monument's design. Not wishing to commit at this point, the committee proposed that it be a preliminary competition. A number of Polish sculptors protested over this and other conditions stipulated by the organizers.[16] Some of their demands, however, such as the desire that both sculptor and materials be Polish, were misdirected patriotism—at least according to Kraszewski, who wrote the poet's son that "the monument should be of bronze and, above all, artistically beautiful."[17] This desire for a beautiful monument, one that befit a Pole of Mickiewicz's stature, was complicated by the lack of consensus on what constituted beauty. Artists balked at the stylistic terms imposed by the committee, which decreed that the bronze monument was to be in Renaissance style, a condition that clearly thwarted the committee's intention of gathering as many varied ideas as possible.

The competition, held in the spring of 1882, proved disappointing. From April 12 through 18, twenty-seven submissions were exhibited in the room of the National Museum in Old Cloth Hall, where the general (paying) public could examine them. Many Poles were bewildered to learn of the jury's decision to reward Tomasz Dygas's rather conventional project of a seated Mickiewicz with allegorical figures.[18] Although the projects had not been identified by author, that precaution did not prevent the public from suspecting that committee members were familiar with certain works and treated them accordingly. An outcry led to the works being exhibited in Warsaw, where assessments were no more favorable. Later statements seem to indicate that at least some committee members were treating the competition in a rather cavalier fashion, opining that, at one thousand francs (the value of the award), it was hardly worth fussing over the decision.[19] A divide clearly separated the notables on the committee, for whom one thousand francs was an insignificant sum, from the Polish sculptors and artists (not to mention much of the public), who struggled to make ends meet. Instead of providing the nation with varied options for a monument that it could proudly erect to its famous son, the competition led to arguments, accusations, and acrimony.

The preliminary competition took place before the committee had solved yet another problem connected with the monument: where to put it.[20] The most logical place, for many, seemed to be the Rynek—the market square—in the center of Cracow. Even Zyblikiewicz admitted, "when the entire nation raises a monument to its greatest bard from public donations, then our city must offer for that monument its choicest location—thus, the Rynek."[21] The democrats campaigned vigorously for the site. "The heart of Poland is Cracow, the heart of Cracow [is] the Rynek. That is where Adam's monument is to stand."[22] Supporting this view were numerous Warsaw residents, who submitted a formal request that Mickiewicz be honored with a freestanding monument in the market square, that its style not be determined by that of nearby buildings because it was to outlast those structures, and that it be the work of a Pole. In May 1882, a majority of committee members voted for the Cracow Rynek.[23]

The Rynek was not the only possible location, however. Many different spots within the confines of the medieval city were suggested: Plac Franciszkański, Plac Dominikański, Plac Szczepański, and others.[24] The most zealous campaign, however, was waged for a square that did not yet exist. That same spring, it was decided that a new university building would be constructed on a plot at the edge of the Planty (then known as Plantacye), the park established where the medieval fortifications had once stood. One of the town councilors, the photographer Walery Rzewuski, suggested that a Mickiewicz Square adjoin that neo-Gothic building (today's Collegium Novum). Thinking a university location most appropriate for the poet, since he was so beloved by Polish youth—this despite the fact that the university students were among the most fervent supporters of the Rynek location—he set out to gain the support of influential men, Poles and Austrians alike, for this project.[25] In addition to ideological and stylistic arguments, Rzewuski likewise voiced aesthetic and, perhaps, even patriotic reasons for not wanting the Rynek site:

> A poet . . . requires . . . open space, air, greenery and flowers. The Rynek will not give him this. It would give at best a whole rabble in yarmulkes and without them, which, having sat down at the foot of the monument (like today in front of houses), would carry out transactions in the open; it would give a view of the squalor of market stalls and . . . shops, which in another dozen years will doubtless be in the hands of those who already have soiled Grodzka Street today.[26]

The image of an idyllic vernal site for Mickiewicz was contrasted with a not very pretty picture of the center of the city, which the photographer depicted as overrun with moneygrubbing Jews for whom the poet had no significance. Yet, one wonders about the validity of Rzewuski's argument. First, this vision of the downtown area does not square well with the picture usually painted of a refurbished Cracow, as we recall from the discussion of the renovation of Old Cloth Hall. Second, the suggestion that Jews did not appreciate the Polish bard contradicts the positive attitude toward Mickiewicz of various Jewish organizations in Cracow during the translation and of the Jewish "men of the eighties" who—like Mickiewicz—found parallels between the fate of the Jewish and Polish nations.[27] Last but not least, it happens that Mickiewicz likely had Jewish blood in him—a matter never discussed (one assumes, not generally known or not acknowledged) during this period.[28]

Rzewuski's position led to a furious intellectual battle. Members of the Cracow-based Circle of Artists and Writers (Koło artystyczno-literackie) in particular summoned an arsenal of counterarguments. Placing the monument squarely in the national interest, they de-emphasized any local or particularist connections of the bard. Save the university square for a monument to Długosz or Copernicus, wrote Kazimierz Bartoszewicz, Rzewuski's most vocal opponent. The Mickiewicz monument had a different role to play: not simply a monument to a "master of the pen," it was to honor "the most outstanding representative of the national idea after 1831."[29] As the main poet who took the place of great leaders and statesmen and carried the national banner, Mickiewicz deserved the greater glory, "the greater significance, not in the history of literature alone but in the history of the nation." It was the duty of the entire nation to erect a monument to him; the effort would be a "manifestation of national unity" not unlike that during the Kraszewski jubilee.[30] Activists underscoring the all-national significance of the Mickiewicz monument desired not a pretty spot for a poet but a central location for the nation's spiritual leader. And, indeed, a decision was made in favor of the Rynek in September 1883.

The opponents to the Rynek site did not give up the fight, however. They retrenched and repositioned themselves for a new attack in February 1890. This coup was launched by the men who now held the reins of the preparations in their hands. To follow these developments, first we must return briefly to the activities of the committee. In 1885 the second of the competitions was held. The jury infuriated the nation once again by choosing yet another Dygas project. While pleasing to the eye (if lacking anything that would make it distinctly Polish), the design was neither imposing nor uplifting; it was definitely not the expected apotheosis of the bard. The publication of the protocol of the proceedings further aggravated public opinion, for it became clear that "neither the conditions of the competition, nor aesthetic considerations, nor the idea of the bard was taken seriously into account."[31] Unbelievably, only two models were actually discussed at all (neither systematically), and no justification was given for rejecting models. The jury seemed almost reluctant to judge the models, and the committee's organization again proved inept, all of which infuriated the public.[32]

This second debacle led to the intervention of the former mayor of Cracow turned provincial marshal, Mikołaj Zyblikiewicz. Years before, in private correspondence, he blamed the endless debate over the monument on the Poles' very nature:

> Polonia, in every matter touching the general public [ogół], needs debates, criticism, polemics, projects, various concepts, etc. Whether all this is wise or not, effective or not, discussion is necessary, for our society would sulk and be angry if a monument, even the most splendid, was erected without prior noise and fuss. Only a small handful of serious and genuinely patriotic people would be satisfied, but the general public would shout at the top of its voice that something was done without its advice and opinion.[33]

Given this state of affairs, Zyblikiewicz intended to let the Poles talk themselves out before taking control over the proceedings. Now, he played his trump card. If no geniuses of Polish sculpture had emerged, why not turn to the genius of the paintbrush, Jan Matejko? The latter had submitted a late entry to the last competition, presented to the jury on the day of its decision-making session—too late to be taken into consideration. Matejko's sketch had favorably impressed the viewers. It called for the symbolic representation of Polish virtues and vices, a series of figures depicting characters from the bard's works, as well as a statue of Mickiewicz atop a high column. Unfortunately, Matejko's proposal proved not to be the panacea the committee so desperately needed—something the Poles learned the hard way, after two sculptors vainly attempted to render Matejko's idea in three-dimensional form. That Poland's preeminent artist could not provide a workable project was disappointing, for Matejko was one of few figures who everyone thought should have some say in the matter of the monument.[34]

After this failure and much more foot-dragging, the committee abdicated its responsibility for the monument, choosing in the fall of 1886 to invest Zyblikiewicz with "dictatorial" powers that might enable him to carry through the matter.[35] His death later that year left the committee rudderless. Still intent on passing responsibility for the monument to someone else, it opted for a directorate of sorts, apparently patterned after the commission that was to keep tabs on the realization of Matejko's idea: the More Select (*Ściślejszy*) Executive Committee for the Construction of the Adam Mickiewicz Monument.[36] If democracy within the full committee had proved ineffective, the danger of absolute rule proved absolute in the case of the Select Committee. Not bound by any of the decisions made by the full committee, it proceeded to turn the entire matter of the Mickiewicz monument on its head. First, it ignored the results of the 1888 "new and final" competition, which for once found Polish society supporting the decision of the jury to award Cyprian Godebski first place, Teodor Rygier second. Instead of contracting for one of these two top projects, the Select Committee engaged Rygier to realize not his winning but his weaker entry, a project carrying only two votes out of twenty. Society once again was shocked by the choice of a colorless monument that, were the main figure to be replaced, might equally well serve, in the words of one critic, as a tribute to Bismarck.[37]

To make matters worse, controversy over the monument's location resurfaced. The Select Committee took advantage of a decision of the Cracow city council dating from December 1883, in which it informed the (full) committee that the city would give whatever piece of land was desired for the monument. Now, with the dimensions of the actual monument in mind, committee members voted to reject the chosen site for the monument—the Rynek—and locate the Mickiewicz monument on the outskirts of the medieval town: on the edge of the Planty, near Sławkowska Street.[38] This change of location was unexpected, as the choice of the Rynek had seemed definitively settled. Despite the torrents of criticism leveled at the committee, its most active member, Konstanty Przezdziecki of Warsaw, exuded an unbowed confidence in the powers invested in the committee. The wealthy art lover, who funded the mosaic for the Mickiewicz crypt later that same year, was personally blamed for both the choice of Rygier's second design as well as the change in location.[39] One satirical paper opined that Przezdziecki should be turned into a living monument—if they could decide where to stick him![40]

These new developments shed light not only on perceptions of the bard and his place in Cracow but also on the politics of such a monument. Reasons given for the change in location included the need to save the Rynek to commemorate "political facts" connected with that site.[41] That Mickiewicz would be relegated to a spot outside the Rynek suggests a hierarchy of both monuments and heroes. In Cracow, figures of local importance were given preference over those of "foreigners"—that is, non-Galicians. A sense of the Mickiewicz monument as being for Poles from outside Galicia pervaded the decision: the last of the justifications for the new location provided by the Select Committee stated that, located on the northern side of Cracow, the monument would be nearer to the train station, the arrival point of those "from other provinces of Poland."[42] Mickiewicz and his ideals, thus, were to be kept from penetrating far into the "heart of Poland."

The Select Committee nonetheless found its designs thwarted by what must have seemed an unlikely quarter: the local Cracow government. Objections to the new location came at the ground level from the civil servants who would be asked to implement the necessary changes in the urban environment, for, among other things, the Select Committee's plans called for the creation of a new square, depriving the city of more of its greenery. Ultimately, the decision was overruled at a session of the urban economic section and commission for the Planty.[43] Local democratic opinion was elated, seeing the refusal of the city to change the location of the monument as "just recompense, given the opinion of the entire country, in defiance of which the committee thus far willfully acted."[44]

While the general public seemed to win this half of the battle in 1891, the other half—over the shape of the monument—had been lost irredeemably. Another seven years would pass before a flawed Mickiewicz monument would be unveiled in the Cracow market square. This convoluted process involved the relocation (some would say escape) of the sculptor to Rome; a lack of oversight on the part of the committee, which proved inept and sluggish; and the casting of the bronze figures, several of which—including that of Mickiewicz himself—were rejected by both public and committee and had to be redone.[45] In fact, the monument might never have been unveiled had it not been for members of the Cracow city

council, who in 1897 pressed for the completion of the monument in time for the one hundredth anniversary of Mickiewicz's birth the following year.

MICKIEWICZ UNVEILED

In the end, thus, it took the pressure of the approaching anniversary to mobilize those in charge of readying the monument for its public debut. Years before, a satirical journal had joked that Mickiewicz should be located on ulica Długa—Long Street—because the nation had waited so long for him.[46] By 1898, the centennial of Mickiewicz's birth, interest in the fate of the Cracow monument had all but ceased. After years of controversy over its design and ultimate public resignation to its mediocrity, any unveiling would be anticlimactic. It was common knowledge that the Mickiewicz monument would be a blight on Cracow's main square, and the nation would have to put a good face on a bad deal. A conversation at the unveiling between Stanisław Badeni, the Galician provincial marshal, and Władysław Mickiewicz tells the story. Asked how he liked the monument, Mickiewicz's son replied, "It's very bad," to which Badeni responded, "It could have been worse."[47] (The recast figures clearly did not improve the monument much.) Mickiewicz was of the opinion that the whole thing should be melted down.

But was it an utter loss? Its lack of distinction notwithstanding, the Mickiewicz monument erected in Cracow had both symbolic and real value for the Polish nation. In a way, what it stood for was more important than how it looked—or even that it stood at all. Stanisław Witkiewicz was right: the one hundred thousand guldens gathered from the poor nation were the real monument, showing how much Mickiewicz was worth to the Poles.[48] Yet the monument was also put to use by the nation. If nothing else, it placed a distinctly Polish imprint upon the Cracow Rynek. Here was a spot that belonged to the Poles, a place where they could make a statement. The nation had acquired an open-air forum of sorts, one that would prove useful in the ensuing years.

Thus, despite problems with the monument, Poles representing various social groups were eager to celebrate the one hundredth anniversary of Mickiewicz's birth and demanded a say in the process.[49] Organized by the Cracow city council, not the provincial authorities, the celebration seemed to have more of a local character, despite the participation of Galician authorities such as Stanisław Badeni, whose presence and comments have already been noted. Of course, Badeni and his predecessors, as members of the Select Committee (which always included the person who served as provincial marshal), had failed to deliver up the monument the nation had desired; the authorities may have wished to let others take the blame should the festivities also be disappointing. Even so, the authorities could no longer retain control of the two-day celebration as they had in years past. With the increased politicization of society, many groups lobbied for a voice at the monument's unveiling.

Fifty years after peasant emancipation, Mickiewicz proved to have popular appeal. The peasant politician Jakub Bojko was permitted to speak at the unveiling of the monument on June 26, and populist strains found their echo in the speech of the student representative Maciej Szukiewicz as well as in ludic features such as wreaths on the Vistula River with acetylene lights. Artists involved in the commemoration included members of "Young Poland" like Lucjan Rydel and Stanisław Wyspiański, whose "poetic fantasy" also noted the nation's concern with the fate of Poles of the borderlands, east and west—a concern reflected in the establishment at this time of an Adam Mickiewicz Fund for the Construction of Polish Schools for the *kresy* to counter the German Schulverein, the work of the People's School Society.[50] That Silesians were present at the unveiling of the Mickiewicz monument was considered a step in the right direction, showing that they as well as villagers back in Galicia took interest in broader Polish affairs.[51] Mickiewicz had become a tool for the nationalization of the folk.

While folk and student representatives were given a chance to speak, the same opportunity was not offered to the increasingly visible Polish socialists. Their recent political gains were seen in the newly diverse composition of the Austrian parliament: with the addition in 1897 of a fifth electoral curia, permitting universal male suffrage, both peasants and socialists had entered into the political arena formerly monopolized by Polish elites. Their presence nonetheless irked both conservatives and democrats: unlike Bojko and the populists, the socialists had refused to enter the Polish caucus, forming instead an oppositional bloc in the parliament under the leadership of Ignacy Daszyński, the young and dynamic socialist tribune. Daszyński's haranguing of the "Polish" government in Vienna—led by the former viceroy Kazimierz Badeni, a figure familiar to us from earlier commemorations—helped to undermine its authority and lead to its downfall. Poles who had been proud to see one of their own as Austrian prime minister were upset that a Polish socialist would have attacked him.[52] Socialists clearly had incurred the enmity of many Cracovians, for letters of protest at their inclusion in the planning stages of the event flooded the city council.[53] In the end, socialists were kept from playing a role in the official celebration.

They nonetheless were among the first to avail themselves of the monument's existence to attest to their own. Socialists from all three partitioned lands assembled in Cracow to honor the bard, holding their own private celebration on June 28, two days after the unveiling. Coincidentally, that same day a state of emergency was declared in thirty-two western districts of Galicia, ostensibly because of a "Jewish problem."[54] Even then, despite the fact that this anti-Semitic outburst was attributable in part to Stojałowski's agitation, socialists and Jews found themselves linked in the public mind.[55] Having learned of the authorities' intent to declare a state of emergency, Daszyński implored Viceroy Leon Piniński to postpone the declaration so as not to show visiting socialists this less pleasant face of the Galician regime—to no avail. Back in Cracow, where a police cordon blocked the entrance of the socialists to the center of town, the leader of the Polish Social-Democratic Party took matters into his own hands. His threat that blood would be shed if the socialists were unable to place wreaths at the foot of the Mickiewicz monument led to a compromise with the local authorities: traveling not by foot but by carriage, the socialists were able to deposit, under the watchful eyes of the Cracow police, fifty-four wreaths to the "poet revolutionary."[56] Before long other protesters deposited wreaths at Mickiewicz's feet bearing more disquieting, anti-Austrian messages.[57] These testimonies to the bard's revolutionary legacy—for was that not why this site was chosen?—helped to turn the Mickiewicz monument into a place for Polish protests.

Despite these tensions, Galician conservatives still retained a high profile at the unveiling and managed some crowd-pleasing effects. Provincial Marshal Stanisław Badeni and Stanisław Tarnowski dressed for the occasion in old Polish style, albeit adorned with Austrian medals;[58] and bravos reportedly greeted Tarnowski's remark that there should be more monuments.[59] But the scholar who had once said that Mickiewicz's poetry had done more harm than good also seemed to criticize the nation for not having erected monuments to its warriors first.[60]

Perhaps the crowds did not hear those later remarks—or chose to ignore them, dining selectively upon the smorgasbord of ideas that such festivities presented. What seems to be truer of the proceedings is that each group took from them what it sought. The university president's Mickiewicz had been sent from God to strengthen hearts (*na serc pokrzepienie*) and encourage his compatriots on to "noble work."[61] Father Józef Pelczar, who gave the sermon at the celebration, underscored Mickiewicz's faith while warning youth that even great minds can lose their way if they stray from the Church.[62] The socialists called the "real" Mickiewicz "a revolutionary, a defender of the people's interests, [and] a socialist."[63] Various Mickiewiczes, thus, were celebrated within the space of one commemoration.

BRONZED—OR TARNISHED?

The Mickiewicz festivities in Cracow were full of public statements related more to current political trends than to the commemoration of the bard. As usual, the actions of the Polish ruling elites underscored aspects of their triloyalism. Two aspects gained publicity—one, notoriety—during the celebration. The first concerned Polish-Czech relations, which were extremely cordial at this time. That the previous Austrian prime minister, the Pole Kazimierz Badeni, had attempted to place the Czech language on a par with German in the Czech lands was appreciated by these Slavic brethren (if not by the Germans, who hounded him out of office). This mutual sympathy was played up in Cracow: already in December 1897 a "Slavic day" was held during which equal rights for all nationalities were demanded.[64] At the Mickiewicz celebration, numerous Czech politicians as well as the poet Jaroslav Vrchlický made their appearance, participating in the parade and depositing a silver linden branch in the Wawel crypt in homage of the bard; they were later feted and encouraged at a banquet organized by the Circle of Artists and Writers.[65] It was as though the Poles, imitating Mickiewicz, were coming to the defense of weaker Slavic nations. At the same banquet, however, the happy Slavic boat was rocked by Professor Roman Brandt of Moscow, a guest brought by the ever-controversial Włodzimierz Spasowicz. The Russian (a professor of Slavic linguistics) not only criticized both Mickiewicz and Galician parliamentarism, but also offered a poem touting the brotherhood of Poles and Russians. While a group of youth present at the banquet walked out in protest, a member of the old guard commented that it would be nice to see Brandt's "cordial words" turned into "equally cordial actions."[66] Slavic solidarity proved a tricky business, indeed.

Proof of this is the fact that the other Slavic "tribe" in Galicia, the Ukrainians, had not participated in the Mickiewicz commemoration. The relationship between Poles and Ukrainians had recently reached a nadir. This stage was both reflected in and aggravated by an article penned by Ivan Franko. A socialist, Franko had been one of the leaders of the Ukrainian Radical movement in the 1870s. The Ukrainian was also a talented literary writer and publicist, writing in Ukrainian, Polish, and German. He moved about with ease in the Polish-language world of Galicia, writing for Lwów papers—especially the democratic *Kurier Lwowski,* of which he was an editor—and playing a role in the formation of the Polish Peasant Party. Nonetheless, his politics and heritage inclined Kazimierz Badeni to prevent this well-educated, competent scholar from obtaining a position at the University of Lwów.[67]

In his writings, Franko had often given proof of his familiarity with Polish literature, which he read and reviewed regularly, and he had praise for many Polish writers. No one would have expected, then, that in 1897, the year before a major Mickiewicz anniversary, he would express views of the bard that would shock and anger Poles. Published in the Viennese socialist paper *Die Zeit,* Franko's article, "Ein Dichter des Verrathes," offended from its first words. The Ukrainian called Mickiewicz a "poet of treason," citing the bard's own works—in particular, the epic poem *Konrad Wallenrod*—as evidence. This was the tale, set in medieval times, of a young Lithuanian who joined the ranks of the nation's great enemy, the Teutonic Knights, in order to undermine them from within. Franko argued that Mickiewicz idealized treachery. (The effect of this particular work had indeed been "treacherous," if you will: published in 1828, *Konrad Wallenrod* emboldened Poles to rise up against Russian rule two years later.) The Ukrainian argued that the bard's continued popularity among the Poles resulted in the poisoning of young minds: "The times must have been melancholy indeed if a poet of genius could stray on such erroneous paths, and it is a sad state of affairs if a nation considers such a poet . . . to be its greatest national hero and prophet, and feeds its young generations with the poisonous fruits of his spirit."[68] Instead of being a good example for the peoples of Europe and his own nation, Mickiewicz was a subversive and a questionable influence.

Why did Franko suddenly choose to attack the most highly regarded Polish poet? The timing of the incident provides one answer. Besides being the year prior to the great Mickiewicz anniversary, 1897 saw the introduction of the new fifth curia and the secret ballot into imperial politics, which should have resulted in vastly improved chances for the masses to elect their own representatives. As it turned out, the elections that year to the Galician Sejm and the Council of State were unusually corrupt, even by Galician standards. In the course of the elections, nine people died, thirty-nine were wounded, and eight hundred arrested.[69] Franko termed the elections "manifestations of moral depravity" resulting from an ethical double standard.[70] Justifying his article, he wrote of his fascination with the psychological underpinnings that allowed the Poles, so sensitive to the tiniest slight against their own nation, to treat other nations so ruthlessly. That Franko targeted Mickiewicz in this context was a more complex matter. It has been suggested that the charge of treason stemmed from Franko's own personal dilemma: the writer was caught uncomfortably between Polish and Ukrainian culture and was himself suspected, or even accused, by both sides of being a "Wallenrod."[71]

Poles responded to the article by closing their ranks to Franko: he was expelled from the Historical Association (Towarzystwo Historyczne) in Lwów and lost his job at *Kurier Lwowski*.[72] They also closed their ranks to Ukrainians in general, as witnessed by the renaming of the Unification Association of Progressive Youth the Unification Association of *Polish* Progressive Youth.[73] None of this boded well for Polish-Ruthenian cooperation, nor did it improve the Poles' reputation in Vienna during Badeni's embattled tenure as head of the government. The figure of Mickiewicz, revered by so many Poles, made him the most effective of targets by those who found reason to criticize the "patriots" of Galicia. As in the case of the statue, his symbolic value far transcended the reality of either man or monument.

MONUMENTALIZING THE BARD
IN WARSAW

The symbolic value of yet another monument would prove to be greater than the sum of its parts. In the words of Stanisław Witkiewicz:

> The history of the Mickiewicz monument in Warsaw is one of the most wonderful, sublime and invigorating signs of collective existence, . . . one of the great victories in the unceasing . . . battle for the existence of the Polish

nation. Under the oppression of the strictest police surveillance . . . , under the oppression of censorship . . . , this miraculous plebiscite took place with lightning speed, in the face of which the mighty state stood amazed, helpless, and lacking courage to prevent and suppress.[74]

The "miraculous plebiscite" that led to the unveiling of the Warsaw monument, the only legal national celebration in Russian Poland in this period, contrasts sharply with the construction of the Mickiewicz monument in Cracow. While Galicia sometimes seemed to suffer from a proliferation of celebrations, a dearth of national events characterized life in the Russian Empire. Poles under tsarist rule did not have the liberty of expressing themselves freely in the public sphere. Tsarist officials dictated the circumstances under which Polishness struggled: the language of public life, of education, was Russian. Monuments erected in tsarist-controlled Warsaw glorified Polish oppressors, not freedom fighters; the city's public space belonged to the gendarmes, not to the common man. Here, with the erection of a monument to Mickiewicz, was a chance to establish a purely Polish space, to turn a square in the center of the city into a Polish haven.

While there was ample room for controversy, debate, even delay in Galicia, these could hardly be countenanced in Warsaw. Many Poles in the Russian Empire had followed the course of the Cracow preparations, and the Warsaw committee was able to draw lessons from that fiasco. The centennial celebration of Mickiewicz in Warsaw likewise illuminates the dilemma of tri-loyalism. It came to mark the end of an era of resignation and signaled the rise of new forces within the nation.

The Mickiewicz anniversary came at an auspicious time, the so-called New Course. The accession of Nicholas II to the throne in 1894 had mobilized loyal conservatives, who seemed willing to settle for a degree of cultural autonomy within the Russian Empire. They prepared a gift of a million rubles for the tsar, presented to him during his visit to Warsaw in September 1897. One of the concessions awarded the Poles for this demonstration of loyalty was permission to erect a monument to Mickiewicz. Dmowski maintained that permission for the celebration was granted as a concession to the Poles, among whom illegal activities had been increasing (as seen in 1891 and 1894), given that they had no legal outlet for their patriotism. The Moscow government had decided to broaden the "public arena," with the hope that such scope for legal actions would give the upper hand to Polish loyalist and conservative circles.[75]

Even here, though, the history of interest in honoring the bard does not lack a connection to Poles elsewhere. While the monument to Mickiewicz in Galicia seemed to be inspired by a Prussian connection, impetus for the Warsaw monument came from a former student at Jagiellonian University. The chairman of the committee organizing the first Mickiewicz evening in

Cracow in 1873, Henryk Hugo Wróblewski, raised the idea of celebrating the centennial of Mickiewicz's birth in this way in his newspaper, *Gazeta Radomska* (Radom gazette).[76] The Warsaw press soon seized upon the idea, and the nation began to contemplate how best to honor the bard.

The figure most responsible for the success of these plans, however, was the Polish novelist Henryk Sienkiewicz.[77] The writer had asked that plans for his upcoming jubilee be postponed in order that the nation might concentrate "all its energies and means on the monument."[78] He also was the most active of the committee members. Although the loyalist Prince Michał Radziwiłł chaired the committee, it was Sienkiewicz—his deputy—who orchestrated the undertaking. Sienkiewicz knew of the perils of erecting monuments, having served as a member of the Select Committee for the Cracow monument in 1884–85. This awareness doubtless colored his approach to the Warsaw monument, which we know he envisaged already in 1883.

The Warsaw organizers apparently learned from the mistakes of the Cracow committee. Unlike the Cracovians, they also worked within strict time limits. The monument was to be completed by December 24, 1898, the one hundredth anniversary of Mickiewicz's birth. That left them with less than two years—not even a year and a half once approval for the final project was obtained in October 1897.[79]

Little could be done until preliminary permission for the monument was received from Governor General Imeretinskii in April 1897. In addition to allowing the Poles to collect donations, he approved the composition of the committee, selecting twelve Poles from a list of potential committee members. Once constituted, the committee set to work immediately: it established a practical system of administration for day-to-day matters and summoned a technical commission to supervise the execution of the project. It also settled on a site: a square on the much-trafficked Krakowskie Przedmieście, near the Carmelite church and not far from the historic Old Town and Castle Square. In contrast to the Cracow organizers, the Warsaw committee avoided all "discussion and plebiscites" and made its decisions by itself.[80]

The same held true for the design of the monument. Unlike the pattern followed in Cracow, no competitions were held for the Warsaw monument. Still, the Warsaw committee seems to have benefited from the Cracow competitions: it selected as its sculptor Cyprian Godebski, who won first prize in 1888. The committee nonetheless requested a simpler monument than Godebski's winning project, one without any allegorical figures. Unlike its lackadaisical Cracow counterpart, the Warsaw committee kept track of the artist's work and made timely recommendations. This more dictatorial style got the job done in Warsaw to the committee's liking, even if the resulting work still attracted criticism.[81]

The efficiency of the committee notwithstanding, all these efforts would have come to naught had the project not engaged the rest of the nation. But amassing the necessary funds proved easy. The response in donations for the Warsaw monument, "a kind of manifestation of the national spirit," was remarkable.[82] In the course of two months, the entire sum necessary—over two hundred thousand rubles—was collected, with peasants and workers as well as the middle and upper classes making donations.[83]

This apparent Polish unity surprised the tsarist authorities, which doubtless would have preferred that the monument interest only a narrow stratum of society. That so many villagers and workers showed signs of identifying with the Polish nation left the authorities seeking ways to undermine the concessions they had granted the Poles. To counter the "miraculous plebiscite," tsarist officialdom began to impose limitations on how the Poles could celebrate the bard: they increased censorship, refused permission to publish inexpensive commemorative publications or editions of Mickiewicz's works, and ordered pictures of the bard removed from public view.[84]

A counterweight to Mickiewicz was provided in the form of another monument. Unveiled in Wilno in November 1898, it honored a man known in Polish circles as the Hangman: Mikhail Nikolaevich Muraviev. Muraviev was the Russian responsible for punishing the Poles after the January Insurrection—or, in the words of his supporters, for "freeing the north-west land [of the Russian Empire] from Polish-Catholic bondage."[85] Given the poet's connection to Wilno, a place where he had lived and studied (in contrast to Warsaw and Cracow, neither of which he had ever visited), the choice of location for the Muraviev monument was particularly painful. Ironically, the city had hoped to gain permission for a Mickiewicz monument in 1858, after a visit from Tsar Alexander II, who at the time seemed well disposed to the Poles; yet the mood of the nation, and of the tsar, soon changed, effectively discouraging such plans. Forty years later, news of the impending monument to Muraviev rallied Poles to construct, in secret, a symbolic tombstone for Mickiewicz in Saint John's Church in Wilno. The marble and sandstone monument, mounted high up in the church, could hardly counterbalance this desecration of their city with a tribute to the persecutor of the Poles. Still, they worked valiantly to erect their monument before the Muraviev statue was unveiled.[86]

Although public, the Warsaw unveiling could not rival the showy and pomp-filled ceremonies of Cracow. Restrictions placed upon the festivities themselves made it a celebration hardly worthy of the name. The committee had planned a simple unveiling, fearing that a more ambitious program might jeopardize the event. The ceremony would consist of speeches by Radziwiłł and Sienkiewicz, the blessing of the square by a Catholic clergyman, and the playing of several well-known national musical compositions.[87] No deputies, wreaths, or gatherings: the only official invitations would be sent to Mickiewicz's children abroad. Predistributed tickets would authorize the select thousands (about twelve thousand) able to witness the unveiling and designate the route they should take to the square. The police, augmented by the military, would assure that order was maintained by cordoning off the area.[88]

Yet even this modest proposal proved too much. The Russians insisted that the planned speeches be preceded by the playing of the hymn "Bozhe tsaria khrani"—"God Save the Tsar." Even the most conciliatory of committees could not stomach this profanation of a Polish ceremony, so the speeches were canceled. In the end, the fifteen-minute celebration of the centennial of Mickiewicz's birth passed without the language of the bard being heard. No Polish prayer, poem, or speech resounded in the square. The only sounds to be heard that cold, cloudy morning were the Latin blessing intoned by the priest, both preceded and followed by two short musical compositions of Moniuszko.[89] After the ceremony, the crowds were allowed to process in front of the monument, and some tossed flowers in its direction. Enclosed by an ornate iron fence, the newly created national space was filled with the same silence that had characterized the unveiling of the Poznań monument to Mickiewicz four decades earlier.

The only words connected with the event came in the form of telegrams sent to the committee by various well-wishers, Poles and non-Poles. Many came from the Czech lands, with the city council of Prague even sending a silver laurel branch. A number of telegrams were later published in a commemorative volume prepared by Zygmunt Wasilewski.[90] Naturally, the Poles in charge of the unveiling tried to cast the festivities in a positive light. Sienkiewicz, whose own planned speech had been censored by the authorities, later remarked pointedly, "people here are silent all the more profoundly, the more profoundly they feel collectively" and that it had been a great day for "our social life."[91]

The Mickiewicz celebration in Warsaw is significant for another reason. It marked the first clash between the leaders of the two main camps of Polish politics of the period (and ensuing decades): Roman Dmowski and Józef Piłsudski. While neither of the young activists had any illusions as to why permission had been granted for the monument, they opted for different strategies. Dmowski and his National League decided to participate in the unveiling; Piłsudski's socialists boycotted the event. Both ploys, interestingly enough, were designed to raise the profile of the respective political group.

The unveiling of the Mickiewicz monument in Warsaw witnessed a new emphasis on peasant involvement in the lands under Russian control. Despite Dmowski's initial distrust of the Russians' concessions, his Na-

Uroczystość odsłonięcia pomnika

Fig. 5.2 "The Celebration of the Unveiling of the [Mickiewicz] monument [in Warsaw]." *From Zygmunt Wasilewski,* Pomnik Mickiewicza w Warszawie, 1897–1898 *(Warsaw: nakładem Komitetu Budowy Pomnika, 1899). Note the bilingual business signs in this large Russian metropolis.*

tional League joined in the celebration, organized lectures and performances for youth and workers, as well as facilitated contacts between peasants from various parts of the old Polish Commonwealth. Peasants from a range of the former Polish territories—from Silesia, the Lithuanian and Belarusian regions, even from the Tatra Mountains on Galicia's southern border—assembled the day before the unveiling.[92] The coming together of these peasants from all corners of Poland for the purpose of recognizing the nation's preeminent poet was significant, according to Dmowski. In a letter to Zygmunt Miłkowski, in which he acknowledged the shortcomings of many of the league's initiatives, he nonetheless strongly defended its latest achievement:

> if you had been in Warsaw during the unveiling of the Mickiewicz monument and had seen those 400 peasant delegates from all parts of the Kingdom [of Poland] and the seized land [*kraju zabranego*], if you had heard them speaking at the secret Vigil gatherings (in which one counted 160 people), then you would admit that the result attained in this regard may redeem many mistakes.[93]

The significance of the gatherings, termed by one Warsaw observer the "first peasant congress organized on a larger scale," was not lost on the socialists: the National Democrats were winning over some of the more nationally conscious peasants.[94]

This new age of national outreach and increased activism did not favor the conciliationists who organized the event, as witnessed by the muzzling of the Poles at the unveiling. Indeed, their policy was soon to be proven deficient by another faction involved in the commemoration: the Polish Socialist Party (Polska Partia Socjalistyczna, or PPS). The socialism of the PPS, like that of Limanowski, emphasized patriotism; like the insurrectionaries before them, they wished to free the Poles from tsarist rule and restore their independence.[95] The socialists' protest against the official Warsaw celebration of the bard stemmed in part from the incongruities of the propertied classes working in tandem with the tsarist government. By choosing to celebrate Mickiewicz as poet and not as revolutionary, they presented a distorted view of Mickiewicz, "who was not only a genius but also the personification of our one-hundred-year struggle against bondage."[96] Thus, the leader of the PPS, Józef Piłsudski, organized a counter-commemoration after the unveiling, marching a small group of radical intellectuals and workers from Aleje Ujazdowskie in the direction of the monument.[97]

Far surpassing the effect of this tiny demonstration was another move. The socialists had gained possession of a secret document, the so-called Imeretinskii memorial, that unmasked the bad faith on the part of the Russian officials who had seemed so accommodating. Published by the PPS, the memorial and other secret documents showed the true nature of the new, supposedly more conciliatory Russian government, whose reforms were intended to keep Polish peasants from falling under the spell of the Polish intelligentsia (whether of socialist or other persuasion).[98] The dissemination of their contents dealt a severe blow to the New Course and to tri-loyalism in Russian Poland, thus making other options of political behavior—such as those represented by Dmowski and Piłsudski—seem more attractive.

COMPETING CLAIMS
ON SYMBOLIC SPACE

If the square containing the Mickiewicz statue, protected by an ornate iron fence, was destined to become a kind of a "national sanctuary" and focal point for the Poles in Warsaw, its unveiling illustrated the incongruities of the Poles trying to remain loyal Russian subjects while retaining their own national identity.[99] Not all Poles would settle for an exclusively cultural or ethnographic identity or resign themselves to the fact of partition. Many were unwilling to sit back and allow the conciliationists alone to profit from the occasion, as seen from the initiatives of the parties associated with Dmowski and Piłsudski. The Mickiewicz celebration in Warsaw marked the swan song of tri-loyalism in that region of the former Polish state.

While the events in Cracow and Warsaw reflected the different conditions for national activity within the two empires, they do not lack parallels. The Varsovians had taken interest in the work of their Cracow brethren, and vice versa. Socialists in both empires made near-immediate use of the monuments. In both cases, political groups found themselves at odds with each other. In Cracow, however, those allied with Galician officialdom expelled the socialists from the official celebration and from the newly created national space, while in Warsaw the socialists themselves decided to boycott the tainted commemoration and organize their own. Preoccupation with the peasantry and its sense of belonging also characterized both regions. The masses increasingly were being wooed by members of various political parties and encouraged to play a more active role.

The Mickiewicz celebrations underscore the dead bard's fate as a national bone of contention. Various groups sought their own reflections in the bronzed Mickiewicz, who became a mirror of the Poles' miscellaneous hopes and ideals. An all-purpose figure, he was for schoolteachers "the first teacher of his nation in the nineteenth century," presented to Polish youth and villagers as a "propagator of temperance."[100] Conservative and clerical forces peppered their ringing endorsements of a pious Mickiewicz—God's gift to the nation—with calls for self-improvement. Democrats tried to show how reading Mickiewicz could change one's life from one based on words to one of deeds: it reportedly had made a fervent patriot, who ended up fighting in the 1863 insurrection, out of a Frenchified young man.[101] Socialists praised him as a revolutionary and precursor of socialism; radical elements in Galicia founded an Adam Mickiewicz People's University to promote knowledge among the uneducated masses.[102]

Extraordinary in all these endeavors was the extent to which all levels of Polish society took an interest in this dead poet. The controversies surrounding the monuments led some groups of Poles to produce tributes to Mickiewicz that would be more lasting than bronze or marble. The Adam Mickiewicz People's University was only the brightest star in this Polish firmament.[103] Numerous smaller endeavors led to the creation of libraries, folk schools, stipends, the publication of popular works and portraits, the erection of lesser monuments and tablets, "Mickiewicz" trees and mounds, even the naming of new varieties of plants or fruits after the bard. Mickiewicz had found his way into the Wawel crypt, public squares, and peasant huts; now his name was being associated with the best efforts of the Polish nation. Mickiewicz had truly been nationalized; the figure of the bard stood for the people as a whole. This suggests that what most Poles desired was "not a statue but a monument" that would attest to the unity of the nation.[104]

This national unity may have grown even stronger as a result of the attack on Mickiewicz from one outside the nation. Ivan Franko had mastered the Polish language and was intimately acquainted with its culture. He knew which Polish icons to smash; his criticism of Mickiewicz offended and angered Poles. That a scholar of Franko's caliber would take on the most highly regarded Polish poet likewise testifies to the pain he and other Ukrainians felt as the younger brothers within Galicia. If rigged and corrupt elections kept them from power, they would have to find less pleasant ways of gaining attention in the province.

Of the project for the Warsaw monument, *Gazeta Warszawska* (Warsaw gazette) complained, "Our bourgeois age is not capable of extraordinary things."[105] Less critical of these efforts than contemporary Poles, we might ask whether a truly monumental sculpture to the bard could have been erected while the nation remained partitioned, or even whether that was the most important issue for the stateless nation. Ultimately, it mattered little that the symbolic figures around which they rallied were not great works of art. Their very existence testified to the extraordinary things of which Poles were capable at this time. And monuments continued to be erected, the potent symbolism of which far outweighed any aesthetic considerations. Their value lay in their testimony to the continued interest of the nation, despite the challenges it faced, in its heroes and sources of inspiration.

Part Three

THE FIRST YEARS
OF THE
TWENTIETH CENTURY

SIX

Teutons versus Slavs?
Commemorating the Battle of Grunwald

Events of the first years of the twentieth century exacerbated conflicts between the inhabitants of Central and Eastern Europe. The rise of a more aggressive German nationalism since the birth of the German Empire in 1871 posed problems for the Poles as well as for the rest of Europe. Poles constituted a significant national minority in the east of the empire. By the turn of the century, the Poles of Poznania, Pomerania, Silesia, Warmia, and Mazuria were increasingly perceived as a cancer on the German national state that diluted its national content and weakened its eastern border. Pressures to Germanize the eastern territories of the Reich were exerted by a proliferation of new associations, such as the Eastern Marches Association (Hakata) and the Pan-German League, trying to shape the German state and dictate policies that were ostensibly in the national interest.[1] Antipathy toward the Polish nobility and clergy began to encompass the broader masses, the peasants and their children.

How Poles dealt with this situation is the subject of the present chapter. Could Poles under German rule resist the increasing pressure to abandon their language and culture for German? This challenge to the integrity and identity of the nation put the Poles on the defensive at the turn of the century, a time when some kind of international conflict seemed imminent. The search for potential allies commenced, as Poles considered their prospects for the future. Given German hostility, would such considerations boil down to simplistic dichotomies: Teutons versus Slavs, the West versus the East? Or did Russia represent the greater threat? Such determinations were bound to have repercussions for the situation of Poles within one or more of the empires, all the more so as alliances between the three partitioning powers were themselves undergoing revision in the first decade of the twentieth century.

SHORTHANDS FOR GERMAN OPPRESSION

Although the anti-Catholic, anti-Polish *Kulturkampf* ended in the 1880s, the connection between Polishness and Catholicism was strengthened by yet another governmental measure—this time, one that concerned the language in which Polish citizens of the German Reich were taught religion. Although most subjects in Prussia's denominational schools had been taught in German for decades, religious education was the one exception. Polish-language instruction had long been justified by the clergy, which feared that, if pupils could not understand the principles of their faith, they might more easily become prey to socialist agitation. By the turn of the century, however, Prussian authorities were more concerned with the slow process of Germanization in the eastern provinces of the Reich than with any socialist threat.[2] The new Prussian minister of education, Konrad Studt, decided to phase out the use of Polish in religious education: it would be allowed only in the lowest level of religious education in the elementary schools.[3]

Bismarck's attack on Catholicism during the *Kulturkampf* had helped to strengthen the national consciousness of the Poles in his state; this new attack brought about unexpected protest. By mandating German for religious language instruction, the authorities were perceived as impinging upon the Poles' culture and seeking to undermine the connection between Polishness and Catholicism. Their weak knowledge of German making it hard to assess the curriculum, some parents feared that their children would be taught Lutheranism, not Catholicism.[4] These concerns led to what has been termed the school strike of 1901. This was actually a form of passive resistance, according to Kulczycki: students confronted with the new policy declined to use their new German textbooks, answer questions, or say their prayers in German.[5]

While pupils resisted in numerous locales, the town of Września (Wreschen) will forever be associated with the 1901 school strike.[6] A confrontation erupted in this predominantly Polish town one day as a group of adults, having heard the cries of uncooperative pupils being beaten, entered the school building and approached the offending faculty; someone later threw a rock through the window of one particularly detested teacher's house. This threatening of teachers proved the last straw for the local authorities.[7] Those who had entered the school that day were put on trial, found guilty, and given sentences of up to two and one-half years in prison.[8]

The harshness of the sentences elicited an uproar. The Września school incident was brought to the attention of Poles (and others) worldwide, as news of it was broadcast by Henryk Sienkiewicz, Zygmunt Miłkowski, and Maria Konopnicka, among others. Much was made of the fact that innocent children were beaten for preferring to pray and receive religious instruction in their mother tongue. Polish victimhood was underscored by these activists; they sought sympathetic ears in the West, hoping that pressure might be exerted on those who oppressed members of the partitioned nation. Września became a catchword for German injustice.[9]

Another response to the German oppression combined demonstrations with commemorations. Once again, Sienkiewicz played a pivotal role. The writer's twenty-fifth jubilee, postponed so as not to detract from the efforts of erecting the Mickiewicz monument in Warsaw, was finally celebrated in 1900. Sienkiewicz's moment in the national limelight happened to coincide with the completion of the serialization in the press of his newest historical novel, *The Teutonic Knights* (*Krzyżacy*).[10] The subject of the novel, perhaps Sienkiewicz's best, had relevance for the Poles of this period, who drew parallels between the current clash between Poles and Germans and a much earlier encounter.

The Teutonic Knights focused on the relationship between the medieval Polish state and the powerful Teutonic Order. The religious order (formerly based in Palestine) had been invited by Conrad of Mazovia in the first half of the thirteenth century to help defend his lands against the pagan Prussians along the Baltic Sea. Over the next century or two, the knights' "conversion" of these pagan peoples decimated their population while gaining for the order a territorial stronghold on the Baltic. Before long, the Teutonic Order turned its attention to the Lithuanians in the east, whom it hoped to convert and dominate. The fact that the Lithuanians had undergone mass conversion after the royal marriage of Grand Duke Jagiełło (Jogaila) to Jadwiga, the young heir to the Polish throne, in 1386 did not keep the Teutonic Order from pressing both countries. The conflict reached a head in the 1410 Battle of Grunwald, also known as the Battle of Tannenberg.[11] The Teutonic Knights were defeated by a united force comprised of Poles, Lithuanians, and other inhabitants of East and Central Europe: Ruthenians (roughly equated with today's Belarusians and Ukrainians), Tartars, Czechs, and Moravians, as well as Moldavian vassals of the Polish state. This victory not only strengthened the Polish state; cooperation in defeating the Teutonic Knights brought the peoples of East-Central Europe closer together and raised the stature of the Jagiellonian dynasty, which, a century later, ruled Bohemia and Hungary as well as Poland and Lithuania.

Thanks to Sienkiewicz's latest novel, the scene of the victory at Grunwald began to work its way into collective memory. On numerous occasions the author read aloud his version of the battle to the crowds that gathered to honor him in cities throughout the Polish lands. This juxtaposition of events—jubilee and oppression—encouraged twentieth-century Poles to turn a loose historical parallel into a firm equation: the oppressors of the Poles in the new Germany were modern Teutonic Knights. Their way was deemed one of brutality: while centuries earlier, "at the point of a sword . . . [they] wanted to bring the light of the Gospels to baptized Lithuania," they now beat Polish children for refusing to respond in German.[12]

No figment of a hypersensitive Polish imagination, the sense of being heirs of the Teutonic Knights likewise absorbed Prussians at the turn of the century. In 1901 an inscription (on a stone that lay at the battle site) in honor of the slain Grand Master of the Teutonic Knights, Ulrich von Jungingen, announced that he had died "fighting for *German* existence and *German* law"—this despite the multinational composition and religious mandate of the order.[13] The renovation of the castle at Malbork (Marienburg), its former stronghold, also strengthened the connection. A speech given by Emperor William II at the rededication of the (now Lutheran) chapel on June 5, 1902, provides further evidence that that the Teutonic past was being embraced by the Hohenzollerns, and that the common enemy of both was the Poles.[14] The emperor claimed that "Polish impudence wants to tread too near to Germandom and I am forced to call my people to defend our national property." More threateningly, he also spoke of "German tasks in countries to the east of the Vistula" and expressed a desire to support the German element beyond the borders of the country.[15]

William II's speech sparked anti-German demonstrations, particularly in Galicia, this time in the form of celebrations of the approaching anniversary of the Battle of Grunwald. The tide of popular outrage in June led Poles in both Lwów and Cracow to establish commemorative committees and hold celebrations in July.[16] They had already been reminded a half-year earlier of the old, pre-partition tradition of commemorating the battle each July 15, which ceased only with the Prussian occupation of Cracow in 1794.[17] Still, the celebrations of 1902 were inspired mainly by Sienkiewicz, who both popularized Grunwald and spread news of German oppression, and by Germans such as William II, acting like the successors of the Teutonic Knights.[18] In Cracow, Poles took note of the participation of members of the Polish Merchant Congregation, historically descended from Germans but Polonized over the centuries.[19] And, although imperial, provincial, and local dignitaries were present for the festivities, Cracovians gave a hero's welcome to the Czech Václav Klofáč, one of the Czechs and Slovenians who—unlike the loyal Polish deputies—had spoken out in the Austrian parliament against William II's speech.[20]

Where Września had become a byword for German injustice, Grunwald was rapidly becoming a synonym for resistance against Germanization. A populist paper read widely by peasants in Russian Poland, *Gazeta*

Świąteczna (Holiday gazette), explained that "each [Polish] outpost in Silesia is Grunwald. It is also each inch of Poznanian land, snatched from the jaws (*pysk*) of Hakata."[21] The threat to Poles in the German Empire was seen as crucial at this time, as the following statement by Jan Ludwik Popławski attests:

> We must look at the next dozen or so years in the Prussian zone as at a critical moment, in which it will be decided whether the German element [*niemczyzna*] will manage to gain ultimate ascendancy over us. And only a great, comprehensive effort of the entire nation, not only of the section of it that suffers Prussian oppression, can tip the scale of victory to our side.[22]

These developments had a tremendous impact on the National Democrats and their view of the Polish question. The National Democrats originally had not considered the Germans to be the Poles' greatest enemy. The events of the first years of the twentieth century, however, convinced Dmowski otherwise. Evidence for this he found in the focused German response to the next series of Polish school strikes, which were much bigger (approximately eighty thousand children participating) and better organized.[23] In contrast, Russia had been forced to make concessions—religious, linguistic, economic, and political—in the wake of the Russo-Japanese War and "revolution" (in the Polish lands) of 1904–1906, even to the extent of allowing for a constitution and parliament (the Duma).[24] It looked as though Poles might be able to turn Russian weakness to their advantage. In Germany, on the other hand, legislation passed in the years 1904–1908 further limited the Poles' opportunities. Prohibitions on the creation of new agricultural settlements famously kept the peasant Michał Drzymała from building a house on his newly acquired land, on which he set up a used circus wagon instead. A new law made it possible for Germans to expropriate Polish landholdings in Poznania and West Prussia, despite the Poles' vigorous campaign in the West for support against this move. And an otherwise progressive law on associations and meetings had the effect of outlawing the use of the Polish language in the pre-election campaigns in many districts, forcing Poles to resort to so-called mute rallies.[25] The pillars of Polish national identity—language, land, religion—were threatened in the new Germany.

REMEMBERING GRUNWALD IN 1910

Given their increasing preoccupation with the situation of Poles in the German Empire, it should come as no surprise that Polish activists turned the five hundredth anniversary of the Battle of Grunwald into a major national celebration. Plans for the commemoration were initiated by the Cracow city council in 1907.[26] The well-practiced commemoration mechanism, fine-tuned over the preceding decades, cranked up to prepare this three-day event. A host of subcommittees were formed to deal with various aspects of the celebration, including arrangements made for accommodations, publications, decorations, exhibitions, excursions, a parade, and entertainment for the folk. Yet other parts of the festivities were prepared by other groups and organizations; these included various theatricals (including performances by highlanders), the celebration of wreaths (a midsummer night's festival of pagan origin with illumination and entertainment on the Vistula), two days of exercises on the Błonia field by the Falcons, as well as congresses, rallies, and meetings of various kinds.[27] While the Cracow committee did most of the work, a provincial committee, headed by Cracow mayor Juliusz Leo, eventually took over—thus ensuring the participation of provincial dignitaries.

The celebration of the Battle of Grunwald in 1910 turned out to be the largest of the pre-1914 commemorations. An estimated one hundred fifty thousand to one hundred sixty thousand guests from out of town as well as forty thousand Falcons traveled to Cracow for the three-day festivities.[28] Whether in organized groups or as individual travelers, Poles came from all three empires as well as from elsewhere in Europe and America.[29] The parade from the Błonia field to the Wawel on July 17, the final day of the celebration, took over six hours, as over one hundred thousand participated in the eight-kilometer-long procession.[30] Images from these Grunwald festivities reached the broadest audience of all the commemorations of this period, thanks to the latest technological innovation: motion pictures. The oldest known film document of pre–World War I Poland in existence, newsreel clips of the ceremonies were viewed by theatergoers in Galicia and, possibly, wherever the Parisian Journal de Pathé was distributed.[31] A number of foreign correspondents—most notably from France and England—were also present, a special bureau for the press in Cracow having been established for their convenience during the festivities.[32]

The events of 1910 outclassed the commemorations of 1902 in both fame and scope. Yet a very different mood prevailed. While the festivities of 1902—spontaneous, nationalistic, and popular—were closely connected to German persecution, the events of 1910 downplayed the clash of Germans and Poles. Not wishing to antagonize the partitioning powers, the organizers strove to bolster a fragile national unity, sorely tried by the veritable civil war within the Kingdom of Poland in 1904–1906.[33] In the course of the celebrations, Grunwald metamorphosed from a tool of protest into one of more restrained nation-building. How this more moderate stance came to be is the story of Grunwald 1910.

PADEREWSKI'S MONUMENT
AND POLISH NATION-BUILDING

The Cracow celebration was notable for its centerpiece: a gift of a famous Pole to the nation. The Polish pianist Ignacy Jan Paderewski commissioned a bronze monument to the victors at Grunwald, which was unveiled on July 15, 1910. By this time his name was well known to audiences worldwide. After a series of successful concerts in Vienna, Paris, and England as well as in Cracow and Lwów in the late 1880s, the next decade brought Paderewski repeatedly to America, making his name a household word and symbol of Poland abroad. That he was associated with the Polish nation was truly justified, as by the turn of the century the pianist was recognized back home not only for his musical virtuosity but also as a benefactor. Paderewski donated the proceeds from many concerts to social causes, organizations, institutions, and individuals; sponsored competitions among the Poles for literary as well as musical accomplishments; and supported other national endeavors.[34] While curiosity about Paderewski's present may have inspired many Poles to travel to Cracow for this occasion, the monument did more than make the anniversary celebration more festive. It was seen as important not only to the festivities but to the underlying idea of Grunwald, for which "the gigantic weight of this colossal monument . . . serves as ballast [*balastuje*], . . . secures a lasting place . . . among the ideals that enliven us: in a word, embodies them in granite and bronze."[35]

Paderewski claimed he came up with the idea for the monument to the victors at Grunwald at the age of ten.[36] While this seems farfetched, clearly the first years of the century were viewed by Paderewski as a crucial period for the Polish nation. In 1907 he had come to its defense when the Danish novelist and Nobel laureate Bjørstjerne Bjørnson wrote critically of the Poles.[37] The following year, Paderewski asked a young Polish sculptor residing in Paris, Antoni Wiwulski, to sketch out some ideas related to the subject of Grunwald; the pianist secretly commissioned the work at the beginning of 1909.[38]

The project was a high-risk proposition, politically as well as financially. Bronze monuments did not come cheaply, and Paderewski had entrusted preparations to an unproven artist. Doubtless aware of the controversy that had surrounded the erection of and projects for the Mickiewicz monuments discussed earlier, the Polish pianist shrouded the monument in secrecy. Other concerns may also have caused the pianist to keep his project private. One word from the Austrian authorities would have rendered moot Paderewski's ambitious plans for the 1910 anniversary. Would they permit the Galician Poles to erect a monument to the victors at Grunwald—that is, against the ancestors of the Habsburgs' political allies?

According to an anecdote published many years later, the viceroy of Galicia, Michał Bobrzyński, came to Paderewski's rescue. Paderewski's plenipotentiary, Tadeusz Jentys, traveled to Cracow at the beginning of 1910 with photographs and a model of the monument to try to secure approval. Without consulting his superiors in Vienna, Bobrzyński decided to give his permission. This account of the viceroy's deed had him placing the historical significance of the monument over any risk to his career. "Do not forget," said Bobrzyński, "that I am a historian, thus I must have respect for history. What would history say of me if I did not do everything I could (*gdybym całym sobą nie dopomógł do tego*) so that a monument to the glory of Grunwald would stand on Polish land?"[39] That the viceroy was a historian may have made all the difference in this case; a number of conservatives opposed the celebration, fearing that it would prompt German retaliation in the form of the awaited expropriation of Polish estates.[40]

A more serious objection came from an unexpected quarter. Some Poles who acknowledged the significance of the Battle of Grunwald still fretted over the Cracow celebration. They feared that a group of Poles would take advantage of the festivities to push its own political agenda. Among them was Sienkiewicz, who worried that the event would be politicized by the "jamboree"—the Falcon Jamboree, specifically timed to coincide with the anniversary celebrations.[41] The Falcons were a gymnastic organization, not unlike the German Turnervereine but even closer to the Czech Falcons, which began the fashion for such clubs in the Slavic East.[42] The organization had gained enormous popularity among Poles in the three empires (although it functioned underground in the Russian Empire) and the United States.[43] That the jamboree was frowned upon by the Galician authorities is evident from the various hurdles the Falcons had to overcome, including gaining access to housing and equipment.[44] This was due in part, one expects, to the traditional anti-German stance of the organization as well as to the Falcons' training with lances, clubs, and rifles, demonstrations of which were bound to be commented upon unfavorably by the Poles' enemies.[45]

People like Sienkiewicz were also alarmed by the strident anti-Germanism of nationalistic groups. In 1909, a celebration of the Grunwald anniversary had been organized in Cracow by Straż Polska (Polish Guard). Although it considered itself a distinct organization, Straż Polska was suspiciously close to the National Democrats in both approach and principles.[46] In addition to sponsoring historical commemorations, it too advocated national self-defense, boycotted German goods, and sought to defend the Polish language.[47] Even its expressed desire to transcend party politics made it seem closer to the National Democrats, whose claim to be a pan-Polish party often blurred conveniently with preexisting moves in the same direction.[48] The agendas of these increasingly nationalistic organizations emphasized the value of strong and disciplined bodies, economic self-sufficiency, and Polish unity; they seemed intent on making patriotism the monopoly of the nationalist right as well. While many Poles thought the nation should strive for unity, some worried that it would come at the cost of letting one political orientation dominate Polish society.

An incident that same year illustrates the divisiveness that the Poles hoped to avoid during this internationally turbulent period. Like Paderewski, the painter Jan Styka also concocted a contribution to enhance the Grunwald celebration. However, his proposal of erecting a panorama of the Battle of Grunwald in the Barbakan (the round medieval fortification that stands directly outside the Florian Gate and across the street from Matejko Square) led to heated debates and its ultimate rejection—quite a story in itself. In the end, the Barbakan came to house not a panorama for the masses, but a genuine sign of the German/Polish conflict, Drzymała's famous wagon, transferred there specifically for the celebration.[49]

The "almost Homeric battles" over Styka's project contributed to the atmosphere of divisiveness, leading some to believe that the "Grunwald [festivities] w[ould] not succeed (*nie uda się*) because there is no harmony in our society"—a concern that had been troubling Poles since 1904–1906.[50] Fears that Polish nationalists would politicize the festivities likewise spurred Sienkiewicz, whose ill health prevented him from attending, to write that he joined with "all those who believe . . . that celebrations of past great victories can bear blessed fruit only when they become not a boastful cry but an ark of the covenant between children of one Fatherland, a stimulus to improve one's own soul and an encouragement to work, to public virtue and self-sacrifice."[51] The anniversary was not for gloating over past greatness, but for thoughtful introspection that would inspire greater identification with the nation and its fate and strengthen the collectivity.

Of importance were not just battles and military virtues but also cultural values. Medieval Poles had the virtue of a simple life, which Sienkiewicz underscored in *The Teutonic Knights;* in his view, their more austere habits made them better defenders of their country.[52] But more significant than the unencumbered lifestyle of the Poles was the nation's mission. While connected to Western Europe, the nation saw itself as improving upon it: "Five hundred years ago, fertilized by the culture of the West, we repulsed . . . the rapacity of the same West."[53] Poles fought in self-defense, not for the sake of territorial acquisition. Territory and allies were gained through other means, as indicated in the union of the Polish and Lithuanian states through the marriage of Jadwiga and Jagiełło: "Teutonic Knights conquered pagans with the sword, Poles with good and unforced will."[54]

Bringing civilization to the East via peaceful means seemed to be that rai-
son d'être for the Poles. The symbolism of Grunwald, thus, implied a clash
of approaches, even of civilizations. Polish historians saw it this way as
well: "Here two worlds stood face to face, two cultures were at grips with
each other, two political and ethical ideas, two distinct, collective spirits,
which had been formulated on two completely different bases, and which
contradicted each other at every point."[55] The Poles claimed to represent
something different: but to what extent were they successful in convincing
themselves as well as the broader world of their unique mission and position in East-Central Europe?

Such considerations helped to transform the anniversary celebration.
The Grunwald celebration of 1910 was no longer a simple matter of
protest, as in 1902. Instead, the event was to be held, as expressed in the
inscription on Paderewski's monument, "For the glory of our forefathers,
for the encouragement of our brothers" (*Praojcom na chwałę, braciom na
otuchę*). The festivities did not become an anti-German demonstration. Instead, they appeared to have metamorphosed into a nation-building exercise.

The actual Grunwald celebrations of July 15–17 turned out to be a
crowded yet joyous affair.[56] Each day brought thousands more Poles to Cracow. The committee had received numerous requests for assistance with
housing arrangements and tickets from all over the Polish lands and beyond; a bureau was set up at the train station to direct those arriving, and
many other organizations were ready to receive their own guests as well.[57]
Field kitchens had been established to provide sustenance to the crowds,
whose needs could not have been handled by the local restaurants. Cracow's
streets hummed as the guests, many dressed in folk garb or Falcon uniform,
took in the glories of Poland's spiritual capital.

As with so many Polish celebrations, the solemnities began with a
church service and sermon in Saint Mary's Church. Tickets proved insuffi-
cient to guarantee holders a space in the church, as many Poles had occupied seats long before the official guests arrived. Churchgoers then proceeded from the market square to what by then was a very crowded but
festive Matejko Square. Across from the Barbakan, festooned in red carnations, the square held several grandstands, one for dignitaries and deputa-
tions, another for the four-hundred-strong orchestra and choir. Most spectators simply stood throughout the music and speeches, eager to get a
glimpse of the monument; many others peered from the windows and
roofs of nearby buildings. The united choirs began the program of the unveiling by singing "Bogurodzica," an ancient hymn dating back to the age
of Grunwald and likely sung by those warriors. Addressing the crowds, the
provincial marshal, Stanisław Badeni, praised Jagiełło before the yellow

Fig. 6.1 The unveiling of the Władysław Jagiełło Monument on 15 July 1910 in Krakow. The photograph appears to be taken from the Barbakan or part of the walled fortress surrounding the medieval town. The crowd and decorations, of course, are of a much later vintage. *From* Księga pamiątkowa obchodu pięćsetnej rocznicy zwycięstwa pod Grunwaldem w dniu 15, 16, i 17 lipca 1910 r. w Krakowie z dodaniem albumu literacko-artystycznego poświęconego wielkiej rocznicy dziejowej, *ed. K. Bartoszewicz (Kraków: nakładem Franciszka Terakowskiego, 1911).*

curtains, suspended from enormous garlanded poles, dropped to unveil Paderewski and Wiwulski's labor of love: the Grunwald, or—as it was more commonly referred to at this time—the King Władysław Jagiełło Monument. At that moment, the choirs broke into song.

The crowds were now able to see the much-anticipated monument. Towering above the square was a five-meter-high figure of Jagiełło on horseback, perched atop a four-sided rough granite block eight meters tall. Other figures surrounded the granite block: in the front of the monument a pensive Witold (Vytautas), the leader of the Lithuanian forces, stood above the vanquished Grand Master of the Teutonic Knights. To the monument's left, a Lithuanian warrior sounded the victory on a horn, as he held a Teutonic Knight captive on one knee. On the opposite side, Polish knights were seen gathering the banners of the vanquished. To the rear of the monument stood a peasant breaking out of his chains—"a picture of the future," according to one commentator.[58] Thus, although ostensibly a monument to Jagiełło, it clearly identified the king with the event whose anniversary was being celebrated that day.

Following the applause elicited by the sight of the monument, Paderewski addressed the crowd in a brief speech—in many ways a Polish Gettysburg address[59]—which began as follows:

> The work we see before us did not originate from hatred. It was born of profound love for our country, not only in her former greatness and present helplessness, but also in the strength and brightness of her future. It was born of our love and gratitude to those ancestors who went into battle not for plunder and booty, but took up arms and conquered in defense of a good and just cause.

Paderewski declared that the monument was a "pious votive offering" and implored the spirits of those ancestors to intercede with God to inspire the inhabitants of this land with love and harmony, among other gifts. Entrusting the monument to the care of the nation, he added: "Let every Pole and every Lithuanian, from all the former provinces of our country and from across the Ocean, see this Monument as a symbol of our common past, a testimony of our common glory, a stimulus to joint effective work."[60] The pianist was as dynamic a speaker as he was a musician, and the speech—its tenor as well as its delivery—was much praised.

Paderewski's speech illustrated the new, understated approach to the Grunwald anniversary. No hatred motivated the monument, claimed Paderewski, who refrained from mentioning the Germans or Teutonic Knights by name. Instead, the greater Polish nation was called to see the monument as a symbol of what its members had in common—a shared, glorious history—and to take inspiration to work together toward a common goal. The speech reflected the desires of the organizers for a gently constructive approach to the festivities, one that would not antagonize the Germans. In this, the tone of Paderewski's speech contrasted markedly with other, much sharper statements made by him earlier.[61]

In the speech cited above, one can see the influence of the conservatives who ran Galicia—to whom, incidentally, Paderewski was indebted for permission to erect his monument. As early as 1902, the conservatives had tried to stress that the Poles were above hatred, which had a demoralizing effect.[62] Others developed this theme further in 1910: hatred was not a collective feeling of the Polish soul, and Poles did not hate Germans or anyone.[63] Commenting on Polish-Prussian relations, the historian Szymon Askenazy cast the matter in a slightly different light. Blind hatred—such as hatred for the Prussians—was characteristic of small nations. The Poles were a great nation.[64]

THE JAGIELLONIAN IDEA REVISITED?

The greatness of the Polish nation perceived by Askenazy was closely connected to the victory at Grunwald. The Cracow committee's announcement underscored the fact that the victory at Grunwald had facilitated the Union of Horodło.[65] The union, signed in 1413, reconciled the Polish and Lithuanian states, which prior to the Battle of Grunwald had been unsure of their mutual relationship. Horodło was the first concrete step toward a more lasting union. Lithuanian nobles were granted the same political and economic rights as their Polish counterparts, emphasized further by the bestowing of membership in Polish heraldic clans. In one step, the political members of the two states literally became one family.

Grunwald, thus, contributed to the making of the unique state that came to be known as the Polish-Lithuanian Commonwealth. In later times this vision of the state—and state-building—was often referred to as the Jagiellonian idea. The Jagiellonian idea represented a different approach to empire, one that brought peoples together voluntarily, not by force. One commemorative brochure defined it as "the unification of the peoples of east and south-east Europe under the motto of liberty and progress in one great federation."[66] In these ideals lay the attractiveness of Jagiellonian rule, which in earlier centuries had led both Czechs and Hungarians to choose monarchs from that dynasty for themselves.

In the face of twentieth-century German aggression, the broader implications of Grunwald for the Slavic nations of Europe did not pass unnoticed. According to this same source, a united Slavdom could defend itself, but it would have to be united "not in Muscovite style [*po moskiewsku*] with the help of the knout and handcuffs, but in Polish style [*po polsku*], with the help of liberty."[67] In other words, the Jagiellonian idea challenged a doctrine with a long pedigree in the East: Pan-Slavism.[68] In earlier incarnations, Russian-sponsored Pan-Slavism had been unattractive to the Poles, who continued to chafe under tsarist rule. The advent of Neo-Slavism in 1905 augured some improvement in this regard, which seemed to be borne out by the Prague Slav Congress of 1908.[69] Present in Prague, Dmowski found a common language with the Russians, perhaps as a result of his own ideas on Eastern Europe: that same year, he published a book entitled *Germany, Russia and the Polish Question,* in which he advocated rapprochement between Russia and Austria-Hungary to hold German expansion at bay. Interestingly, the anniversary of Grunwald—July 15—was celebrated in Prague during the congress. A festive meeting of the Poles and Russians present was arranged by the Czech organizer of the congress, Karel Kramář, who realized that Neo-Slavism required an alliance between the Poles and the Russians to succeed. The little anniversary celebration brought no real progress, however, although conciliatory sounds were made by both sides.[70]

The Prague Pan-Slav Congress marked the zenith of Neo-Slavism. By 1910, there was little hope of a Polish-Russian rapprochement. The anti-Polish faction within the Russian movement, represented by Vladimir Bo-brinskii, Ivan Filevich, and Dimitrii Vergun, came to dominate the congress in Sofia in 1910. That summer, Slavic forces essentially became polarized: Slavs allied with the Russians went to Sofia, while those supportive of the Polish cause attended the Grunwald celebration in Cracow.

Yet the split was not a clean one. A handful of Russians traveled to Cracow for the anniversary. Their attendance proved more problematic than the presence of Habsburg Slavs, in the form of delegations from Prague, Ljubljana, and Zagreb.[71] Indeed, responses to the Russian presence demonstrate the lack of consensus on the part of Cracovians. The Slavic activist Marian Zdziechowski wanted Russians sympathetic to the Polish cause to participate in the Grunwald celebration. However, Cracow mayor Leo protested: "we are on the eve of war with Russia, thus they should not be here."[72] (The Galician authorities were concerned about appearances of pro-Russian sentiment in the face of approaching international conflict, which likely would pit Austria-Hungary against the tsarist regime.) Yet that did not deter several Russian supporters of Polish autonomy: Fedor Iz-mailovich Rodichev, a founder and member of the Kadet Party, the *Rech'* journalist Aleksandr Stakhovich, and Professor Aleksandr Lvovich Pogodin. Pogodin and Rodichev even gave impromptu speeches after the unveiling of the Grunwald monument. While Pogodin, a former professor at Warsaw University, addressed the crowds in Polish, Rodichev was allowed to speak in Russian—quite a novelty: this apparently was the "first time, on the street, before a crowd, here in Cracow, that Russian was spoken."[73]

It has been suggested that the two Russians may have been prompted to speak by Roman Dmowski.[74] If so, this may have been the only direct involvement of the Polish politician in shaping the Cracow celebration. Despite the attractiveness of the anniversary for the National Democrats, given their vision of the Polish future, the Grunwald commemoration was the work—and triumph—of Paderewski. Although Dmowski was in close contact with Paderewski, the former's relations with the Polish pianist were fraught with mistrust and even envy, given the relatively weakened status of his party at that moment: its continued depiction of Germans as the Poles' major enemy had led to major hemorrhaging, and the Neo-Slav movement was also foundering.[75] By contrast, Paderewski's star was rising within the national firmament, as seen from the ovations and praise bestowed upon the bestower of such a generous, "royal" gift,[76] during the festivities by the organizers as well as by local and international dignitaries and associations.[77] While Paderewski was acclaimed as the "first citizen of Cracow" by Mayor Leo, the populist paper *Wieniec-Pszczółka* thought that too weak a tribute: it declared that Paderewski was the "first citizen of Poland," showing the Poles how to love their fatherland and nation.[78] The nation had a new hero in Paderewski, while the National Democrats had fallen from favor.

The participation of Rodichev and his compatriots in the Grunwald festivities nonetheless gave hope to observers in Russian Poland, who drew analogies between their situation and that of the Habsburg monarchy in 1867 and wondered whether the question of Polish-Russian relations would "be resolved by Rodichev in Jagiellonian fashion or Bobrinskii according to the Teutonic Knights' formula."[79] This formulation seems to turn the Slavs versus the Teutons question on its head. Russian Pan-Slavs of Bobrinskii's ilk, thus, were being compared to the Teutonic Knights. Even the liberal Prince Evgenii Trubetskoi spoke despairingly of the "German character of Russian nationalism," which prevented Russia from convincing Poles and the Slavs of Austria-Hungary that it was the "bulwark against Pan-Germanism."[80] This depiction of Russia as Germanic was echoed by Poles of the "Jagiellonian" persuasion: "Russia never was nor is now a Slavic state, despite the fact that it has a huge majority of Slavic population. The court is German, the ruling family is German in blood and spirit, the bureaucracy is German in spirit and to a great part in blood as well—and the spirit of the culture that controls Russia is some strange mix of Tatar-Byzantine-German influences."[81] Had the Grunwald festivities, instead of gathering Slavs under one anti-German banner, metamorphosed into a competition for Slavic hegemony? Had Slavdom become polarized, with both Poles and Russians poised to take on a leadership role?[82]

If the Grunwald festivities were to be considered a Slavic conference, they were defective on a number of counts. One was the participation of nearly one hundred Hungarians, who, although they came uninvited, apparently were well received by the public.[83] Hungarians, of course, were not Slavs, and in fact oppressed the Slavic minorities within their half of the Habsburg Empire. Historically, however, the Hungarians had close ties with the Poles, and this friendship apparently continued. Another deficiency was the increasing emphasis on Grunwald as an exclusively Polish victory, rather than as one reflecting the cooperation of equal partners.[84] Without the Poles, wrote the historian Wiktor Czermak, Lithuania would have been overrun in 1410; this realization led the Grand Duchy to seek union with Poland at Horodło in 1413. And, as we have seen, King Jagiełło and not Lithuanian Grand Duke Witold had pride of place in the Grunwald monument. Supporters of Neo-Slavism still tendered hopes for the "Slavic idea" based upon Polish culture and policies; the Polish state had been great, they claimed, as long as it took an interest in the lives of the various Slavs within its borders as well as its Slav neighbors.[85]

Polish perceptions of their historic mission placed them squarely in a leadership role in Eastern Europe—and at loggerheads with both Germans and Russians. Amazing for a partitioned nation, Poles seemed to be vying for hegemony in East-Central Europe: they strove to keep the Germans at bay on the one hand, while trying to win over converts to the Jagiellonian idea on the other. In this scenario, both Germans and Russians were identified with the Teutonic Knights—the "bad German cause" fighting the "good Polish cause."[86]

Yet, did the partitioned Poles truly have a chance to strengthen their position within the larger East European space in 1910? While it has been argued that the Polish-led Grunwald celebration in Cracow was more successful than the Russian-led Pan-Slavic congress in Sofia, this did not resolve the question of genuine influence within the region.[87] More important was the reaction of other descendants of those who fought the Teutonic Knights, such as the Lithuanians: how did they view this episode from the past? What happened in more recent years to the unprecedented relationship of the Lithuanians and the Poles can be seen through their respective attitudes toward the anniversary celebration. For many residents of the former Grand Duchy were not interested in being part of the Cracow celebration. Unfortunately for the Poles, despite their positive, inclusionary, "statesmanlike" rhetoric, the 1910 celebration did not bring the desired result: the participation of the Poles' historic allies, the Lithuanians and the Ruthenians.

Yet here one must beware the fallacy of ambiguity: for these terms—Lithuanian and Ruthenian—had multiple meanings. The old geographical and regional allegiance that allowed Poland's preeminent Romantic poet, Mickiewicz, to begin his epic poem "Lithuania! My homeland!" (in Polish) or allowed noble citizens to identify themselves as *gente Ruthenus, natione Polonus* still prevailed among the Polonized ruling classes and intelligentsia in these eastern borderlands—the descendants of those who fought at Grunwald. They saw themselves much as did one of the Slavic enthusiasts, Marian Zdziechowski, who felt in his heart of hearts "a citizen of the Grand Duchy of Lithuania, indissolubly linked in union with Poland."[88]

A resident of Cracow, the same Zdziechowski authored a carefully worded invitation to those who fit the modern definition of Lithuanian: that is, the ethnic Lithuanians, whose young intelligentsia was emerging from the ranks of educated villagers. These "descendants and heirs of those, without whom there would not have been any Grunwald," who were now the "guests closest to us and most desired," chose, however, to boycott the Cracow celebration.[89] Some, such as the progressive democrats of *Lietuvos*

Žinios, feared for their young culture and worried about being "decoration" at the festivities.[90] Doubtless others suspected this was part of a Polish conspiracy to Polonize them: such were the reactions to the Lubomirski family's donation, this anniversary year, of forty-two thousand crowns to support lectures of Lithuanian history and literature at Jagiellonian University.[91]

Other reactions indicate to what extent national alliances had changed since 1410. In rebuffing Polish overtures, some sought not to harm the relatively congenial relations with the new Germany. The Lithuanians of East Prussia, for example, did not respond to the invitation to attend the Cracow festivities, although one group celebrated, by itself, in Tilsit. These Lithuanians even restricted their reports on the Cracow celebrations to reprints from German newspapers.[92] An old enemy had now become the Lithuanians' ally.

Lithuanians, too, were learning new lessons from their former brethren. Having seen the usefulness of the press as a "force that creates the opinion of the civilized world and sometimes compels even stubborn governments to cease oppressing conquered peoples," they waged a small campaign in the foreign press against the Poles.[93] One Mister Rankus published an article in the Parisian paper *La Croix,* in which he asked "why Poles, persecuted by Russians and Germans, have themselves become persecutors." The irony here is that the Poles were receiving worse press than the tsarist regime, which after all ruled both nations in the empire's western guberniias. Still, the perception of Polish persecution prevailed, as Poles—in this instance, Polish clergymen—were blamed for the language of church services in certain localities being changed from Lithuanian to Polish.[94] If this was how Poles took care of their neighbors, ethnic Lithuanians would seek out new, more promising, allies.

Poles, thus, were faced with a predicament. While their own self-perception focused on their status as a persecuted nation, as well as on their historical attractiveness within East-Central Europe, their image was tarnished. By the early twentieth century, the Poles' nearest neighbors, those accustomed to living within the same state—Lithuanians and Ukrainians—actively campaigned to show the Poles in a different, less favorable light. As the Ukrainian paper *Dilo* attested, "today, in the 500th anniversary of the Grunwald battle . . . those who hated Poland most were her allies from Grunwald: Ruthenia and Lithuania, seeing in [Poland] the synonym of their bondage."[95]

THE CHURCH AND GRUNWALD

While the Poles were unable to convince their former brethren from the Commonwealth to join in their celebration, the festivities engendered an unexpected backlash from within an entity generally identified closely with the nation: the Catholic Church. The clergy's attitudes toward the Grunwald anniversary and festivities sent mixed signals to the Polish faithful. Were they to be Catholics first or Poles? The course of events suggests a growing dissonance between the views of the Church and the nation.

Prior to the partitions of Poland, Grunwald anniversaries had been celebrations of both Church and state. Religious and political themes were entwined in representations of the event, dating from the earliest historical sources. Even more recent images such as Matejko's painting of the battle had their religious side: the artist painted Saint Stanislas in the heavens. While the canvas had been spirited off to Warsaw, where it became part of the collection of the Society for the Encouragement of the Fine Arts in 1902, reproductions soon were made available for mass distribution and would figure in the iconography of 1910.[96]

The fervent Catholicism of the Polish monarchy should have made it easy for the Church to find a way to celebrate the anniversary. It had already celebrated the anniversary of Jagiełło's baptism in 1886.[97] The person of the queen provided another opportunity for religious engagement. After all, many had attributed the victory at Grunwald to the young Jadwiga, whose acquiescence in marrying Jagiełło brought about the Christianization of Lithuania and the end of "paganism" in Europe.[98] Instrumental in raising the profile of Queen Jadwiga was the suffragan bishop of Lwów, Władysław Bandurski. Encouraged by the beatification of Joan of Arc in 1909, enabled in part by a massive public initiative in France, Bandurski proclaimed, "Let the Grunwald anniversary be the point of departure for a broad campaign in honor of Queen Jadwiga."[99]

Yet even the possibility of furthering the cause of Jadwiga's beatification did not win over the entire clergy to the Grunwald celebration. The Poles' partitioned status had always posed various problems for the hierarchy in the Polish lands, as the Vatican had dealings with the imperial powers to consider as well. This meant, for example, that in 1901 no support for Polish-language religious instruction in the Prussian lands was forthcoming from the Vatican, which had not wanted to antagonize Protestant Germany. The case of the Grunwald celebration was complicated by the fact that the combined forces had fought a religious order. Those who saw the Teutonic Knights as defenders of Christianity—and these included priests of both German and Polish descent—were uncomfortable with the idea of celebrating the victory.[100]

When support for the celebration was not forthcoming from the highest-ranking clergyman in the Polish lands, however, the whole nation took note. Cracow bishop since 1894 and cardinal since 1901, Jan Puzyna was no supporter of Polish national demonstrations. Approached in 1902 for permission to hold a church service and procession to the Wawel, the conservative Puzyna first refused—and reportedly was applauded by several pan-German dailies for doing so.[101] Too soon, however, for a second visit of the committee resulted in permission being granted for masses in Saint Mary's and Wawel Cathedral as well as for the laying of wreaths on Jagiełło's sarcophagus.[102] The Polish press duly corrected the record, noting that the cardinal had said "that every Catholic is permitted to order a holy Mass, and the faithful to attend it"—not exactly a ringing endorsement of the event.[103] Indeed, Puzyna's position calls to mind that of his former boss, Archbishop Seweryn Morawski, who had not been favorably disposed to the 3 May celebration in 1891. Puzyna's reputation in patriotic Polish circles plummeted further when he denied a Wawel burial to the Polish bard Juliusz Słowacki in 1909, the centennial of his birth.[104]

By the time of the Grunwald preparations, hopes that Puzyna would be supportive of the commemorative efforts were few, and rightly so. No special concessions were wrested from the cardinal, who denied requests for an outdoor mass that would accommodate the Falcons on the Błonia.

Puzyna was not the only Polish clergyman to voice reservations about the festivities. Apparently some in the Catholic press actually declared that Catholics who took part in the Grunwald celebration in Cracow would be sinning: "Catholics are not allowed to subordinate their Catholic convictions to patriotism, for what would the Fatherland gain by this, if in honoring it we simultaneously offended the Lord God. . . ."[105] Many of the same clergy objected to the undesirable company participants would be keeping in the procession: that is, to the presence of socialists. Indeed, thousands of socialists, with red carnations in their boutonnieres, took part in the procession on July 17, led by Daszyński and the elderly Limanowski.[106]

The clergy's animosity toward socialists may have been related to the hard times it was experiencing. Anticlericalism among Poles was growing, particularly in Russian Poland.[107] Pertinent for the commemoration, it also surfaced in Galicia, on the campus of Jagiellonian University. At a rally in 1910, students insisted that their university celebration of the Grunwald anniversary have a secular character and thus not include church services.[108] (It seems that the demographic changes wrought since 1905, when the school strikes in the Kingdom of Poland brought a great influx of students [many of whom were more radically inclined] to the universities of Galicia, were being felt.[109]) This desire of the students to secularize their commemoration scandalized the authorities, both university and provincial: as a result, Jagiellonian University students were denied permission to hold their planned celebration and apparently were also not assigned a place in the parade that was part of the larger Grunwald festivities. In protest, the students organized an anticlerical rally at Wawel Castle, arguing that "academic youth, which soon will occupy various posts in society, must be permeated with the Polish spirit, not the clerical."[110] They proceeded to the Mickie-wicz statue, then headed toward the bishop's palace with the intent of sere-nading him with revolutionary songs, but their way was blocked by po-lice.[111] This episode underscores the problematic relationship of nation and Church: could Poles remove themselves from the influence of the Church without weakening one of the pillars upon which the nation stood?

While these and other events left certain members of the clergy less well inclined to the commemorating public, others supported the Grunwald celebrations, in turn reinforcing the Polish-Catholic connection. Outdoor masses, forbidden by Puzyna in Cracow, were permitted in east Galicia by Archbishop Józef Bilczewski of Lwów. Sambor and Jarosław as well as Lwów took advantage of the opportunity. In Lwów, an outdoor mass at the Falcon field was celebrated by the archbishop himself, with a sermon by Bishop Bandurski. Bishop Józef Pelczar of Przemyśl also proved favorably inclined toward the Grunwald anniversary celebration.[112]

The clergyman most identified with the Cracow festivities was Bishop Władysław Bandurski. He provided the sermons for the services in Saint Mary's Church on the morning of the unveiling as well as in Wawel Cathe-dral at the mass for Queen Jadwiga.[113] Bandurski also participated in the events organized by the Falcons, which caused some to accuse him of harm-ing the authority of the Church and (even) wanting to be popular, for he addressed the crowds out-of-doors on the Błonia field after Cardinal Puzyna forbade the clergy to take part in celebrations held outside of Church prop-erty.[114]

Although his superiors may have been unhappy about Bandurski's par-ticipation, the general public's reaction to Bandurski was enthusiastic in the extreme. He was already much loved by Cracovians, who knew him as a moving preacher, and was often featured in the local calendars.[115] In various commemorative publications, Bandurski was termed the spirit of the cele-bration, even "the spiritual primate of Poland."[116] During the three-day event, the public showed its appreciation of the bishop by signing copies of a formal letter of thanks at the various Cracow bookstores and newspaper offices.[117] Credited with the strengthening (*krzepienie*) of hearts and spirits, Bandurski also helped to win over more converts to the national cause. Take the example of Ferdinand Machay. The seminarian from Orawa (Orava), who spoke Polish at his village home but was educated in Slovak and Hungarian, had come with the Hungarian delegation to the Grunwald festivities. The eloquence of Bandurski and others at the celebration and the sense of belonging to something larger—to a Poland in which peasants figured as well as lords—wrought magic. Upon his return to Hungary, Machay lectured on the Grunwald festivities, which he termed his "first open *credo* of Polishness."[118] In this way, Bandurski more than compensated for the lackluster reaction of Puzyna and other clergymen.

MODERN-DAY POLISH KNIGHTS

While acknowledging that the celebrations represented the beginnings of historical consciousness for many a villager and worker, Bandurski helped to bring past and present together. This is seen not only in his inspirational sermon at Saint Mary's, which was included in a number of commemorative publications, but in the encouragement he gave to the Falcons. Indeed, Bandurski strengthened their national pedigree and image by situating them firmly within the Polish historical tradition. This becomes clear from his speech at the site of the Falcon Jamboree, with its large grandstands and vast crowds. The knights of the past were now knighting the Falcons, Bandurski said, turning them into knights of Poland. The connection between the Falcons and the knights of yore, incidentally, was precisely what the Falcons wanted to promote: the poster advertising the Falcon Jamboree—Jan Styka's (actual) contribution to the 1910 festivities—shows the figure of an armor-clad Zawisza Czarny, perhaps Poland's most famous medieval warrior, knighting a kneeling Falcon against the background of the Wawel, with the inscription "Be vigilant" (*Czuwaj*).[119] However, Bandurski softened the militaristic tones by emphasizing the nation's more peaceful accomplishments: included in his litany was Poland's role as bulwark of Christianity in the East, baptizer of Lithuania, protector of Ruthenia. Poland was also, the bishop emphasized, "one of the brightest lands that had no blood or injustice on itself, only stripes received from evil-doers."[120]

Bandurski's words refocused Polish attentions away from anti-German sentiments—no small feat. Certainly the Falcon program, lasting longer and witnessed by larger crowds than the official part of the celebration, had the potential to set a different tone. The gymnasts were a visible group: members of the Falcons spent four days (July 15–18) in Cracow, most of the time clad in club uniform. At the same time, they formed an enclave within the city confines: they had their own campsite, post office, field kitchen, and supplies on the Błonia field, the site of their drills.[121]

Demonstrations of Falcon fitness began on Saturday, July 16: despite the rain and mud, a crowd of about twenty-five thousand turned out to observe the various drills and exercises. Falcon "nests," male and female, from the three empires as well as from as far away as the United States, traveled to Cracow for the festivities; many members demonstrated their physical prowess, coordination, and ability to follow orders. The exercises, according to Emil Bobrowski, "demonstrated considerable efficiency and left the impression, or at least the illusion, of maneuvers of a force organized

Fig. 6.2 Falcon Jamboree. Large crowds thrilled to the exercises in unison—some conducted with clubs or guns—of this international assembly of Polish Falcons. *From* Księga pamiątkowa obchodu pięćsetnej rocznicy zwycięstwa pod Grunwaldem w dniu 15, 16, i 17 lipca 1910 r. w Krakowie z dodaniem albumu literacko-artystycznego poświęconego wielkiej rocznicy dziejowej, *ed. K. Bartoszewicz (Kraków: nakładem Franciszka Terakowskiego, 1911).*

for battle."[122] The socialist regretted that it was only a show, "for it would have been not a bad army at all," and wished that the working classes could gain access to such drilling.[123] Yet another observer, a young villager from outside Galicia, found the Falcons the best part about the trip: with the Falcons on the Poles' side, he exclaimed, "Poland will not perish!"[124]

Although the crowds present for the Falcon Jubilee seemed to keep any anti-German sentiments they may have harbored under wraps, the festivities did allow the conflict to be voiced—literally, if in a less obvious way than in the speeches given. This is demonstrated by the jamboree song, the Falcons' marching tune. For the anniversary, the director of the Cracow Music Society set to music the lyrics the Falcons had designated for this purpose: a poem written by Maria Konopnicka in 1908 protesting against German oppression. Not an innocuous hymn, the jamboree song had a distinctly anti-German crusading spirit: the Polish singers take an oath not to leave the land of their birth or be turned into Germans. This "Grunwald Hymn" was sung by the choir at the unveiling. Although hardly heard over the din of applause then, it later was adopted by the Polish scouts as well as by other similarly minded organizations as their anthem. As a result, the song—known today as "Rota"—became known far beyond the confines of the Falcon organization.[125]

This musical interlude notwithstanding, the Falcon exercises, parade, as well as the behavior of the crowds during the Grunwald festivities made favorable impressions on many visitors, Poles and non-Poles alike. Paderewski's gift may have attracted them to Cracow, but they left with a greater sense of the modern Polish nation. The large number of peasants and workers present attested to the growing engagement of the lower classes in national endeavors. Parliamentarians of peasant extraction, such as Bojko and Wójcik, proudly wore regional peasant attire, and plenty of villagers were in attendance at the various events, participating as well as observing.[126] Photographs invariably depicted the Cracovians on horseback, the highlanders with their distinctive garb; the backdrop for Paderewski's speech, a group of young girls from the progressive village of Albigowa stood near the podium at the unveiling. The folk so impressed one visitor from the Russian Empire that he raised a toast to the peaceful, composed, dignified "Cracow crowd."[127]

Members of the foreign press also waxed enthusiastic about the nation, with compliments making their way into foreign periodicals such as *Journal de Genève, Gazette de Lausanne,* and the Parisian weekly *L'Illustration.*[128] At the same banquet, the editor of *Gil Blas* declared that "in no other country in the same situation could one see, with the same harmony of hearts and hopes, a peaceful army, composed of such a brotherly union of all social strata."[129] Similar praise came from the Russian editor of the recently suspended *Rech.* Maurice Muret ended his article in *L'Illustration* with the words: "If Poland at present has ceased to be a great state, the Poles nonetheless remain a great nation."[130] This, of course, is precisely what the Poles wanted the world to think.

FIVE HUNDRED YEARS LATER . . .

The twentieth century brought new challenges to the Polish nation. Denationalization and expropriation loomed in Prussian Poland, where Polish children were to be brought closer to "Germandom" (*Deutschtum*) by means of a German education.[131] Growing Prussian animosity toward Poles residing within the borders of a unified German state sparked the resurrection of annual celebrations of the anniversary of the Battle of Grunwald in 1902. Unlike so many of the celebrations discussed to date, commemorations were resumed not in an anniversary year but as a response to perceptions of injustice by the heirs of the Teutonic Knights, the Prussian-led

German Empire. Poles both protested and publicized their plight, abroad as well as among themselves, in this way fighting to defend their own national existence, as had their ancestors.

While outrage characterized the commemorations of 1902, a veneer of moderation was applied to the 1910 festivities—this despite the anti-German stance of the National Democrats. The gentler approach to the celebration for the five hundredth anniversary of the Battle of Grunwald was dictated by both political and pragmatic considerations: the Poles wished to avoid antagonizing the Austrian authorities, who allowed the nation its celebration, while shoring up national unity in a period of increasing political fragmentation.

During the Grunwald celebrations in Cracow, Poles avoided the extremes of noisy patriotism and the quenching of national spirit, exhibiting, according to reports, more equanimity and seriousness than before.[132] The celebration was treated as a nation-building exercise, one that stressed Polish strengths and solidarity rather than the German menace. Still, the public focus on national unity and nation-building could not help but build upon the earlier layers of protest.[133] Past images of oppression, if only in the form of Drzymała's wagon within the Barbakan (its presence not advertised), provided the context for the new monument across the street.

In this context, the Poles' self-perception contrasted with their view of Germans: they saw themselves as a Slavic nation that had brought unity and peace to Eastern Europe. Poles had fought not for territorial aggrandizement but to defend themselves. These characteristics left them with a moral advantage over the German nation, one that they hoped would someday bear fruit. Yet had they already lost that moral advantage? The Polish-German conflict produced a new type of mentality among a certain segment of the nation that included Roman Dmowski and his supporters. Poles were learning more than the German language from the empire to the west. Paradoxically, given their concern with the German threat, these fervent nationalists began to pattern their own behavior toward other nations after the German example. In a way, thus, vigorous national defense—of the type that led ethnic Lithuanians and Ukrainians to recoil from the Poles' outstretched arms—could be considered a kind of "Germanization," particularly when contrasted with the type of inclusive Polish nationalism that preceded it. It may seem odd to describe what we know today as integral nationalism in these terms. But that kind of "denationalization" appeared to be an unavoidable by-product of the battle for existence that beset the twentieth century. In this regard, all nationalists—whether Polish, Lithuanian, Ukrainian, Russian, or German—were becoming more "German," that is, more egoistic, more concerned with ethnicity, language, and bloodlines than with shared pasts and ideologies.

The Grunwald commemoration had its successes and its failures. Its moderation and tact helped to portray the Polish nation in a favorable light, both at home and abroad. Certain issues, such as the relation of the Catholic Church to the nation, remained unresolved, as Poles for the most part strove to emphasize the positive role played by clergymen such as Bandurski while downplaying opposition on the part of others. Nor was the victory at Grunwald, in its 1910 incarnation, "Jagiellonian": the Poles' historic allies, the Lithuanians and Ukrainians, did not join in the celebration. It was one thing to talk about cooperation in the past, another to practice it in the present. The ethnic, exclusive view of the nation appeared to be trumping the historic, inclusive one. In 1910, these regional minorities saw the Poles as a denationalizing or oppressing entity, much as the Poles saw the Germans. Avoiding Polish overtures, they chose to fight for their own languages and their own rights.

This largest and most elaborate of the Polish pre-independence commemorations brought about some positive results as well. Other neighbors—Czechs, Croatians, Slovenians, Hungarians, and a handful of Russians—were shown to support the Poles. The commemoration also turned a pianist into a national hero. Paderewski's involvement in the festivities sheds further light on the national leadership role often played by Polish notables from literary and artistic fields and suggests traits—as a self-made man, national benefactor, and ambassador to the rest of the world—that the Poles valued most. At any rate, the perceived German threat was held at bay, and the Poles remained a distinct nation.

SEVEN

Poles in Arms:
Insurrectionary Legacies

In the first years of the twentieth century, the specter of war loomed large. The Great Powers were engaged in an arms race: Germany hurried to build up its navy to compete with that of Great Britain. The annexation of Bosnia and Herzegovina by Austria-Hungary in October 1908 and the outbreak of the First Balkan War four years later rocked the international scene. The very real threat of impending European war cast a new shadow upon the Polish past, particularly its insurrectionary legacy. Half a century had passed since the nation's last armed struggle. Could Poles extract lessons from earlier battle experiences that would guide them toward independence?

The last major public commemorations preceding the outbreak of World War I were characterized by a new approach to commemorations. While previous events provided Poles with occasions for cultural enrichment and cross-partition networking, now a more practical set of goals took priority. The final celebrations of this period featured the actions of armed Poles in the previous century. The year 1913 provided Poles with opportunities to relate to two episodes connected with the nation's insurrectionary past: the January Insurrection and the Napoleonic Wars.

Poles had memorialized military victories a number of times in the previous decades, the battles at Grunwald, Vienna, and Racławice receiving the greatest attention. Now they were to celebrate significant military defeats. Paradoxically, "celebrate" *is* the appropriate verb in this case, for while Polish activists were aware of the historical outcomes, they managed to single out positive aspects of the two defeats as well. A mix of Romanticism and pragmatism, of hero worship and lessons extracted from past mistakes, of concern with deeds as well as with words contributed to a new model for armed struggle. The fiftieth anniversary of the January Insurrection and the centennial of the death of Prince Józef Poniatowski not only inspired Poles;

they helped to prepare them—physically and mentally, individually and collectively—for the approaching international conflict.

To understand the new, pragmatic approach to commemorations visible in 1913, one needs to have a sense of the underlying causes—domestic, national, and international—that not only propelled the Poles in this direction but also facilitated the rise of Polish militarism. New factors helped to transform the commemorative landscape. These included the rising Polish-Ukrainian conflict in Galicia as well as the lessons learned from the events of 1904–1906 in Russian Poland. Both led to the creation of paramilitary groups. The new celebrations likewise built upon the Grunwald festivities of 1910, with the Falcons' well-attended field exercises that raised the issue of not only physical fitness but military preparedness as well. While providing the Poles with their usual outlets for commemoration, Galicia also proved to be the one place where these paramilitary organizations might be transformed—at least in the imagination of the commemorators—into the nuclei of national armies.

The anniversaries celebrated in 1913–14, the last before the outbreak of world war, provide insight into various movements and desiderata regarding the nation's future. By superimposing the insurrectionary past on a rapidly changing present—by connecting the living and the dead—these commemorations helped to set the stage for Polish military exploits during World War I. These final commemorations marked the transition from the now traditional celebration of national anniversaries to the accumulation of new deeds worthy of commemoration in the future.

PREPARING FOR COMBAT,
OR THE REVENGE OF THE VETERANS

The next major celebratory milestone after the Grunwald festivities of 1910 was the fiftieth anniversary of the January Insurrection of 1863–64. That Poles in the Kingdom of Poland had revolted in the early 1860s illustrates the maxim of the danger of a little reform. In the early 1860s, Tsar Alexander II's penchant for reforms had emboldened his Polish subjects to press for change. A series of patriotic demonstrations, funerals, and anniversary celebrations set a new tone in the public sphere and prompted the tsarist authorities to make some concessions to the Poles. The reforms, combined with repressive measures, ultimately proved unpalatable, however, and in January 1863 a group of conspirators decided to initiate guerrilla war.

The January Insurrection ultimately proved to be a failure. The underground National Government directing the Polish efforts, armed with its own seal and offices and run by an invisible network of conspirators, proved no match for the Russian army. The insurrection resulted in the deaths of the most dedicated Polish cadres, the exile of thousands more to Siberia, and it caused Russia to complete the transformation of the separate Polish kingdom into a Russian province. Only over the course of the next decades were Poles able to recover, slowly and incompletely, from those tremendous setbacks.

That the January Insurrection became a major national celebration in Galicia in 1913 was paradoxical. That subject had been taboo in certain circles for the last fifty years. The January Insurrection was the especial bugbear of the Cracow conservatives, who could not stomach any kind of Polish conspiracy. In the words of one observer, "where the year 1863 was concerned, no word of condemnation seemed sharp enough" to them.[1] Their principled censure had kept past attempts to commemorate the insurrectionary past in Cracow small and guaranteed surveillance by the police, who made note even of church services commemorating the insurrection.[2] Not only conservatives were wary of glorifying insurrection, however. Many Poles continued to fear that another half-baked, inept attempt at insurrection would set the nation back further.

Yet the January Insurrection was the formative experience of a whole generation. Its veterans had suffered ever since for their support of the failed endeavor; conservatives, positivists, and tri-loyalists questioned the approach, means, and sanity of the democrats and romantics who had initiated it. In a way, thus, the large public anniversary celebration of the January Insurrection represented a kind of revenge of the insurrectionaries: the message that they had been trying to keep alive, that Poland needed to be fought for, had not perished.

This sea change was made possible by new circumstances that helped to alter attitudes toward the idea of Poles in arms. The Falcons' participation in the Grunwald celebration of 1910 already hinted at this new development. This resemblance of the Falcons to a military force was not a coincidence contrived especially for the festivities. Support for movements that not only strengthened but trained bodies had been spurred on by developments that predated the Grunwald celebration. These included worsening relations between Ukrainians and Poles in Galicia. At the dawn of the twentieth century, Polish nationalists made clear their discomfort with the growth of Ukrainian national consciousness in eastern Galicia. They opposed plans that would expand educational opportunities for Ukrainians, particularly at the high school or university level, and condemned universal, equal suffrage because it would have an adverse affect on the Polish minority in the east. What resulted was Galician civil war, to a great extent fought by the young intelligentsia of both nations at the University of Lwów. In 1907, Ukrainian students demanded the right to be sworn in as students in their own language; this demand unrequited, they occupied the main administrative building, wreaking havoc on signs of Polish control over the university. As a result of their actions and immediate arrest, five students received short prison terms; these soon began a hunger strike. Rising tensions, in part fed by international press reactions and their repercussions, led to violence. In the spring of 1908, a young Ukrainian socialist, Myroslav Sichyns'kyi, assassinated the Galician viceroy, Andrzej Potocki.[3]

The message of Sichyns'kyi's act was clear to Polish Galicians: Poles would have to defend themselves. Less than a month after Potocki's assassination, the authorities approved the statute of a new Polish organization, the Bartosz Squads (Drużyny Bartoszowe). Formed by one of the nationalist splinter groups, with financial assistance from the east Galician conservatives known as the Podolians, the squads were designed to strengthen the Polish element in east Galicia. While the original statute gave pride of place to gymnastics exercises and firefighting readiness, it also made room for celebrations of national holidays and other educational initiatives. The organizers sought to continue the work begun in the 1894 celebrations of the Battle of Racławice, of "plac[ing] Poland in the heart of the peasant," by drawing a connection between national pride and local customs.[4] The focus on distinct regional characteristics, ironically, resulted in the Bartosz Squads resembling their competition: the Ukrainian Sich associations (founded in 1900, outlawed in 1903, but relegalized in 1908 by Potocki's successor, Michał Bobrzyński).[5] Both Sich and Bartosz Squads served as means for Galician peasants to see themselves less as "the emperor's people" and more as Poles and Ukrainians. Before long, they would become offensive as well as defensive weapons.

While the situation inside Galicia prompted these developments in associational life, an international event further altered Polish perceptions. This was the annexation of Bosnia and Herzegovina by Austria-Hungary in October 1908. Although Austria-Hungary had occupied and administered Bosnia and Herzegovina since 1878, the seizure of these lands—counter to the provisions of the Berlin Congress of 1898—was designed to weaken the position of independent Serbia, perceived as the Piedmont of the South Slavs (Yugoslavs) and dependent upon Russia for support. An international crisis ensued, as Russia protested the annexation and prepared itself for a military confrontation. That Germany declared itself on the side of Austria-Hungary convinced the Russians to back off, and war eventually was averted—not before the threat of war captured the Polish imagination, spawning a plethora of rumors and speculation that conservatives tried to dispel.[6]

The work of the local "firefighters" did not prevent Poles from preparing for the eventuality of European war. With the specter of armed conflict looming (and the chance at regaining independence apparently so close), various Polish factions in Galicia found it expedient to downplay partisan differences and seek a common denominator for joint operation in the case of war. It happened that Viceroy Bobrzyński and various socialist groups within Galicia shared a common goal of gaining Polish independence through a political alliance with the Habsburgs. While socialists of both the Galician PPSD and the PPS Revolutionary Faction (the wing of the Polish Socialist Party most interested in Polish independence) saw in Austria and Germany potential allies en route to Polish independence, this political orientation is associated primarily with the figure of Józef Piłsudski.[7]

Piłsudski's view of the future was based on his assessment of the recent past. The failure of revolution in 1904–1906 and the experience of the PPS's fighting squads proved to the socialist leader that his party was incapable of leading the Poles to freedom. He devised a new strategy by which Poles could benefit from conflict in Europe, predicated on his belief that Russian Poland would become a battlefield. Piłsudski concluded that the left bank of the Vistula River (as opposed to the fortified right bank) would be the proper place of entry for Polish troops; that their arrival would inspire massive numbers of volunteers—the makings of a Polish army—to sign up; and that these forces would have to be led by officers trained in the one place where Polish activities of this sort were feasible: Galicia.[8] What was needed, thus, was an independent military-type organization that would prepare cadres for war—a paramilitary organization.[9] This led to the creation in June 1908 of a secret organization called the Union for Active Struggle (Związek Walki Czynnej). Staffed for the most part by youth of a socialist or radical-populist bent, at home and abroad, it sought to prepare for a future armed uprising against the tsarist regime.[10]

As a result of growing international tensions, legal paramilitary organizations proliferated during the next several years. The secret Union for Active Struggle spawned two separate legal societies, the Riflemen's Union and the Rifleman Society, founded in Lwów and Cracow in April and December of 1910. Ostensibly these were sport and gymnastics organizations (the Polish equivalent of *Jungschützenvereine*), although they were allowed privileges of which the secret Union for Active Struggle could only dream: the use of military shooting ranges and permission to hold exercises and lectures as well as obtain arms and ammunition. Before long, other new organizations received official Galician approval, while preexisting organizations such as the Bartosz Squads modified their statutes to allow for paramilitary operations. Ukrainians likewise took their cue from Piłsudski. Toward the end of 1913, the numerous Ukrainian Sich were transformed into a military youth organization, the Sich Riflemen (Sichovi Striltsi). To avoid sparking any objections to a Ukrainian paramilitary group, the leader of the

Sich, Kyrylo Trylovs'kyi, simply translated the statute of the Polish "Rifle-man" into Ukrainian for his group, thus guaranteeing official authorization (since the Polish version had been approved by the authorities).[11]

In Piłsudski's conception, the new focus on armed struggle was part of a larger strategy to regain Polish statehood. An informer's account of a secret meeting in Cracow at the end of December 1911 at which Piłsudski was present provides insights into the mentality of the period.[12] While discussion of plans to translate the remains of Słowacki to the Wawel and those of the writer Maria Konopnicka to Skałka suggests some continuity with the nation-building impulses of the past, the main thrust of the meeting seemed to be in a new direction. Those present advocated fighting—literally—for Poland (*wywalczyć Polskę*). The preparations involved preparing parallel underground institutions—legislature, executive, treasury, army, and the like—for that future state.[13] Part of this program was realized the following summer, when a diverse group of Polish party leaders voted to create the Polish Military Treasury (Polski Skarb Narodowy), which would subsidize military preparations such as military courses, publications, and the like. This coordinated effort seemed to bode well for Polish paramilitary development, which soon gained funds from Poles all over the world, most significantly from the New World.[14] Interestingly, the Russian government seemed to have a better sense of the significance of these new developments than did the Austrian authorities, as seen from this comment by the Russian minister of the interior: "the political center of the Polish question currently lies not in the Kingdom [of Poland], but in Galicia. In the Kingdom, everything is peaceful; in Galicia, however, everything is boiling: there riflemen divisions are being organized half-openly and openly under the leadership of Józef Piłsudski," he added, "whom we foolhardedly allowed to escape from prison."[15]

PIŁSUDSKI AND
THE LESSONS OF 1863

The rise of Polish paramilitary organizations at this time is related to an early but significant impulse to celebrate the fiftieth anniversary of the January Insurrection. Even the formation of the treasury did not pass without reference to this legacy: as one participant in the congress stated, it "would not be the nucleus of . . . a National Government, but would be a swallow foreshadowing it."[16] The National Government had been the organization that proclaimed the insurrection on January 22, 1863, and coordinated the actions of the insurrectionaries.

In the period immediately following the creation of the Union for Active Struggle, Józef Piłsudski engaged in a close study of the history of the

January Insurrection and military history in general, the results of which he shared with the general public on numerous occasions in 1912, 1913, and 1914.[17] (He himself sought to learn from experiences of previous insurrectionists and military leaders, for, although he served as military commander of the rifleman groups in Lwów and Cracow, the PPS leader had no formal military training.) While not as broadly public as commemorative parades, Piłsudski's lectures in a way inaugurated the 1913 anniversary year. Piłsudski was making a name for himself as one who spoke in a clear, logical fashion, with "an uncommon strength of conviction and directness of expression," which contrasted favorably with the impressions left by many commemorative speakers.[18] He was a sought-after lecturer and took advantage of opportunities to reach people through this medium of communication. His lectures on the January Insurrection also set the tone for presentations given by other similarly minded Poles in this period, for example, at a series of summer courses offered in Zakopane in 1913, which were heavily attended by Poles from the Russian Empire.[19]

While no written trace remains of many of his speeches, we do have stenographic notes from Piłsudski's series of ten lectures at the prestigious School of Social and Political Science in Cracow in 1912 on the January Insurrection, later published as *A Military History of the January Insurrection*.[20] Piłsudski's keen eye for military and organizational detail was evident in the lectures. These were commemorative lectures, as Piłsudski himself commented: "the fiftieth anniversary [of the January Insurrection] is approaching and I would like to contribute to the celebration of this anniversary."[21] He set out to provide a systematic and objective evaluation of the historical evidence available from the Insurrection of 1863, beginning with the preconditions that inspired Poles to revolt and concluding with the insurrection's collapse in April 1864. In his analysis of the technical and organizational foundations of the insurrection, Piłsudski singled out two institutions that, according to him, facilitated the conduct of the insurrection and became a source of pride: the officers' training school in Genoa (later in Cuneo), attended by a number of the Polish insurrectionaries, and the underground National Government, already in place before the onset of the insurrection. These clearly inspired the military leader to found his own training ground (the riflemen organizations) and see the need for political centralization—something recognized by others as well. For, not long after war broke out in the Balkans in October 1912, the Provisional Commission of Confederated Independence Parties (Komisja Tymczasowa Skonfederowanych Stronnictw Niepodległościowych, or KTSSN) was created, bringing together working-class parties, populists, and the progressive intelligentsia.[22] With Piłsudski and his friends at the helm, the KTSSN was to serve as an umbrella organization that could coordinate a Polish response to further developments—that is, metamorphose into that longed-for National Government.

While these and other points of Piłsudski's analysis underscore his practical assessment of the Insurrection of 1863–64, the speaker also wished to convey to his audience his emotional assessment. This he saved for the very end of the final lecture of the ten-part series. Piłsudski emphasized that he was not one of the critics of the insurrection who considered it a crime against the Polish nation. He believed that it had not been fought in vain, that it could, and should, provide a lesson for the new generation. Indeed, Piłsudski said that he wished "to build a bridge between the current generation and the generation of 1863."[23] Piłsudski perceived Polish history as one long continuum, a fateful yet glorious series of ups and downs that could not conquer the hardy nation. Despite the loss of statehood, the Poles retained their unique position in world history by remaining faithful to their nation and maintaining their "moral force." Piłsudski appeared intent on righting the course of Polish history: having absorbed its lessons, he intended to complete the Insurrection of 1863 successfully.

THE LIVING AND THE DEAD: REMEMBERING THE JANUARY INSURRECTION

By the fiftieth anniversary of the January Insurrection in 1913, thus, Poles had undergone major changes in their political outlook. War had begun in the Balkans, paramilitary groups proliferated in Galicia, and the future held the promise of change. The threat of impending European war cast a new shadow upon the Polish past, particularly its insurrectionary legacy. Half a century had passed since the January Insurrection. Would the festivities amount to more than a dutiful recounting of a painful moment in Polish history?

The time seemed right for Poles to remind the world of their past and potential military prowess. The Balkan wars and the creation of the new state of Albania gave the nation hope, while the inroads made into Ottoman-controlled territory suggested that the conventions governing international politics were not as rigid as they had seemed. "In such moments," mulled the editors of one Cracow paper, "the heroism of deeds . . . may remind the world of the name of Poland." But, importantly, the Poland to be remembered was "not that which wallows in penitential dust, but that which, over the corpses of its oppressors, striking in the ignominious signs of tsarist autocracy, rises from the dust of oblivion to avenge its injuries, to head towards the dawning daybreak of Freedom."[24] A commemorative medal from this anniversary year encapsulates this active stance: we see a youth straining to free the bowed Polonia, her arms in stocks (figure 7.1).

Fig. 7.1 Commemorative medal for the fiftieth anniversary of the
January Insurrection. *By W. Jastrzębowski; photo courtesy of the
National Museum, Kraków, Numismatic Bureau.*

The fiftieth anniversary celebration was different from previous commemorations in a number of ways. For example, festivities were planned throughout the anniversary year.[25] The winter months had never been favored for commemorations, as they complicated travel plans for guests coming from a distance. Still, January was not ignored. Theatricals, lectures, and formal gatherings would be scheduled around the January 22 date, while various congresses (complete with their own special events) would be scheduled during the warmer months of summer and early fall. Certain activities reached an even broader audience. Competitions for songs, dramatic works, historical monographs, and popular books allowed Poles from the three zones to provide their own interpretations of the insurrection and its significance. An anniversary exhibition commemorating the 1863 insurrection would open abroad, in Rapperswil, then travel to Lwów, where the Palace of Art (familiar to us from the 1894 exposition and restored expressly for this purpose) would house the tens of thousands of exhibits. The mass of memorabilia—uniforms, banners, battle plans, photographs, documents with the seal of the National Government, as well as artifacts from the period of Siberian exile of these veterans—brought home the reality of war to the visitors.[26]

The anniversary was to provide the organizing principle for the year's events. "Each collective endeavor, each initiative of general significance," according to the committee organizing the commemoration, "should take place in the entire jubilee year under the sign and slogan of the January Insurrection."[27] Some programs were strategically scheduled so as to coincide with commemorative events. As in 1910, the Falcons would hold their jubilee in the summer, to coincide with the opening of the exhibition of memorabilia from 1863. A congress of Polish singers and festival of Polish music would follow. Finally, veterans of 1863 "from all of Poland" would be invited to attend a congress in September. The main committee in Lwów saw its goal as "the creation of conditions that would give the jubilee celebration a nation-wide character, without regard to border cordons and posts [*bez względu na kordony i słupy graniczne*]."[28] There was also a sense that 1913 should be a year of taking stock. Numerous congresses scheduled for Lwów, the main commemorative site for this anniversary, were to demonstrate the progress made by the nation over the past fifty years. The various parts of the commemoration would provide a "reckoning of the work of the generation which, after the war, persevered in a different battle, no less difficult, augmenting forces and detachments for the great national future."[29]

Given the anti-Russian nature of the January Insurrection, it may come as a surprise that the moving force behind these commemorations came from the National Democratic camp. Franciszek Rawita-Gawroński, Ernest

Adam, Witold Lewicki, and Tadeusz Dwernicki occupied the main offices within the committee, apparently in order to control as much as possible what might be perceived as the anti-Russian nature of the event. To be sure, the composition of the honorary presidium relied heavily on local (Lwów) dignitaries less wedded to a particular ideology: Bishop Władysław Bandurski, Professor Oswald Balzer, parliamentarian and president of the National Council in Lwów Tadeusz Cieński, university president Ludwik Finkel, Lwów mayor Józef Neumann, and Princess Jadwiga Sapieżyna.[30] Together, both groups allayed fears of the authorities in Vienna, who worried that the Riflemen might be in charge. That the nationalists, who did not wish to antagonize Russia, were in charge of the commemoration seemingly guaranteed that the anniversary would avoid provoking cross-border conflict.

The main celebrations of the 1863 anniversary were scheduled for Lwów. This was not because the organizing committee was based in the Galician capital. Rather, the honor to be the "central point of the celebration" reflected Lwów's connection to the insurrectionary past.[31] Of all Polish cities in this period, Lwów had provided the most congenial asylum for veterans of the January Insurrection. As early as the mid-1860s, a symbolic cross in honor of those who had fallen was erected at Łyczakowski Cemetery; once veterans began to return home after Siberian exile (from 1867), various individuals and organizations came to their assistance.[32]

For the most part, the Lwów festivities at the end of January 1913 followed the time-honored tradition of church services and sermons, lectures, meetings, choral performances, and plays. Noteworthy this time was the presence of aged veterans: for example, the most moving part of one assembly was deemed to be the appearance onstage of Ludomir Benedyktowicz. The armless veteran had made a career for himself as an artist, using a metal device attached to his limbs to hold a brush or a pencil. Here, he recited a poem he had written, after which the audience showered him with flowers and applause. And, while the idea of self-sacrifice in the name of the nation was brought home, there was no reason for it to be perceived as an exclusively male virtue. Three women—Henryka Pustowojtówna, Marya Piotrowiczowa, and Zofia Dobronoki—fighting alongside male soldiers during the 1863 insurrection represented one extreme example of women's engagement in national issues. Fifty years later, women wrote booklets and plays—and, in the case of Marya Raczyńska's *Cienie* (Shades), won awards in the anniversary competition. They also took on other, perhaps more traditional duties: the General Committee of Polish Women called for all women to sell commemorative pins and transparencies as well as participate in the festivities, and the women's branch of the People's School Society scheduled its own celebration.[33]

What made the fiftieth anniversary of the January Insurrection so unusual, however, was its proximity to the past. A mere fifty years had passed, in contrast with the centuries separating so many of the anniversaries of the last decades from their sources of inspiration. The idea of national continuity, thus, took on a peculiar significance, as veterans could be portrayed as "living monuments to the sublimity of the collective Polish spirit."[34] In 1913, the nation undertook to honor these "living monuments." Feeling collectively responsible for the last Poles who fought for the nation's freedom, commemoration organizers sought donations for a veterans' home that would provide housing and care for these aged warriors. To this end, they offered inexpensive commemorative memorabilia for sale. The cause elicited a universal response, as seen from the paper trail of requests from one branch of the organizing committee. In the first weeks following the announcement, requests came from several dozen locales and a wide variety of organizations: schools, fire departments, TSL reading rooms, Falcons, and the clergy and religious orders. The nation had a responsibility for those "who, standing today above the grave, are still the only eyewitnesses of the last efforts for a better future for the nation."[35]

Memory and history intersected most poignantly at the prime spot for commemoration: Łyczakowski Cemetery, the place where the living encountered the dead. One reason why the choice of Lwów was most apt for the main festivities in 1913 was that a special section of the cemetery had been reserved for veterans of the January Insurrection. This "hill of the 1863–4 insurrectionaries" was the most famous section of Łyczakowski Cemetery at that time. It was also the greatest collection of insurrectionary tombs from the January Insurrection anywhere. Close to 140 veterans already lay there in 1913.[36]

What the Wawel was to Cracow, Łyczakowski Cemetery was to Lwów. Redolent of the past, its romantic, forested location at the far eastern side of the cemetery provided a moving site for a celebration. In January 1913, the commemoration of the insurrection was held at dusk. A crowd of about ten thousand made its way through the cemetery, up the winding alleys that led to the remote hill covered with iron crosses—the insurrectionaries' graves, each lit with candles. The darkness awash in candlelight, flickering like the souls of the dead, must have recalled the traditional All Souls' celebration. Yet, instead of honoring family members, the participants commemorated a collective hero: the Polish nation in armed struggle.[37]

Particularly well lit was the distinctive tomb of Szymon Wizunas Szydłowski at the entrance to the insurrectionaries' hill. Here was a monument to the man, known to all of patriotic Lwów and to the collectivity he represented. In his youth a tsarist officer and apparently descended from the princely family of Światopełk-Mirski, Wizunas had joined the insur-

Fig. 7.2 Wizunas's tomb in Łyczakowski Cemetery. Even today, one finds wreaths and candles at this site, now in Ukrainian L'viv. *Photo by Mary Baker.*

rection as the standard-bearer of the region of Witebsk (Vitsebsk).[38] When, after years of exile, he settled down in Lwów, the elderly veteran donated the precious, tattered banner in his care to the Lwów Society of Veterans of 1863. In turn, he was designated the standard-bearer of the veterans' organization for life. Wizunas became a potent symbol of the January Insurrection. Owing his survival to peasants, who cared for his wounds and hid him from the Russians during the insurrection, Wizunas donned traditional peasant garb at all public appearances in his capacity as standard-bearer. He, thus, was a latter-day Kościuszko, the incarnation of the slogan uniting the Polish nobility and folk.

In 1909, a monument was erected over Wizunas's grave, part of which consisted of granite tablets inscribed with the names of those who had perished in various battles in 1863–64 (see figure 7.2). The standard-bearer was immortalized in stone, not in words, "the figure of the putative nobleman in peasant coat, holding the banner of the Witebsk Land with the Eagle, Chase, and Archangel and pointing with his right hand the way to an independent Poland."[39] Like the banner, the monument depicted the coats-of-arms of the three parts of the pre-partition state: Poland proper (with the Polish eagle), Lithuania (the Chase, or knight on horseback), and Ruthenia (signified by its patron, Michael the Archangel). Doubtless this symbolism—of peasants with the nobility, and of a united Commonwealth—was not lost on the Leopoldians, who hoped for a future Poland that would embrace all social classes as well as all regions of the former state.

In this public celebration of the January Insurrection, the monument on Wizunas's grave was the first sight to greet pilgrims to this part of the cemetery. After a long, uphill procession along the winding lanes of the verdant cemetery park, the committee deposited a metal wreath and two laurel wreaths at the site; other organizations left theirs as well. Veterans, Falcons, scouts, committee members, and several thousand spectators gathered nearby. At dusk, under the light of lanterns, the committee vice president recalled Warsaw, summoning dark thoughts of their brothers still in bondage in the former Polish capital. Veterans made the trek as well, with one—a Mr. Webersfeld—speaking, as did the president of the Falcons, Ksawery Fischer. As the smoke from the lanterns and candles wafted upward, the group assembled sang "With the Smoke of Fires" (Z dymem pożarów) before returning to town. There, speeches were made in front of the Mickiewicz monument. Many took part in a dinner in honor of over one hundred veterans assembled there.[40]

The connection between the living and the dead was underscored in other ways. Liberals emphasized the connection between that past and the present: "what we celebrate in this act is nothing other than the demonstration of the continuity of our developmental line. . . ."[41] Poles in arms were seen to represent a positive side of the national character, one that allowed the nation to survive the partitions. This image, and such statements, received much publicity. The discourse of 1913 focused heavily on the military side of the insurrection, repeatedly referred to as armed struggle or armed battle. January 22 became the "anniversary of the announcement of an armed movement."[42] Nationalists such as Stanisław Grabski emphasized that "the army of 1863 was already a national army in the full sense of the word, it was the *nation in arms* [*było narodem uzbrojonym*]."[43]

The emphasis on armed Poles manifested itself more concretely as well. On January 22, 1913, the link between the insurrectionaries and the paramilitary formations was completed. After his speech before a working-class audience in the town hall, Piłsudski led his riflemen through the town to place a wreath at Wizunas's tomb in the Łyczakowski Cemetery: "This was the first marching past of uniformed Polish divisions through Lwów—the first such march from the time of the November Insurrection."[44] How controversial an act this was is indicated by the careful silence the conservative Cracow paper maintained: it did not even mention Piłsudski's name as a lecturer in the town hall, let alone note the march of his riflemen.[45]

The Falcon jubilee, as well as Falcon and scout participation in the various celebrations, also maintained the image of an armed nation. The first large military exercises of the Falcons took place at the jubilee in early July 1913. Reportedly over eighty thousand (more likely eight thousand!) Falcons participated. Like a regiment in training, they camped overnight on a hill near Hołosko (in the rain) and, after additional Falcons arrived in the wee hours of the morning from west Galicia, took part in a "battle" until ten o'clock. Exercises for the public were held that same day in the afternoon. The event impressed viewers, with one newspaper complimenting the Falcons on how fresh they looked that afternoon despite the lack of a night's sleep, another gushing about "the Falcon army."[46] Falcons also took part in the September 7 celebration: during a congress of 1863 veterans, the horseback divisions of the Falcons and scouts performed before a crowd of several thousand.

OTHER CELEBRATIONS, OTHER TRADITIONS

Celebrations of the anniversary of the January Insurrection were not restricted to Lwów, although those in the Galician capital were the largest and most successful. In Poznań, festivities in the Poznań Bazaar were interrupted by police commissioners, who declared the meeting a public one—and, thus, to be conducted in German. Only Polish youth escaped police supervision, singing national songs at the Mickiewicz monument and managing to disperse before the police arrived.[47]

Cracow's celebration involved the usual preparations by the municipal authorities, university, and other groups. Perhaps the city was losing its grip over celebrations, as even the organizers had some doubts whether various aspects, such as the traditional procession, would succeed.[48] Here, too, a military presence was felt: the horseback division of Falcons participated in the parade together with Cracow and Podgórze Falcon squads.[49] One newspaper nonetheless castigated the organizers, claiming that a "false chord of insincerity, lack of will and shameful submission to the orders and 'directions' of servile elements in the province" marred the celebration.[50] Other criticisms of the traditional celebratory mode came from an unexpected quarter: the folk. The popular press commented negatively on the patriotic platitudes. The celebrations gave rise to discussions of the celebrations and of the anniversary.

Peasants celebrated the January Insurrection variously. In some places, such as in the mountainous region to the south of Cracow, peasant veterans spoke of their exploits. For example, a Mr. Ciszek of Czarny Dunajec read his memoirs in several locales in the vicinity. Yet others demonstrated their connection to the larger nation in a different way. To commemorate the January Insurrection, the Zakopane division of the Riflemen's Union held night exercises on January 24–25. Battle practice was obviously preferred over speech making.[51] The popular press drew a direct connection between the anniversary and the new paramilitary organizations. The message was clear: "Let the fiftieth anniversary of the last insurrection find all of us in the ranks of the Riflemen."[52] Given the wide reach of *Przyjaciel Ludu*— twenty-three thousand copies and at least twice as many readers—such exhortations could have an impact on the Polish peasantry.[53]

Those in the populist camp also sought to reinforce this connection of the peasantry and the broader Polish nation through yet another commemoration, that of the Chochołów Insurrection of 1846.[54] This was not the famous Galician massacre, in which peasants turned on the "Poles" (landlords and nobility), but a kind of peasant version of the larger Insurrection of 1863; its celebration underscored the reliability and the readiness of the peasantry, certainly of those from the highlands, to fight as part of the larger nation. That the sixty-seventh anniversary of this other insurrection should be celebrated in 1913 can be attributed to increased national work in the highlands since the Grunwald anniversary. A highlanders' union (*Związek Podhalan* or *Związek Górali*) had been founded, its goal being to work and fight "not only for the future of the mountain people, but for the future of Poland."[55] It held congresses in 1911, 1912, and 1913 and also sponsored the celebration of the Chochołów insurrection, which was scheduled as an extraordinary congress. That same year, highlanders began to create Podhale Squads.[56] Their establishment marked a change in focus from agitation and celebration to military exercises and civic culture.[57]

Those celebrating the Chochołów anniversary on February 23, 1913, relied on various images to establish the leadership role of the highlanders. The famous Tatra legend of King Boleslas and his knights asleep under the mountains was modified to imply that the knights were the Podhale folk, an independent peasantry not easily swayed by influence peddlers: "For while the folk in the lowlands in '46 allowed themselves to be lured by evil promptings, our mountaineers followed good inspiration: the Polish Weal against oppressors."[58] The mountaineers who reached for their scythes to chase the Germans out of the country saved the honor of the Polish peasant in general.[59] A good example could be found in the highlands: "the figure of a peasant-Pole, a peasant-patriot, nationally and educationally enlightened . . . a new peasant race . . . of heroes" that would order the rest of the peasantry to follow in its footsteps.[60] In the same vein, a proclamation was made by those gathered on the anniversary on February 22: all Poles were asked to "desist from partisan battles and concentrate all forces in striving to liberate the Polish nation from the shackles of bondage."[61] The highlanders had begun to advise—or direct—the nation. Still a distinct group in the early twentieth century, highlanders were making the transition from regional particularism to a larger Polish consciousness. The celebration of the Chochołów anniversary was a way for them to claim their larger patrimony, the Poland for which their ancestors had fought—and for which their twentieth-century descendants would soon be called to fight.[62]

PONIATOWSKI:
THE ULTIMATE NOBLE SACRIFICE

At the final celebration of the January Insurrection in the first days of September, participants in a meeting of the Mutual Assistance Society decided that they would take part in another celebration the following month.[63] For fast approaching was the centennial of the death of Prince Józef Poniatowski. The leader of the army of the Duchy of Warsaw (the Polish political entity under French protection, 1807–15), Poniatowski fought valiantly and faithfully under Napoleon, preferring to drown in the Elster River near Leipzig than surrender.

Falling within this year of national remembrance, the anniversary of Poniatowski's death can be treated in part as a continuation of the 1863 celebration. Although the anniversary festivities themselves had a relatively short gestation period,[64] the Poniatowski commemoration highlighted a growing trend in Polish history that had important repercussions for views of the insurrectionary past, particularly the initiatives—such as the Polish Legions of General Jan Henryk Dąbrowski who fought for and with Napoleon—of the early nineteenth century.[65]

The commemoration of October 1913 spoke to more than just the Polish nation. The significance of the Wars of Liberation and the Battle of Leipzig was not lost on those who had fought Napoleon. They celebrated the anniversary of the victory over the French with a full year of festivities.[66] In 1913, a new monument, the Völkerschlachtdenkmal, was dedicated in Leipzig, with forty-three thousand members of the German gymnastics association taking part in festive relay races to the city from various points in the German Empire.[67]

Polish perceptions of the Napoleonic Wars and the Battle of Leipzig naturally differed from those of the Germans. Prussians celebrated the Battle of Leipzig as a national holiday. Having fought on the losing side, one might expect the Poles to have assessed the battle more negatively. Yet they had reasons to associate the Napoleonic era with Polish greatness, for it upset the arrangement of the Polish partitions that had wiped the state off the map of Europe. Had it not been for the existence of the Duchy of Warsaw as well as the Polish legions that fought Napoleon's battles, the Congress of Vienna in all likelihood would never have recreated a Polish state. Furthermore, Poles saw moral victory on their side. In their view, Napoleon was a "symbol of protest against today's Europe, . . . a voice of the past crying out that thrones based upon the oppression of nations are fragile."[68] Nor did they find the outcome of the so-called Wars of Liberation encouraging, as elsewhere they led not to constitutional monarchies but to political reaction.

Positive interpretations of this period were fostered by a new force in Polish historiography. In the first years of the twentieth century, a new school of history began to displace the pessimistic Cracow school. To a great extent this was the achievement of a professor at the University of Lwów, Szymon Askenazy. Askenazy has been seen as a kind of spiritual leader of the Polish freedom fighters of this period.[69] At the Third Congress of Polish Historians in 1900, the Lwów historian had addressed the need to bring the study of Polish history from the Middle Ages and pre-partition period into the modern era. This was a controversial position, for the historical profession still considered events of the nineteenth century to be contemporary history, not removed enough from the present to approach in objective fashion. Askenazy and his students researched more contemporary history, with the master writing on the Polish Legions under Napoleon, the insurrection of 1830–31, and of course Poniatowski.[70]

Askenazy's campaign for informed scholarship on more modern events was not prompted solely by the lack of coverage on these subjects. The historian took an activistic approach to history and sought to engage society more deeply in the fate of the nation. To this end, he believed, history and historians should render service to the nation.[71] Askenazy had specific ideas about what kind of service the historical profession needed to render. For example, he was concerned that the Poles under Russian rule would conclude that a Polish state could not exist unless it were linked in some way with Russia. "It seemed to me necessary to attack that fiction," he wrote.[72]

Askenazy not only thought that Poland had a chance for an independent existence; he was convinced that the nation needed to retain its identification with its chivalric past. This he tried to convey in his biography of Poniatowski. I should note that Askenazy's biography was not read by a narrow audience of specialists: by 1913 the book was in its third edition, which suggests a broader readership.[73] Askenazy presented the nobleman in all his humanity. This did not stop him from calling him "Poland's darling," "a flawless citizen" (*obywatel bez skazy*), terms he used in a commemorative lecture, which was published for audiences in Russian Poland as well as Galicia.[74] Perhaps to counter the trite patriotic verbiage that multiplied with every celebration, Askenazy contended that Poniatowski "showed how hard it really was to be a good Pole; that it is not enough to want to be one—one must know how [to be one]."[75] By choosing to face the rushing waters of the Elster over retreating and surrendering to Alexander I of Russia, who doubtless would have found a post for him, the Polish military leader refused to put personal gain over the nation's fate. He truly was a symbol of "national honor," as Askenazy declared.[76] As such, Poniatowski was revered by the nation, resulting in a cult of the general and his burial in the Wawel.

The preexisting cult of the Polish military leader, together with the approaching anniversary of his death, suggests why Poniatowski might be a figure worthy of particular attention in the fall of 1913. It also demonstrates why the anniversary festivities centered upon Cracow, the site of his burial. In a way, the Poles had come full circle in their celebration of the past: the first important commemoration of the previous century had been the 1817 translation of Poniatowski's remains to the Wawel crypt.

There were other reasons why Poniatowski would be attractive to a number of Poles at this time. For those for whom history was the story of influential individuals, the Polish general clearly was a significant historical actor. If the anniversary celebration of the 1863 insurrection proved to be the revenge of the insurrectionaries, and Chochołów strengthened the national image of the highlanders, the celebration of Poniatowski featured another segment of society: the cream of the nobility, the influential Polish aristocracy.

This example of a nobleman's dedication to the cause was valued by the Cracow conservatives. *Czas* declared, "of all our heroes, he is the most Polish."[77] In part, this reflects Askenazy's own scholarship, which singled out Poniatowski as the national character incarnate, more lovable than Kościuszko's "stern virtue."[78] His youth spent in Vienna, Poniatowski was introduced to his homeland by his uncle, Stanislas Augustus Poniatowski, the last king of Poland. The nephew resigned his position in the royal army upon learning of his uncle's accession to the Targowica confederation; like many of his generation and position, the dashing nobleman spent the next years in dissolute living in Prussian-occupied Warsaw. Returning to military affairs under Kościuszko, Poniatowski distinguished himself as general of the newly formed Duchy of Warsaw, annexing Western Galicia to its hold-

Ksiąźę Józef Poniatowski
1813–1913.

Fig. 7.3 Transparency from the Poniatowski celebration "Prince Józef Poniatowski, 1813–1913." These colorful transparent images were placed in windows and illuminated for the benefit of passersby. *Photo courtesy of the Library of the Historical Museum of the City of Cracow.*

ings after the Battle of Raszyn. The Galician campaign led to his rehabilitation. And, with his death at the Battle of Leipzig, "this son and nephew of the Poniatowskis ma[de] of himself high expiation for the [sins of the] previous generation."[79] That a wealthy and well-connected aristocrat could make the ultimate sacrifice for his nation was something in which the descendants of the Targowica traitors could take pride.[80] The ancient chivalric tradition was incarnate in this "first prince of Poland," who, while gallant, young, and handsome, nonetheless demonstrated what the Polish spirit was capable of.[81] The Cracow conservatives also placed a premium on Poniatowski's fidelity to Napoleon and his cause, perhaps with a subtext for the pro-Austrian political orientation of many Galicians in this period.

The festivities in Cracow on October 18 and 19 built upon the military theme already prevalent that year. The first day of the commemoration resembled many other similar celebrations, with a gathering at Jagiellonian University and theatricals. At a session in the municipal theater, Professor

Ignacy Chrzanowski cited the prince several times in his speech. The sentence "The time has come for the Polish army to become useful for the country" may have had additional resonance for listeners, many of whom were involved in paramilitary operations. The professor likewise mentioned Poniatowski's contribution of restoring honor to the nation by quoting the oft-mentioned words attributed to him: "God entrusted me with the honor of the Poles, to him alone will I return it."[82] This latter was the message engraved on a commemorative coin produced on the occasion of the anniversary.

The festivities of the second day, the main day of commemoration, involved a number of paramilitary groups that had traveled to Cracow for the festivities.[83] The presence of nearly two thousand Falcons, six hundred scouts, three hundred members of the newly formed Podhale Squads (Drużyny Podhalańskie) in Nowy Targ, and one hundred Bartosz Squad members from the Bochnia district as well as two hundred fifty participants from the Tarnów district, other cities, Silesia, and the Poznań region was noted in the press.[84] The paramilitary groups took part in a relatively new aspect of Polish commemorations: night exercises. Participants were divided into two opposing sides. Each side carried out reconnaissance on horseback, and in the gray of morning the first shots were fired and a battle for a knoll known as Piaskowa Skała, near Borek Fałęcki, began. The victorious side occupied the knoll and dug trenches, thus holding its position. The exercise lasted from three until eight o'clock in the morning, after which the troops filed past Mayor Leo and Falcon president Turski en route to the Błonia field. The Błonia field had been readied for a field mass, with an altar erected in the form of an open tent made out of colorful carpets. This improvement over the public Grunwald celebration was due at least in part to the new (since 1911) occupant of the Cracow see, Prince-Bishop Adam Stefan Sapieha. At the Poniatowski celebration, the descendants of the old Polish nobility, in national dress, were out in full force. Delegates of the Bartosz Squads, scouts, and Falcons also assisted the clergy.

From the Błonia, the assembled delegations proceeded to the Wawel. At the head of the parade rode the Cracow fire chief, who for this occasion wore the full uniform of the Fourth Cavalry Regiment from 1809. He was followed by three hundred peasants on horseback, the horseback division of the Falcons, leading Falcons from the German and Austrian zones (twelve towns represented in the latter); Falcon Field Squads (from thirty-four locales); and around a thousand scouts. A group of about five hundred highlanders (men and women) bore a pine wreath with the inscription "From your ashes will come an avenger"—the type of sentiment we might expect from these new national activists. Half a company of Riflemen came on horseback, albeit without their weapons, which the authorities had ordered them to leave in a building at the racetrack. Another several dozen organi-

Po obchodzie ku czci ks. Józefa.

Skauci.   Strzelcy.

Fig. 7.4 "After the Celebration in Honor of Prince Józef," *Illustrowany Kurier Codzienny* no. 244 (1913). This is how the popular Cracow daily presented the event: Scouts on the left, Riflemen on the right, a standard-bearer at the center with the slogan "God save Poland"—clearly not as censurable a sentiment in 1913 as it had been in decades past.

zations, including gymnastic organizations from the Kingdom of Poland and Falcons from the Poznań region, a particularly extensive representation of agricultural societies from all over Galicia, and the traditional Cracow guilds and other local corporations, participated.

The sight of all the paramilitary troops in their uniforms (the Falcons and scouts also held exercises later at the racetrack) inspired much gushing on the part of the local dailies: it was said that "a Polish armed force for the first time presented itself massively." Those participating were called "modern Polish legions"—a reference to the insurrectionary history of the Napoleonic era.[85] The paramilitary forces had been awaited with great anticipation: "When numerous regiments and squads of young Poland preparing to assume, as the inheritance of their ancestors, the legacy of the national banner" pay homage at the tomb of "the last of the defenders of independent Poland, that moment will be a great strengthening of hearts, a renewal of the covenant with the spirit of the Fatherland, awaiting sacrifices from its sons."[86]

Yet this was not the first military celebration of Poniatowski this year. As befit the commemoration of Poland's most famous cavalry general, on

October 5 the Falcon horseback division commemorated him by organizing their first horseback competition for members from Cracow and Lwów, with awards given to the winners of various events. Prior to the competition a new Falcon banner for the Cracow division, featuring images of Our Lady of Częstochowa and the Polish eagle, was blessed in Wawel Cathedral. A special drill was prepared by the Lwów Falcons, dressed in uniforms of the First Cavalry Regiment of the Polish Army of 1830. Their charge with lances at full speed reportedly thrilled the crowds.[87]

In sum, the press wrote of the "extraordinary character" of the Poniatowski anniversary celebration: while homage was given to the Polish hero, the festivities included a "program of exercises of a military nature, which were to testify to the physical robustness of the nation."[88] The commemorations almost seemed an excuse for military exercises in some quarters.

They also afforded another occasion to provide positive examples for the young to emulate. Not all Poles, after all, had great faith in the Polish national character; some desperately wanted to nurture those traits that would prepare cadres better for the discipline of war—or find a leader who could do the same. That explains why Michał Sokolnicki, in his lecture on Prince Józef in Cracow on October 5, cast the military leader in accordance with twentieth-century needs. He depicted Poniatowski as a strong leader, trying to elucidate the source of his strength in order that others might become like him. At the same time, Sokolnicki thought that the nation had already found its leader of the future: a simple, strong Pole, like so many great sons of the nation, from the Lithuanian lands—Józef Piłsudski.[89]

A LAST "COMMEMORATION"
OF THE LAST INSURRECTION . . .

Despite appearances, the anniversary celebration of the January Insurrection was not quite finished in 1913. The insurrection, after all, did not end until 1864. In conjunction with this came what might be considered the most atypical celebration of this period—a military tribute, perhaps, to the insurrectionaries of the past as well as an attempt to carry to completion their aims.

This was made possible by the events of June 28, 1914. The heir to the Habsburg throne, Francis Ferdinand, and his wife picked a poor day to travel to Sarajevo. June 28 happened to be Vidovdan, the anniversary of the fourteenth-century battle of Kosovo Pole, a day of historic reckoning for the Serbs. The assassination of a Habsburg on such a day would certainly be perceived as a national deed. While this is not the place to discuss the convoluted calculations that led to the outbreak of the First World War, events over the next month turned the likelihood of war into certainty. On

August 2, Piłsudski obtained permission from the Austrian military authorities to begin the mobilization of his riflemen. The next day, Piłsudski formed the first company of cadres (*kompania kadrowa*) in Cracow.

In the wake of the recent celebrations of the Napoleonic era, this transformation of paramilitary organizations into genuine fighting forces recalled to mind the Polish legions of old. On August 4, Cracow mayor Juliusz Leo addressed the soldiers at their swearing in. Exhorting them to fight bravely, he said: "You are following the path of those whose name you inherit, the path of those, among whom for the first time rose the cry '[Poland] has not yet perished!' The knights of '31 and warriors of '63 are watching you. Be the heirs of their heroic blood!"[90] Leo obviously had attended numerous commemorations during his tenure as mayor. In these few sentences, he managed to invoke the legacy of three insurrectionary generations: the insurrectionaries of November and January as well as Dąbrowski's Polish Legions. The impending war brought other historic connections to the fore. That same day, the Podhale Squads command called upon Cracovians to fight against "Muscovy." The announcement read, "Do you remember Chochołów? Remember our grandfathers, who in 1846 rose up in arms to win independence for the Fatherland."[91] Echoes of the recently celebrated commemorations, thus, continued to resound.

On August 5, Austria-Hungary declared war on Russia, and Piłsudski was given permission to invade Russian Poland the following day. His company set off from the Riflemen training school at Oleandry (Cracow) to the Kingdom of Poland at dawn on August 6. Polish forces, thus, were the first to invade Russia. Piłsudski remained behind in Cracow to attend a meeting of the KSSN. He had an announcement to make: a National Government had been formed in Warsaw, and it demanded that the military command of the KSSN submit to it. Piłsudski asked that the KSSN give its approval.[92]

News of a National Government naturally brought to mind the January Insurrection, during which such an organization had coordinated the insurrectionary effort. Piłsudski's announcement, however, was bogus. No National Government had been formed, in Warsaw or elsewhere. Indeed, later that evening, Piłsudski approached Leon Wasilewski, asking him secretly to compose an announcement, dated "Warsaw, 3 August," and have a seal designed and made as well.[93] Piłsudski played on the Poles' knowledge of their own national history, which suggested that the outbreak of war could conceivably prompt a new generation of Poles to respond as had the generation of 1863. The military leader sought to put his own plans into action—the same plans presented in his *Military Geography of the Kingdom of Poland,* discussed earlier. Piłsudski intended to make history: he wanted to wage the battle fought in 1863 but win it.[94]

The timing of the invasion of the Polish forces proved fortuitous. Although August 5 marked the declaration of war against Russia by Austria-Hungary, it was also a date of importance in the history of the January Insurrection. Exactly fifty years earlier, the leaders of the National Government of 1863–64—Romuałd Traugutt, Rafał Krajewski, Józef Toczyński, Roman Żuliński, and Jan Jeziorański—had been hanged. Was it simply a coincidence that the Riflemen prepared to cross the Russian border that same night?

Doubtless preoccupied with plans for the invasion, Piłsudski seems not to have made mention of the anniversary.[95] Still, it did not go unnoticed among another group of Riflemen. Sokolnicki, who was in charge of Riflemen forces in Lwów, says that his memory was jogged by the daily newspaper, in which it was noted that a mass in memory of the slain leaders was scheduled for that morning. He ordered his company as well as the local Rifleman Squads to attend the service—the first real participation of the Riflemen in such celebrations, according to Sokolnicki: "So far we have not taken part in celebrations . . . not anniversaries and commemorations interested us, but modest work for future operations. . . . Now it is different . . . we are going to stand up to the enemy, we are going to fight . . . we thus have the right to honor those Poles who for the same cause suffered death."[96] The patriotic Bishop Bandurski received the armed forces enthusiastically. Sokolnicki observed that the Riflemen's attendance at the service had a positive effect on the attitudes of the Lwów public, which generally had been more supportive of the nationalist paramilitary organizations. No "show" or "holiday" army, the Riflemen had focused on practical matters, such as gaining the skills and materials needed for the job ahead of them. Still, they were hardly indifferent to the nation's past. These were, after all, the same riflemen who sang the patriotic 1863 insurrectionary hymn "Hey, Riflemen Together, above Us the White Eagle" ("Hej, strzelcy wraz, nad nami Orzeł Biały") upon their return to the Błonia field in Cracow after field exercises in April 1913.[97] Their identification with 1863 was undeniable.

Ultimately, whether the timing of the Polish troops' invasion of Russian Poland was a coincidence was unimportant. The foray of the Riflemen turned Legionnaires itself had commemorative significance. As Urbankowski notes, Piłsudski enlivened the legend of the January Insurrection, writing, as it were, a victorious epilogue, despite the fifty years separating the events.[98] The deed would forge a new link in the chain of Polish history. Before long, it would become part of the anniversary calendar, a legend of Polish efforts that single-handedly restored independence to the country. This first small force bore the seeds of the wartime legends to come: the legend of the Polish Legions, of the Polish Brigades (in particular, of Piłsudski's own First Brigade), and of Piłsudski himself. In the coming years, the identification of these Polish efforts during World War I with those of the insurrectionists of 1863–64 would be strengthened by speeches given by Piłsudski in 1919 and 1920; by his meetings with veterans; by his decision to award the first orders of Virtuti Militari on January 22, 1920; by allowing the veterans of the January Insurrection to wear the military uniform of the army of independent Poland.[99] In sum, August 6 initiated a new era, yet one hearkening back to the January Insurrection, defining itself in the terms of the other while extending, improving upon the legend of armed Poles striving for liberty.

PREPARING (FOR) THE FUTURE

Fraught with increasing international tension, the second decade of the twentieth century cast Polish commemorations of the January Insurrection and Prince Józef Poniatowski in a different light. Seizing the opportunity, the nascent paramilitary organizations in Galicia engaged in military exercises as well as demonstrated their physical and military prowess in front of the public. This new means of honoring the past reflected the challenge of the day: to prepare Poles for the eventuality of a world war that, pitting the partitioning powers against each other, could decide their fate.

The pre-1914 festivals served national military preparedness by providing the organizations with opportunities to demonstrate their skills, often in tandem with other such organizations, in the context of a celebration. Commemorations were the best kind of advertisement, providing both increased visibility and positive press coverage. By popularizing paramilitary organizations such as the Falcons, Bartosz Squads, and Podhale Squads, the festivities attracted new recruits. More broadly, they raised hopes: perhaps the Poles were able to become a more disciplined nation, to put the common good before individual comfort or profit.

The commemorations helped prepare Poles, mentally and physically, for war as well as gave evidence of the growing dedication to the national cause and concomitant acceptance of the eventuality of bodily harm or death. The nation was offered a number of heroes for emulation: the collective hero of the January Insurrection, evoked in the sea of iron crosses at the Łyczakowski Cemetery in Lwów; the highland peasant as hero, promoted by the highlanders themselves in their celebration of the sixty-seventh anniversary of the Chochołów rebellion; and the heroic individual, epitomized by the attractive figure of Prince Józef Poniatowski. Each of these historical events and heroes contributed to a greater consciousness of the nation's legacy of armed struggle.

In a sense, the years 1913–14 were one big national commemoration of Poles in arms, from its beginning on January 22 through the hanging of the members of the National Government on August 5 the following year. Distinctions between past and present, between celebrating history and making it, were becoming increasingly blurred. Traditional commemorations were enlivened by the presence of paramilitary forces, which in turn transformed the events by personifying a hope on the part of so many Polish patriots of the last several decades: that a new generation was ready to continue the battle for Polish freedom. In these celebrations, there was room for Poles of all political persuasions. While the bulk of the festive public events of 1913 had been organized by Polish nationalist organizations, the outbreak of World War I allowed a different group of Poles to build upon those festivities in their own unique way. The new Polish fighting forces—Piłsudski's contribution to Polish nation-building—became even more closely identified with the insurrectionary tradition.

Regardless of the partisan differences reflected in the celebrations, the general mood of the nation was changing in favor of armed struggle. Various groups responded to one or another of these legacies and their representative commemorations, all of which were invoked during the war as well as in 1913–14. This was a time when all pertinent historical examples were invoked, in the hopes that they would aid the Polish cause. The insurrectionary legacy was underscored by parties and organizations across the board. Even socialists who earlier had opposed Piłsudski, like Bolesław Drobner, signed up as Riflemen or styled themselves as such, despite their civilian status; and Ignacy Daszyński bought himself a Rifleman's uniform, which he wore while serving as military commissar.[100]

All of this provides evidence of the emergence of a Polish "Myth of the War Experience," to use George Mosse's term.[101] In independent Poland, the Legions were depicted as another link in the chain of Polish post-partition history, one in which Poles rose up in arms to fight for their independence. The invasion of Piłsudski's troops on August 6, 1914, had been no more successful militarily than the uprising of 1863, despite Piłsudski's study of past uprisings. The riflemen's attempt nonetheless bore marks of the same lineage: a relatively small group of dedicated cadres strove to undo the partitions by themselves. This effort allowed Poles to interpret the recreation of a Polish state after the war as their own accomplishment, not a feat of diplomatic work or wartime alliances.

The nation had come a long way since 1879. The gains in national identity were impressive, as were the military skills visible those last years in Galicia. As one commentator noted, "The Polish armed force . . . made . . . a particularly strong impression on visitors from the other side of the cordon."[102] It hoped to make a similarly strong impression on the powers that, by beginning World War I, were about to change the face of this part of Europe.

Conclusion

While the Polish predicament remained—the Poles were still a nation without a state in 1914—much had been accomplished over the space of thirty-odd years. The anniversary celebrations that preceded the reestablishment of an independent Polish state were not simply "pageants." Nor were they unhealthy signs of national activity, as some conservatives and their allies would have us believe, speaking of a "mania of celebrations of national holidays and anniversaries, those demonstrations that keep society in a kind of ferment, pulling it away from reality into a world of imagination."[1] It was the reality of partition that was unpalatable, activists would maintain; should we be surprised that they sought other alternatives? They needed to be able to imagine a different scenario, one that showed a nation united in action and ready to regain its independence. In this regard, commemorations were especially valuable. Not only did they help, as Rousseau had imagined, to "raise souls to the pitch of the souls of the ancients."[2] They reoriented the nation, emboldening it to prepare, in very concrete ways, for a future Poland.

A "historic" nation, the Poles did not lack a past; what they wanted, however, was a future. In the years following the Insurrection of 1863, groups of democratically minded activists strove to keep the memory of the nation's past alive through public celebrations of noteworthy historical events and exemplary Poles. These commemorations inspired additional efforts: new social initiatives and organizations, tangible representations of the past that served as pedagogical tools in the proselytizing of the masses. In the process, broader masses—including peasants—came to feel part of the Polish nation as well as to acknowledge their ultimate responsibility for the nation's future. The new conceptions of the Polish nation expounded in public discourse became the backbone of their understanding of what it meant to be a Pole.

In time, a new generation of Poles, keen on exerting its influence over the nation, came to embrace commemorations. These "defiant ones," to use Cywiński's term, were on a crusade to change the face of Polish politics.[3] Despite the continued oppression of their compatriots in both the German and Russian Empires, they refused to settle for the limited ethnographic (apolitical but cultural) existence for which many in the previous generation had toiled. The doctrine of tri-loyalism was jettisoned in favor of a new focus on nation-building that extended or even transcended the boundaries of what was permitted by the imperial authorities. At the same time, these new activists, especially those in the National Democratic camp, redefined Polishness through their manipulation of the national discourse that accompanied the commemorations.

Given the limited opportunities for Poles to act as Poles *tout court* (not Galician, not Russian, not Prussian or German), national celebrations had much to offer. In a way, they represented a more flamboyant approach to organic work, designed to enlighten by engaging hearts, minds, and souls and winning them over to the national cause. By focusing on a shared past, they transcended the partitions, gathered Poles of various political persuasions under the national banner, and roused, not doused, national sentiment. As one observer put it, "those 'pageants' are our bread for entire years of hard labor, . . . they connect us, divided into . . . cliques, parties and partitions, . . . attract the indifferent, warm the cold; they are a debt paid to the memory of heroes whom we wish to imitate."[4] With commemorations, the Poles found a way to express and develop their national identity under conditions of partition.

Many advantages accrued to the members of this stateless nation as a result of these national celebrations. These may be grouped under six headings: as aspects of horizontal, vertical, temporal, and symbolic integration, as well as the ability to produce national leaders and raise the nation's international profile. While my discussion of these contributions is based on the case I know best (the one researched here), I believe that other nations in circumstances similar to the Poles could derive similar benefit from such celebrations.

First, commemorations provided a valuable forum for cross-border communication and contact. They brought together Poles from the various empires as well as abroad—an aspect of commemorations not to be underestimated. Whether out of necessity, convenience, or preference, Poles sharing a profession or avocation often ended up gathering or even rooming together during such festivities. Horizontal integration was further facilitated within Polish society by the planned coincidence of congresses, so many of which were appended to the larger celebrations we have examined: for example, the first Polish historical congress, the first all-Polish Congress of Writers and Artists, and dozens of similar gatherings during the Lwów Exposition and beyond. Not only opportunities for celebration, such events afforded occasions for reflection, as with the series of congresses commemorating the January Insurrection that was designed to sum up the nation's progress over the last fifty years.

Increased contact with Poles from other regions often facilitated more tangible achievements: the founding of institutions as well as the construction of monuments. Among others, these included the National Museum in Cracow, the People's School Society, Bartosz Squads, even the Mickiewicz University organized by the socialists. That these gatherings and accomplishments were connected with the commemorative impulse has often passed almost unnoticed. Dealt with individually, they have been viewed as by-products of organic work within one or another partition. Yet meetings held in conjunction with national celebrations did not promote the development of the various partitioned lands in isolation. They helped Poles to transcend political boundaries and focus on not only what they had in common but what they could achieve if they worked together. In a period of noted regional distinctiveness, commemorations helped to elide the differences in attitudes, perceptions, and experience that often characterized the various partitions. By transcending regionalisms, enforced or habitual, commemorations helped to strengthen the common bonds that united all Poles.

Second, commemorations integrated Polish society vertically. The festivities brought together people of different social backgrounds, classes, and estates, underscoring the fact that they were all part of the same nation. This growing national inclusiveness had both symbolic and real dimensions. No longer monopolized by the nobility, the nation included the entire social spectrum. This could be seen in the colorful processions that so often were part of the festivities. A similar mix of folk, townspeople, and gentry jostled in the crowds at the unveiling of monuments and tablets, perused the same exhibitions, bowed their heads together in the same churches or under the same sky during field masses. More structured interaction was facilitated by the work of numerous commemoration activists, beginning with Father Stojałowski, who reached out to the common folk. They placed a premium on broad folk participation and sought to show that the Polish peasant was mature and cognizant of his membership in the nation.

Commemorations were uniquely suited to increase the interaction between activists and peasants. Their pageantry, color, and novelty provided an unforgettable sight for unsophisticated eyes (and not only for them). The unveiling of tablets, monuments, or busts elicited shared public excitement. Together with commemorative paintings, they continued to inspire viewers long after the festivities. Folk participants were exposed to stirring speeches and songs, occasionally treated to meals, and provided with mementos that would serve as permanent reminders of the experience: commemorative books and brochures, broadsides, pins and medallions, postcards. These simple souvenirs, treasured by many participants, inspired tales of the festivities, of trips to the big city, of sights and sounds and feelings. Like the public sites and monuments, they too were teaching tools designed to interest the folk in their Polish heritage.

The inclusion and increasing participation of the peasantry in national matters is one of the successes of this Polish commemorative age. With their piety depicted as a value shared by the nation as a whole, peasants were led on a new kind of pilgrimage, gaining exposure to relics and images of the Polish past as well as of saints. In time, villagers organized their own outings to such sites and came to see themselves as full-fledged, even invaluable members of the nation. Peasants increasingly made the leap from a primary identification of themselves as "locals," "Mazurians," "Catholics," or "the emperor's people" to calling themselves Poles and assuming the rights and responsibilities connected with that identity, even to the extent of taking up arms to fight for a Polish state. While no more than a minority of peasants was reached in these decades, those who felt themselves Poles were no less dedicated to the cause than their urban counterparts. According to Tadeusz Krawczak, 70 percent of the members of the Riflemen's Unions and the Riflemen were peasants, as were 30 percent of the Polish Riflemen Squads, 88 percent of the Bartosz Squads, and over 90 percent of the Falcon Field Squads. Galician peasants also comprised one-fourth of the Polish Legions, making them an important addition to the national fighting force.[5] Compare this level of engagement with the attitudes of Russian peasants during the World War I, and the significance of this achievement becomes even clearer.

An oft-overlooked but unique benefit of commemorations concerns their relation to time—the third nation-building aspect, one I term temporal integration. Anniversary celebrations focused the attention of the nation on specific dates and events of particular importance to the Poles. The sense of a connection in time with the nation at large played a crucial role for those unable to participate in the public festivities. The very thought that, elsewhere on the planet, thousands or perhaps even millions of Poles were honoring the same deeds or personages lent credence to notions of a Polish nation united in spirit, if not yet in reality.

These ideas were buttressed by knowledge of the larger events covered in the press as well as in commemorative publications that showed how Poles of different regions were able to celebrate these anniversaries. Yet even the illiterate could share in the sensation, as countless times during the course of the celebrations various speakers called to mind the brothers who were not free to celebrate openly. Moreover, those Poles present at the festivities could be imagined as but the tip of the iceberg: they were delegates, official or otherwise, of the masses of Poles who did not travel to the commemorative center but who likewise made note of the date. In this way, commemorations were superior to the imagined communities conjured up through the process of reading that have been described by Benedict Anderson and by Thomas and Znaniecki before him.[6]

Existing in a sphere separate from the realities of partition and imperial rule, these anniversary remembrances fostered what could be considered a notion of "Polish" or "national" time, a time that transcended partition and geography. An entire calendar could be devised to recall the events of the past, one that, to borrow David Cressy's phrase, could "operat[e] as an annual mnemonic."[7] Recollections of a common legacy removed from their lives as imperial subjects were most necessary for the Poles of Galicia: not persecuted for their Polishness, they could become complacent in their more favorable conditions. Galicians needed to be reminded that there were things more important than their own relative comfort—things such as national unity and the hope that one day Poles might again be masters of their own destiny.

Related to the issue of time was a blurring of distinctions between past and present. The Polish poet Cyprian Norwid once stated that the past was "today, only somewhat farther away" (*dziś, tylko cokolwiek dalej*). This sense of national time as a fuzzy continuum was shared by many Polish activists, whose interpretations of the past were often shaped by the requirements of the moment. During this period, the dead had as great a significance as the living; in Urbankowski's words, it was a "mythic time."[8] Not only did the activists see the past through the prism of the present. They often sought to imbed themselves, as heirs to a praiseworthy history, within that continuum, to claim a lineage for their own views. In the process, a host of images was superimposed upon the Polish past by commemorators of various backgrounds and persuasions. Gazing at the past, these Poles saw the future as well.

Fourth, commemorations helped shape the symbolic vocabulary of the nation, a process I term symbolic integration. Some of these symbols, which Pierre Nora would term "realms of memory," had a physical basis. In the course of these anniversary celebrations, the Poles managed to demarcate or even establish national spaces. Places such as the Wawel crypts, Old Cloth Hall, the Skałka crypt, the rotunda of the Racławice Panorama, the insurrectionaries' hill at Łyczakowski Cemetery, and the vicinity of various national monuments (a number of which were erected during this period) were invested with national significance. While many were located in Galicia, these sites were perceived not as Austrian but as Polish by those who participated in the festivities.

The city of Cracow proved to be a national space par excellence. Its historic value as well as the accessibility of its national sites to the general public helped to elevate it to the status of a living national relic. We have seen how Polish aspects of the city were reinforced. Cracow was the site of important burials and reburials; home to the National Museum; a place where national colors and symbols were visible on a daily basis; a city that Poles from all the partitions increasingly came to call home. The establishment of Cracow as national space helped to provide an atmosphere in which the nation could come together to work as well as to celebrate. A critical mass of nationally self-conscious Poles, engaged in celebrations of the past, could turn even a city under foreign rule into a surrogate homeland, a Poland in the minds of the masses, an imagined Poland. Of course, that this city had been the medieval capital of Poland and was still full of signs of the nation's past was a special advantage.

The most obvious symbols, of course, were the events and persons being celebrated. In many instances, they were given a physical locus in the form of monuments, tombs, and other physical markers. The role played by such symbols in Polish discussions of the past, present, and future was crucial. Commemorations provided both the subject matter and the forum for a national discourse. Public commemorations often initiated the discussion of the national past, its interpretations, as well as suggestions for ways in which the nation could develop, in some cases raising issues that had long been dormant. (The Warsaw activists behind the 1891 celebrations, for example, claimed that their demonstration overcame apathy and turned the attention of society toward a national politics that transcended the partitions.[9]) This is also visible in the extensive press coverage of the anniversaries and their celebrations. These symbols could be thought of as the most basic of national building blocks. They provided a shared vocabulary for a national discourse, a set of symbolic terms common to all Poles claiming the nation's heritage. At the same time, the symbols allowed for an important eliding of differences. As we saw in the case of Mickiewicz, many could agree to celebrate him; what they could not agree upon was why. Perhaps this explains the longevity of so many national symbols. Perennially open to a degree of recasting or redefinition, they allowed for interpretations of them to change even as history was changing.

Fifth, the celebrations contributed to an enhanced authority and visibility of national leaders. One of the arguments used by activists in Galicia to justify the public commemoration of the Polish past was that the multinational empire of the Habsburgs allowed national traditions to be cultivated. In certain instances, of course, it behooved Poles to act as though their anniversaries were innocuous expressions of ethnographic identity. Such a reading of the events, however, misrepresented the reality. Under this veneer of national tradition or culture lay a profoundly political dimension. Polish celebrations broadcast as well as helped shape the configuration of power within society. Power and status were indicated by the placement of groups in the processions, the choice of public speakers, the breadth of participation (local, regional, national), as well as by the relative success of a given celebration. Given their high profile, these public events ended up featuring certain individuals, parties, and organizations, sometimes to the advantage, sometimes to the detriment of the local notables or authorities. They also provided a means for both individuals and groups to gain public notice.

Commemorations, thus, afforded a rare opportunity for the partitioned nation to display or develop genuinely national leaders. This was particularly important for a major group of activists coming from the intelligentsia—the segment of society most likely to be found criticizing the status quo. As we have seen, artists, writers, and other members of the Polish intelligentsia involved in the celebrations gave the lie to the idea that politicians functioning within the three partitions directed the development of the nation. Rather, those who created, shaped, or publicized images were the real rousers of the nation. Many well-known Polish artists and writers—including Adam Asnyk, Maria Konopnicka, Józef Ignacy Kraszewski, Ignacy Jan Paderewski, Henryk Siemiradzki, Henryk Sienkiewicz, Jan Styka, and Kornel Ujejski—took an active interest in national development and contributed their own special talents to the effort. Countless others produced the souvenirs—broadsides, booklets, medals, and postcards—that concretized the memories the participants brought home. Commemorations also inspired important political leaders of the future such as Ignacy Jan Paderewski, Roman Dmowski, and Józef Piłsudski to make their first forays into the public sphere and express their views of the nation. By placing new groups and individuals who did not represent the imperial centers in the limelight, commemorations counteracted the centripetal force of imperial politics and laid the basis for an all-Polish politics.

Last but not least, public celebrations were occasions to gain international attention and advertise the Polish cause abroad. This in part explains why the pan-Polish efforts known as commemorations were not dismissed as quaint provincial gatherings by the partitioning powers. That many of the artistic and literary figures influential in the festivities had already gained international notice lent their words and deeds greater weight and often garnered the commemorations publicity on an international scale. This, in turn, raised the international profile of the nation.

Commemorations could also serve as a pretext for a national foreign policy otherwise denied the stateless Poles. Matejko's unexpected gift to the pope of *Sobieski at Vienna* was the first such event. The theme of Teutonic oppression that permeated the various Grunwald festivities likewise lent itself to international use, as the Poles attempted to publicize their plight in the German partition. (The importance of this theme is underscored by the fact that renewed celebration of the anniversary of the Battle of Grunwald began not in a round anniversary year but was sparked by the German persecution of Polish children in Września nearly a decade earlier.) The militarization of the final series of celebrations also boosted the Poles' standing within the empires, lending credence to their self-depiction as well-trained military cadres ready to fight—cadres that were increasingly viewed by the imperial authorities as potential contributors to their own war efforts. Commemorations, thus, served notice to the world that the Polish question had not ceased to exist.

Lest the connection between commemorating and nation-building seem too cozy, let us recall to mind other uses of such fetes. As discussed in the introduction, commemorations could just as easily support the political status quo or even imperial goals. They could just as easily divide as integrate the various members of a nation. Public celebrations provide opportunities to air diverse and conflicting interpretations of the commemorated events and figures, which represented various concepts of the nation, its legacy and future. In some cases, conflicts surfaced repeatedly, as seen in the tension between the Church hierarchy and commemoration organizers. For example, both Church and nation sought to retain or gain control over the symbolically important site of the Wawel Cathedral and crypts. And, on more than one occasion the heads of the Roman Catholic Church in Cracow and Lwów criticized or even squelched celebrations that seemed to place patriotism above piety.

Such conflicts were even more numerous in the realm of partisan politics. The past became the contested territory of a number of groups or individuals, each trying to shape the Polish national agenda. That national issues should give rise to a degree of national discord should not be surprising, given the very personal relationship of each individual to the concept of his own identity. As the sociologist Stanisław Ossowski noted, "Whoever participates in the national collectivity is, in the idea of national ideology, connected with it identically, if ideological divergences do not come into play; but then each active patriot strives to thrust his concept of the fatherland upon the entire nation, for that—his—fatherland is understood by him as the general fatherland."[10] In a way, this is what my investigation is really about: how Polish patriots reconceptualized their fatherland in the last decades of partitioned status, and how they managed to popularize their interpretations of that fatherland, its past, present, and future, in ways that would affect the nation as a whole.

MEMORY, HISTORY, INVENTION

I have argued that remembrances of the Polish past were induced by anniversary celebrations recalling noteworthy events and national figures. The use of commemorations to broadcast views of the nation lent itself to creative manipulations of the past. The past being remembered, it turns out, was to a great extent invented, or reinvented, in the course of commemorating.

The creative nature of this phenomenon stems in part from the process itself. The entirety of Polish history, in all its rich detail, could not be enumerated in the celebrations, which commemorated selected moments from the past. That Polish historiography was still in its infancy did not make the work of organizational committees any easier; public knowledge of the Polish past was sketchy at best and relied heavily on legends and traditional tales. Furthermore, given the limitations of time, effort, and resources, activists had to choose which events and personages to champion on a national scale. The natural occurrence of certain round anniversaries provided some direction for those intent on rallying the nation. Still other anniversaries—such as that of the November Insurrection of 1830—received short shrift, for political as well as other reasons. In other words, the past being presented was streamlined, simplified, and selective.

Selectivity extended also to interpretations of the anniversaries' significance. The organizers popularized certain versions of events and sought to present the national figures honored in ways that would contribute to Polish nation-making. The broader concept of the nation, comprised of noblemen, burghers, peasants, and workers, became a Procrustean bed to which all events and heroes worthy of a major commemorative effort would have to conform. The most popular interpretations of history were those that illustrated national virtues and provided encouragement and inspiration, or otherwise caused participants to identify with figures from the past. Thus, the failed Kościuszko Insurrection was transformed into a positive symbol by focusing on its first and most spectacular victory, the Battle of Racławice. The legacy of Mickiewicz was fought over by Poles of all imaginable political persuasions, each wanting to justify his own vision of nation and its future. The failure of the January Insurrection was overshadowed by its significance as a link in the chain of historic encounters in which Poles fought for their freedom. In these and other instances, commemorators sought to cast the past in, above all, a useful light.

This tailoring of history to fit the needs of the present, carried out by these activists, did not always square with the memory of those who maintained an uninterrupted sense of continuity with that past: the aristocracy. Commemorations presented a reinterpretation of the past, one that was to serve the needs of a new elite and redefined nation. This inventiveness or creativity in celebration, it should be noted, came primarily from those further removed from noble status. Indeed, nineteenth-century conservatives—for the most part, scions of the old nobility—decried the fact that various traditional elements were being lost, altered, or distorted by those who hoped to reinvigorate the Polish nation. For example, the wearing of confederate hats by women during festivities of the early 1890s elicited a comment of "how superficially, how childishly, and how unsatisfactorily we take care of our memories."[11] Such concerns for historical veracity suggest that these interpretations of the Polish past may have had less to do with a search for historical "truth." One might speak instead of an expropriation of historical memory in the name of the modern Polish nation.

That the old aristocracy, the conservatives, and other tri-loyalists might react negatively to aspects of invention in these fetes, of course, is hardly surprising. A statement made by Pierre Nora provides insight into their view of the past. He wrote, "If we still dwelled among our memories, there would be no need to consecrate sites embodying them. *Lieux de mémoire* [places of memory] would not exist, because memory would not have been swept away by history."[12] The Polish aristocracy still dwelled among its memories. It had retained its landed estates, its family treasures, and its archives despite the partitions and in some cases had even managed to salvage a degree of political influence. Constantly surrounded by the past, it found it difficult to distinguish between memory and history and most likely assumed that they were one and the same. The conservative upper nobility objected to modish interpretations of the history with which they claimed to be more familiar. These old-fashioned Poles realized that the past touted in the commemorations was often incomplete, distorted, inauthentic.

This view of the past influenced the attitudes of the aristocracy toward commemorations. Considering themselves the repository of Polishness, the conservatives had no reason to wish to avail themselves of the nation-building potential of public celebrations. As Szujski implied in his 1879 "firefighting" speech, the nation would persist; it did not require artificial stimulation to bring it back to life. In other words, those for whom the past remained present saw no reason to worry about the future.

This attitude hints at the true role played by the conservatives. In response to the commemorative desires of their political opposition, the conservatives ultimately learned to make use of the past for their own purpose in order not to jeopardize their control over the public sphere or—worse—politics. We saw how local and provincial authorities took control over the festivities, thus gaining in stature when the results were considered a success: an example of this was the career of Mikołaj Zyblikiewicz. Concerns for the political fate of the elites occasionally prompted restrictions designed to depoliticize, limit, upstage, or even undermine the celebrations. Conservatives, nonetheless, were not the ones who came up with the idea of celebrating national anniversaries publicly. This is why I take exception to accounts of the Polish past that present the conservatives and their allies as providing the impetus for the commemorations.

The liberal democratic opposition deserves the credit for advocating public commemorations and popularizing them to the extent that the regional elites felt a need to be involved. In Cracow, Poles affiliated with the opposition daily *Nowa Reforma*—men such as Adam Asnyk and Tadeusz Romanowicz—took the initiative. They established independent citizens' committees and occasionally gained additional leverage through contacts with Poles outside of Galicia. While close relations with the partitioning powers did not worry the political elites, the liberal democratic intelligentsia was concerned that the Galician masses would become complacently imperial—that they would see no reason to identify themselves above all with Polishness and the Polish national cause. These liberals strove to foster interaction with other Poles across political borders, to develop a sense of shared heritage that could overcome the differences of recent experience. Contemporaries such as Wilhelm Feldman knew this: although not a liberal democrat himself, he acknowledged that they had been responsible for keeping the memory of past dates alive in late-nineteenth-century Galicia.[13] In a way, thus, it is right that the first commemoration honored one of their own: Józef Ignacy Kraszewski, to whom Kieniewicz attributed the role of spiritual guardian and "father confessor" of the Polish democrats.[14] This investigation of the commemorative impulse makes it easier to understand why it took political outsiders—the democrats of the 1870s and 1880s—to rouse the nation in this fashion.

This is not to say that either liberal democrats or conservatives emerged as the dominant political group during this period. With the advent of the 1890s, both found themselves increasingly marginalized. Initially, the democratic ranks were broadened by younger members of society, men such as Ernest Adam, Włodzimierz Lewicki, and Michał Danielak. The Cracow democratic daily *Nowa Reforma* even served as the press organ of the nascent national democrats in the Kingdom of Poland for a while.[15] Yet for many of these students, as well as for others, liberal democracy increasingly lost its charms. Conservatives and democrats alike found their positions under attack by members of these new political movements—by a generation that had not personally experienced the tragedy of the January Insurrection—for being too passive and conciliatory vis-à-vis the partitioning powers. Some of the "defiant ones" joined the ranks of the populists; others aligned themselves with the two most powerful political forces to emerge during this period: nationalism and socialism. These groups—particularly the last two—came to dominate the national discourse not only on commemorations but also on the shape of and prospects for a future Poland.

The ability of members of the new political movements to move to the fore was in part a function of the growth of mass politics, which placed a premium on winning support among the masses. In this, commemorations were also helpful, as they often allowed representatives of various groups to gain a voice—legally or illegally—in the public sphere. The nation-building rhetoric that accompanied them also provided a means for political leaders and masses to find common ground. Celebrations prompted Poles to think of themselves in national terms as well as to become more responsive to calls to place the nation's fate once again in the forefront of national consciousness. I must emphasize once again that these new groups did not create this situation but rather took advantage of the change. A new type of politics—noisier, more national, more public—had begun even before the advent of true mass political parties in the 1890s, as we have seen from the support given the commemorative urge in the late 1870s and 1880s. (In much the same way, the twentieth-century impulse to military exercise was developed and systematized, not invented: secret clubs of Polish youth had long required their members to learn how to use weapons.[16]) Rather, these new political forces saw the value of commemorations as a way of getting their message into the public sphere.

The new movements nonetheless reinterpreted (one might say modernized) the major task that faced the nation. The restoration of an independent Poland, while important, was not enough for this generation. What the nation needed, they argued, was a reconfigured Poland, a revamped Polish nation. While populists desired social justice and socialists hoped to create a "Peoples' Poland," the nationalists sought to provide conditions under which the Polish nation could realize its potential, with independence being but "the most important condition for broad national development."[17]

WHAT KIND OF A "POLAND" DID THESE MODERN POLES DESIRE?

The resultant "Poland," primarily the work of the nationalists, was a far cry from its earlier incarnation. The premodern state that was partitioned at the end of the eighteenth century was *not* Poland—certainly, not formally. Its official name was the Commonwealth of Both Nations (Rzeczpospolita Obojga Narodów), although I have chosen to refer to it as the Polish-Lithuanian Commonwealth. To find a country with Poland in the official title, one would have to go back to the medieval Polish kingdom. The name given to the western half of the Commonwealth, "the Crown"—short for the Crown of the Polish Kingdom (Corona Regni Poloniae, or Korona Królestwa Polskiego)—reflected this historical past.[18] For the most part, the

Crown consisted of the ethnic Polish territories that had comprised the medieval state—a fact not immaterial for my conclusion.

The Commonwealth, on the other hand, was a multi-ethnic, multi-denominational political nation. One could argue that, like the modern nation, the nation identified with this earlier entity, the noble nation, was likewise a construct, one dating from the sixteenth century. The first invention of a Polish nation, albeit a premodern one, was designed to solve the problem of the heterogeneity of the nobility within its borders. How were Polish and Lithuanian Catholics, Ruthenian Orthodox, German Protestants, and others inhabiting this vast and fragmented territory to gain a sense of unity? Ultimately, a Polish national identity was superimposed over preexisting regional identities, and a myth of common Sarmatian ancestry was extended to the totality of the nobility. All noble citizens came to see themselves as belonging to the Polish nation (*natione Poloni*), regardless of their ethnic heritage. The establishment of this myth—this useful fiction—to unite various peoples into a self-conscious political whole was the first "inventing" of Poland.

If a multi-ethnic, multi-denominational political nation was the result of the first invention of Poland, over the course of this period of commemorations the modern nation assumed a quite different form. If we review the earliest celebrations, much stock was placed in the breadth of their appeal. They publicized the attractiveness of Polish strengths—in arts and letters (Kraszewski), military prowess (Sobieski), and freedom-fighting instincts (Mickiewicz)—that transcended the more narrow confines of the nation. In a way, images connected with these events presented what was best in the old Poland. Even the focus on turning peasants (of whatever ethnic heritage) into citizens could be viewed as a continuation of the reforms connected with the Constitution of 3 May 1791. The new "Poland" comes into focus as one examines later commemorations, the 1890s being a period of transition. It had a broader social base—part of the democratic legacy. Indeed, that aspect of the populists' desiderata was realized: no longer could anyone argue that peasants had no right to think of themselves as Poles. Polishness had become a quality applied to the masses: villagers, workers, even women patriots dressed in confederate hats.

Although the new Poland gained a broader social base through the inclusion and elevation of the peasantry, it—paradoxically—became narrower in a different sense. For the sentiments popularized by the commemorations led toward a more exclusively ethnic definition of Poland. Again, this was not seen in the earliest commemorations. There the historic prerogative to claim a certain ethnic or regional status (for example, Lithuanian or Ruthenian) while professing Polish nationhood was maintained: recall the discussion of the tablet commemorating the presence of "Polish [meaning Polish and Ruthenian/Ukrainian] villagers" at the 1883 festivities. At the same time, the belief grew that Poles living outside of the borders of the Commonwealth in 1772—including the Silesians in both Austria-Hungary and the German Empire and the Mazurians of East Prussia—were also part of the nation.[19] These "Poles" had been lost to "Poland" since the Middle Ages; that is, they had never been part of the Polish-Lithuanian Commonwealth. Their only connection came through the first Polish state, the Poland ruled by the Piast dynasty, and the fact that the locals spoke a dialect that could be considered Polish. That, however, sufficed for late-nineteenth-century national activists. We have seen how those involved in the commemorations underscored the Polishness of Silesians as well as how the People's School Society worked to strengthen the Polish element in such border regions.

That these Poles had managed to retain their language and customs despite being surrounded by non-Poles suggests another facet of the reinvented Poland. The process of nation-building is a zero-sum situation. What one nation gains, another nation loses. Or, to use Roman Szporluk's phrase, "One nation's fall is another nation's rise."[20] This has important implications for the way we perceive nation formation: this process does not take place in a vacuum but has consequences of an international, inter-national (between nations), even intra-state nature.

In the case of the Poles, this process affected nations on both sides of East-Central Europe. Let me begin with the western side and work eastward. The end of the nineteenth century marked a turning point in the reshaping of Polish national identity, in part influenced by the German attempts at self-definition. The inability of Prussia to assimilate the Poles within, as Rogers Brubaker has noted, was of great consequence here.[21] A growing number of Germans sought to deny the Poles within the German Empire the right to be loyal citizens without renouncing their Polishness. Activists watched with amazement how such pressure—seen in the *Kulturkampf* and various pieces of legislation—created so many nationally conscious Poles out of those who, under milder conditions, might eventually have assimilated into the German majority. They learned an important lesson: Germans were not going to let Poles forge their nation in peace, so they had better become accustomed to less-than-ideal conditions for nation-building.

German action in the West inspired a Polish reaction in the East. Finding the German method brutal but bracing, Polish nationalists in turn applied similar tactics to areas in which Polish culture had the upper hand: the "western frontier" of imperial Russia. As some recent scholarship has demonstrated, the Polish problem within likewise bedeviled a Russia that found it hard to come to grips with its multinational nature.[22] As we saw from the discussion of the Grunwald anniversary, late-nineteenth-century Poles had began to exert additional pressure on the other peoples inhabiting former Commonwealth territory, who might choose to side with the partitioning powers instead of the Poles. All signs of allegiance to any but the Polish cause were to be regarded with suspicion. Polish nationalists increasingly made clear their attitude toward ethnic minorities: if they did not assimilate (that is, adopt Polish language and culture), they should anticipate a fight for their continued existence or development as a nation. In other words, diversity was no longer acceptable. The nation had to be united in the face of attacks from outside.

Nation-building was becoming a zero-sum game played out in terms of what Szporluk has termed intra-state relations: that is, when "an old ('large') nation disintegrates and is reconstituted into two (or more) new nations."[23] In the case of old Poland, the nation ultimately disintegrated along ethnic lines. The premodern concept of the Polish nation as an overarching political construct for a citizenry differentiated ethnically, denominationally, and regionally was abandoned by nationalistic activists for an ethno-linguistic definition. Whereas "Polishness" had once been an inclusive term, uniting disparate people (*gentes*) under the larger nation (*natio*), identification markers characteristic of the Polish/"Mazurian" ethnic element were increasingly considered essential: language (Polish), religion (Catholic), and identity (Polish). *Gente Ruthenus, natione Polonus* types would no longer be considered Poles unless the former designation was merely a sentimental remnant, not a primary source of identity.

This development had an impact on the way the remaining peoples of the former Commonwealth were treated. As Daniel Beauvois has noted, in addition to the Polish "noble nation," there were at least five societies aspiring to modern nationhood on the territory of the Polish-Lithuanian Commonwealth: Lithuanian, Belarusian, Ukrainian, Jewish, and Polish peasant.[24] Given their ethno-linguistic definition of the nation, Polish nationalists essentially concerned themselves with only the last of these. Indeed, the main accomplishment of these modern nation-builders seems to have been the unification of the old Polish noble and new Polish peasant options.

The rest posed a dilemma for the newly emerging modern Polish nation. Were these peoples—descendants of inhabitants of the Polish-Lithuanian Commonwealth but not ethnic Poles—a domestic (internal) problem, or should relations be defined in inter-national terms?[25] The resulting situation in part explains why ethnic Lithuanians refused to participate in the Grunwald festivities organized by the Poles. We had noted their disbelief that the Poles would do anything beneficial for them; clearly some had come into contact with Poles who wanted the Lithuanians to assimilate fully into Polish culture, to abandon their language and customs for those of the (previously) noble majority. The same approach was applied to the Belarusian population, which, given its less well developed sense of identity, could be thought of as an easier mass to convert. It was expected that the upward mobility connected with the process of modernization, the move away from villages to the cities, and improved access to education would show these "peasant" nations that superior options for self-definition existed. That is precisely what some members of these minorities feared.

Given the preponderance of commemorations in Galicia, changing Polish perceptions of Ukrainians can be fleshed out more fully. Initially, the so-called Ruthenes were treated as a subset of the Polish nation, as the tablet noting peasant presence at the 1883 commemoration attests. Differences in views of the Ruthenian question surfaced during the Mickiewicz translation. Still, the celebrations of 1894 witnessed a number of attempts to bring Poles and Ukrainians together, with choreographed interaction— the effort of local women's groups—between peasant children attending the Lwów Exposition. Such efforts could not counterbalance the discrimination these "younger brothers" faced in Galicia, however. Franko's criticism of Mickiewicz prior to the 1898 anniversary of the bard marked a sharp deterioration of Polish-Ruthenian relations. From that point on, Galician Ukrainians continued to differentiate themselves from their Galician Polish brethren, to the point of not acknowledging the common past as holding any attraction for them (as in the Grunwald anniversary year). By the outbreak of war, there were separate Polish and Ukrainian paramilitary groups, each intent on fighting for its own nation. Again, out of the ruins of the old Polish noble nation we find two fledgling ones, each struggling to establish itself in the region.

The situation of Jews in the lands of the former Commonwealth changed even more radically. For, while it was thought possible for Lithuanian, Belarusian, or Ukrainian peasants to switch their allegiance to the Polish nation (linguistically and culturally), these options were increasingly denied Jews. This despite the fact that many Galician Jews, certainly those who functioned in the larger society, had demonstrated their allegiance to the Polish nation by participating in the commemorations. The anniversary of the Third of May seems particularly noteworthy in this regard. Of course, one could add that, in Galicia, the Poles were the ruling nationality, thus it behooved Jewish organizations to maintain cordial relations. These Jews were fighting an uphill battle for acceptance by the majority Poles, however, as anti-Semitism and the sense that Jews could never become real Poles increased with time. This situation was exacerbated in the former Kingdom of Poland by the massive influx of Russified Jews fleeing Russian persecution. The electoral troubles of the most influential Polish nationalist, Roman Dmowski, who failed to win a seat in the Russian Duma late in this period on account of the Jewish vote, only reinforced his already pronounced anti-Semitism. Mickiewicz's image of the patriotic Jankiel, thus, ultimately gained little ground for his nineteenth-century coreligionists.

THE DOMINANCE OF THE NATIONAL

The subject of the "break-up of Poland"—to twist the title of Tom Nairn's well-known book—deserves further study. I have only begun to sketch some of its contours, suggesting that the change between the old and new Poland was more radical than may have been thought. While the terms "Poland," "Pole," and "Polish" continued to be used, in many cases they were infused with a new meaning. The new Polish nation was becoming less welcoming of diversity, less inclusive than its earlier incarnation. While it feted dates from the pre-partition past, it was selective in what it chose to highlight.

Yet it also had a special relationship with a part of the distant past: the Poland of the Piasts. When the ethnic Polish nation is plotted on the map, one sees a definite geographic shift toward the west, compared to the 1772 (pre-partition) borders. Silesia and Pomerania become part of the equation; the lands in the East belong only insofar as Polish culture succeeds in making inroads there or Polish force dominates the smaller nations. Yet was this really a return to Piast Poland? Not exactly. For modern perceptions of what it meant to be part of that state were superimposed upon the reality. The Piast rulers, after all, were oblivious to the "national question" as we know it. They had not fought to regain the "Polish" territories of Silesia and Pomerania, nor was their expansion into the lands of old Rus'—the Kievan patrimony—considered an aberration. They probably had even less of a sense of being Polish than did the nobility under Jagiellonian rule, for whom noble "Polish" status and the Sarmatian myth were of much greater value.

More important for this modern version of Piast Poland was a reassuring, if in part imagined, homogeneity. Whereas the premodern state had been a kind of noble anarchy, in which the dissent of an individual carried great weight, now Poles were instructed to subordinate everything to the national interest. This single-mindedness was one of the by-products of the commemorations. These celebrations placed the fate of the nation in the foreground and helped to establish a national, even a nationalistic, discourse of sorts. Those who were accused of being more concerned with what Vienna, Berlin, or St. Petersburg thought were easily marginalized. One had to be shown to have the interest of the nation at heart, or at least spout the proper platitudes.

This in part explains why I maintain that the nationalists had the greatest impact on the shaping of a modern Polish identity. Neither populists nor socialists could challenge their preeminence. The situation of the populists was paradoxical: while the broadening of the nation upgraded the status of the peasantry, it nonetheless lessened their political impact. For the populists had no monopoly on the subject of the importance of the *lud*, the folk, for the nation: all these modern political groups professed concern with the masses. Individual peasants, thus, could veer in the direction of either socialism or nationalism, and many did. Peasants were also handicapped by the sharp opposition of many clergymen to their organization, which left them struggling and divided. As regards the patriotic socialists, we have likewise seen their concern for the nation and its fate. In some ways, however, they appeared quite similar to the nationalists—especially when contrasted with the tri-loyalists. They too were intent on changing the face of the nation, albeit their concerns lay more in creating a Poland in which the working masses would feel at home. We have seen how the Warsaw student activists of the early 1890s, of both nationalistic and socialistic bent, were more united in their opposition to the status quo than opposed to each other, and often worked together during that period.

In later years, as the commemorative focus shifted back once again to Galicia, socialists found themselves at a disadvantage. They had always had trouble gaining a broader audience for their views during the commemorations, courtesy of the authorities. Given suspicions as to their loyalty and fears of internationalism, socialists were long marginalized and persecuted by the Galician authorities, and their activities were played down or even ignored by the nonsocialist press. Recall that the interest of socialists in a certain historic figure, such as Kraszewski or Mickiewicz, was thought by more conservative elements to taint the men being honored; indeed, in the case of Mickiewicz, the socialists' laying of wreaths at his Cracow monument led some to call for the destruction of any of the poet's papers that might allow him to be associated with such doctrines.[26] The situation was complicated, as we know, by the diversity of the socialists themselves: some saw no reason to think of themselves in national terms or link their aims to a future Poland, while others certainly did so and, like Ignacy Daszyński, imagined a "People's Poland." Even "pro-Polish" socialists often managed to irritate other committee members or officialdom, resulting in their being kept from playing a more prominent public role in either planning or speaking at the festivities. As the lesser of two evils (in the eyes of the authorities), nationalists profited from antisocialist discrimination and were able to maneuver themselves into stronger positions.

The changes in the Polish Socialist Party after 1905 also contributed to a situation in which both main parties could be viewed as working toward a national goal. The socialists' ultimate desire for Polish independence caused them to subordinate the social question to the national one; this in turn enabled the nationalist discourse on the nation to retain the upper hand. After all, Piłsudski and his followers were obsessed with tactical preparations: military training, the establishment of an underground national government, and the like. They remained vague on the composition of the nation, in the name of which they were preparing to fight. Instead, they popularized the freedom-fighting legacy they hoped would inspire new national cadres to join them in action. Piłsudski's camp ultimately focused on the narrowest goal, independence, without spending much time imagining the shape that desired Polish state would assume. Thus, while Poles across the political spectrum became enamored of the insurrectionary legacy promoted by Piłsudski and his camp, they were able to imagine it in terms of the newly broad (socially) yet newly narrow (ethnic) Polish nation. This situation doubtless was reinforced by the fact that the nationalists increasingly came to dominate not only the national discourse, but also many pan-Polish and seemingly nonpartisan organizations such as the Falcons or even the People's School Society—the latter, as we recall, a by-product of the commemorative process.

There is one other group whose impact on nation formation cannot be ignored: the Catholic Church. The relation of the Church—by which I mean the clergy—to the nation, as seen through this study of commemorations, remains a vexing problem, one worthy of further study. The true extent of its involvement in celebrations is admittedly skewed by my omission of any discussion of Church celebrations separate from these specifically national commemorations. With the exception of a brief mention of the Saint Stanislas anniversary, no saints' holidays figured in this work—and there were plenty during this period.[27] My choice of festivities, however, has provided ample opportunity to examine the involvement of the Church in festivities of an unambiguously national nature. It was influenced by a number of factors. The clergy and conservatives were worried by the growing secularization of Polish society. No less troublesome was the indiscriminate use of religious ceremony in conjunction with commemorations. At times, it seemed that Poles were defining themselves as Poles first, then Catholics (or—even worse—they only paid lip service to Catholicism on account of the pious masses). Even the word "pilgrimage" now embraced not only religious sites, but places of national significance as well.[28]

The clergy responded in various ways, its participation ranging from nonexistent, lackluster, or peripheral to engaged, fervent, and inspiring. Despite this troubling variance, the involvement of the Church remained a desideratum for much of Polish society, as seen from the habitual choice of a holy Mass as the appropriate way to begin an anniversary celebration.

Generally speaking, the Polish activists behind the commemorations wanted to retain a link to the Catholic Church, so closely associated with Polishness. Their faith was tried on a number of occasions by the grudging support of so many important clergymen, who found themselves facing an uneasy trinity: Nation-Empire-Rome.

At times it seemed that the Church hierarchy wished to upstage the national event. Recall Bishop Albin Dunajewski's blessing of Old Cloth Hall and not Kraszewski; his elevation to cardinal right before the Mickiewicz translation; the Church's promotion of the Brotherhood of the Immaculate Conception of Our Lady, Queen of the Polish Crown, and celebration of Mary, Queen of Poland, over the centennial of the Constitution of the Third of May; and the timing in 1894 of the peasant rally (not the Church's work, if to its benefit) to coincide with the anniversary of Saint Hyacinth's canonization. In other instances, various bishops (among them, Dunajewski, Seweryn Morawski, and Jan Puzyna) protested, boycotted, or vetoed the celebrations planned by the laity. Lesser clergymen often had to toe the line or risk being persecuted like Father Stojałowski—the latter an example of how the Church could support national (or populist) development. For an age for which it has generally been assumed that Church and nation went hand in hand, there was a great deal of ambiguity on both sides. To what degree should allegiance to one come before allegiance to the other?

Commemorations, as well as the new concept of the nation, exacerbated this predicament. The elevation of national figures and events in the public sphere threatened to place the Church in a subordinate role. Prior to this age, celebrations traditionally had a sizable religious component or were simply manifestations of what sometimes appeared to be a Church-state condominium, a mixing of the sacred and the profane.[29] During the late nineteenth century, a period in which the nation remained partitioned and under foreign rule, many Poles chose to value patriotism over piety. The relationship between the nation and religion has been examined by scholars from Durkheim to Mosse. The words of yet another scholar shed light on the controversy raised by the rise of the former: "In celebrating symbols of their histories, societies in fact worship themselves."[30] From the point of view of the Church, thus, the specter of the people worshipping the nation—that is, themselves—bordered on idolatry. While paying lip service to the Church, the new Polish patriotism nonetheless threatened to supplant religion in the minds of some of the faithful. Given the close relationship between Polishness and Catholicism, this was no idle threat.

The connection between the religious and the national nonetheless persisted. We have seen how it was used to draw the peasants more fully into the nation. It also permeated Polish commemorations, in which religious imagery and rhetoric abounded. Catholicism likewise remained an important defining factor for the Poles, who, regardless of their own religiosity, could not deny the effect the Church had had on Polish nation formation. The history of the Polish nation would continue to be plagued by conflicting images and the shifting relations of political actors and the Church hierarchy.

THE POWER OF POLISH SYMBOLS

Regardless what the Church thought, the idea of celebrating the nation was here to stay. The national past had become a source of inspiration for further action. Its value, as well as the value of its imagery, was appreciated by both the Poles and the partitioning powers. This is seen in the staging of celebrations during World War I by various parties; a telling example is the 1914 speech of the Russian grand duke, Nikolai Nikolaevich, in which he expressed his hope that "the sword that routed the enemy at Grunwald had not rusted."[31] In the interwar period, the new Polish state—the so-called Second Republic—recognized the value of commemorations of past events and illustrious figures. The anniversary of the Constitution of the Third of May became a national holiday. The state also took care of unfinished business: the remains of a second Polish bard, Juliusz Słowacki, were buried in the Wawel crypt.[32] It was no coincidence that this event took place in 1927, one year after a coup d'état brought Józef Piłsudski to power. (Słowacki turns out to have been Piłsudski's favorite Romantic poet.) And the Wawel proved to be the resting place of Piłsudski himself after his death in 1935. Further links in the chain of Polish history, thus, continued to be forged.

Interest in the Polish past as well as in the relics of that past continued through the next international conflagration, World War II, and beyond. During the war, the image of Grunwald once again came to the fore, with the Nazis this time seen as modern-day Teutonic Knights. That Hitler's forces systematically destroyed Polish national monuments during the occupation attests to the fact that the Germans realized how important such symbols were for the Poles. An appreciation of the Polish past—at least certain elements of that past—was also fostered after the war. Although it may seem paradoxical, the communists who came to rule the new "People's Poland" were careful to play the national card. They preferred to keep the image of Grunwald in the minds of Poles so as to be able to depict the Soviet Union as the Poles' best and most reliable friend. They also sought to emphasize the legacy of the medieval Polish state over the Jagiellonian legacy; this would justify the new borders of the postwar state, which had been readjusted westward. The postwar state proved in a way to be the incarnation of the nation-state desired by generations of earlier Polish nationalists, fitting more nearly the image of an ethnically homogeneous Piast Poland.

The communists' understanding of the importance of the past for the Poles is also seen in their attitudes toward the reconstruction of various Polish symbols. A number of national monuments, destroyed by German forces during the war, were rebuilt under communist rule. This reconstruction lent them a new air. To give one example, this process transformed Cracow's undistinguished Mickiewicz monument. Despite the chance to improve on this artistic failure, Rygier's Mickiewicz was rebuilt to the last unfortunate detail. The significance of the monument was altered, however, through its reconstruction by a new generation: no longer remembered as the flawed outcome of a flawed process, it now was presented as a testimony to the perseverance of the Polish nation.

Other nineteenth-century relics and holidays were to take on even greater significance. The Racławice Panorama became a symbol of renewed national vigor. Transferred from the no-longer-Polish L'viv to the newly Polish city of Wrocław as a result of the postwar territorial revision, the painting of peasants fighting the Russian forces was not exhibited in the postwar period until the Solidarity movement took up its cause in 1980. Pressure from the new movement also led the communist government to celebrate the Polish national May 3 as well as the communist international May 1 in 1981.

Solidarity likewise made great use of both freedom-fighting and religious motifs familiar to us from so many commemorations. The ubiquitous crosses and lapel pins of Our Lady of Częstochowa and outdoor masses became part of the imagery of the movement. As an example of the Poles' continued sense of mission, consider a statement prepared by the first Solidarity Congress in the fall of 1981. The assembled activists composed their "Message to the Working People of Eastern Europe," in which the Poles offered to share their experience of free trade unions with the entire region. Once again, a Polish act reflected the nation's peculiar place between East and West, called to mind the old Polish Romantic messianism as well as the slogan "for our freedom and yours"—and was seen as threatening by the communist authorities in Poland and elsewhere. Even after the imposition of martial law on December 13, 1981, when all public gatherings were outlawed, Poles still managed to commemorate: by coordinating the placing of candles in windows, huge crosses of light adorned the facades of apartment buildings on the 13th of each month.[33]

Many more examples could be provided, but it should be clear from our discussion that a number of nineteenth-century symbols retained their potency into the twentieth century, and the value of establishing new links in the chain of Polish history was not lost on the nation or successive governments. At various times, political developments helped new generations to seek a connection to the people and events popularized at the end of the partition period, to draw parallels between the distant past and the present. The past had not lost its relevance for a nation still steeped in its history and all too conscious of the vagaries of fate.

PASTS (IM)PERFECT

The Polish past had provided the raw materials from which a new Poland was shaped. The late nineteenth century offered the Poles an opportunity to showcase episodes of their history and establish models of great individuals for emulation. The nation did not have to begin an insurrection in order to express its concern for its past, present, and future. Other strategies and other tasks needed to precede the taking up of arms, if that was to have any lasting impact on the state of the nation. Unlike the Italians, the Poles needed to create—to reinvent—their nation before they could expect any success in attaining, or maintaining, statehood.

The past was important to the Poles. In the words of one contemporary, Polish ideals and civilization were "considered in every corner of the former Poland as the general property of the entire nation and represent . . . the most valuable legacy rescued from the defeat [of partition]."[34] We have seen that this legacy was nonetheless subject to modification, the Poles' past subject to reinvention. The events of the previous century in particular prompted ruminations on the fate of the nation and suggested future actions. Commemorations of the past provided a forum for dialogue, a shared vocabulary of events that united Poles of different backgrounds and states. They also inspired the Poles to dream of the future, to imagine a Poland they could call home.

Views of the Polish past, of Polish history, had changed enormously over a relatively short period. The history of the Polish-Lithuanian Commonwealth had been expropriated by those less familiar with its details. The noble emphasis on familial relations and connections had been abandoned for an emphasis on shared deeds, particularly on the insurrectionary acts that attested to the Poles' dissatisfaction with foreign rule and dedication to the national cause. As a result of the bias of historical interpretations, the past increasingly was claimed by the common people, the folk—the Polish folk, seen to be its future and its salvation. This was but one facet of the new Poland, one that had been a long time in coming, but one foreseen by Polish reformers of a much earlier age.

More radical was the recasting of the multi-ethnic and multi-denominational Commonwealth as a national Polish state. Polishness was reduced from a political to an ethnic designation. One may think of this as a retroactive nationalization of Poland. Polish nationalists superimposed their narrow definition of Polishness upon the multi-ethnic past; this in turn would lead other ethnic groups from the old Commonwealth—including Lithuanians, Ukrainians, and Jews—to jettison that common past in favor of something uniquely theirs. We have, in short, witnessed the reinvention of Poland.

That this nation and later state took a narrower view of the past than had prevailed in premodern times was in part the function of the rise of modern nationalisms. For nations are forged in interaction with each other. Nineteenth-century Polish nation-building was a reaction to the state of partition. Glimpses of a tantalizing, half-real, half-mythologized past inspired the Poles to formulate their own ideas about the continuum of Polish existence. In the process of remembering and forgetting, they got some things wrong, as so many other nations did. They also got some things right, rousing legions of new Poles to national consciousness and the fight for political independence.

NOTES

Unless otherwise stated, all translations are my own.

INTRODUCTION

1. In his study of the commemoration, Józef Buszko fleshes out the varied reactions to the discovery of liberal and conservative Poles as well as the concerns of the religious and secular authorities. (Józef Buszko, *Uroczystości kazimierzowskie na Wawelu w roku 1869* [Kraków: Ministerstwo Kultury i Sztuki, Zarząd Muzeów i Ochrony Zabytków, 1970].)

2. Buszko termed this a "counter-manifestation on the part of tsardom" (ibid., 86). While the decision to remove signs of Polishness from the school had been made earlier, the immediate sending of a telegram to Warsaw underscored the desire of the authorities to link the undesirable Polish commemoration with the new anti-Polish decree.

3. [Józef Ignacy Kraszewski], *Rachunki z roku 1869 przez B. Bolesławitę*, from 7 July 1869, 300–301, cited in ibid., 13.

4. See *Invention of Tradition*, ed. Eric Hobsbawm and Terence Ranger (Cambridge: Cambridge University Press, 1983), especially the concluding chapter by Hobsbawm, "Mass-Producing Traditions: Europe, 1870–1914," 263–307; and David Cannadine, "The Context, Performance and Meaning of Ritual: The British Monarchy and the 'Invention of Tradition', c. 1820–1977," in ibid., 138. Cannadine called this period a "golden age of 'invented traditions.'" The term "official nationalism" (originally from Hugh Seton-Watson's *Nations and States*) is discussed by Benedict Anderson, *Imagined Communities: Reflections on the Origin and Spread of Nationalism,* rev. ed. (London and New York: Verso, 1991), chap. 6.

5. Eric Hobsbawm, "Introduction: Inventing Traditions," in *Invention of Tradition*, 4–5.

6. The more patriotic Polish priests sidestepped the intent by reading the announcements in Latin—or by mumbling such that the faithful could hardly hear.

7. Daniel Unowsky nonetheless suggests that imperial ceremonial in the Habsburg lands was transformed after 1848—if not in a national vein. (Daniel Louis Unowsky, "The Pomp and Politics of Patriotism: Imperial Celebrations in Habsburg Austria, 1848–1916" [Ph.D. diss., Columbia University, 2000].) Similar conclusions are presented in idem, "Reasserting Empire: Habsburg Imperial Celebrations after the Revolutions of 1848–1849," in *Staging the Past: The Politics of Commemoration in Habsburg Central Europe, 1848 to the Present,* ed. Maria Bucur and Nancy M. Wingfield (West Lafayette, Ind.: Purdue University Press, 2001), 13–45.

8. Cannadine, "British Monarchy," 111.

9. Richard Wortman, "Moscow and Petersburg: The Problem of Political Center in Tsarist Russia, 1881–1914," in *Rites of Power: Symbolism, Ritual, and Politics since the Middle Ages,* ed. Sean Wilentz (Philadelphia: University of Pennsylvania Press, 1985), 244–71, esp. 250–51. For more on the Russian case, see idem, *Scenarios of Power: Myth and Ceremony in Russian Monarchy,* 2 vols. (Princeton: Princeton University Press, 1995–2000).

10. English-language works include Maurice Agulhon, "Politics, Images, and Symbols in Post-Revolutionary France," in *Rites of Power,* 177–205; Charles Rearick, "Festivals in Modern France: The Experience of the Third Republic," *Journal of Contemporary History* 12 (1977): 435–60; Alon Confino, *The Nation as a Local Metaphor: Württemberg, Imperial Germany, and National Memory, 1871–1918* (Chapel Hill and London: University of North Carolina Press, 1997); Michael Kammen, *Mystic Chords of Memory: The Transformation of Tradition in American Culture* (New York: Alfred A. Knopf, 1991).

11. Marcus C. Levitt, *Russian Literary Politics and the Pushkin Celebration of 1880* (Ithaca, N.Y.: Cornell University Press, 1989); Charles Rearick, "Festivals and Politics: The Michelet Centennial of 1898," in *Historians in Politics,* ed. Walter Laqueur and George L. Mosse (London and Beverly Hills, Calif.: Sage Publications, 1974), 59–78; Rainer Noltenius, "Schiller als Führer und Heiland: Das Schillerfest 1859 als nationaler Traum von der Geburt des zweiten deutschen Kaiserreichs," in *Öffentliche Festkultur: Politische Feste in Deutschland von der Aufklärung bis zum Ersten Weltkrieg,* ed. Dieter Düding, Peter Friedemann, and Paul Munch (Reinbek bei Hamburg: Rowohlt, 1988), 237–58.

12. Anderson, *Imagined Communities,* 194.

13. This was the journal *Kwartalnik Historyczny.*

14. John R. Gillis, "Introduction: Memory and Identity: The History of a Relationship," in *Commemorations: The Politics of National Identity,* ed. John R. Gillis (Princeton: Princeton University Press, 1994), 5.

15. Jonathan Sperber, "Festivals of National Unity in the German Revolution of 1848/49," *Past and Present* 136 (1992): 138; Rearick, "Festivals in Modern France," 437.

16. Peter Carrier, "Historical Traces of the Present: The Uses of Commemoration," *Historical Reflections* 22, no. 2 (1996): 435.

17. This wonderful metaphor comes from Anderson, *Imagined Communities,* 86.

18. Miroslav Hroch, *Social Preconditions of National Revival in Europe: A Comparative Analysis of the Social Composition of Patriotic Groups among the Smaller European Nations,* trans. Ben Fowkes (Cambridge: Cambridge University Press, 1985), esp. 23–30.

19. Ibid., 9. Hungary also shares this appellation.

20. The use of ethnic/linguistic/national adjectives in this brief review of the partitioned lands is intended only to give a sense of the relative diversity of the population of the different regions, not to impute to those populations any sort of national consciousness—particularly any predetermined kind. For a discussion of the pitfalls of "ethnicism," which Jeremy King defines as "a vague, largely implicit framework that holds the nations of East Central Europe to have sprung primarily from a specific set of mass, mutually exclusive ethnic groups defined by inherited cultural and linguistic patterns," see Jeremy King, "The Nationalization of East Central Europe: Ethnicism, Ethnicity, and Beyond," in *Staging the Past,* 123.

21. The East Slav population of this region—today's Belarusians and Ukrainians—were considered Russian by the imperial government. In his subtly argued monograph, Theodore R. Weeks shows that, although there was no official policy of Russification, security and other concerns certainly led the Russian government to strive to keep power out of the hands of the Poles. (Theodore R. Weeks, *Nation and State in Late Imperial Russia: Nationalism and Russification on the Western Frontier, 1863–1914* [DeKalb: Northern Illinois University Press, 1996].)

22. The exception here is the Revolution of 1905, the subject of a monograph by Robert E. Blobaum, *Rewolucja: Russian Poland, 1904–1907* (Ithaca, N.Y., and London: Cornell University Press, 1995).

23. Jean-Jacques Rousseau, *The Government of Poland,* trans. Willmoore Kendall (Indianapolis and New York: Bobbs-Merrill, 1972), 10. See the chapter "Rousseau's Poland" in Larry Wolff, *Inventing Eastern Europe: The Map of Civilization on the Mind of the Enlighten-*

ment (Stanford: Stanford University Press, 1994), 235–83, for an interesting discussion of Rousseau's views on this subject.

24. Hobsbawm and Ranger, eds., *Invention of Tradition;* Anderson, *Imagined Communities.*

25. Rousseau, *Government of Poland,* 14, 13, and passim.

26. Discussion of the two is connected in Jan Krukowski, "Komisja Edukacji Narodowej wobec setnej rocznicy zwycięstwa pod Wiedniem," *Studia Historyczne* 26, no. 4 (1983).

27. Hroch, *Social Preconditions,* 14.

28. Tadeusz Łepkowski, *Polska—narodziny nowoczesnego narodu, 1764–1870* (Warsaw: Państwowe Wydawnictwo Naukowe, 1967), 508.

29. King, "The Nationalization of East Central Europe."

30. According to Walicki, approximately 9 to 10 percent of the Commonwealth population belonged to the *szlachta,* or gentry, although regionally the situation looked quite different, with up to 25 percent of the population (for example, in the ethnically Polish and Catholic region of Masovia) being recorded as noble. The majority (50–55 percent) of the nobility were landless, 35–45 percent classified as petty gentry, and less than 5 percent genuinely wealthy. (Andrzej Walicki, *Philosophy and Romantic Nationalism: The Case of Poland* [Oxford: Clarendon Press; New York: Oxford University Press, 1982], 29.)

31. Eugen Weber, *Peasants into Frenchmen: The Modernization of Rural France, 1870–1914* (Stanford, Calif.: Stanford University Press, 1976). Regarding the German case, Harold James has written how early-nineteenth-century Germans "engaged in what might be termed the promiscuous construction of a national image, a national identity, and a national mission." (Harold James, *A German Identity, 1770–1990* [New York: Routledge, 1989], 6.)

32. There is a vast literature on the subject of the transformation of peasants into Poles during the nineteenth century. Polish titles include Helena Brodowska, *Chłopi o sobie i Polsce: Rozwój świadomości społeczno-narodowej* (Warsaw: Ludowa Spółdzielnia Wydawnicza, 1984); Tadeusz Krawczak, "Kształtowanie świadomości narodowej chłopów polskich w Galicji w latach 1864–1914," *Przegląd Humanistyczny* 11 (1978): 135–50; Jan Molenda, *Chłopi, naród, niepodległość: Kształtowanie się postaw narodowych i obywatelskich chłopów w Galicji i Królestwie Polskim w przededniu odrodzenia Polski* (Warsaw: Wydawnictwo NERITON, 1999); Józef Ryszard Szaflik, "Czynniki kształtujące świadomość narodową chłopa polskiego w końcu XIX i w początkach XX wieku," *Przegląd Humanistyczny* 26, no. 12 (1982): 1–15, and 27, no. 4 (1983): 43–82; idem, *O rząd chłopskich dusz* (Warsaw: Ludowa Spółdzielnia Wydawnicza, 1976). In English, see the new book by Keely Stauter Halsted, *The Nation in the Village: The Genesis of Peasant National Identity in Austrian Poland, 1848–1914* (Ithaca, N.Y.: Cornell University Press, 2001).

33. From diary entry of Sunday, 13 January 1889. (Stefan Żeromski, *Dzienniki,* ed. Jerzy Kądziela, 2d. rev. ed. [Warsaw: Czytelnik, 1963–70], 6:75.)

34. These terms are taken from ibid. Kościuszko's significance will be discussed in chapter 4, that of Mickiewicz in chapters 3 and 5.

35. Following new Italian research, Confino (in his *Nation as a Local Metaphor,* 15, 221, n. 47) attributes the statement to Ferdinando Martino, the secretary of education, not to Massimo d'Azeglio, who is usually credited with the famous words.

36. The most pronounced statement of this position is Adam Bromke, *Poland's Politics: Idealism vs. Realism* (Cambridge: Harvard University Press, 1967).

37. See, for example, Marek Czapliński, "Poczynania organicznikowskie a problem niepodległości Polski, " in *Między irredentą, lojalnością a kolaboracją: O suwerenność państwową i niezależność narodową (1795–1989)* (Toruń: Wydawnictwo Adam Marszałek, 2001), 121–35.

38. Among the most valuable are Anderson, *Imagined Communities;* Ernest Gellner, *Nations and Nationalism* (Ithaca, N.Y., and London: Cornell University Press, 1983); Hroch, *Social Preconditions;* Eric Hobsbawm, *Nations and Nationalism since 1780: Programme, Myth, Reality* (Cambridge, New York, Port Chester, Melbourne, and Sydney: Cambridge University Press, 1990, Canto edition 1991—the latter used here). For nation-specific works of particular value, see Rogers Brubaker, *Citizenship and Nationhood in France and Germany* (Cambridge and London: Harvard University Press, 1992); Linda Colley, *Britons: Forging the Nation, 1707–1837* (New Haven and London: Yale University Press, 1992); Caroline Ford, *Creating the Nation in Provincial France: Religion and Political Identity in Brittany* (Princeton: Princeton University Press, 1993); Peter Sahlins, *Boundaries: The Making of France and Spain in the Pyrenees* (Berkeley and Los Angeles: University of California Press, 1989); James Sheehan, "What Is German History? Reflections on the Role of the *Nation* in German History and Historiography," *Journal of Modern History* 53 (March 1981): 1–23, and the works cited in the next three notes. For the Polish case, see Peter Brock, "Polish Nationalism," in *Nationalism in Eastern Europe,* ed. Peter F. Sugar and Ivo John Lederer (Seattle and London: University of Washington Press, 1994), 310–72; and Tomasz Kizwalter, *O nowoczesności narodu: Przypadek Polski* (Warsaw: Wydawnictwo naukowe Semper, 1999).

39. Mona Ozouf, *Festivals and the French Revolution,* trans. Alan Sheridan (Cambridge: Harvard University Press, 1988); Lynn Hunt, *Politics, Culture and Class in the French Revolution* (Berkeley and Los Angeles: University of California Press, 1984); Rearick, "Festivals in Modern France," 435–460; Carrier, "Historical Traces"; *Commemorations: The Politics of National Identity; Öffentliche Festkultur;* Emil Brix and Hannes Stekl, eds., *Der Kampf um das Gedächtnis: Öffentliche Gedenktage in Mitteleuropa* (Vienna: Böhlau, 1997); David Cressy, *Bonfires and Balls: National Memory and the Protestant Calendar in Elizabethan and Stuart England* (London: Weidenfeld and Nicolson, 1989).

40. George Mosse, *The Nationalization of the Masses: Political Symbolism and Mass Movements in Germany from the Napoleonic Wars through the Third Reich* (New York: H. Fertig, 1975); Wilhelm Hansen, *Nationaldenkmäler und Nationalfeste im 19. Jahrhundert* (Lüneburg: Niederdeutscher Verband fur Volks- und Altertumskunde, 1976); Thomas Nipperdey, "Nationalidee und Nationaldenkmal im 19. Jahrhundert," *Historische Zeitschrift* 206 (1968): 577–79; Mircea Eliade, "Sacred Architecture and Symbolism," in *Symbolism, the Sacred and the Art,* ed. D. Apostolos-Cappadona (New York: Crossroad, 1986); Agulhon, "Politics, Images, and Symbols."

41. There is a wealth of works dealing with memories of the twentieth-century past, in particular of World War II and its aftermath. See Iwona Irwin-Zarecka, *Frames of Remembrance: The Dynamics of Collective Memory* (New Brunswick, N.J.: Transaction, 1994); Charles S. Maier, *The Unmasterable Past: History, Holocaust, and German National Identity* (Cambridge: Harvard University Press, 1988); Henri Rousso, *The Vichy Syndrome: History and Memory in France since 1944,* trans. Arthur Goldhammer (Cambridge: Harvard University Press, 1991); *Realms of Memory: Rethinking the French Past,* ed. Pierre Nora, 3 vols. (originally published as *Les Lieux de mémoire* [1984–92]); Yael Zerubavel, *Recovered Roots: Collective Memory and the Making of Israeli National Tradition* (Chicago: University of Chicago Press, 1994).

42. General works on myths range from Claude Levi-Strauss, *Structural Anthropology,* trans. Claire Jacobson and Brooke Grundest Schoepf (New York: Basic Books, 1963), to *Myths and Nationhood,* ed. Geoffrey Hosking and George Schöpflin (London: Hurst and Company, 1997); in addition to Norman Davies's survey of a number of Polish myths in *Myths and Nationhood,* the Polish use of myths is discussed systematically in *Polskie mity polityczne XIX i XX wieku,* ed. Wojciech Wrzesiński (Wrocław: Wydawnictwo Uniwersytetu Wrocławskiego, 1994).

43. This is a pitfall into which Porter falls in *When Nationalism Began to Hate: Imagining Modern Politics in Nineteenth-Century Poland* (New York and Oxford: Oxford University Press, 2000); for a survey and critique of some of the most recent literature (including Porter), see Patrice M. Dabrowski, "What Kind of Modernity Did Poles Need? A Look at Nineteenth-Century Nation Making" (book review article), *Nationalities Papers* 29, no. 3 (September 2001): 509–23.

44. The most synthetic works specifically on the Polish case remain articles by Adam Galos ("Obchody rocznicowe na prowincji zaboru austriackiego," in *Studia z dziejów prowincji galicyjskiej*, ed. Adam Galos [Acta Universitatis Wratislaviensis, no. 1532, Historia 111] [Wrocław: Wydawnictwo Uniwersytetu Wrocławskiego, 1993], 89–112; and "Z zagadnień roli rocznic historycznych w Polsce w XIX w.," in [n.t.], ed. Adolf Juzwenko and Wojciech Wrzesiński [Acta Universitatis Wratislaviensis, no. 543, Historia 36] [Wrocław: Wydawnictwo Uniwersytetu Wrocławskiego, 1981]: 137–53); Józef Buszko, "Uroczystości patriotyczne na Wawel w latach Rzeczypospolitej Krakowskiej i w dobie autonomii galicyjskiej," in *Annales Universitatis Mariae Curie-Skłodowska Lublin—Polonia*, vol. 51, 4, sectio F (Lublin: nakładem Uniwersytetu Marii Curie-Skłodowskiej, 1996), 31–41; and Stanisław Grodziski, "Nationalfeiertage und öffentliche Gedenktage Polens im 19. und 20. Jahrhundert," in *Der Kampf um das Gedächtnis*, 203–15. Galos has authored many articles on individual commemorations. His and other articles will be cited in the relevant chapters. As regards the scholarship on this subject in English, a book on commemorations in the Habsburg empire (in which one can find chapters concerning Polish-run Galicia) is a welcome addition: Bucur and Wingfield, eds., *Staging the Past*.

45. Ernest Renan, *Qu'est-ce qu'une nation?* (*What Is a nation?*), trans. Wanda Romer Taylor (Toronto: Tapir Press, 1996). Benedict Anderson, *Imagined Communities*, 199ff., makes much of this aspect of national identity formation.

46. In an oft-cited lecture, Stanisław Estreicher credits the Cracow school of history—which pessimistically assessed the Polish past—with the "cult of the past and desire to take advantage of the values inherent in it for the use of present generations." (Stanisław Estreicher, *Znaczenie Krakowa dla życia narodowego polskiego w ciągu XIX wieku: Odczyt wypowiedziany w "Klubie Społecznym" w dniu 21 października 1931 roku* [Kraków: W. L. Anczyca i spółki, 1931], 23.) Following Estreicher's lead, Jacek Purchla claims that the conservatives (*Stańczyks*) were the ones who initiated the great national anniversary celebrations. (Jacek Purchla, *Matecznik polski: Pozaekonomiczne czynniki rozwoju Krakowa w okresie autonomii galicyjskiej* [Kraków: Wydawnictwo Znak, 1992], 63.)

47. As the desire to reach Poles everywhere was common to many people and groups, I prefer to use the phrase "pan-Polish" instead of the more commonly used "all-Polish"; in this way, we avoid the immediate association with the *All-Polish Review* (*Przegląd Wszechpolski*) and a particular nationalistic camp—neither of which, incidentally, existed in the first decade or so of this study. The political rise and fall of German notable elites is ably described by David Blackbourn, "The Discreet Charm of the Bourgeoisie: Reappraising German History in the Nineteenth Century," in *The Peculiarities of German History: Bourgeois Society and Politics in Nineteenth-Century Germany,* by David Blackbourn and Geoff Eley (Oxford and New York: Oxford University Press, 1984).

48. Henryk Wereszycki, "Międzynarodowe echa jubileuszu Kraszewskiego w 1879 roku," *Dzieje Najnowsze* 6, no. 3 (1974): 4–5.

49. Richard Pipes, *Russia under the Old Regime* (New York: Charles Scribner's Sons, 1974), 298.

50. Wereszycki, "Międzynarodowe echa," 6–7.

51. The term "second metropolis" is borrowed from Blair Ruble (*Second Metropolis: Pragmatic Pluralism in Gilded Age Chicago, Silver Age Moscow, and Meiji Osaka* [Washington, D.C., New York, and Cambridge: Woodrow Wilson Center Press and Cambridge University Press, 2001]).

1. POLISH PHOENIX

1. Wilhelm Feldman, *Dzieje polskiej myśli politycznej, 1864–1914,* 2d ed. (Warsaw: Instytut Badania Najnowszej Historji Polski, 1933), 240.

2. "Znaczenie jubileuszu Kraszewskiego" (in the original, "Die Bedeutung der Kraszewski-Feier,") *Fremden-Blatt* no. 294 (25 October 1879), cited in *Księga pamiątkowa jubileuszu J. I. Kraszewskiego 1879 roku* (Kraków: nakładem komitetu wydawniczego, 1881), 261.

3. St[anisław] Tarnowski, "Zjazd krakowski z powodu jubileuszu J. I. Kraszewskiego," *Przegląd Polski* 14 (November 1879): 293.

4. *Księga Kraszewskiego,* 3.

5. Piekarski (T. J. Rola, pseud.), *Józef Ignacy Kraszewski z powodu pięćdziesięcio-lecia pracy i zasługi jego dla społeczeństwa* (Warsaw: drukiem Józefa Ungra, 1878), 48; K[arol] Estreicher, *Feniks polski* (Lviv: nakładem autora, 1887), 18.

6. *Księga Kraszewskiego,* 3–4. Celebrations were held in both 1878 and 1879 at different times, as the nation was not sure when exactly Kraszewski, who had written under numerous pseudonyms, had first published. Ultimately the librarian of the Jagiellonian University, Karol Estreicher, determined that the writer's first work (under the pseudonym of Kleofas Pasternak) was published in *Kuryer Wileński* (Wilno courier) in July 1829, making 1879 the real jubilee year. (According to the minutes of the first meeting of the Cracow committee for the Kraszewski jubilee on December 4, 1877, APŁ, Archiwum Bartoszewiczów 492, fols. 1–2; *Księga Kraszewskiego,* 13.)

7. *Księga Kraszewskiego,* 6, 12–15. The marble tablet was the work of the father of artist and writer Stanisław Wyspiański.

8. Cited in ibid., 13.

9. Cited in ibid., 5.

10. The words of the third (anonymous) speaker [Mr. S.—Henryk Sienkiewicz, perhaps?] at a jubilee celebration held in Zakopane, cited in ibid., 14.

11. Eljasz, "Józef Ignacy Kraszewski," 29.

12. His words are cited in *Księga Kraszewskiego,* 5.

13. From the speech of Father Józef Martusiewicz, who spoke at the Kraszewski celebration in Zakopane, cited in *Księga Kraszewskiego,* 10.

14. Much of this section is based upon the minutes of the Cracow Kraszewski committee found among the personal papers of Kazimierz Bartoszewicz, the young man who compiled the notes. (APŁ, Archiwum Bartoszewiczów 492.)

15. Ibid., fols. 1–2, 3–5, 13–15.

16. Kraszewski may also have been considered a rival to the conservatives' hegemony in the ancient capital, having been a candidate for the chair in Polish literature (eventually given to Tarnowski) as well as the editor's seat at the daily *Czas.* (Wincenty Danek, *Józef Ignacy Kraszewski: Zarys biograficzny* [Warsaw: Ludowa Spółdzielnia Wydawnicza, 1976], 242–43.)

17. It affected events with which the writer was connected, such as the Cracow congress of the Lwów Pedagogical Society to celebrate the one hundredth anniversary of the National Education Commission: it was moved to Lwów, ostensibly because of an outbreak of cholera. (Reports of plague often served the politics of the Galician conservatives.) See the report from the Historical-Literary Commission's session of 8 January 1973, when Wincenty Danek presented his work "Setna rocznica Komisji Edukacji Narodowej w r. 1873 i udział w niej J. I. Kraszewskiego," *Sprawozdania z posiedzeń Komisji Naukowych PAN Oddz. w Krakowie* 17, no. 1 (1974): 30–31.

18. Letter of 20 September 1877 of Kalinka to Stanisław Tarnowski, BJ przyb. 38/53, cited in Izabella Lankosz, "Wokół jubileuszu 50-lecia działalności literackiej Józefa Ignacego Kraszewskiego" (master's thesis, Jagiellonian University, 1995), 27.

19. The words of Walerian Kalinka in a letter of 17 September 1877, BJ przyb. 38/53, cited in Stanisław Burkot, "O jubileuszu J. I. Kraszewskiego," *Dziesięciolecie Wyższej Szkoły Pedagogicznej w Krakowie* (Kraków: Państwowe Wydawnictwo Naukowe, 1957), 278.

20. Irena Homola, *Kraków za prezydentury Mikołaja Zyblikiewicza (1874–1881)* (Kraków: Wydawnictwo Literackie, 1976), 61ff., 73–75, 81. Clearly a talented linguist, Zyblikiewicz was famous for giving splendid speeches in German at sessions of the Council of State in Vienna.

21. Ibid., 48; Władysław Luszczkiewicz, "Sukiennice krakowskie" (dalszy ciąg), *Kłosy* 30, no. 774 (1880): 275–77; Homola, *Kraków za prezydentury,* 150–64.

22. Homola, *Kraków za prezydentury,* 256; Jerzy Piekarczyk, "Veto prezydenta," *Kraków* 3 (1985): 18.

23. A notation that Zyblikiewicz had informed the viceroy of his intent was made in a Cracow police report of 18 January 1879, APKr, DPKr 24, 703/pr/79, 61/pr/79. Potocki would be informed of the course of the jubilee by the director of the Cracow police, from whom he requested two reports a day for the duration as well as a daily telegram outlining the main points. (Letter of 30 September 1879, APKr, DPKr 24,703/pr/79, 691/pr/79; letter from the Prezydium Namiest. Ł. 7566 [5 September 1879], APKr, DPKr 24, 703/pr/79, 636/pr/79.)

24. September 1879 letter of Zyblikiewicz to Kraszewski, BJ rkps 6545 IV, fols. 607–609. Other controversies concerned the timing of the celebration. See Patrice Marie Dabrowski, "Reinventing Poland: Commemorations and the Shaping of the Modern Nation" (Ph.D. diss., Harvard University, 1999), 62–63.

25. *Księga Kraszewskiego,* 22, 25. The details of the commemoration presented here are taken mainly from *Księga Kraszewskiego* and the Cracow daily *Czas.*

26. Tarnowski, "Zjazd krakowski," 297–98.

27. Commented upon by many sources, including Spasowicz, "Jubileusz Kraszewskiego," *Ateneum* 4 (1879): 385; K. D., "Khronika. Pis'mo iz" Krakova: Iubilei Krashevskago, 3–5 oktiabria, 1879," *Vestnik Evropy* 6 (November 1879): 410.

28. BJ 224642 V, 15–17, Rara; *Czas,* 1 October 1879 and 3 October 1879; Rachunek Nr I: Wydatki na uroczystość jubileuszową J. I. Kraszewskiego, APKr, IT 1022/I; Lankosz, "Wokół jubileuszu," 26.

29. One Poznań commentary noted the positive influence the minister for Galician affairs, Florian Ziemiałkowski, had on the emperor. (*Goście krakowscy w Poznaniu: Jubileusz Kraszewskiego w Krakowie* [Poznań: druk. W. Simona, 1881], 94.)

30. *Księga Kraszewskiego,* 25.

31. One Warsaw correspondent wondered whether the delay with the posters was designed to prevent the crowds from assembling. ("Korespondencya Gazety Warszawskiej," *Gazeta Warszawska,* 24 September/6 October 1879.)

32. *Księga Kraszewskiego,* 24–25.

33. Cited in Homola, *Kraków za prezydentury,* 262.

34. Letter (n.d., around 20 September 1879), cited in Danek, *Kraszewski: Zarys biograficzny,* 294.

35. He later confided to a friend that during his stay he took morphine at night to fall asleep, quinine during the day to keep up his strength. (Letter of 20 October 1879 to Celina Dominikowska, cited in ibid., 365.)

36. See Kraszewski correspondence, BJ rkps 5312, fol. 34.

37. Stanisław Dobrzanowski, *Restauracja diecezji krakowskiej w latach osiemdziesiątych XIX wieku* (Warsaw: Akademia Teologii Katolickiej, 1977), 57.

38. Draft of police report, APKr, DPKr 24, 703/pr/79, 691/pr/79.

39. As was true for many such endeavors in the nineteenth century, this renovation was not devoid of innovation: the architect, Tomasz Pryliński, added neo-Gothic arcades and an imposing central entranceway.

40. The text of Dunajewski's benediction was reproduced in the papers, if not in the commemorative volume that followed. Here I cite the version given in *Przegląd Polski* ("Mowa X. Biskupa Krakowskiego przy poświęceniu Sukiennic," *Przegląd Polski* 14 [November 1879]: 304–305).

41. Ibid.

42. The underscorings of an abbreviated version of Dunajewski's benediction in a book printed by visitors to the jubilee emphasized the obvious omissions of the bishop. (*Goście krakowscy,* 94–95, 97.)

43. *Księga Kraszewskiego,* 26. The dress of the dignitaries was not without significance. Badeni was in uniform, the provincial marshal in Polish dress, the former playing an official Austrian role, the latter an official Polish one.

44. See Kraszewski letter, BJ rkps 5312, fol. 34. Also mentioned in Danek, *Kraszewski: Zarys biograficzny,* 287. This is discussed further in Dabrowski, "Reinventing Poland," 75–76.

45. Dobrzanowski, *Restauracja,* 57; Purchla, *Matecznik,* 88.

46. Earlier, Dunajewski had supposedly stated that he would have taken part, but claimed, "I am too young a bishop, thus in Rome they would have tripped me up [*by mi z Rzymu stołka podstawiono*]." (From a letter of 29 September 1879 of Alfred Szczepański to Kraszewski, BJ rkps 6536, cited in Burkot, "O jubileuszu," 277.)

47. Purchla, *Matecznik,* 88.

48. Helena Hempel, *Wspomnienia z życia ś.p. ks. Stanisława Stojałowskiego* (Kraków: Związek Ludowo-Narodowy, 1921), 28. See also Ziejka, "Krakowscy pątnicy," *Klejnoty i sekrety Krakowa,* ed. Róża Godula (Kraków: Wydawnictwo Wawelskie, 1994), 21–23; and Keely Stauter-Halsted, "Rural Myth and the Modern Nation: Peasant Commemorations of Polish National Holidays, 1879–1910," in *Staging the Past,* 157–58.

49. Maciej Szarek, "Bieg mego życia" (typewritten manuscript), BJ przyb. 110/76, fols. 7–11, 16.

50. Three times as many people wanted tickets than could have them. ("Kronika miejscowa i zagraniczna," *Czas,* 1 October 1879.)

51. Maciej Szarek, "Bieg mego życia," 18.

52. Ibid., 19.

53. This event is chronicled fully in *Księga Kraszewskiego,* which enumerates even those speeches and gifts that, due to a lack of time, could not be presented during that ceremony.

54. K. D., "Khronika," 412. Perhaps this was in response to Wodzicki, who had seen fit to advertise his "Polishness" in the church.

55. *Księga Kraszewskiego,* 26.

56. The gifts he received were later exhibited in the Old Cloth Hall, the proceeds from which were earmarked for the Mickiewicz monument (discussed in chapter 5). The proceeds from the commemorative volume were treated similarly. (*Księga Kraszewskiego,* 2.)

57. Ibid., 32. Regions and cities represented by delegates included the old Lithuanian Żmudź (Samogitia); Grodno (Hrodna), Minsk, Pinsk, and Mohilew (Mohilau); Kamieniec (Kamyanets), Kiev (Kyïv), Łuck (Lutsk), Żytomierz (Zhitomyr), Kharkov (Kharkiv), Odessa (Odesa), Polesie; the Bessarabian town of Chocim (Chutin, Chotin); Łomża, Ostrołęka, Piotrków, Kielce, and Kalisz; Riga, Petersburg, and Siberia.

58. Danek, *Kraszewski: Zarys biograficzny,* 331. Many telegrams were published in *Księga Kraszewskiego,* 201–31.

59. Letter to Agaton Giller, 17 March 1879, cited in Danek, *Kraszewski: Zarys biograficzny,* 293.

60. Ibid.

61. *Księga Kraszewskiego,* 38. The other direct quotations in this paragraph come from ibid., 37–43.

62. Kraszewski did not allude to them in his speech.

63. This is a paraphrase of Luke 2:29–30.

64. *Księga Kraszewskiego,* 42–43.

65. While Burkot calls the socialists the "third partner in Galician contests," this assessment seems a bit premature. (Burkot, "O jubileuszu," 273.)

66. See, for example, a letter of Kirkor of 17 March 1879, BJ rkps 6509, cited in ibid., 272.

67. Witold Piekarski bragged that their activity during the celebration was irritating the conservatives in a letter of 24 October 1879 to his father, Teodor Piekarski, BJ rkps 6525, cited in ibid., 273. See their leaflet: Odezwa socjalistów polskich wystosowana do Józefa Ignacego Kraszewskiego z powodu Jubileuszu prac Jego na polu literackiem, BJ 224642 V 63 Rara.

68. From Witold Piekarski, *Listy z więzienia (1879)* (Wrocław: Zakład Narodowy im. Ossolińskich, 1953), 43–44, cited in Danek, *Kraszewski: Zarys biograficzny,* 311.

69. "Obchód w Krakowie jubileuszu pięćdziesięcioletniej pracy literackiej J. I. Kraszewskiego," supplement to *Czas,* 5 October 1870. This speech is published in *Księga Kraszewskiego,* 45–46, albeit minus several of the metaphors cited above.

70. For a total cost of 8,020 guldens. (Rachunek nr 2 II: Wydatki na obiad, APKr, IT 1022/I; *Księga Kraszewskiego,* 49.)

71. The jubilee figured in print on one corner of the napkin.

72. Provided, respectively, by the La Ferme factory of Warsaw and a group of Warsaw bakeries. (*Księga Kraszewskiego,* 49–50.)

73. "Obchód w Krakowie jubileuszu pięćdziesięcioletniej pracy literackiej J. I. Kraszewskiego," supplement to *Czas,* 5 October 1879. The toast was also published in *Księga Kraszewskiego,* 50–51. The Czech connection, interestingly, had been cultivated by Kraszewski, and Asnyk had been an honorary guest at the Prague celebration in December 1878. (Ibid., 239, 244.)

74. The text of his toast is reprinted in ibid., 55–56.

75. The diplomatic implications of the Kraszewski jubilee are discussed in Wereszycki, "Międzynarodowe echa," 3–6.

76. Tarnowski, "Zjazd krakowski," 292. This did not mean that all citizens of the Russian Empire were encouraged to fete Kraszewski. A secret order from the chancellery of the curator of the Warsaw school district forbade its subordinates and pupils to take part in the Kraszewski celebration. (BJ rkps 8923 IV, fols. 80–81; *Księga Kraszewskiego,* 236.)

77. *Księga Kraszewskiego,* 57–58.

78. Ibid., 56.

79. According to the police report on the banquet, APKr, DPKr 24, 703/pr/79, 695/pr/79. It is hard to get a sense of this encounter from the press of the time, which found it expedient to gloss over the incident. *Czas* hardly mentions the controversy. The confrontation was completely recast in the commemorative volume so often cited in this section. There it was reported that Spasowicz's speech was as well received as the others; simply some guests had not heard it well and thus misunderstood it. (*Księga Kraszewskiego,* 56–57.)

80. Wereszycki, "Międzynarodowe echa," 10.

81. They also saw it as evidence of nearsighted politics. (*Goście krakowscy,* 102.) Russians responded variously, as seen in Wereszycki, "Międzynarodowe echa," 11–14. On Liske, see Karol J. Nitman, "Ksawery Liske," *Świat* no. 24 (15 December 1890): 600–604.

82. From Męciński's speech, published in *Księga Kraszewskiego*, 64–65.

83. For example, *Czas*. ("Obchód w Krakowie jubileuszu pięćdziesięcioletniej pracy literackiej J. I. Kraszewskiego," supplement to *Czas*, 5 October 1879.)

84. "Obchód w Krakowie jubileuszu pięćdziesięcioletniej pracy literackiej J. I. Kraszewskiego," *Czas*, 7 October 1879.

85. K. D., "Khronika," 423.

86. Józef Szujski alluded to this in his talk at the banquet. The text was given in full in "Obchód w Krakowie jubileuszu pięćdziesięcioletniej pracy literackiej J. I. Kraszewskiego," *Czas*, 7 October 1879.

87. Józef Dużyk, *Henryk Siemiradzki życie i twórczość* (Wrocław: Zakład Narodowy im. Ossolińskich, 1984), 19–20. Despite Siemiradzki's assertions that he was a Pole, Russians claimed him as one of their own.

88. *Pochodnie Nerona,* also known as *Świeczniki Chrześciaństwa* (Christianity's candlesticks). Kraszewski, who had met the artist in 1872, had reviewed the painting (exhibited in Munich) in the Polish periodical *Biesiada Literacka* (Literary feast).

89. According to Alfred Szczepański, Siemiradzki claimed that he had painted the work for the Poles and, when it became clear that they understood the significance of the martyrs, he could not do other than make a present of the painting to them. (From a police report on the dinner at the Sharpshooters' Hall, 9 October 1879, APKr, DPKr 24, 703/pr/79.)

90. "Obchód w Krakowie jubileuszu pięćdziesięcioletniej pracy literackiej J. I. Kraszewskiego," *Czas*, 7 October 1879.

91. "Wiadomości bieżące zagraniczne," *Gazeta Warszawska*, 29 September/11 October 1879.

92. *Księga Kraszewskiego*, 81.

93. The words of the president of the Towarzystwo Sztuk Pięknych, Count Henryk Wodzicki. (Ibid., 81–82.) As will be seen in later chapters, this designation—a royal gift—seems to be the height of praise. Poles making a significant, and expensive, contribution to the nation could be thought of as a sort of self-made Polish royalty.

94. Was he thus atoning for the excesses of the Cracow conservatives? It certainly does not appear that Siemiradzki intended any slight to Kraszewski, whom he had met years before and for whom he had great respect. (See excerpt from Siemiradzki's correspondence cited in Dużyk, *Siemiradzki*, 11.) After the celebration had ended, Siemiradzki also wrote very respectfully to the honorand and requested permission to promote one of Kraszewski's projects: a Polish daily in Vienna. (18 October 1879 letter of Henryk Siemiradzki to Kraszewski, BJ rkps 6531, fols. 547–48.)

95. Tadeusz Chruścicki, introduction to *The National Museum in Cracow: A Historical Outline and Selected Objects,* trans. Elżbieta Chrzanowska (Warsaw: Arkady, 1987), 5; *Księga Kraszewskiego*, 80–81.

96. Alfred Szczepański, cited in *Księga Kraszewskiego*, 83.

97. Akt fundacyjny "Macierzy Polskiej," BJ rkps 6902 IV, fols. 12–13.

98. In his letter to Zyblikiewicz of September 1882, Kraszewski said that "We all belong to the folk" and that education was to be "not only for the village huts, town houses and workshops, but also for the noble manors and Jewish houses . . ." (Danek, *Kraszewski: Zarys biograficzny*, 335–38).

99. Letter of 6 November 1881 to Władysław Bełza, Ossolineum, rkps 12424/I, cited in ibid., 335.

100. Tadeusz Krawczak, "Udział chłopów galicyjskich w ruchu niepodległościowym, 1912–1918" (master's thesis, Warsaw University, 1976), 46.

101. From a letter to Giller (n.d., after the commemoration), cited in Danek, *Kraszewski: Zarys biograficzny*, 296.

102. February 1882 letter of Zyblikiewicz to Kraszewski, BJ rkps 6545 IV, fols. 616–17; 20 April 1882, BJ rkps 6545 IV, fol. 618.

103. They also took sustenance from thirty-two platters of venison, an unspecified amount of wine, thirty-two cakes, and twelve hundred pastries from four bakeries. (Rachunek nr 3 III: Wydatki na Bal, 25 October 1879, APKr, IT 1022/I.)

104. "Obchód w Krakowie jubileuszu pięćdziesięcioletniej pracy literackiej J. I. Kraszewskiego," *Czas,* 7 October 1879.

105. Telegram to the viceroy's presidium, APKr, DPKr 24, 703/pr/79, 696/pr/79.

106. Perhaps for this reason Kraszewski wrote that this evening left Zyblikiewicz peevish. (Letter to Agaton Giller [n.d.; after the Cracow commemoration], published in Danek, *Kraszewski: Zarys biograficzny,* 296.)

107. From police report on the dinner at the Sharpshooters' Hall, 9 October 1879, APKr, DPKr 24, 703/pr/79.

108. Ibid. These phrases were not included in the text of Chodźkiewicz's speech published in *Księga Kraszewskiego,* 87.

109. Wereszycki, "Międzynarodowe echa," 3.

110. "Kronika Krakowska," *Jozefa Czecha Kalendarz Krakowski* (1906), 79–83.

111. This process, more complicated than it seemed at the outset, took decades: the Wawel did not pass into Polish control until 1905.

112. "Obchód w Krakowie jubileuszu pięćdziesięcioletniej pracy literackiej J. I. Kraszewskiego," *Czas,* 4 October 1879.

113. In Kraszewski's words, "Many opponents holed themselves up, others had to play a double role, others pretended to be converted. One could sense wavering and those, who during the first days still stood cold, were in the end forced at least to pretend that they had warmed up." (From a letter to Agaton Giller [n.d.; after the Cracow commemoration], published in Danek, *Kraszewski: Zarys biograficzny,* 296.)

114. Burkot, "O jubileuszu," 271.

115. "Kochani bracia Krakowianie!" (signed "Jubilee Guests") (Kraków: nakł. zbiorowym, druk. W. L. Anczyca i sp., 1879); BJ 224642 V Rara, 52.

116. From a poem in Stojałowski's *Pszczółka:* "Rozhowor Wandy z Wisły z powodu Jubileuszu obchodzonego w Krakowie w Październiku 1879," *Pszczółka* 5, no. 21 (23 October 1879): 163–64. Stojałowski eventually gave the event good press and even published Kraszewski's speech in full. (Ibid., 161–63.)

117. *Księga Kraszewskiego,* 2.

118. The comment comes from an article in *Golos* (no. 295 [1879]), a selection of which is found in *Pisma iuzhnorussa po povodu iubileia Krashevskago* (Izdanie redaktsii "Kievlianina") (Kiev: v universitetskoi tipografii [I. Zavadzkago], 1879), 5.

119. From a letter of 5 December 1879 of Karol Estreicher to Maria and Feliks Faleński, cited in Danek, *Kraszewski: Zarys biograficzny,* 324.

2. THE RELIEF OF VIENNA, 1683–1883

1. Credit for the idea is given to the group "Ognisko." (A. Nowolecki, *Uroczystości ku uczczeniu pamięci Jana III w dzielnicach polskich i za granicą: Na pamiątkę 200-letniej rocznicy odsieczy Wiednia 1683 r.* [Kraków: staraniem "Wydawnictwa Czytelni Ludowej," 1883], 21–22.)

2. Viscount [Edgar Vincent] d'Abernon, *The Eighteenth Decisive Battle of the World: Warsaw, 1920* (London: Hodder and Stoughton, 1931), 11.

3. Michał Rożek, *Tradycja wiedeńska w Krakowie* (Kraków: Krajowa Agencja Wydawnicza, 1983), 32–33.

4. Ibid., 33–34; Halina Florkowska-Frančić, "Emigracyjne obchody dwóchsetnej rocznicy wiktorii wiedeńskiej," *Przegląd Polonistyczny* 10 (1984): 78.

5. Rożek, *Tradycja wiedeńska*, 30.

6. Józef Chociszewski, *Sobieski pod Wiedniem dnia 12 września r. P. 1683: Na pamiątkę 22-letniego jubileuszu*, 4th ed. (Poznań: nakł. Księgarni Katolickiej, 1883), 32.

7. J. L[ouis], "Pierwszy obchód zwycięstwa pod Wiedniem w Krakowie," *Czas*, 28 February 1883.

8. "Przegląd polityczny," *Przegląd Polski* 18 (October 1883): 157.

9. Ibid. Hard to translate, with its sense of "gathering spiritual strength," this last phrase later finds a strong echo in the *pokrzepienie serc* (literally, the strengthening of hearts), the motivation for writing historical novels attributed to the writer Henryk Sienkiewicz. If, in the old phrase, city air made Germans free (*Stadt Luft macht frei*), then Cracow air made Poles stronger, more Polish.

10. [N.t.], *Czas,* 7 August 1883, also cited in Galos, "Obchody rocznicy odsieczy," 128.

11. Ibid. Dabrowski, "Reinventing Poland," 116–18, has more on these smaller (if significant) celebrations, in Galicia as well as abroad.

12. Involving a novena of preparation, the church festivities actually began 2 September. How they were tied into the commemoration will be addressed later.

13. A number of treatments of the events of 1883 were published in commemoration of the centenary of the celebration. These include articles by Wiesław Bieńkowski, "Obchody 200-lecia Wiktorii Wiedeńskiej w Krakowie," *Zeszyty Naukowe Stowarzyszenia PAX* (Seria: Kultura, Oświata, Nauka) 6/7 (1983); Wiesław Bieńkowski, "Rok 1883 w Krakowie (Uroczystości 200-lecia odsieczy Wiednia)," *Rocznik Krakowski* 51 (1987): 97–118; Adam Galos, "Obchody rocznicy odsieczy wiedeńskiej w Galicji w 1883 r.," in *Z dziejów i tradycji srebrnego wieku,* ed. Jerry Pietrzak (Acta Universitatis Wratislaviensis, no. 1108, Historia 75) (Wrocław: Wydawnictwo Uniwersytetu Wrocławskiego, 1990): 123–43; Adam Galos, "Obchody rocznicy wiedeńskiej w XIX w.," *Śląski Kwartalnik Historyczny Sobótka* 35 (1980): 437–39; Rożek, *Tradycja wiedeńska,* esp. 41–51; J. Szablowski, "Obchody jubileuszowe zwycięstwa pod Wiedniem w 1683 roku w ciągu trzech stuleci," in *Odsiecz wiedeńska 1683: Wystawa jubileuszowa w Zamku Królewskim na Wawelu w trzechsetlecie bitwy* (Kraków: Państwowe zbiory sztuki na Wawelu, 1990), 1:7–40; Celina Bąk-Koczarska, "Rada Miejska organizatorem obchodu 200-lecia odsieczy Wiednia w Krakowie," *Zeszyty Naukowe Muzeum Historycznego Miasta Krakowa: Krzysztofory* 9 (1982): 38–55; Florkowska-Frančić, "Emigracyjne obchody," 69–79; Adam Galos, "Władze pruskie wobec obchodów rocznicy wiedeńskiej w 1883 r.," *Śląski Kwartalnik Historyczny Sobótka* 36 (1981): 267–78; and Grażyna Lichończak, "Pomnik króla Jana III Sobieskiego w Ogrodzie Strzeleckim w Krakowie," *Zeszyty Naukowe Muzeum Historycznego Miasta Krakowa: Krzysztofory* 9 (1982): 56–65. A more recent work focusing on activities in Lwów is by Paweł Sierżęga, "Centralny komitet jubileuszowy w przygotowaniach obchodów 200. rocznicy odsieczy wiedeńskiej w Galicji" (in *Z przeszłości Europy Środkowowschodniej*, ed. Jadwiga Hoff [Rzeszów: Wydawnictwo Uniwersytetu Rzeszowskiego, 2002], 76–99.) I have been unable to consult his new monograph about the 1883 commemoration, which has been published in the series Galicja i jej dziedzictwo.

14. Letter of 4 March 1880 of Zuzanna Czartoryska to Rada Królewskiego głównego Miasta Krakowa, Bibl PAN Kr, 10425. She supposedly was acting on a suggestion made by photographer and Cracow city councilor Walery Rzewuski. (Bąk-Koczarska, "Rada Miejska," 38.)

15. Stanisław Tarnowski, "Obchód wiedeńskiej rocznicy," *Przegląd Polski* 18 (October 1883): 7.

16. Bąk-Koczarska, "Rada Miejska," 40.

17. Bieńkowski, "Rok 1883," 105; "Kronika," *Nowa Reforma,* 11 September 1883; Stanisław Tomkowicz and Jerzy Mycielski, "Wystawa pamiątek i zabytków z epoki Jana III w Krakowie," *Przegląd Polski* 18 (October 1883): 82.

18. *Odsiecz wiedeńska 1683,* 1:19.

19. Words of Fryderyk Zoll, deputy chairman of the exhibition section, cited in "Uroczysty obchód jubileuszu Sobieskiego w Krakowie," *Nowa Reforma,* 12 September 1883. Figures taken from Bieńkowski, "Obchody 200-lecia," 160.

20. From the text of Zyblikiewicz's speech, in Polkowski, "Kronika dni wrześniowych," 89–90.

21. Tarnowski, "Obchód wiedeńskiej rocznicy," 14.

22. Tadeusz Chruścicki, introduction to *The National Museum in Cracow: A Historical Outline and Selected Objects,* trans. Elżbieta Chrzanowska (Warsaw: Arkady, 1987), 8.

23. Tarnowski wrote that only one other work, Weloński's sculpture of a gladiator, was outstanding. (Tarnowski, "Obchód wiedeńskiej rocznicy," 16.)

24. Protokół obrad komisyi jubileuszu Sobieskiego, 27 August 1883, APKr, IT 1023/14.

25. His *Das Jahr 1683 und der folgende grosse Türkenkrieg* (Graz: Verlagsbuch, Styria, 1882) was criticized by X., "Nowy zamach na chwałę Jana Sobieskiego," *Czas,* 12 November 1882.

26. The dilemma of presentation facing historians of Austria, it seems, was how loyally to celebrate the memory of the duke of Lorraine. For example, in a footnote in his *Handbuch der Geschichte Oesterreichs,* Graz professor Franz Krones "confesse[d] that the joy of the patriotic researcher of the history of the siege of Vienna is marred by the extolling of the deeds of the Polish king and the Poles, as the real liberators of Vienna" to the detriment of the imperial and German armies. (Józef Szujski, "Przed rocznicą Odsieczy Wiedeńskiej," *Czas,* 26 May 1882.)

27. X., "Nowy zamach na chwałę Jana Sobieskiego" (cont.), *Czas,* 15 November 1882.

28. Józef Szujski, "Przed rocznicą Odsieczy Wiedeńskiej."

29. [Władysław Wisłocki], *Sobiesciana: Bibliografia jubileuszowego obchodu dwóchsetnej rocznicy potrzeby wiedeńskiej z r. 1683, z ryciną Apoteozy króla Jana III dłuta P. Welońskiego* (Lviv: nakładem centralnego komitetu jubileuszowego, 1884).

30. "Kronika," *Nowa Reforma,* 10 July 1883; *Sobiesciana,* 62–65.

31. "Obchód Sobieskiego. Lwów, 12 czerwca," *Nowa Reforma,* 15 June 1883; Karl Weiss, *Herr Onno Klopp und das Verhalten der Bürger Wiens im Jahre 1683* (Vienna: Rudolf Lechners Verlagsbuchhandlung, 1882); Selma Krasa, "Das historische Ereignis und seine Rezeption: Zum Nachleben der Zweiten Türkenbelagerung Wiens in der österreichischen Kunst des 19. und 20. Jahrhunderts," *Die Türken vor Wien: Europa und die Entscheidung an der Donau 1683* (Salzburg and Vienna: Residenz Verlag, 1982), 13.

32. While the Poles do not come out and say this directly, the Czechs do. See the Czech comment in the lead article, "Die Sobieski-Feier mit Hindernissen," *Politik* (Prague), 7 September 1883, cited in "Głos czeski o obchodzie jubileuszu Sobieskiego," *Nowa Reforma,* 11 September 1883.

33. From *Dziennik Poznański,* 25 July 1883, cited in Joanna Oleszczuk, "Wokół jubileuszu 200-lecia odsieczy wiedeńskiej w Krakowie" (master's thesis, Jagiellonian University, 1994–95), 110.

34. For the text of the Viennese invitation, see "Historyczna wystawa miasta Wiednia r. 1883," *Czas,* 4 March 1883; the words of the Polish committee were published in "Komitet jubileuszowy dla Komitetu jubileuszowego dla uczczenia 200-letniej rocznicy Wiednia," *Nowa Reforma,* 1 May 1883. It should be noted, in all fairness to the Viennese, that the mayor praised Sobieski's leadership at the actual celebration, and his speech was reproduced and distributed to the public. (Rożek, *Tradycja wiedeńska,* 39.)

35. Protocols of the committee are preserved in APKr, IT 1023/14.

36. Ibid., 38–39, 41–42, 50.

37. "Sprawy miejskie: Posiedzenie Rady miejskiej d. 22 stycznia," *Czas,* 24 January 1883; Tarnowski, "Obchód wiedeńskiej rocznicy," 3–4.

38. "Uroczysty obchód jubileuszu Sobieskiego w Krakowie," *Nowa Reforma,* 14 September 1883. Compare Krieger's 1883 photograph in Bąk-Koczarska, "Rada Miejska," 52.

39. To gain as many volunteers for the honor guard as possible, a local paper played on readers' patriotism, implying that the Poles ought to desire a successful celebration in 1883 at least as much as during the emperor's visit in 1880. ("Jubileusz Sobieskiego," *Nowa Reforma,* 4 September 1883.)

40. Polkowski, "Kronika dni wrześniowych," 98–99.

41. Tarnowski, "Obchód wiedeńskiej rocznicy," 14.

42. Minutes of the committee meeting, 1 September 1883, APKr, IT 1023/14; "Kronika miejscowa i zagraniczna," *Czas,* 22 August 1883.

43. Bąk-Koczarska, "Rada Miejska," 48.

44. Polkowski, "Kronika dni wrześniowych," 102. Emphasis from the original.

45. "Jubileusz Sobieskiego," *Nowa Reforma,* 29 August 1883; "Jubileusz Sobieskiego," *Nowa Reforma,* 6 September 1883; Bieńkowski, "Rok 1883 w Krakowie," 111.

46. Barbara Kuczała, "Odsiecz wiedeńska w twórczości Jana Matejki," *Zeszyty Naukowe Muzeum Historycznego Miasta Krakowa: Krzysztofory* 9 (1982): 34.

47. Maryjan Gorzkowski, *Wskazówki do nowego obrazu J. Matejki "Sobieski pod Wiedniem"* ([Kraków]: nakładem autora, Druk W. Korneckiego, [1883]), 256. The designation "rp." stands for "in the year of the Lord," and "Polonus" is Latin for "Pole." The constant labeling of Poles as Austrians, Germans, or Russians, depending on their location, frustrated many artists and writers during this period.

48. Marian Gorzkowski, *Jan Matejko: Epoka od r. 1861 do końca życia artysty z dziennika prowadzonego w ciągu lat siedemnastu* (Kraków: Towarzystwo Przyjaciół Sztuk Pięknych w Krakowie, 1993), 258.

49. Published in "Kronika miejscowa i zagraniczna," *Czas,* 7 August 1883.

50. Stanisław Pigoń, *Z Komborni w świat: Wspomnienia młodości* (Kraków: Spółdzielnia wydawnicza "Więź," 1946), 98. The younger Pigoń later became professor of Polish literature at Jagiellonian University, a notable example of upward mobility among the peasantry.

51. Galos, "Obchody rocznicy odsieczy," 135, 139.

52. The history of Polish coronations as well as copies of documents connected with the 1883 ceremony are found in Polkowski, "Kronika dni wrześniowych," 68–76.

53. For more on this subject, see Patrice M. Dabrowski, "Folk, Faith and the Fatherland: Defining the Polish Nation in 1883," *Nationalities Papers* 28, no. 3 (2000): 387–416.

54. See John-Paul Himka, *Religion and Nationality in Western Ukraine: The Greek Catholic Church and the Ruthenian National Movement in Galicia, 1867–1900* (Montreal: McGill-Queen's University Press, 1999).

55. Bieńkowski, "Rok 1883," 108; *Pamiątka pielgrzymki ludowej do Krakowa urządzonej staraniem Redakcyi pism ludowych "Wieńca" i "Pszczółki" w wrześniu 1883 na uroczystość koronacyi cudownego obrazu N.P. Maryi na Piaskach i na uroczystość obchodu dwuchsetnej rocznicy zwycięstwa króla polskiego Jana III. pod Wiedniem* (L'viv: z drukarni Towarzystwa imienia Szewczenki, 1883), 27–28.

56. This was noted in *Pamiątka pielgrzymki ludowej,* 5.

57. Polkowski, "Kronika dni wrześniowych," 68–69.

58. *Wieniec* 9, no. 18 (30 August 1883): 137; Bieńkowski, "Rok 1883," 109; "Kronika," *Nowa Reforma,* 11 September 1883.

59. "5236 włościan," *Pszczółka* 9, no. 17 (23 August 1883): 129; "Kronika," *Nowa Reforma,* 11 September 1883.

60. *Pamiątka pielgrzymki ludowej,* 21.
61. "Kronika," *Nowa Reforma,* 11 September 1883.
62. Tarnowski, "Obchód wiedeńskiej rocznicy," 10–11, 13.
63. *Pamiątka pielgrzymki ludowej,* 27–28.
64. A number of committee members came from liberal democratic, literary-artistic, and intelligent, not conservative, circles more associated with the opposition paper *Nowa Reforma* than with the conservative *Czas.* Many of these activists would serve on commemoration committees for years to come. The leadership of the citizens' committee included Kazimierz Bartoszewicz, Walery Gadomski, Eminowicz, Kornecki, Juliusz Kossak, count Mieroszowski, Adam Mikłaszewski, Father Ignacy Polkowski, Tadeusz Romanowicz. ("Kronika," *Nowa Reforma,* 9 August 1883.)
65. "Jubileusz Sobieskiego," *Nowa Reforma,* 23 August 1883.
66. See the report on the committee meeting ("Jubileusz Sobieskiego," *Nowa Reforma,* 24 August 1883).
67. Among the speakers at the folk gathering were Władysław Kołodziejczyk, a peasant from Mogiła; Jakób Kot, a Ruthene from Olesko, where Sobieski was born; Michał Ostrowski, a Ruthenian merchant from Ruda; and Ruthenian villager Hrehory Skoblik (vel Skabłyk) of Daszowa in the province of Stryj. ("Obchód uroczysty jubileuszu Sobieskiego w Krakowie," *Nowa Reforma,* 12 September 1883.) The texts of their speeches are in *Czas,* 13 September 1883.
68. For more details of the complaints, see Dabrowski, "Folk, Faith, and the Fatherland," 406.
69. Letter of Paweł Popiel to the Cracow mayor, published in "Ostatnie wiadomości," *Czas,* 22 August 1883. The original letter, dated 18 August 1883, is in APKr, IT 1023/14.
70. Minutes of the committee meeting, 23 August 1883, APKr, IT 1023/14. This last item infuriated the conservatives, who objected to the representation of only one class while suspecting that the villager's speech was inspired by the democrats. (Tarnowski, "Obchód wiedeńskiej rocznicy," 20.)
71. "Jubileusz Sobieskiego," *Nowa Reforma,* 31 August 1883.
72. Józef Pelczar, *Kazanie miane dnia 12 września 1883 r. jako w dwusetną rocznicę zwycięstwa pod Wiedniem, przez . . . rektora Uniw. Jag., kanonika katedr. krak.* (reprint from *Czas*) (Kraków, 1883), 3.
73. Nowolecki, *Uroczystości,* 3; *Odsiecz wiedeńska 1683,* 1:17.
74. That Poles continued to be perceived as a threat is demonstrated by Witold Rodkiewicz, *Russian Nationality Policy in the Western Provinces of the Empire (1863–1905)* (Lublin: Scientific Society of Lublin, 1998).
75. From a speech given by Dr. E. Czerkawski in Lwów on 11 September, cited in "Obchód jubileuszowy we Lwowie," *Nowa Reforma,* 14 September 1883.
76. Even the governor of Illinois recognized the Poles as defenders of human rights and freedom during the 1883 celebration, the first time Poles assembled in a visible demonstration of unity on the streets of America (Chicago). One of the main organizers of the Chicago festivities was Karol Chłapowski, husband of actress Helena Modrzejewska, who had been present in Cracow in 1879. (Florkowska-Frančić, "Emigracyjne obchody," 72; Galos, "Obchody rocznicy wiedeńskiej w XIX w.," 437.)
77. These facts were underscored by the Ruthenian villager from Daszowa, in his speech to the peasants, as reported in "Uroczysty obchód jubileuszu Sobieskiego w Krakowie," *Nowa Reforma,* 13 September 1883.
78. This information comes from a *Gazeta Narodowa* report on the committee meetings of 10 and 21 April, mentioned in "Komitet jubileuszowy dla Komitetu jubileuszowego dla uczczenia 200-letniej rocznicy Wiednia," *Nowa Reforma,* 1 May 1883.
79. BJ Druki ulotne jub., 224784 IV Rara, I/3.

80. Words of Director Maciołowski, cited in *Nowa Reforma,* 13 September 1883.

81. "Obchód uroczysty jubileuszu Sobieskiego w Krakowie," *Nowa Reforma,* 12 September 1883.

82. Ibid.

83. From the speech of Jan Czesak, a villager from Szczurowa, at the farewell to the village delegates. ("Kronika," *Nowa Reforma,* 15 September 1883.)

84. "Uroczysty obchód jubileuszu Sobieskiego w Krakowie," *Nowa Reforma,* 14 September 1883.

85. That the Polish nation prior to the partitions had been a political, not an ethnic, nation has been convincingly shown by Walicki, *Philosophy and Romantic Nationalism.*

86. The Ukrainian paper *Dilo* said the jubilee had the character of a Polish national manifestation (per Nowolecki, *Uroczystości,* 51); *Prolom* and *Slovo* were also opposed. For other views of the siege, see the "Ukrainophile" Stefan Kachala's book on 1683, reviewed in *Reforma,* 23 June 1882.

87. Such figures as Platon Kostecki and Father Jan Guszalewicz wrote poems ("Kronika," *Nowa Reforma,* 12 September 1883), as did J. Szaraniewicz ("Jubileusz Sobieskiego," *Nowa Reforma,* 31 August 1883).

88. "Obchód Sobieskiego: Lwów, 12 czerwca," *Nowa Reforma,* 15 June 1883.

89. Galos, "Obchody rocznicy odsieczy," 142; more on him in Galos, "Władze pruskie wobec obchodów," 273–74.

90. For more on these gatherings, see Dabrowski, "Reinventing Poland," 168–70.

91. The words of the Landrat in Wągrowiec, Unruh, in a statement dated "September 1, 1883, Sedan Day." (Published in *Gazeta Toruńska,* cited in Oleszczuk, "Wokół jubileuszu," 103.) Reportedly 189 towns held some kind of commemoration, although in places the authorities exerted pressure on the Poles to remove the tablets. (Galos, "Obchody rocznicy odsieczy," 135; Galos, "Władze pruskie," 275.)

92. "Przegląd polityczny," *Przegląd Polski* 18 (October 1883): 159.

93. Nowolecki, *Uroczystości,* 37; "Jubileusz Matejki," *Nowa Reforma,* 26 July 1883.

94. Words of Stanisław Tarnowski, cited in Bieńkowski, "Rok 1883," 106.

95. The text of Matejko's speech was published in numerous places, including Polkowski, "Kronika dni wrześniowych," 105. Reactions to Matejko's decision are covered in greater depth in Dabrowski, "Reinventing Poland," 184–89.

96. Readers who find this confusing are in good company, for Matejko's rather cryptic announcement required much clarification.

97. Jerzy Pietrzak, "Podarowanie obrazu 'Sobieski pod Wiedniem' Papieżowi Leonowi XIII: Prawda i myti," in *Z dziejów i tradycji srebrnego wieku,* ed. Jerzy Pietrzak (Acta Universitatis Wratislaviensis, no. 1108, Historia 70) (Wrocław: Wydawnictwo Uniwersytetu Wrocławskiego, 1990), 156–59.

98. Gorzkowski, *Matejko,* 268.

99. Published in *Kurier Poznański,* 21 December 1883, cited in Pietrzak, "Podarowanie obrazu," 160.

100. Such sentiments were reflected in a speech given by Lucyan Tatomir in Lwów, 11 September, cited in "Obchód jubileuszowy we Lwowie," *Nowa Reforma,* 14 September 1883.

101. "Dwuchsetletnia rocznica chwały," *Nowa Reforma,* 11 September 1883.

102. From a speech given at the Ruthenian Boarding-School (*Internat Ruski*) run by the Resurrectionists in Lwów, reported in "Kronika miejscowa i zagraniczna," *Czas,* 13 March 1883.

103. "Przegląd polityczny," *Przegląd Polski* 18 (October 1883): 158.

3. ELOQUENT ASHES

1. William W. Hagen, *Germans, Poles, and Jews: The Nationality Conflict in the Prussian East, 1772–1914* (Chicago and London: University of Chicago Press, 1980), 132. A photograph of the tsarist monument can be found in Szczepan Zachariasz Jabłoński, *Jasna Góra: Ośrodek kultu maryjnego (1864–1914)* (Lublin: Redakcja wydawnictwa KUL, 1982).

2. The impact of Miłkowski's brochure is discussed in Bogdan Cywiński, *Rodowody niepokornych* (Warsaw: Świat Książki. 1996), 346. The history of the league and Zet are detailed in Stanisław Kozicki, *Historia Ligi Narodowej: Okres 1887–1907* (London: Myśl Polski, 1964), 37–85, with pertinent documents—the originals of which were destroyed during World War II—reproduced on pp. 487–516. For a recent discussion of *Głos,* see Porter, *When Nationalism Began to Hate.*

3. This is argued by Halina Bursztyńska in *Henryk Sienkiewicz w kręgu oddziaływania powieści historycznych Józefa Ignacego Kraszewskiego* (Katowice: Uniwersytet Śląski, 1977), 9.

4. Żeromski, *Dzienniki,* 2:440–41, cited in Julian Krzyżanowski, *Henryk Sienkiewicz: Kalendarz życia i twórczości,* 2d rev. ed. (Warsaw: Państwowy Instytut Wydawniczy, 1956), 116.

5. Krzyżanowski, *Sienkiewicz: Kalendarz,* 8.

6. Together with Juliusz Słowacki and Zygmunt Krasiński. (Henryk Markiewicz, "Rodowód i losy mitu trzech wieszczów," in *Badania nad krytyką literacką: Seria 2,* ed. M. Głowiński and K. Dybiak (Wrocław: Zakład Narodowy im. Ossolińskich, 1984), 53.

7. It is sometimes left in its Polish original. See, for example, Roman Robert Koropeckyi, "Recreating the 'Wieszcz': Versions of the Life of Adam Mickiewicz, 1828–1897" (Ph.D. diss., Harvard University, 1990).

8. Maria Janion and Maria Żmigrodzka, *Romantyzm i historia* (Warsaw: Państwowy Instytut Wydawniczy, 1978), 33.

9. "Dlaczego jest Adam Mickiewicz naszym największym poetą?" *Wiek Młody,* 20 May 1898.

10. The subject of Polish messianism receives masterful treatment in part 3 of Andrzej Walicki's *Philosophy and Romantic Nationalism.*

11. Jacek Kolbuszewski, "Rola literatury w kształtowaniu polskich mitów politycznych XIX i XX wieku," in *Polskie mity polityczne,* 48.

12. Janion and Żmigrodzka, *Romantyzm i historia,* 11.

13. The citation is taken from the commemorative speech of the representative of the Lithuanian society Zelmu, Bohdanowicz, in Zdzisław Hordyński, "Sprowadzenia zwłok Adama Mickiewicza na Wawel," *Pamiętnik Towarzystwa Literackiego imienia Adama Mickiewicza* 4 (1890): 364–65. Interestingly, no one mentioned the Jewish heritage of Mickiewicz's mother, who was of Frankish (that is, baptized Jewish) origin.

14. Julian Krzyżanowski, *Dzieje literatury polskiej* (Warsaw: Państwowe Wydawnictwo Naukowe, 1879), 248–50, 257.

15. The Polish phrase is missing a verb. In English, it could be rendered approximately as "We all . . . from him." The missing verb might be construed as "come" or "stem" or perhaps even "owe our existence/identity," according to the Polish poet and literary scholar Stanisław Barańczak. (Letter to the author, 27 January 1997.)

16. See the announcement in the Cracow daily *Kraj* (23 June 1869), published in Krystyna Stachowska, "Materiały," in *Kraków Mickiewiczowi,* ed. Danuta Rederowa (Kraków: Wydawnictwo Literackie, 1956), 181.

17. Ibid.

18. Michał Rożek, *Królewska katedra na Wawelu* (Warsaw: Wydawnictwo Interpress, 1981), 160, 166; Stanisław Windakiewicz, *Dzieje Wawelu* (Kraków: Krakowska Spółka Wydawnicza, 1925), 216–17.

19. See, for example, Karol Suchodolski [KS, pseud.], *Pamiątka podniesienia relikwij Adama Mickiewicza z dodatkiem najpiękniejszych wyjątków z jego Ksiąg Narodu Polskiego i Pielgrzymstwa Polskiego z 4-ma obrazkami* (Kraków: nakł. Karola Suchodolskiego, 1890), 3.

20. Jeż, *Zwłoki Mickiewicza,* cited in Stefan Kawyn, *Ideologia stronnictw politycznych w Polsce wobec Mickiewicza 1890–1898* (L'viv: Nakładem Filomaty, 1937), 31–32.

21. Roman Wapiński, *Polska i małe ojczyzny Polaków: Z dziejów kształtowania się świadomości narodowej w XIX i XX wieku po wybuch II wojny światowej* (Wrocław: Zakład Naukowy im. Ossolińskich, 1994).

22. Windakiewicz, *Dzieje Wawelu,* 217.

23. Żeromski, *Dzienniki,* 6:188.

24. More on this in chapter 5.

25. Maria Świątecka, "Sprowadzenie zwłok Adama Mickiewicza do kraju," in *Kraków Mickiewiczowi,* 29–30. Interestingly, a 1890 account identified this development with the year 1883—the year of the Siege of Vienna celebration. (*Pamiątka złożenia zwłok Adama Mickiewicza w katedrze na Wawelu w Krakowie dnia 4 lipca 1890 r.* [Kraków: nakładem księgarni J. K. Żupańskiego i K. J. Heumanna, 1890], 73.)

26. Władysław Mickiewicz, *Pamiętniki* (Warsaw, Kraków, Łódź, Poznań, Wilno, and Zakopane: nakład Gebethnera i Wolffa, 1933), 3:300.

27. A short summary of the event has been written by Zofia Wielebska, "Obchody 400-lecia śmierci Jana Długosza," in *Jan Długosz: Wpięćsetną rocznicę śmierci; Materiały z sesji (Sandomierz 24–25 maja 1980 r.)* ed. F. Kiryk (Olsztyn: Polskie Tow. Historyczne, 1983), 197–201.

28. From letter of 10 December 1879 of Kraszewski to Władysław Mickiewicz, BJ przyb. 101/65, cited in Danek, *Kraszewski: Zarys biograficzny,* 333–34.

29. W. Mickiewicz, *Pamiętniki,* 1:270–71.

30. Stachowska, "Materiały," 185–86.

31. Reprint of the 1884 article, in BJ, Druki ulotne jubileuszowe, T. XIV/6-1. Also found in APŁ, Archiwum Bartoszewiczów, 1212, fol. 32.

32. Świątecka, "Sprowadzenie zwłok," 31. See also the speech of Stanisław Bouffał, the representative of the Union of Polish Student Societies Abroad (*Zjednoczone Towarzystwa Młodzieży Polskiej za granicą*), printed in Hordyński, "Sprowadzenie zwłok," 363–64.

33. Karol Korta, *Gimnazjum św. Anny w Krakowie: Wspomnienia ucznia z lat 1888–96* (Kraków: druk W.L. Anczyca i Spółki, 1938), 155–56; Halina Winnicka, "Socjaliści polscy wobec Adama Mickiewicza: Przewiezienie zwłok poety do kraju (1890 r.)," *Przegląd Humanistyczny* 21, no. 9 (1977): 53; Bartoszewicz, "Z dziejów pomnika," *Przegląd Literacki,* 10 June 1898.

34. Świątecka, "Sprowadzenie zwłok," 32.

35. See the letter of 12 May 1890 of Stanisław Tarnowski to Michał Bobrzyński, asking the latter to gather signatures on an announcement calling for the funeral to be organized at state expense (and for this to be channeled through the provincial marshal, not the viceroy), BJ rkps 8077 III, fols. 11–12. This did not prevent the Tarnowski family from keeping a facsimile of the exhumation document from Montmorency, which until early 1996 was on loan to the Archiwum PAN w Krakowie, KII-13, 113. Whether it is the copy or is merely a copy of the copy that supposedly was deposited in the Wawel treasury but is not there (see Maria Świątecka, "Sprowadzenie zwłok," 221–22, n. 22) is not certain.

36. "Uwagi śledziennika," *Djabeł,* 4 June 1890; *Djabeł,* 6 March 1890. This satirical weekly harbored no illusions on the subject.

37. See the letter of Jan Tarnowski to Stanisław, 31 May 1890, BJ rkps 8077 III, fols. 15–17.

38. "Uwagi śledziennika," *Djabeł,* 4 June 1890.

39. Per subcommittee meeting of 9 June 1890, as reported in *Kurjer Polski,* 10 June 1890.

40. Letter of 29 June 1890, in APKr, IT 876, fol. 359.

41. See letter of 15 June 1890 of Franciszek Siedlecki, chairman of the committee, to the university president, in AUJ, SII 964 A.

42. Adam Mickiewicz, "Księgi narodu polskiego," in *Dzieła* (Mikołów: nakł. Spółki Wydawn. K. Miarki, 1921), 5:99.

43. W. Mickiewicz, *Pamiętniki,* 3:306–307. Naturally, no mention of imperial opposition was made at the time in the press.

44. As per Badeni letter of 17 June 1890 and related correspondence, APKr, DPKr 37, 390/pr/90.

45. Winnicka, "Socjaliści polscy," 57.

46. Jan Lorentowicz, *Spojrzenie wstecz* (Kraków: Wydawnictwo Literackie, 1957), 109.

47. Reporting the purported views of the "cardinal's circles in Cracow" ("Uroczystość 4. lipca," *Kurjer Lwowski,* 27 June 1890); XX, "Wrażenie (z pogrzebu M.)," *Przegląd Polski* 25 (1890): 203.

48. My translation of the original French of Renan's speech, published in Hordyński, "Sprowadzenie zwłok," 355.

49. Renan, *What Is a Nation?* 47, 49.

50. From Renan's speech, published in Hordyński, "Sprowadzenie zwłok," 355. See also W. Mickiewicz, *Pamiętniki,* 3:322.

51. Renan, *What Is a Nation?* 47.

52. This issue was raised by Kazimierz Waliszewski in the periodical *Kraj.* (Waliszewski, cited in Winnicka, "Socjaliści polscy," 56.)

53. W. Mickiewicz, *Pamiętniki,* 3:330–31.

54. For more on Limanowski's interaction with democrats abroad during this period, see Kazimiera Janina Cottam, *Boleslaw Limanowski (1835–1935): A Study in Socialism and Nationalism* (Boulder, Colo.: East European Quarterly, 1978), 98–99, 111.

55. Bolesław Limanowski, *Pamiętniki* (Warsaw: Książka i Wiedza, 1958), 2:694. While excerpts of the latter speech were deemed publishable by the Galician censor, the purely socialist speech was rejected in its entirety, as was the speech of Barański, the editor of *Pobudka.* (Hordyński, "Sprowadzenie zwłok," 360.) Texts of both are found in Limanowski, *Pamiętniki,* 2:692–94.

56. The role played by Cracow students is discussed in greater detail in Dabrowski, "Reinventing Poland," 222–25.

57. Winnicka, "Socjaliści polscy," 56.

58. *Kurier Lwowski,* 4 July 1890.

59. Cottam, *Limanowski,* 111. The same held true for the Cracow celebrations (yet to come), where members of a conspiratorial youth organization met with representatives of similar organizations from the Russian and Prussian empires. (Jerzy Myśliński, *Grupy polityczne Królestwa Polskiego w zachodniej Galicji, 1895–1904* [Warsaw: Książka i Wiedza, 1967], 21.)

60. Hordyński, "Sprowadzenie zwłok," 366. Lévy did much for keeping Mickiewicz's profile high abroad, as seen in Jerzy W. Borejsza, *Sekretarz Adama Mickiewicza (Armand Lévy i jego czasy 1827–1891),* 2d rev. ed. (Wrocław, Warsaw, Kraków, and Gdańsk: Zakład Narodowy im. Ossolińskich, 1977).

61. Hordyński, "Sprowadzenie zwłok," 366–37; "Korespondencya 'Nowej Reformy': Wiedeń, 2 lipca," *Nowa Reforma,* 4 July 1890.

62. Kawyn, *Ideologia*, 1.

63. Mickiewicz, *Pamiętniki*, 3:301.

64. Program uroczystego złożenia zwłok, 30 April 1890, APKr, IT 976, fols. 453–55.

65. Nonetheless in 1890, Towiański's son reportedly swore—doubtless in an attempt to whitewash the bard's unorthodox past—that "Adam Mickiewicz, that man of exemplary piety and religiosity," was never "inclined, even for a moment, toward any kind of religious sect." (Adam Towiański, in a letter of 3 July 1890 published in *Nowa Reforma*, 4 July 1890.)

66. "Kronika krakowska z Roku Pańskiego 1890," *Józefa Czecha Kalendarz Krakowski* (1891), 65–73; *Czas*, 3 July 1890.

67. Even the inscription on the sarcophagus was the minimal "Adam Mickiewicz," per decision of the executive committee on 24 June. ("Sprowadzenie zwłok Mickiewicza," *Czas*, 25 June 1890.) Count Konstanty Przezdziecki funded the expensive Venetian work, which was installed in the Wawel crypt in May 1891. ("Kronika: Kraków, 3 lipca," *Nowa Reforma*, 4 July 1890; *Nowa Reforma*, 3 May 1891.)

68. Per 19 June session of executive committee. ("Z powodu sprowadzenia zwłok Mickiewicza," *Nowa Reforma*, 21 June 1890.)

69. "Złożenie zwłok Mickiewicza na Wawelu," *Czas*, 5 July 1890.

70. See Dabrowski, "Reinventing Poland," 241 n. 150, for more information on the composition of this group.

71. Per telegram signed by Tarnowski and Edward Jędrzejowicz in late June 1890, AUJ, S II 964.

72. Bibliographic information on Lewicki from "Słowo do wszystkich ludzi sprawiedliwych: W Imię Boga prawdy!" *Wieniec Polski* 24, nos. 16 and 17 (1 June 1898): 260–62.

73. APKr, DPKr 37, 498/pr/1890; Kawyn, *Ideologia*, 41–42.

74. The letter of Jan Wacław Machajski to Żeromski is reproduced in Stefan Żeromski, *Dziennikow tom odnaleziony*, ed. Jerzy Kądziela (Warsaw: Czytelnik, 1973), 116. Interestingly, he made no mention of Lewicki's speech, which should have been more to his liking.

75. Chotkowski's sermon was published in full in Hordyński, "Sprowadzenie zwłok," 388–400. The citations come from pp. 394 and 399.

76. The similarities are discussed in Dabrowski, "Reinventing Poland," 244–46.

77. Hordyński, "Sprowadzenie zwłok," 400.

78. Lorentowicz claims that the youth present cut up what remained of the Constantinople coffin. (Lorentowicz, *Spojrzenie wstecz*, 111.) Stanisław Rosiek (*Zwłoki Mickiewicza: Próba nekrografii poety* [Gdańsk: Słowo/Obraz Terytoria, 1997]) takes the other view.

79. Maria Szeliga, "Uroczystości pogrzebowe Adama Mickiewicza w Montmorency," cited in Rosiek, *Zwłoki Mickiewicza*, 22.

80. Although listed in many newspapers, a more complete compilation is found in *Złożenie zwłok Adama Mickiewicza na Wawelu dnia 4-go lipca 1890 roku: Książka pamiątkowa z 22 ilustracyami* (Kraków: nakł. i czcionkami Drukarni Związkowej, 1890), 126–36. The citations in this paragraph all come from this source.

81. From the text of the 19 May 1890 appeal of the Wadowice committee to the entire Polish folk (*lud*), reprinted in *Złożenie zwłok*, 46.

82. "Uroczystości pogrzebowe nieśmiertelnej pamięci wieszcza narodu naszego Adama Mickiewicza w Krakowie," *Pszczółka Illustrowana* 16, no. 13 (13 July 1890): 213; *Złożenie zwłok*, 51–52.

83. In Polish: Adamowi Mickiewiczowi lud wszystkich ziem Polski.

84. A loose rendition of Mickiewicz's verse: "O gdybym kiedyś dożył tej pociechy, / żeby te księgi zbłądziły pod strzechy" (Oh, if I should live to know the consolation / of these books wandering into thatched huts), cited, inter alia, by Jan Tarnowski in his speech of 4 July (Hordyński, "Sprowadzenie zwłok," 376).

85. "Uroczystości pogrzebowe nieśmiertelnej pamięci wieszcza narodu naszego Adama Mickiewicza w Krakowie," *Pszczółka Illustrowana* 16, no. 13 (13 July 1890): 12.

86. See the telegram in cypher from Badeni to the Cracow Director of Police, 2 July 1890. (APKr, DPKr 37, 430/pr/90.)

87. APKr, DPKr 51, 925/pr/98, 3; Franciszek Kącki, *Ks. Stanisław Stojałowski i jego działalność społeczno-polityczna* (L'viv: Kasa im. Rektora J. Mianowskiego, 1937), 1:154.

88. "Uroczystość Mickiewiczowska," *Nowa Reforma,* 2 July 1890; *Odezwa do ludu polskiego przed obchodem złożenia prochów Adama Mickiewicza na Wawelu,* ed. Stanisław Stojałowski (Gródek, 1890), found in BJ 543768 II.

89. APKr, DPKr 37, 427/pr/90.

90. Zygmunt F. Miłkowski (T.T. Jeż), "Głos pielgrzyma," *Kurjer Lwowski,* 4 July 1890.

91. Ibid.

92. XX, "Wrażenie (z pogrzebu M.)," *Przegląd Polski* 15 (1890): 203–11.

93. W. Mickiewicz, *Pamiętniki,* 3:301.

94. Kalinowski, "Na Wawel," 3.

95. John-Paul Himka, *Socialism in Galicia: The Emergence of Polish Social Democracy and Ukrainian Radicalism (1869–1890)* (Cambridge: distributed by Harvard University Press for the Harvard Ukrainian Research Institute, 1983), 166.

96. The Association's announcement was published in "Z Towarzystwa oświaty ludowej," *Nowa Reforma,* 4 July 1890.

97. Marya Ploderówna, "Dzień 4-go lipca r. 1890 w Krakowie (Wspomnienie)," *Wiek Młody* 6, no. 10 (20 May 1898): 87–88.

98. Hordyński, "Sprowadzenie zwłok," 383; also Świąteczka, "Sprowadzenie zwłok," 59.

99. Ploderówna, "Dzień 4-go lipca," 87–88.

4. "POLAND HAS NOT YET PERISHED"

1. A good brief English-language introduction to the heady last years of the Polish state is chapter 10, "Reform, Reaction and Revolt" in Jerzy Lukowski, *Liberty's Folly: The Polish-Lithuanian Commonwealth in the Eighteenth Century, 1697–1795* (London and New York: Routledge, 1991), 239–47.

2. Cited and translated in Andrzej Walicki, *Poland between East and West: The Controversies over Self-Definition and Modernization in Partitioned Poland* (Cambridge: distributed by Harvard University Press for the Harvard Ukrainian Research Institute, 1994), 14.

3. The words of Ewald Friedrich von Hertzberg, chief minister of Frederick William II, cited in Lukowski, *Liberty's Folly,* 253.

4. From a speech given by Ludwik Finkel to the Legal Association in Lwów, printed in *Gazeta Narodowa,* 3 May 1891; annnouncement of 29 April 1891 in the name of the Cracow citizens' committee, APKr, IT 873, Druki, pisma.

5. See, for example, the words of Wojciech Dzieduszycki, printed in *"Polonia" obraz Jana Styki zakupiony dla gminy miasta Lwowa ku uczczeniu setnej rocznicy ogłoszenia konstytucji Trzeciego Maja 1791* (L'viv: nakładem i drukiem I. Związkowej drukarni, 1891), 7; Eustachy Śmiałowski, *Trzeci maj: Wspomnienie w stuletnią rocznicę* (Kraków: nakładem autora, druk W. Korneckiego, 1891), 16; or the sermon of Father Tadeusz Chromecki given during the centennial celebration (*Mowa na obchód rocznicy konstytucyi dnia 3 Maja 1791 roku, miana w kościele OO. Bernardynów w Krakowie przez Ks. Tadeusza Chromeckiego, rektora XX. Pijarów w Krakowie* [Kraków, 1890], 4).

6. Andrzej Garlicki, "Łódź—Rok 1892," in *Pierwsze maje,* ed. Andrzej Garlicki (Warsaw: Iskry, 1984), 15.

256 | *Notes to pages 103–106*

7. Ibid., 16; "Święcenie pierwszego maja," *Nowa Reforma*, 2 May 1890; Feldman, *Dzieje polskiej myśli*, 229.

8. Feliks Perl [Res, pseud.], *Dzieje ruchu socjalistycznego w zaborze rosyjskim* (Warsaw, 1910), 304.

9. The degree to which the police spied on these various groups is evident from the reports and correspondence found in APKr, DPKr 38, 450/pr/91.

10. A copy of the resolutions from that meeting can be found in APKr, IT 873. Bartoszewicz also kept track of the 1891 correspondence between the government and the provincial committee. (APŁ, Archiwum Bartoszewiczów, 1375, fols. 9–15.)

11. Decree of 18 March 1891, cited in "Kronika," *Nowa Reforma*, 4 April 1891. This did not prevent Jewish residents of Galicia from organizing their own local celebrations or publishing a hymn sung by the Jewish population at the first anniversary of the Constitution in 1792 translated into Yiddish, Polish, German, and French.

12. Epsilon, "'Zakazuję' i 'zabraniam,'" *Trybuna* nos. 12 and 13 (1891): 11.

13. Stanisław Tarnowski, *Z doświadczeń i rozmyślań*, 2d ed. (Kraków: Druk. "Czasu" Fr. Kluczyckiego, 1891), 371.

14. Letter of 13 April 1891 (L. 3782/pr) from Badeni to the sheriffs, in APKr, DPKr 38, 450/pr/91. Without his permission, only invited guests would be allowed to attend the events in question.

15. APKr, DPKr 38, 450/pr/91.

16. Delta, "Mikado z 'pięknej Heleny,'" *Trybuna* nos. 12 and 13 (1891): 9–10.

17. Information on these celebrations has been published by Kazimierz Bartoszewicz in *Księga pamiątkowa setnej rocznicy ustanowienia Konstytucji 3 Maja zebrał i wydał Kazimierz Bartoszewicz*, vol. 2, ed. K. Bartoszewicz (Kraków: Nakładem K. Bartoszewicza, 1891); Franciszka Sawicka, "Setna rocznica Konstytucji 3 Maja w świetle wydawnictw pamiątkowych," in *Konstytucja 3 Maja z perspektywy dwusetnej rocznicy (1791–1991)*, ed. Teresa Kulak (Wrocław: Wydawnictwo Uniwersytetu Wrocławskiego, 1993).

18. So it was declared in the case of Drohobycz. See *1863 Jednodniówka* (Drohobycz: staraniem Towarzystw polskich, 1913), 23.

19. This was Juliusz Miklaszewski's *Odczyt w stuletnią rocznicę Konstytucji 3 maja* (Kraków: nakł. Ign. Żółtowskiego, 1891), the publication of which was funded by Ignacy Żółtowski, according to Kazimierz Langie: see Langie's letter of 20 June 1891 to the 3 May commemoration committee in Cracow, APKr, IT 873, Korespondencye.

20. *Księga pamiątkowa setnej rocznicy*, 2:209–28.

21. Outside of Galicia, celebrations were described for thirteen sites in German Poland (not including the German Empire proper, where gatherings were noted in Leipzig and Berlin), Warsaw, and many major European cities as well as twelve locations in the United States and Canada. (Ibid., vols. 1 and 2.)

22. Maria Wysłouchowa, *O Konstytucji trzeciego Maja i przyczynach, które ją wywołały* (L'viv, 1891), 1, cited in Adam Galos, "Ewolucja tradycji trzeciomajowej w obchodach historycznych," in *Konstytucja 3 Maja z perspektywy dwusetnej rocznicy (1791–1991)*, 44–45.

23. For more on this canvas, see Jarosław Krawczyk, *Matejko i historia* (Warsaw: Instytut Sztuki Polskiej Akademii Nauk, 1990), 116–215; Wanda Nowakowska, "3 Maja w malarskiej legendzie," in *Konstytucja 3 Maja w tradycji i kulturze polskiej*, ed. Alina Barszczewska-Krupa (Łódź: Wydawnictwo Łódzkie, 1991), 572–83.

24. A presentation of the painting was made on 21 April 1892. ("Kronika," *Świat* 5, no. 9 [1 May 1892]: 218–19.)

25. Cited in Aleksander Małaczyński, *Jan Styka (szkic biograficzny)* (L'viv: Drukarnia Uniwersytecka, 1930), 22. Styka may have been inspired by the famous panorama of Alfred Stevens and Henri Gervex encompassing the history of the century (*L'histoire du siècle*), ex-

hibited at the World Exposition in France in 1889. (Franciszek Ziejka, *Panorama Racławicka* [Kraków: Krajowa Agencja Wydawnicza, 1984], 31.)

26. Cited in *"Polonia" obraz Jana Styki*, 1.

27. Małaczyński, *Styka*, 23–24.

28. This section is based upon a manuscript of Bishop Seweryn Morawski justifying his behavior during the celebration of the centenary of the Third of May, Bibl PAN Kr, 5559.

29. Ibid., fol. 7.

30. Teofil Merunowicz, "Obchód trzeciego maja wobec współczesnych prądów społecznych," *Dziennik Polski*, 3 May 1891.

31. See APKr, IT 873, Protokoły.

32. The only monograph on the subject of the TSL (Maria Jolanta Żmichrowska, *Towarzystwo Szkoły Ludowej [1891–1939]* [Olsztyn: Wyższa Szkoła Pedagogiczna w Olsztynie, 1992]) does not go into details on the organization's beginnings (that is, before it was approved by the authorities), nor did the author consult the archival materials on the Third of May anniversary (APKr, IT 873) that would have shed further light on the subject.

33. Announcement of the Cracow branch of the People's School Society dated 27 April 1892, Bibl PAN Kr, 2064, vol. 4, fol. 657.

34. Bibl PAN Kr, 2064, vol. 4, fol. 657; BJ przyb. 189/90, fol. 4; Ryszard Terlecki, *Oświata dorosłych i popularyzacji nauki w Galicji w okresie autonomii* [Wrocław: Zakład Narodowy im. Ossolińskich, 1990], 161.

35. The decision to let all present sign the statute was made during a committee meeting on 24 April. (APKr, IT 873, Protokoły.)

36. *Czas*, 1 May 1891; "Kronika," *Czas*, 23 April 1891. See the statute of Father Józef Pelczar's brotherhood: *Statut Bractwa najświętszej Panny Maryi Królowej Korony Polskiej*, APKr, IT 873, Druki, pisma.

37. *Pamiętnik tajnych organizacyi niepodległościowych na terenie byłej Galicji w latach od roku 1880–1897: Zebrał i ułożył . . .*, ed. Wacław M. Borzemski (L'viv: wydany staraniem Komitetu Z. O. N., 1930), 114–17; Krawczak, "Kształtowanie świadomości," 141; Maryan Stępowski, *Towarzystwo Szkoły Ludowej: Jak powstało, co zrobiło i do czego dąży (1891–1911); w 20-tą rocznicę powstania Towarzystwa napisał dr . . .* (Kraków: Nakł. Tow. Szkoły Ludowej, 1911), 49; Krawczak, "Udział chłopów," 51.

38. Terlecki, *Oświata dorosłych*, 165.

39. "Sto lat dochodzących . . ."

40. Perl, *Dzieje ruchu socjalistycznego*, 308.

41. From the announcement of the Polish League calling for a celebration of the one hundredth anniversary of the Constitution of the Third of May, in Kozicki, *Historia Ligi Narodowej*, 506–509.

42. Odezwa Ligi Polskiej.

43. "Sztuczki moskiewskie z powodu Trzeciego Maja" (Muscovite tricks on the occasion of the Third of May), *Djabeł* 23, no. 8 (21 April 1891).

44. Hannes Stekl emphasized this celebration as the first Polish national holiday (Hannes Stekl, "Öffentliche Gedenktage und gesellschaftliche Identitäten," in *Der Kampf um das Gedächtnis: Öffentliche Gedenktage in Mitteleuropa*, ed. Emil Brix and Hannes Stekl [Vienna, Cologne, and Weimar: Böhlau Verlag, 1997], 99).

45. "Kronika: Z Warszawy," *Nowa Reforma*, 2 May 1891; Perl, *Dzieje ruchu socjalistycznego*, 308; Jerzy Pietrzak, "Świątynia Opatrzności Bożej," in *Konstytucja 3 Maja z perspektywy dwusetnej rocznicy (1791–1991)*, 18–19; Andrzej Feliks Grabski, "Program i symbol: 3 Maja w polskiej myśli politycznej," in *3 Maja w tradycji i kulturze polskiej*, ed. Alina Barszczewska-Krupa (Łódź: Wydawnictwo Uniwersytetu Łódzkiego, 1991), 2:225.

46. Kozicki, *Historia Ligi Narodowej*, 72–74; Perl, *Dzieje ruchu socjalistycznego*, 308; A. L. Pogodin, *Glavnyia techeniia pol'skoi politicheskoi mysli, 1863–1907 gg.* (Sankt-Peterburg: Prosvieshchenie, n.d.), 308; Ignacy Matuszewski, "Obchód stulecia konstytucyi 3-go maja w roku 1891 w Warszawie: Garść wspomnień naocznego świadka," *Tygodnik Illustrowany* 48, no. 18 (4 May 1907): 367–68; Władysław Pobóg-Malinowski, *Najnowsza historia polityczna Polski*, 2d ed. (London: B. Świderski, 1963), 1:221–22 n. 65. Bruliński's funeral at the Powązki cemetery led to further clashes and reprisals.

47. For more on the arrests, see Tomasz Ruśkiewicz, *Tajny związek młodzieży polskiej w latach 1887–1893: Na podstawie urzędowych dokumentów rosyjskich i własnych wspomnień skreślił* . . . (Warsaw: Drukarnia Przemysłowa, 1926), 31–48; Kozicki, *Historia Ligi Narodowej*, 73–75.

48. According to one of Dmowski's biographers, this decision was also helped along mainly by Dmowski's personal encounter with those who ran the Polish League from abroad, after which he concluded that a different strategy should be used to engage the nation. (Roman Wapiński, *Roman Dmowski* [Lublin: Wydawnictwo Lubelskie, 1988], 45–48.)

49. "O święcie 'Trzeciego maja' i o obchodach narodowych w ogóle," *Z dzisiejszej doby* 4:3–7.

50. Ibid. Łączność was founded in 1888 for members of Zet within the Russian Empire who finished their studies or for other reasons were separated from their universities or schools. (Andrzej Micewski, *Roman Dmowski* [Warsaw: Wydawnictwo "Verum," 1971], 53, 55.) The most thorough treatment of the organization I have found is in Tadeusz Wolsza, *Narodowa Demokracja wobec chłopów w latach 1887–1914: Programy, polityka, działalność* (Warsaw: Ludowa Spółdzielnia Wydawnicza, 1992), 29–46.

51. "O święcie," 5–7.

52. Matuszewski, "Obchód stulecia," 368.

53. Pobóg-Malinowski, *Najnowsza historia*, 1:222–23 n. 69.

54. *Pamiętnik tajnych organizacyi*, 57, 76, 83–85, 132, 153–58. There are two different accounts of the cap incident, one claiming that Stanisław Badeni, son of the provincial marshal, was also involved.

55. For police actions against those suspected of wishing to celebrate it, see APKr, DPKr 42, 37/pr/93. A vote in favor of national mourning by the Student Union at the Jagiellonian University led to its dissolution. (APKr, DPKr 45, 903/pr/94.) Some students in Lwów were also prosecuted. (*Pamiętnik tajnych organizacyj*, 97.)

56. *Rodacy!* (leaflet), November 1892, APKr, DPKr 42, 37/pr/93.

57. Announcement, Lwów, 22 December 1891, BJ 224781 IV, vol. 3, 1889–1900, fol. 10. See also Bibl PAN Kr, 7797, fols. 28–32.

58. *Nowa Reforma*, 23 February 1894.

59. *Rodacy!* (leaflet), dated November 1892, in APKr, DPKr 42, 37/pr/93.

60. APKr, DPKr 42, 37/pr/93; APKr, DPKr 45, 690/pr/94.

61. *Pamiętnik tajnych organizacji*, 87–97, 155–58.

62. Franciszek Magryś, *Żywot chłopa działacza* (Warsaw: Ludowa Spółdzielnia Wydawnicza, 1987), 67–68.

63. Ibid. This same trip was also attended by another peasant, later to become quite famous: Jakub Bojko.

64. Maciej Szarek in a letter of 27 May 1893 to Maria Wysłouchowa, published in Janusz Albin and Józef Ryszard Szaflik, "Listy Macieja Szarka z lat 1861–1904," *Ze skarbca kultury* 39 (1984): 110.

65. Many recent works have addressed the figure of Kościuszko. These include Krystyna Śreniowska, *Kościuszko bohater narodowy: Opinie współczesnych i potomnych, 1794–1946* (Warsaw: Państwowe Wydawnictwo Naukowe, 1973); *Kościuszce w hołdzie*, ed. Mieczysław

Rokosz (Kraków: Wydawnictwo i Drukarnia "Secesja," 1994), especially Mirosław Frančić, "Kopiec Kościuszki—historia znaczeń," 185–237. Of particular interest is Magdalena Micińska, *Gołąb i orzeł: Obchody rocznic kościuszkowskich w latach 1894 i 1917* (Warsaw: Wydawnictwo NERITON, 1997).

66. From the introduction to *Pieśni narodowe, staraniem młodzieży na pamiątkę setnej rocznicy bohaterstwa ludu wydane* (Kraków: nakładem dra Z. Kostkiewicza i K. Wojnara, 1894), 3. An interesting modern look at the historiography on the peasant connection can be found in Jacek Kochanowicz, "Powstanie i chłopi: Cztery interpretacje," in *Kościuszko— powstanie 1794 r.—tradycja: Materiały z sesji naukowej w 200-lecie powstania kościuszkowskiego 15–16 kwietnia 1994 r.*, ed. Jerzy Kowecki (Warsaw: Biblioteka Narodowa, 1997), 77–89.

67. See Kraszewski's comment, cited in [Antoni Kostecki], *Wieniec wspomnień malujących charakter, przymioty, usposobienie i cnoty Tadeusza Kościuszki z różnych autorów zebrany w redakcyi "Kościuszki"* (Kraków: nakładem zakładu introligatorskiego J. Gadowskiego na uczczenie stuletniej rocznicy, 1894), 13–14.

68. Franciszek Ziejka, "Racławicka legenda," in *W kręgu Panoramy Racławickiej* (Wrocław: Zakład Narodowy im. Ossolińskich, 1985), 83–84.

69. Here I disagree with Ziejka, who says that "the centenary of the Kościuszko Insurrection was virtually reduced to the commemorating of the Racławice battle." (Ibid., 84.)

70. These options are downplayed by Dariusz Rolnik, whose account of the celebrations in Cracow and Lwów is generally solid. (Dariusz Rolnik, "Obchody setnej rocznicy insurekcji kościuszkowskiej w Galicji," in *200 rocznica powstania kościuszkowskiego,* ed. Henryk Kocój [Katowice: Wydawnictwo Uniwersytetu Śląskiego, 1994], 218–34.) For more on the folk celebrations, see Keely Stauter-Halsted, "Patriotic Celebrations in Austrian Poland: The Kościuszko Centennial and the Formation of Peasant Nationalism," *Austrian History Yearbook* 25 (1994): 74–95; and Dabrowski, "Reinventing Poland," 316–34.

71. *Nowa Reforma,* 31 March 1894.

72. Tadeusz Chromecki, *Mowa miana w katedrze na Wawelu w setną rocznicę przysięgi Tadeusza Kościuszki przez ks. Tadeusza Chromeckiego dnia 31 marca 1894 r.* (Kraków: nakładem autora, 1894).

73. Andrzej Feliks Grabski, *W kręgu kultu Naczelnika: Rapperswilskie inicjatywy kościuszkowskie (1894–1897)* (Warsaw: Państwowy Instytut Wydawniczy, 1981), 44. For more on the tablet, see "Kronika krakowska z roku pańskiego 1896," *Józefa Czecha Kalendarz Krakowski* (1897), 75–76; Micińska, *Gołąb i orzeł,* 20–21.

74. At the next session of the city council, Friedlein claimed that they had tried to remove the work without harming it. ("Sprawy miejskie," *Czas,* 7 April 1894.)

75. "Uroczystość Kościuszkowska (wiec ludowy w Krakowie)," *Nowa Reforma,* 5 April 1894; Wincenty Witos, *Moje wspomnienia* (Paris: Instytut Literacki, 1964), 1:205 n. 42 (p. 447); Krzysztof Dunin-Wąsowicz, *Dzieje Stronnictwa Ludowego w Galicji* (Warsaw: Ludowa Spółdzielnia Wydawnicza, 1956), 98.

76. A series of documents connected with the suspension as well as Stojałowski's attempts at regaining his privileges in Rome were published in *Czas,* 29 March 1894—just in time, it appears, for the arrival of peasants in Cracow for the celebration.

77. For the police responses, see APKr, DPKr 51, 925/pr/98, 227, 231–44, 255–56, 265; APKr, DPKr 44, 383/pr/94.

78. "'Neue Freie Presse' o uroczystości kościuszkowskiej w Krakowie," *Kurjer Lwowski,* 7 April 1894.

79. "Kronika," *Czas,* 5 April 1894; Rolnik, "Obchody setnej rocznicy," 225.

80. Rolnik, "Obchody setnej rocznicy," 225.

81. "Kronika," *Czas,* 7 April 1894.

82. Micewski, *Dmowski,* 46–47, 51–53, 55; Wolsza, *Narodowa Demokracja,* 46.

83. Roman Dmowski, *Pisma* (Częstochowa: Antoni Gmachowski i S-ka, 1938), 3:247. Original underscoring omitted.

84. The brochure was titled *Our Patriotism* (*Nasz Patriotism*). (Dmowski, *Pisma,* 3:247.) Original underscoring omitted.

85. Cited in "Przegląd polityczny," *Nowa Reforma,* 28 April 1894.

86. Zdzisław Dębicki, *Grzechy młodości* (Warsaw: nakładem Trzaski, Everta i Michalskiego A.S., 1930), 4–7 (PAN archive copy).

87. Citation from *Varshavskii Dnievnik,* published in "Przegląd polityczny," *Nowa Reforma,* 28 April 1894.

88. Dębicki, *Grzechy młodości,* 4–7; Feldman, *Dzieje polskiej myśli,* 250 n. 1; Józef Dąbrowski [J. Grabiec, pseud.], *Dzieje porozbiorowe narodu polskiego* (Warsaw: Towarzystwo Wydawnicze, 1916), 275. Many of those students eventually applied to study at Jagiellonian University. (Józef Buszko, *Społeczno-polityczne oblicze Uniwersytetu Jagiellońskiego w dobie autonomii galicyjskiej [1869–1914]* [Kraków: Państwowe Wydawnictwo Naukowe, 1963], 43.)

89. Bojko, cited in Brodowska, *Chłopi o sobie i Polsce,* 194.

90. Andrzej Rehorowski, "Powszechna Wystawa Krajowa we Lwowie roku 1894 i siły produkcyjne kraju" (master's thesis, Jagiellonian University, 1995), 91; Jacek Purchla, "W stulecie powszechnej wystawy krajowej we Lwowie 1894 roku," *Cracovia Leopolis* 2 (1995): 6.

91. Cello, "Wystawa w 1894 roku," *Świat* (1893): 505.

92. *W kręgu Panoramy Racławickiej,* 151.

93. From Sapieha's speech at opening of Wystawa krajowa, cited in Rehorowski, "Powszechna Wystawa Krajowa," 72.

94. Purchla, "W stulecie," 6.

95. Cello, "Wystawa w 1894 roku," 537–40.

96. *Objaśnienia do panoramy bitwy pod Racławicami* (n.p., 1894), 11.

97. Rehorowski, "Powszechna Wystawa Krajowa," 58.

98. "Kronika (Plakat wystawy krajowej)," *Nowa Reforma,* 6 January 1894.

99. Konstanty M. Górski, *Polska sztuka współczesna 1887–1894 na Wystawie krajowej we Lwowie 1894 r. przez . . .* (Kraków: drukarnia "Czasu" Fr. Kluczyckiego i sp., 1896), 63.

100. Cello, "Wystawa w 1894 roku," 505.

101. From Sapieha's speech at opening of Wystawa krajowa, cited in Rehorowski, "Powszechna Wystawa Krajowa," 72.

102. "Kronika galicyjska," *Biblioteka Warszawska* 215, no. 7 (July 1894): 120.

103. From letter of emperor to Prince Adam Sapieha, cited in Rehorowski, "Powszechna Wystawa Krajowa," 94.

104. From *Dziennik Polski,* reprinted in Jan and Tadeusz Styka, *Grunwald w Rondlu Bramy Floriańskiej* (Kraków: nakładem Jana Styki, 1909), 26.

105. Words of Emperor Francis Joseph of 7 September 1894, cited in "Cesarz we Lwowie," *Nowa Reforma,* 11 September 1894.

106. "Kronika," *Nowa Reforma,* 4 August 1894.

107. Rehorowski, "Powszechna Wystawa Krajowa," 125.

108. This comparison is not the invention of the author. Contemporary Poles drew a parallel between the Eiffel Tower and the Racławice Panorama, as seen in an article by F. Morawski, "Słowo o wystawie lwowskiej," *Przegląd Powszechny* (1894), cited in Micińska, *Gołąb i orzeł,* 33.

109. Mieczysław Zlat, "Wstęp," in *W kręgu Panoramy Racławickiej,* ed. Bożena Steinborn (Wrocław: Zakład Narodowy im. Ossolińskich, 1985), 10; Stephan Oettermann, *Das Panorama: Die Geschichte eines Massenmediums* (Frankfurt: Syndikat, 1980).

110. Małgorzata Dolistowska, "Panorama 'Bitwa pod Racławicami,'" in *W kręgu Panoramy Racławickiej*, 141–42. Both Jan Styka and the coauthor of the Polish panorama, Wojciech Kossak, were inspired by these panoramas and their artists.

111. Words taken from an article by Wojciech Dzieduszycki in *Dziennik Polski*, 14 January 1895, cited in Małaczyński, *Styka*, 28.

112. Ziejka, *Panorama Racławicka*, 32–34, 45.

113. See discussion of the competing trends—between Styka the idealist and Kossak the realist—in ibid., 40–44.

114. See the views of Maurycy Mochnacki cited in Jerzy Szacki, *Ojczyzna, naród, rewolucja: Problematyka narodowa w polskiej myśli szlacheckorewolucyjnej* (Warsaw: Państwowy Instytut Wydawniczy, 1962), 214.

115. "Bitwa Racławicka," in Bolesław Twardowski [BT, pseud.], *Historya Powstania Kościuszki 1794 r: Z dodaniem spisu osób, które brały udział w powstaniu, oraz dołączeniem życiorysów głównych przywódców*, 2d ed. (Poznań: Nakładem Księgarni Katolickiej, 1896), 8; Dolistowska, "Panorama 'Bitwa pod Racławicami,'" 144; Jan Poniatowski, *Panorama racławicka: Przewodnik* (Wrocław: Krajowa Agencja Wydawnicza, 1987), n.p.; section after illustrations.

116. Zlat, "Wstęp," 11. This seems a cautious estimate, as much higher figures have been cited elsewhere.

117. Styka, *Grunwald w Rondlu*, 33; see also Ziejka, *Panorama Racławicka*, 44.

118. *Nowa Reforma*, 29 May 1894; Ziejka, *Panorama Racławicka*, 56.

119. Ziejka, *Panorama Racławicka*, 56.

120. *Nowa Reforma*, 29 May 1894.

121. Jan Kasprowicz [Jan-Ka., pseud.], "Dzieci na wystawie," *Kurjer Lwowski*, 6 July 1894. Together with several other villagers, Bojko had visited the Czech exposition in 1891 (Bibl PAN Kr 4268, fols. 1–16).

122. APŁ, Archiwum Bartoszewiczów, 1005, fols. 10–11; "Wystawa," *Gazeta Lwowska*, 26 June 1894; *Pamiętnik tajnych organizacyj*, 116.

123. Micińska, *Gołąb i orzeł*, 36.

124. Mrs. Łomnicka had also played a valuable, if secret, role as hostess to many secret youth gatherings and served as the keeper of the statute, seals, and papers of the "Żuawi" (Zouaves). (*Pamiętnik tajnych organizacyi*, 130; also Wojnar's recollections in ibid., 171–72.)

125. "Wystawa," *Gazeta Lwowska*, 19 June 1894.

126. Kasprowicz, "Dzieci na wystawie."

127. This has been noted by Ziejka, *Panorama Racławicka*, 54.

128. See, for example, Albin and Szaflik, "Listy Macieja Szarka," 125 n. 2; Olga A. Narkiewicz, *The Green Flag: Polish Populist Politics, 1867–1970* (London and Totowa, N.J.: Croom Helm and Rowman and Littlefield, 1976), 68–69.

129. From *Kurier Lwowski*, 27 July 1894, cited in Ziejka, *Panorama Racławicka*, 57.

130. Ibid., 47.

131. "Kornel Ujejski do włościan," *Nowa Reforma*, 29 August 1894.

132. "Wystawa," *Gazeta Lwowska*, 28 August 1894.

133. "Z wystawy krajowej: Lwów 26 sierpnia," *Nowa Reforma*, 28 August 1894; "Wystawa," *Gazeta Lwowska*, 28 August 1894 and 29 August 1894; "Wiec chłopski: Lwów, 27 sierpnia (Posiedzenie poranne)," *Nowa Reforma*, 25 August 1894.

134. At least according to reports in *Nowa Reforma*, 27 August 1894.

135. "W sprawie zlotu Sokołów,'" *Nowa Reforma*, 6 January 1894; *Nowa Reforma*, 15 March 1894; *Nowa Reforma*, 29 June 1894; "Wystawa," *Gazeta Lwowska*, 1 July 1894; *Czas*, 17 July 1894; "Wystawa," *Gazeta Lwowska*, 18 July 1894.

136. "Zjazdy we Lwowie: Lwów, 16 września," *Nowa Reforma,* 18 September 1894; "Kronika," *Nowa Reforma,* 19 September 1894; "Wystawa," *Gazeta Lwowska,* 25 September 1894; BJ rkps 7124 III, fol. 40; Rehorowski, "Powszechna Wystawa Krajowa," 78–84.

137. "Wystawa," *Gazeta Lwowska,* 14 August 1894.

138. "Ślązacy we Lwowie: Lwów, 15 sierpnia," *Nowa Reforma,* 17 August 1894.

139. "Ślązacy we Lwowie: Lwów, 12 sierpnia," *Nowa Reforma,* 14 August 1894; "Ślązacy we Lwowie: Lwów, 15 sierpnia," *Nowa Reforma,* 17 August 1894.

140. Hagen, *Germans, Poles, and Jews,* 171.

141. Kościelski's words on national unity were recorded in "Wystawa," *Gazeta Lwowska,* 19 September 1894; "Kronika," *Czas,* 19 September 1894. The crucial fragment was published, with slight variation, in Feldman, *Dzieje polskiej myśli,* 181.

142. See, for example, *Neue Freie Presse,* 19 September 1894; Ted Kaminski, *Polish Publicists and Prussian Politics (1890–1894)* (Stuttgart: Franz Steiner Verlag, 1988), 212–13, cites some German and Prussian Polish reactions. A thorough history of the organization is Adam Galos, F. H. Gentzen, and W. Jakóbczyk, *Dzieje Hakaty,* ed. Janusz Pajewski (Poznań: Instytut Zachodni, 1966) (also available in German)—"Hakata" being the Polish abbreviation for "H-K-T," the initials of the founders of the organization.

143. Kościelski's letter was printed under the rubric "Die Polen in Preussen und Oesterreich," *Neue Freie Presse,* 22 September 1894. A translated version appeared in many Polish newspapers, including *Nowa Reforma,* 25 September 1894.

144. "Uroczystość kościuszkowska," *Związek Chłopski,* 1 May 1894; more examples can be found in Stauter-Halsted, "Patriotic Celebrations in Austrian Poland."

145. *Wiejscy działacze społeczni* (Warsaw: Kasa im. Mianowskiego, 1937), 1:205 (citation), 209–10.

146. Ibid., 210. While these numbers seem to be exaggerated (Krawczak, "Kształtowanie świadomości," 147, claims around three thousand were present), even lesser crowds would be impressive.

147. *Wiejscy działacze,* 213.

148. This complicated and interesting story has been presented by Grabski, *W kręgu kultu,* in a chapter entitled "O serce Naczelnika," 92–141.

149. Jan Słomka, *Pamiętniki włościanina od pańszczyzny do dni dzisiejszych* (Kraków: Krakowska Drukarnia Nakładowa, 1912), 220–21. It is interesting to note that, the day before the unveiling, the miraculous image of Our Lady of Dzików was crowned in Tarnobrzeg. Shades of other celebrations . . . Two years later, another monument to the peasant scytheman was erected in Lwów.

150. *Pieśni narodowe,* 3–4.

151. Krawczak, "Kształtowanie świadomości," 142–43.

152. Oswald Balzer, "Reformy społeczne i polityczne konstytucyi Trzeciego Maja," *Przegląd Polski* 25 (1891): 496.

153. Miklaszewski, *Odczyt,* 52.

154. For more on what was not celebrated, see Micińska, *Gołąb i orzeł,* 18.

155. Already in 1894, Kossak began work on a scene from the Napoleonic Wars (at Berezina) exhibited in Berlin in 1896–98. After the enthusiastic reception of the Racławice Panorama in Budapest in 1896, the Hungarians commissioned Styka to paint one for them: the Bem-Petöfi Panorama was exhibited in 1897. Styka also painted *Golgotha* (1896, financed in part by the pianist Ignacy Jan Paderewski; now on permanent display at Forest Lawn Memorial Park in Glendale, California) and *The Martyrdom of Christians in Nero's Circus* (1899, exhibited at the 1900 World's Fair in Paris). (Dolistowska, "Panorama 'Bitwa pod Racławicami,'" 138–40; Czesław Czapliński, *The Styka Family Saga; Saga rodu Styków* [New York: Bicentennial Publishing Corporation, 1988], 96–111; Ziejka, *Panorama Racławicka,* 61–79.)

156. Words of Adam Szwajkart, director of the American pavilion and member of the Polish committee in New York, cited in "Kronika," *Nowa Reforma,* 5 September 1894. See also Ziejka, *Panorama Racławicka,* 54.

5. BRONZING THE BARD

1. Jadwiga Jarnuszkiewiczowa, *Pomnik Mickiewicza* (Warsaw: Państwowe Wydawnictwo Naukowe, 1975), 10–12. For more on these monuments, see Hanna Kotkowska-Bareja, *Pomnik Kopernika* (Warsaw: Państwowe Wydawnictwo Naukowe, 1973), and idem, *Pomnik Poniatowskiego* (Warsaw: Państwowe Wydawnictwo Naukowe, 1971).

2. Kazimierz Bartoszewicz, "Z dziejów pomnika," *Przegląd Literacki* 3, no. 11 (10 June 1898): 2.

3. His voice oozing irony, Władysław Bentkowski asked the deputies what they would think if the Danish authorities opposed the erection of a monument to Schiller or Goethe in a cemetery in Denmark, fearing that it would incite the Germans living there to rebellion. (Zdzisław Grot, "Dzieje pomnika Mickiewicza w Poznaniu [1859–1939]," *Przegląd Zachodni* 5 [1949]: 453–56.)

4. Stanisław Schnür Peplowski, "Pomniki Mickiewicza," in *Na odsłonięcie pomnika Mickiewicza w Krakowie* (L'viv: "Słowo Polskie," 1898), 3; Zdzisław Grot, *Dzieje pomnika Mickiewicza w Poznaniu, 1856–1939* (Poznań: Państwowe Wydawnictwo Naukowe, 1956), 24–33.

5. Ignacy Matuszewski, "Z tygodnia na tydzień: Psychologia pomników," *Tygodnik Illustrowany* no. 52 (12 [24] December 1898): 1022.

6. Ibid.

7. Zyblikiewicz to Helena Modrzejewska, cited in Homola, *Kraków za prezydentury,* 259–60.

8. *Czas*'s aesthetic vision of the Rynek of the future circa 1881 is discussed in Jerzy Piekarczyk, "Miejsce dla wieszcza," *Kraków* no. 1 (1986): 33.

9. Much of the history of the erection of the Cracow monument to Mickiewicz has been recounted in Aleksandra Leśnodorska and Zofia Mleczkówna, "Pomnik Adama Mickiewicza w Krakowie," in *Kraków Mickiewiczowi,* ed. Danuta Rederowa (Kraków: Wydawnictwo Literackie, 1956), 89–177, with selected documents prepared by Krystyna Stachowska, "Materiały," in ibid., 198–218. Given the present inaccessibility of some of the materials cited within, including fascicules in the Skład. Akt Prez. M. R. N. Kraków, it has the value of a primary source, particularly for the early history of the preparations. Kawyn, *Ideologia,* is also useful, while Kazimierz Bartoszewicz provides a contemporary, if partisan, account (K[azimierz] Bartoszewicz, "Z dziejów pomnika," *Przegląd Literacki* 3, no. 11 [1898]: 1–7; nos. 12 and 13: 1–6; nos. 14 and 15: 6–10; nos. 16 and 17: 6–11; nos. 18 and 19: 1–5; 4, nos. 4 and 5 [1899]: 6–9). Kraszewski, interestingly, played an important role in gaining Warsaw's support for this endeavor. (Adam Galos, "Wokół jubileuszu Kraszewskiego w 1879 r.," in *Z przeszłości Europy Środkowowschodniej,* ed. Jadwiga Hoff [Rzeszow: Wydawnictwo Uniwersytetu Rzeszowskiego, 2002], 62–63.)

10. Leśnodorska and Mleczkówna, "Pomnik Mickiewicza," 89–95.

11. *Księga Kraszewskiego,* 81.

12. A police telegram sent to the viceroy noted that, on his visit with the local university students, Kraszewski praised them for collecting funds for a Mickiewicz monument. (APKr, DPKr 24, 703/pr/79.)

13. *Księga Kraszewskiego,* 2.

14. From a 10 December 1879 letter of Kraszewski to Władysław Mickiewicz, quoted in Danek, *Kraszewski: Zarys biograficzny,* 333.

15. Bartoszewicz, "Z dziejów pomnika," *Przegląd Literacki* 3 no. 11 (1898): 6–7; Leśnodorska and Mleczkówna, "Pomnik Mickiewicza," 101.

16. Leśnodorska and Mleczkówna, "Pomnik Mickiewicza," 105.

17. Letter to Władysław Mickiewicz, cited in W. Mickiewicz, *Pamiętniki,* 1:270.

18. *Reforma,* 20 April 1882.

19. This comment from *Czas,* cited in *Nowa Reforma,* 2 May 1882, was also published in Leśnodorska and Mleczkówna, "Pomnik Mickiewicza," 109.

20. Only the main points of this decision-making process will be discussed, given its complexity.

21. W., "Kilka uwag w sprawie pomnika dla Mickiewicza," *Reforma,* 2 May 1882.

22. "Kronika," *Reforma,* 4 May 1882.

23. "Kronika," *Reforma,* 4 May 1882; Walery Rzewuski, *Gdzie postawić pomnik Mickiewicza?* (Kraków: nakładem autora, 1883), XI.

24. Leśnodorska and Mleczkówna, "Pomnik Mickiewicza," 133–34.

25. Rzewuski's efforts are chronicled in BJ rkps 4955 as well as in several pamphlets he penned and published, including *Gdzie postawić pomnik Mickiewicza?* and *Jeszcze kilka uwag i dokumentów w sprawie pomnika Mickiewicza* (n.p., 10 December 1883).

26. Rzewuski, *Gdzie postawić pomnik,* 31–32. For those unfamiliar with the reference to Grodzka Street—the street leading from the Rynek to the Wawel—Rzewuski provided a footnote and chart explaining that twenty-six of the thirty-one stores on that street were owned by Jews.

27. Ezra Mendelsohn, "Jewish Assimilation in L'viv: The Case of Wilhelm Feldman," in *Nationbuilding and the Politics of Nationalism: Essays on Austrian Galicia,* ed. Andrei S. Markovits and Frank E. Sysyn (Cambridge: distributed by Harvard University Press for the Harvard Ukrainian Research Institute, 1982), 94–110.

28. For more on this subject, see Jadwiga Maurer, "The Omission of Jewish Topics in Mickiewicz Scholarship," *Polin* 5 (1990): 184–92.

29. "W sprawie pomnika Mickiewicza," *Przegląd Literacki i Artystyczny,* 5 June 1883.

30. Ibid.

31. Karol Matuszewski, "Konkurs na projekt pomnika Mickiewicza w Krakowie," *Biblioteka Warszawska* 178 (April 1885): 137. The protocol of the jury is reproduced in a long footnote to the article (pp. 120–30).

32. Ibid., 139. It also led Matuszewski to believe that influential Cracow circles were genuinely unsupportive of the plan to erect a monument to Mickiewicz.

33. Letter of 4 January 1883 of Zyblikiewicz to Wojciech Eliasz, APKr, IT 876, fol. 1217.

34. Peplowski, "Pomniki Mickiewicza," 5; *Biblioteka Warszawska* 177 (March 1886): 458; Matuszewski, "Konkurs."

35. "Niepoprawni," *Kurjer Krakowski,* 12 November 1887; Leśnodorska and Mleczkówna, "Pomnik Mickiewicza," 121–22.

36. Per decision of 29 October 1886. (Ibid.)

37. Bartoszewicz, "Z dziejów pomnika," *Przegląd Literacki* 3, nos. 18 and 19 (1898): 3.

38. Communiqué of the Select Committee, 28 February 1890, APKr, IT 876, fols. 337–38.

39. See Bartoszewicz, "Z dziejów pomnika," *Przegląd Literacki* 4, nos. 4 and 5 (1899): 7.

40. "Plotki krakowskie," *Djabeł* no. 9 (1890).

41. Communiqué of the Select Committee, 28 February 1890, APKr, IT 876, fols. 337–38 and 465–66. Zaderecki maintains that the Rynek site was being saved for a monument to Emperor Francis Joseph. (Tadeusz Zaderecki, "Pomnik Mickiewicza znów staje w Krakowie," Bibl PAN Kr, 3657, fol. 21.)

42. Communiqué of the Select Committee, 28 February 1890, APKr, IT 876, fols. 337–38.

43. APKr, IT 876, fols. 345–48, 509–16, 519–22.

44. Letter of 10 March 1891 of Adam Asnyk to Helena Modrzejewska and Karol Chłapowski, BJ rkps 9136 III, fols. 59–60.

45. The laurel wreath on the main figure's head was said to resemble an Indian headdress. Details can be gleaned from Bartoszewicz as well as Leśnodorska and Mleczkówna, "Pomnik Mickiewicza."

46. *Djabeł,* 6 March 1890.

47. W. Mickiewicz, *Pamiętniki,* 3:368.

48. Manuscript of Stanisław Witkiewicz, dated Zakopane 15 March 1895, Bibl PAN rkps 2436, fols. 14–25.

49. Materials of the Cracow committee are stored in APŁ, Archiwum Bartoszewiczów, 1211. For a short summary of the festivities, which lasted several days, see Stanisław Libicki, "Uroczystości krakowskie," *Tygodnik Illustrowany* 39, no. 27 (20 June [2 July] 1898): 519–20.

50. "U krypty Mickiewicza," as listed in *Program uroczystości jubileuszowych Adama Mickiewicza w Krakowie w dniach 26 i 27 czerwca 1898* (Kraków: nakład Fr. Pindora, 1898); Lucyan Rydel and Stanisław Wyspiański, *Epilog uroczystego przedstawienia w teatrze krakowskim w dniu 27-go czerwca 1898 na cześć Adama Mickiewicza* (Kraków: W. L. Anczyca i sp., 1898); printed announcement, Cracow, April 1898, APŁ, Archiwum Bartoszewiczów 1005, fols. 90–92.

51. A trip from Upper Silesia, organized by *Katolik,* was planned for the celebration. (APKr, R 48: Wycieczka z Wielkopolski i Górnego Śląska, 1890–1901.)

52. Józef Buszko, *Polacy w parlamencie wiedeńskim, 1848–1918* (Warsaw: Wydawnictwo Sejmowe, 1996), 198 ff.

53. Leśnodorska and Mleczkówna, "Pomnik Mickiewicza," 148; some of these have been published in Stachowska, "Materiały," 212–15.

54. "Mały stan oblężenia w Krakowie," extraordinary supplement to *Głos Narodu* no. 146 (1898).

55. See the observations of Bolesław Drobner, "To już tak dawno," in *Kopiec wspomnień,* 2d ed. (Kraków: Wydawnictwo Literackie, 1964).

56. Ignacy Daszyński, *Pamiętniki* (Kraków: Z. R. S. S. "Proletarjat," 1925–26), 1:151–53. Whether as a reaction to this move or as a sign of continued animosity, the authorities took advantage of the state of emergency to reduce the socialists' influence in Galicia: they closed twenty-nine socialist organizations, "confined" a number of party members, and forced the socialist paper *Naprzód* (Forward) to move to Lwów.

57. For more on the "Free Brothers" (Wolni Bracia), see Dabrowski, "Reinventing Poland," 398–99.

58. *Nowa Reforma,* 28 June 1898; W. Mickiewicz, *Pamiętniki,* 3:344.

59. Stanisław Tarnowski, *Mowa przy odsłonięciu pomnika Mickiewicza w Krakowie dnia 26 czerwca 1898 roku* (Kraków: nakładem autora, w drukarni "Czasu" Fr. Kluczyckiego i spółki, 1898), 3.

60. Ibid., 5; *Djabeł,* 6 March 1890.

61. Announcement by F. Kreutz, 11 May 1897, AUJ, S II 962.

62. Kawyn, *Ideologia,* 173.

63. Per the brochure [M. Zetterbaum and A. Niemojewski], *Adam Mickiewicz 1798–1898: Książka pamiątkowa dla polskiego ludu pracującego* (L'viv: nakł. Redakcyi "Naprzodu," "N. Robotnika," "Prawa ludu" i "Równości," drukiem Artura Goldmana we Lwowie, 1898), cited by Józef Kozłowski, *"my z Niego wszyscy . . .": Socjalistyczne Mickiewicziana z przełomu XIX i XX wieku* (Warsaw: Czytelnik, 1978), 14.

64. Buszko, *Polacy w parlamencie,* 215. For more on the so-called Badeni ordinances, see, for example, Paul Vyšný, *Neo-Slavism and the Czechs, 1898–1914* (Cambridge, London, New York, and Melbourne: Cambridge University Press, 1977), 15.

65. Leśnodorska and Mleczkówna, "Pomnik Mickiewicza," 151–52.

66. Words of Professor Sokołowski, cited in Kawyn, *Ideologia,* 180–82; Leśnodorska and Mleczkówna, "Pomnik Mickiewicza," 155.

67. See, for example, "Meine Habilitation," published in Ivan Franko, *Beiträge zur Geschichte und Kultur der Ukraine: Ausgewählte deutsche Schriften des Revolutionären Demokraten 1882–1915,* ed. E. Winter and P. Kirchner (Berlin: Akademie-Verlag, 1963), 68–71. Interestingly, it has been argued that a fellow Ukrainian, Oleksander Barvinsky, exerted pressure on Badeni in this regard. (Victor Hugo Lane IV, "State Culture and National Identity in a Multi-ethnic Context: Lemberg, 1772–1914" [Ph.D. diss., University of Michigan, 1999], 307–309.)

68. This sentence has been rendered into English by George C. Grabowicz, "The History of Polish-Ukrainian Literary Relations: A Literary and Cultural Perspective," in *Poland and Ukraine: Past and Present,* ed. Peter J. Potichnyj (Edmonton and Toronto: Canadian Institute of Ukrainian Studies, 1980), 123. In addition to translations into Polish and Russian, the article is available in English (Ivan Franko, "A Poet of Betrayal," trans. Adam Hnidj, *Ukrainian Quarterly* 48, no. 1 [spring 1992]: 49–57).

69. Drobner, "To już tak dawno," 32.

70. See Franko's letter to Jan Baudouin de Courtenay (from the second half of February 1898), in Ivan Franko, *Zibrannia tvoriv u p'iatdesiaty tomakh: Lysty (1895–1916)* (Kiev: Vydavnytstvo "Naukova Dumka," 1986), 102–104 (original Polish). Baudouin de Courtenay had himself complained about "Galician morality" in a brochure in 1897. (Drobner, "To już tak dawno," 32.)

71. This has been demonstrated by George C. Grabowicz in a stimulating and insightful essay titled "Franko et Mickiewicz: le 'wallenrodisme' et 'la crainte de l'influence,'" in *Le Verbe et l'Histoire: Mickiewicz, la France et l'Europe* (Paris, Institut d'etudes slaves, 2002), 96–103; also published in an earlier and longer version as "Vozhdivstvo i rozdvojennja: tema 'vallenrodyzmu' v tvorax Franka," *Suchasnist'* (Kyiv), no. 11 (1997): 113–38.

72. *Ivan Franko: Dokumenty y materialy 1856–1965* (Kiev: Naukova Dumka, 1966), 214.

73. Kazimierz Jeziorowski, *Wspomnienia z lat 1886–1924* (Siedlce: nakładem autora, 1933), 73.

74. From manuscript of Stanisław Witkiewicz (1904), Bibl PAN Kr, rkps 2436, fols. 32–33.

75. Letter of R. Skrzycki (alias of Roman Dmowski) to Zygmunt Miłkowski, 28 May 1897; copy in Bibl PAN Kr, 7808, fols. 3–9.

76. Bartoszewicz, "Z dziejów pomnika," *Przegląd Literacki* 3, no. 11 (1898): 3 n. 2. The text of the January 1898 appeal was also published in Zygmunt Wasilewski, *Pomnik Mickiewicza w Warszawie 1897–1898* (Warsaw: nakładem Komitetu budowy pomnika, 1899), 6–7.

77. Krzyżanowski, *Sienkiewicz: Kalendarz,* 204. On the event in general, see Wasilewski, *Pomnik Mickiewicza;* Vesler, "Pomnik Mickiewicza w Warszawie," *Głos Narodu,* 26 June 1898.

78. Letter of 9 April 1897, in Sienkiewicz, *Listy,* ed. Maria Bokszanin (Warsaw: Państwowy Instytut Wydawniczy, 1977), 1:350; also Wasilewski, *Pomnik Mickiewicza,* 11.

79. Wasilewski, *Pomnik Mickiewicza,* 42.

80. Ibid., 18–20, 39.

81. Wasilewski, *Pomnik Mickiewicza,* 56–58. Kawyn, *Ideologia,* 104–105, contains criticisms of the monument's design.

82. Vesler, "Pomnik Mickiewicza," 3.

83. Wasilewski, *Pomnik Mickiewicza,* 28, 33–34. Kawyn has more detail on the donations gathered over eleven weeks by the peasant paper *Gazeta Świąteczna* (Kawyn, *Ideologia,* 107).

84. Zenon Kmiecik, *Prasa warszawska w latach 1886–1904* (Wrocław: Zakład Narodowy im. Ossolińskich, 1989), 20.

85. The words are taken from a telegram sent by Russian professors at Warsaw University on the occasion of the monument's unveiling (cited in Marian Kułakowski, *Dmowski w świetle listów i wspomnień* [London: Gryf, 1968], 1:199). For more on Muraviev and his monument, see Theodore R. Weeks, "Monuments and Memory: Immortalizing Count M. N. Muraviev in Vilna, 1898," *Nationalities Papers* 27, no. 4 (1999): 551–64.

86. Piotr Szubert, "Pomnik Adama Mickiewicza w Wilnie," *Blok-notes Muzeum A. Mickiewicza w Warszawie* 9 (1988): 195, 198. A full account of the erection of the Wilno Mickiewicz monument is contained in a manuscript in the Jagiellonian Library: BJ przyb. 89/58.

87. Wasilewski, *Pomnik Mickiewicza,* 79–80.

88. See reprint of notice in the police gazette in Wasilewski, *Pomnik Mickiewicza,* 81–83.

89. Wasilewski, *Pomnik Mickiewicza,* 84–87. The use of Latin also proved an acceptable alternative to Russian in the case of the foundation act, which the authorities originally had wanted to be written in Russian as well as Polish. (Kawyn, *Ideologia,* 121.)

90. See Wasilewski, *Pomnik Mickiewicza,* 127–28.

91. From his toast to Godebski at a banquet in the latter's honor on 29 December 1898, in Henryk Sienkiewicz, *Pisma zapomniane i niewydane* (Lviv: Wydawnictwo Zakładu Narodowego im. Ossolińskich, 1922), 437–38.

92. BJ przyb. 89/58, fol. 22; Feldman, *Dzieje polskiej myśli,* 294 n. 3. See Wolsza, *Narodowa Demokracja,* 76–77, and Kawyn, *Ideologia,* 118–19, for more on the gatherings, some of which also assembled workers and intelligentsia.

93. Letter of 5 May 1899 of Roman Dmowski [R. Skrzycki, pseud.] to Zygmunt Miłkowski [*Pułkownik,* the colonel], in BJ przyb. 31/62, fol. 13.

94. Dąbrowski, *Czerwona Warszawa,* 155. The Galician peasant Wojciech Wiącek was one of those who traveled to Warsaw.

95. Halina Winnicka, "Socjaliści wobec Adama Mickiewicza: Stulecie urodzin poety," *Przegląd Humanistyczny* 22, no. 1 (1978): 152.

96. From the commemorative brochure *Dzieje pomnika Mickiewicza,* cited in ibid., 156.

97. Ludwik Kulczycki (Mieczysław Mazowiecki, pseud.), *Historya ruchu socyalistycznego w zaborze rosyjskim* (Kraków: Wydawnictwo "Proletaryatu," 1903), 351.

98. These included minutes from meetings of the Council of Ministers on 10 February and 17 February 1898 as well as a note of the chancellery of the same. (*Tajne dokumenty rządu rosyjskiego w sprawach polskich: Memoryał ks. Imeretyńskiego; Protokóły Komitetu Ministrów; Nota Kancelaryi Komitetu Ministrów* [London: drukowane z polecenia Komitetu Centralnego Polskiej Partyi Socyalistycznej, 1898].)

99. T. Münnich, *Pomniki.* Note that *Kraj* criticized the project early on. (See articles cited in Wasilewski, *Pomnik Mickiewicza,* 10–11, 26.)

100. *Pedagogika Mickiewiczowska: Książka pamiątkowa wydana przez Towarzystwo Pedagogiczne ku uczczeniu uroczystego złożenia zwłok Adama Mickiewicza na Wawelu* (Lviv: nakł. Towarzystwa Pedagogicznego, 1890), introduction (no page number); Józef Chociszewski, *Wspomnienie o życiu i pismach Adama Mickiewicza na pamiątkę przewiezienia jego popiołów do ojczystej ziemi w 1890 r.: Dla ludu polskiego i młodzieży skreślił* . . . (Poznań: nakładem Karola Kozłowskiego, 1890), 53.

101. M. Bałucki, "Nasze 'Dziady' (Obrazek z przeszłości)," *Nowa Reforma,* 4 July 1890.

102. In the course of the first two years of the folk university, 751 lectures were given in 33 towns and villages, with 116,573 listeners in attendance. (Edmund Libański, *1899–1901: Dwa lata pracy Uniwersytetu ludowego imienia Adama Mickiewicza* [L'viv: nakł. Uniw. lud. im. A. Mickiewicza, 1901].) See also Terlecki, *Oświata dorosłych,* 165–79. Numerous projects, including the People's University, are discussed in Kawyn, *Ideologia,* 162–68.

103. See Kawyn, *Ideologia,* 162–65 on the People's University, 165–68 on other forms of tribute.

104. From the 2 May 1882 meeting of the Mickiewicz committee, reported in "Kronika," *Reforma,* 4 May 1882.

105. "W sprawie pomnika Mickiewicza," *Gazeta Warszawska* no. 187 (1897), cited in Kawyn, *Ideologia,* 105.

6. TEUTONS VERSUS SLAVS?

1. See, for example, Michael Hughes, *Nationalism and Society: Germany, 1800–1945* (London: Edward Arnold, 1988), chaps. 5–6; Roger Chickering, *"We Men Who Feel Most German": A Cultural Study of the Pan-German League, 1886–1914* (Boston: Allen and Unwin, 1984); Galos, *Dzieje Hakaty.*

2. This, interestingly, in the one part of the former Polish lands where most children completed elementary schooling and where many Poles realized the benefits that knowledge of German could bring. (Lech Trzeciakowski, *Pod pruskim zaborem 1850–1918* [Warsaw: Wiedza Powszechna, 1973], 282.)

3. Ibid., 282, 308; John J. Kulczycki, *School Strikes in Prussian Poland, 1901–1907: The Struggle over Bilateral Education* (New York: Columbia University Press, 1981), 44–45.

4. Kulczycki, *School Strikes,* 70.

5. Kulczycki's book is the best source on the school strike of 1901.

6. Trzeciakowski, *Pod pruskim zaborem,* 330; Kulczycki, *School Strikes,* 67.

7. At least one of them, Koralewski, was a Pole by birth; for his services in promoting the German language he was later given a bonus. (Jürgen Vietig, "Die polnischen Grunwaldfeiern der Jahre 1902 und 1910," in *Germania Slavica II,* ed. Wolfgang H. Fritz [Berlin: Duncker and Humblot, 1981], 245.)

8. Kulczycki, *School Strikes,* 54.

9. Krzyżanowski, *Sienkiewicz: Kalendarz,* 239–40, 243; Dioniza Wawrzykowska-Wierciochowa, *Nie rzucim ziemi, skąd nasz ród . . .* (Warsaw: Wydawnictwo Ministerstwa Obrony Narodowej, 1988), 24–26; Kulczycki, *School Strikes,* 48–54, 62–65, 69.

10. Julian Krzyżanowski, *Henryka Sienkiewicza żywot i sprawy* (Warsaw: Państwowy Instytut Wydawniczy, 1966), 181.

11. For a recent look at the history of the battle, see Sven Ekdahl, "Tannenberg/Grunwald—Ein politisches Symbol in Deutschland und Polen," *Journal of Baltic Studies* 22, no. 4 (1991): 271–324.

12. "Modlitwa w dzień Grunwaldu: Kazanie O. Zygmunta Janickiego," *Głos Narodu,* 15 July 1902.

13. Italics mine. The matter is discussed in Janusz Jasiński, "Polemika wokół Grunwaldu w 1902 roku," *Warmia i Mazury* 27, no. 2 (February 1981): 12–13; Tadeusz Walichnowski, "Grunwald w świadomości współczesnych pokoleń Polaków," in *Grunwald w świadomości Polaków,* by Marian Biskup, Andrzej F. Grabski, Alfons Klafkowski, Henryk Samsonowicz, and Tadeusz Walichnowski (Warsaw and Łódź: Państwowe Wydawnictwo Naukowe, 1981), 56.

14. See Zbigniew Fras, "Obchody rocznicy bitwy pod Grunwaldem w 1902 roku wśród wychodźstwa polskiego w Niemczech i Austrii," in *Tradycja grunwaldzka,* vol. 3.

15. Quotations found in "Telegramy 'Czasu': Cesarz Wilhelm jako hakatysta," *Czas,* 6 June 1902, morning edition; "Toast cesarza Wilhelma," *Czas,* 7 June 1902, morning edition.

16. Galicians likewise supported, financially and otherwise, some of the defendants in the Września case who escaped to Austria-Hungary without serving their prison sentences. (Kulczycki, *School Strikes,* 82–83.)

17. Marian Karol Dubiecki's original article in *Czas* reminding Poles of this tradition was also published as idem, "Rocznice Grunwaldu," in *Obrazy i studia historyczne,* seria 3 (Kijów, 1915).

18. This view is corroborated by Galician police reports, which attribute the Grunwald celebrations to Sienkiewicz's efforts. (Stefan Józef Pastuszka, Józef Ryszard Szaflik, and Romuald Turkowski, "Chłopi i ruch ludowy w obchodach grunwaldzkich przed 1914 r.," in *Tradycja grunwaldzka,* 5:121.)

19. *Tygodnik Illustrowany* 43, no. 30 (2 [13] July 1902): 583; Władysław Wic, "Stosunek Polskiej Partii Socjalno-Demokratycznej Galicji i Śląska do obchodów grunwaldzkich," in *Tradycja grunwaldzka,* 2:152; "Kronika," Czas, 14 July 1902.

20. "Rada państwa (telefonem)," Czas, 11 June 1902, morning edition. After the official celebration, enthusiastic youth carried him from the Wawel to the Mickiewicz monument, where he laid a wreath and spoke about Poles and Czechs working together. ("Z ostatniej chwili," *Głos Narodu,* 12 July 1902; Antoni Giza, "Tradycja grunwaldzka w opinii czeskiej, 1906–1910," in *Tradycja grunwaldzka,* 4:73; "Z ostatniej chwili," *Głos Narodu,* 15 July 1902; "Rocznica Grunwaldu w Krakowie," *Głos Narodu,* 16 July 1902.)

21. Pastuszka, Szaflik, and Turkowski, "Chłopi i ruch ludowy," 147.

22. Cited in Marian Mroczko, *Ziemie dzielnicy pruskiej w polskich koncepcjach i działalności politycznej 1864–1939* (Gdańsk: Wydawnictwo "Marpress," 1994), 94.

23. Trzeciakowski, *Pod pruskim zaborem,* 331. See also Kulczycki, *School Strikes,* esp. chaps. 3 and 4.

24. Invaluable on the events of 1904–1906 is Blobaum, *Rewolucja.*

25. These developments are covered in greater detail in Dabrowski, "Reinventing Poland," 445–54, as well as in works such as Trzeciakowski, *Pod pruskim zaborem,* and Danuta Płygawko, *"Prusy i Polska": Ankieta Henryka Sienkiewicza (1907–1909)* (Poznań: Wielkopolska Agencja Wydawnicza, 1994).

26. A motion had been made by Kazimierz Bartoszewicz to that effect. (*Księga pamiątkowa obchodu pięćsetnej rocznicy zwycięstwa pod Grunwaldem w dniu 15, 16 i 17 lipca 1910 r. w Krakowie z dodaniem albumu literacko artystycznego poświęconego wielkiej rocznicy dziejowej,* ed. K. Bartoszewicz [Kraków: Nakładem Franciszka Terakowskiego, 1911], ix.)

27. Anna Treiderowa, *Obchody Grunwaldzkie w Krakowie (1410–1910)* (Kraków: nakładem Towarzystwa Miłośników Historii i Zabytków Krakowa, 1961), discusses in more detail the work of the committee(s) and subcommittees. Materials on the celebration can be found in the unsorted papers of the Grunwald committee, APKr, IT 881–84, R1, and numerous commemorative volumes and contemporary press. Many scholars have written articles on various aspects of the celebration, most notably in the five volumes of *Tradycja grunwaldzka* edited by Jerzy Maternicki (Warsaw: Uniwersytet Warszawski, Zakład Historii Historiografii i Dydaktyki Historii, 1989–90).

28. Treiderowa, *Obchody,* 31; Henryk Lisiak, "Z dziejów walki o narodowe przetrwanie: Obchody pięćsetnej rocznicy bitwy pod Grunwaldem," *Życie i Myśl* 36 (1988): 12, 32.

29. Contact increased this year between the continents, as a result of the newly erected monuments to Kościuszko and Pułaski in Washington, D.C., as well as on account of the Grunwald festivities, attended by several thousand Poles from America. (Treiderowa, *Obchody,* 28–29.)

30. Cited in Wic, "Stosunek PPSD," 178.

31. The film/newsreel was shown in Lwów, in the "Urania" cinema, from 30 July through the middle of August; in Cracow, from the end of August. (Andrzej Urbańczyk, "To było w 1910 roku: Kto sfilmował?" *Kraków* no. 1 [1990]: 15–17.) The one extant original—with French subtitles and the imprint of Pathé—is in the possession of the Muzeum Historyczne m. Krakowa; a Cracow television station and the Archiwum Wytwórni Filmów Dokumentalnych in Warsaw have copies. It is not clear whether this film has any connection to the written intent of a Pole from America named Kowalski, who wanted to film the festivities in order to share impressions of the event with other Poles back in the States. (Treiderowa, *Obchody,* 29.)

32. *Echa Grunwaldzkie z 1910-go roku,* ed. Józef Paderewski (Kraków, 1910), 25–26. They also offered a feast for the journalists, with plenty of speeches and toasts, the texts of which are included in *Wieniec grunwaldzki z 1910-go roku: Wydawnictwo historyczne, pamiątkowe, ilustrowane; zbiór aktów i dokumentów historycznych z 1910 r.; ku uczczeniu 500 letniej rocznicy wiekopomnego zwycięztwa Polaków nad Krzyżakami,* ed. Józef Paderewski (Kraków: G. Gebethner i Spółka, n.d.), 123–30.

33. For more on this subject, see Blobaum, *Rewolucja.* The idea of civil war is hardly farfetched, as seen from the fact that the PPS's fighting squads initiated terrorist activity not only against the Russian authorities but against their political opponents as well.

34. Henryk Lisiak, *Paderewski: Od Kuryłówki po Arlington* (Poznań: SAWW, 1992), 38; Henryk Przybylski, *Paderewski: Między muzyką a polityką* (Katowice: Wydawnictwo Unia, 1992), 45–47.

35. "Pomnik Władysława Jagiełły w Krakowie," *Tygodnik Illustrowany* 51, no. 29 (16 July 1910): 586.

36. Ignace Jan Paderewski and Mary Lawton, *The Paderewski Memoirs* (New York: C. Scribner's Sons, 1938), 372. The pianist gave the same information in a conversation with a Czas staff member years earlier. (sdl, "Przed odsłonięciem pomnika," Czas, 14 July 1910.)

37. Pływawko, *"Prusy i Polska,"* 124. This concerned the treatment of Ukrainians, discussed in chapter 7.

38. Treiderowa, *Obchody,* 20.

39. Words related by Bobrzyński's interlocutor, Krechowiecki (the editor of *Gazeta Lwowska*), to Adam Grzymała-Siedlecki (A. Grzymała Siedlecki, *Niepospolici ludzie w dniu swoim powszednim* [Kraków: Wydawnictwo Literackie, 1961], 298).

40. This and other objections are discussed in Dabrowski, "Reinventing Poland," 460–65.

41. Cited in Krzyżanowski, *Sienkiewicz: Kalendarz,* 274.

42. See Claire E. Nolte, *The Sokol in the Czech Lands to 1914: Training for the Nation* (New York: Palmgrave Macmillan, 2002).

43. See, for example, Wolsza, *Narodowa Demokracja,* 274–75; Marek Mirkiewicz, "Towarzystwo Gimnastyczne 'Sokół: Mit a rzeczywistość," in *Galicja i jej dziedzictwo* (Rzeszów: Wydawnictwo Wyższej Szkoły Pedagogicznej, 1995), 3:269–81.

44. M., "Dni grunwaldzkie w Galicyi," *Gazeta Warszawska,* 1 July 1910.

45. "Z prasy," Czas, 21 March 1910, evening edition.

46. See correspondence in APŁ, Archiwum Bartoszewiczów, 756; 2086, fols. 8–9, 22–25, 29, 95–98; 2090, fols. 6–7, 60–61; 2085; 2092, fols. 4–5; Ch., "O Straży Polskiej," *Straż Polska* 2, no. 9: 5–6.

47. "Sprawozdanie z działalności Zarządu Głównego 'Straży Polskiej' za czas od 23. marca 1908 do 1. maja 1909" (ciąg dalszy), *Straż Polska* 2, no. 14: 5. See also "Zjazd 'Straży Polskiej,'" *Czas,* 28 June 1910.

48. This is in keeping with Wapiński's statement that the National Democratic doctrine emerged as if in tandem with nationalistic tendencies that were already in existence.

(Adam Wątor, *Działalność Stronnictwa Demokratyczno-Narodowego w zaborze austriackim do roku 1914* [Szczecin: Wydawnictwo Naukowe Uniwersytetu Szczecińskiego, 1993], 14.)

49. Jan Styka and Tadeusz Styka, *Grunwald w Rondlu Bramy Floriańskiej* (Kraków: nakładem Jana Styki, 1909). (The Barbakan was sometimes referred to as the Rondel.) On the wagon, see letter of Dr. Tadeusz Jaworski to Zarząd Muzeum Narodowego of 5 March 1910, as well as the 8 March letter of Dr. Feliks Kopera to the magistrate, both in APKr, IT 881; also discussed in Treiderowa, *Obchody,* 15. Despite the fact that Drzymała's wagon was donated to the National Museum on condition that it be displayed during the commemoration, its presence did not appear to be much publicized during the festivities.

50. K. S., "Grunwald Styki i Barbakan Krakowa," *Tygodnik Illustrowany* 50, no. 48 (27 November 1909): 982–83; letter of 4 July 1910 of Marian Zdziechowski to Aleksander Lednicki, published in Zbigniew Solak, "Obchody grunwaldzkie w listach Mariana Zdziechowskiego," *Studia Historyczne* 36, no. 3 (1993): 364.

51. Sienkiewicz to the mayor of Cracow, Paris, 7 July 1910, APKr, IT 884; published in *Wieniec grunwaldzki,* 72; "List Sienkiewicza," *Czas,* 17 July 1910, morning edition.

52. Mieczysław Giergielewicz, *Henryk Sienkiewicz* (New York: Twayne, 1968), 154–55.

53. Ignacy Grabowski, "15 lipca 1410 roku," *Tygodnik Illustrowany* 51, no. 28 (9 July 1910): 564.

54. From Bronisław Sokalski's introduction to a popular edition of Sienkiewicz's description of the famous battle: Henryk Sienkiewicz, *Grunwald,* commemorative ed. (published by the Committee for the Resurrection of the Commemoration of the Memorable Rout of the Teutonic Knights in 1410) (L'viv: druk. Sz. Bednarskiego, 1902), 5.

55. From the speech of the Polish historian Oswald Balzer, given in Lwów on 29 June 1910, printed in *Słowo Polskie,* 30 June 1910, afternoon edition. Interestingly, similar conclusions were reached by those who compared Russian and Polish approaches—about which more shortly.

56. On the Grunwald commemoration in English, one may consult Marian Marek Drozdowski, *Ignacy Jan Paderewski: A Political Biography in Outline* (Kraków: Interpress, 1979), 54–58.

57. These requests can be viewed in the committee's papers, APKr, IT 881–84.

58. "Pomnik Władysława Jagiełły w Krakowie," *Tygodnik Illustrowany* 51, no. 29 (16 July 1910): 587; *Pomnik króla Jagiełły: Pamiątka uroczystości grunwaldzkich w Krakowie w dniach 15-go, 16-go i 17-go lipca 1910 r.* (Kraków: nakładem i czcionkami drukarni "Prawdy," 1910), 6–7. The bronze depiction of the peasant did not please all observers, as it could be put to use by the socialists to show the treatment of the Polish "proletariat." (See letter of July 1910 of Dr. L. I. L. of Lwów to Paderewski, AAN, Archiwum Paderewskiego, 609, fol. 36.) In 1913, this figure was replaced with a "villager with an energetic expression, his shoulders straining with effort, pulling a plough." ("Kronika," *Czas,* 11 October 1913.)

59. Reactions to the speech suggest that its tone of unity was what was needed after the divisive civil war that took place in the Kingdom of Poland in 1905. See, for example, the letter of 19 July 1910, written by Władysław Reymont, Poland's second literary Nobel laureate, to Paderewski in *Archiwum polityczne Ignacego Paderewskiego,* ed. Halina Janowska et al. (Wrocław, Warsaw, Kraków, and Gdańsk: Zakład Narodowy Imienia Ossolińskich, 1973), 1:28.

60. The text of the speech is found in ibid., 1:27, as well as in many commemorative publications (including *Księga pamiątkowa obchodu pięćsetnej rocznicy zwycięstwa pod Grunwaldem w dniu 15, 16 i 17 lipca 1910 r. w Krakowie z dodaniem albumu literacko-artystycznego poświęconego wielkiej rocznicy dziejowej,* ed. Kazimierz Bartoszewicz (Kraków: Nakładem Franciszka Terakowskiego, 1911); *Pomnik króla Jagiełły,* XXVII, with several words altered; an abbreviated English translation in Drozdowski, *Paderewski,* 55, which nonetheless mistranslates *przyszłość* (future) as "past."

61. See, for example, the text of the foundation protocol (AAN, Archiwum Paderewskiego, 609), published in "Akt fundacyjny pomnika," *Czas*, 14 July 1910, evening edition.

62. "W płaszczu krzyżackim," *Czas*, 6 June 1902, evening edition.

63. Z. D., "Nienawiść i miłość," *Tygodnik Illustrowany* 51, no. 31 (30 July 1910): 626–27.

64. Szymon Askenazy, "Ze stosunków polsko-pruskich," *Tygodnik Illustrowany* 51, no. 37 (10 September 1910): 740–41.

65. Announcement of 26 June 1910, APKr, IT 882; published in *Księga pamiątkowa obchodu pięćsetnej rocznicy*, xii–xiii.

66. *Pomnik króla Jagiełły*, 7.

67. Ibid.

68. As I have argued elsewhere, the Jagiellonian idea was in essence a variant of Pan-Slavism *avant la lettre*. (Patrice M. Dabrowski, "Who to Lead the Slavs? Poles, Russians, and the 1910 Anniversary of the Battle of Grunwald" [unpublished MS].)

69. Vyšný attributes the development of the movement to the political opportunism of the Young Czech leader Karel Kramář (Vyšný, *Neo-Slavism and the Czechs*, 49); see Antoni Giza, *Neoslavism i Polacy, 1906–1910* (Szczecin: Wydawnictwa naukowe Wyższej Szkoły Pedagogicznej w Szczecinie, 1984), for the Polish view of the Congress, and for the Russian view, Z. S. Nenasheva, "Slavianskii s"ezd 1908 g. v Prage i ego mesto v formirovanii ideologii i programmy neoslavisma," in *Slavianskie s"ezdy XIX–XX vv.*, ed. E. P. Aksenova, A. N. Goriainov, and M. Iu. Dostal' (Moscow: Rossiiskaia akademiia nauk Institut slavianovedeniia i balkanistiki, Nauchnyi tsentr obshcheslavianskikh issledovanii, Mezhdunarodnyi fond iugoslavianskikh issledovanii i sotrudnichestva "Slavianskaia letopis'," 1994), 99–112.

70. Antoni Giza, "Neoslawiści wobec obchodów grunwaldzkich w Krakowie w 1910 r.," in *Tradycja grunwaldzka*, 1:256–57. Giza terms the encounter between the Poles and Russians on that anniversary "the culmination point of the congress." (Giza, *Neoslawizm i Polacy*, 118.) Although he discusses Polish-Russian relations at the congress, Vyšný makes no mention of the anniversary.

71. *Wieniec grunwaldzki*, 74–75, 255–56. Although Vyšný, *Neo-Slavism*, covers the congress in Sofia in great detail, he does not mention the Grunwald festivities.

72. Leo's words were noted in letter of 4 July 1910 of Marian Zdziechowski to Aleksander Lednicki, published in Solak, "Obchody grunwaldzkie," 355, 363.

73. July 1910 letter of Marian Zdziechowski letter to his wife, Maria, published in ibid., 366.

74. Drozdowski, *Paderewski*, 55.

75. This view is advanced by Władysław Grabski in an excerpt from his memoirs entitled "Z powrotem we Lwowie," Bibl PAN Kr, 7846, fols. 29–30; Micewski, *Dmowski*, 161–62; Giza, *Neoslawizm i Polacy*, 207–209.

76. Such terms of praise can be found in "Pomnik Władysława Jagiełły w Krakowie," *Tygodnik Illustrowany* 51, no. 29 (16 July 1910): 586; "Kronika miesięczna," *Biblioteka Warszawska* no. 279 (August 1910): 388. Boy mocked Paderewski's new status in a satirical song written for his Green Balloon cabaret, which began with the words "Today I am Poland's king" (Jam dziś Polsce król). (Tadeusz Boy-Żeleński, *Słówka: 26–30 tysiąc* [Warsaw: Instytut Wydawniczy "Bibljoteka Polska," 1925], 278.)

77. *Wieniec grunwaldzki*, 94, 119–20.

78. "Prawdziwa miłość," *Wieniec-Pszczółka* 36, no. 31 (31 July 1910): 466.

79. "Goście słowiańscy w Krakowie," *Prawda*, 30 July 1910, cited in Arkadiusz Kołodziejczyk, "Tradycje walki z naporem krzyżacko-pruskim i zwycięstwo grunwaldzkie na łamach warszawskiej 'Prawdy' 1880–1915," in *Tradycja grunwaldzka*, 2:143. A rabidly

anti-Polish Pan-Slav of the old school, Bobrinskii had served as chairman of the Slav congress in Sofia.

80. E. N. Trubetskoi, "Natsionalizm i slavianskoe edinenie," *Moskovskii Ezhenediel'nik* no. 27 (10 July 1910); parts of this were cited in J. Herbaczewski, "Przegląd prasy słowiańskiej," *Świat Słowiański* 6, part 2 (November 1910): 283.

81. From *Świat Słowiański* 6, part 2 (September 1910): 122, cited in Giza, *Neoslawizm i Polacy,* 210.

82. Such considerations serve as the underpinning for Antoni Giza, "Słowiański aspekt obchodów grunwaldzkich 1910 r. w Krakowie," *Studia Historyczne* 41, no. 1 (1998): 37–48, and they received treatment in earlier works by him as well.

83. Giza, "Neoslawiści," 266–67; *Wieniec grunwaldzki,* 76.

84. See, for example, the articles by Wiktor Czermak in *Czas* and *Tygodnik Illustrowany* ("Dziejowe znaczenie Grunwaldu," *Czas,* 4 July 1910; "Zwycięstwo jagiełłowe," *Tygodnik Illustrowany* 51, no. 29 [16 July 1910]: 579–81).

85. "Na uroczystości grunwaldzkie," *Świat Słowiański* 6, part 2 (July–December 1910): 1–2.

86. "Grunwald," *Rzeczpospolita* 2, no. 36 (9 July 1910): 158.

87. This is the conclusion of Giza, "Słowiański aspekt."

88. Cited in Solak, "Obchody grunwaldzkie," 356. The topic of changing identities in this region receives excellent treatment in Timothy Snyder, *The Reconstruction of Nations: Poland, Ukraine, Lithuania, Belarus, 1569–1999* (New Haven: Yale University Press, 2002).

89. Draft attached to letter of 27 May 1910 to the Cracow president, APKr, IT 884; published in Solak, "Obchody grunwaldzkie," 362.

90. Józef A. Herbaczewski, "Przegląd prasy słowiańskiej: Z prasy litewskiej," *Świat Słowiański* 6, part 2 (August 1910): 105–107.

91. See the suspicions voiced in an article in *Viltis* cited in Józef A. Herbaczewski, "Przegląd prasy słowiańskiej," *Świat Słowiański* 6, part 2 (November 1910): 277; "Fundacya książąt Lubomirskich," *Czas,* 15 July 1910, morning edition.

92. Herbaczewski, "Przegląd prasy słowiańskiej: Z prasy litewskiej," *Świat Słowiański* 6, part 2 (August 1910): 106; Solak, "Obchody grunwaldzkie," 358. In turn, the Germans praised the Lithuanians for not participating in the Cracow festivities. (Lisiak, *Paderewski,* 46.)

93. From *Viltis* no. 112 (1910), cited in Herbaczewski, "Przegląd prasy słowiańskiej," *Świat Słowiański* 6, part 2 (November 1910): 278–79.

94. Mister Rankus, "Polonais et lithuaniens," *La Croix,* 13 August 1910, also discussed in Herbaczewski, "Przegląd prasy słowiańskiej," *Świat Słowiański* 6, part 2 (November 1910): 278–79.

95. Cited in "Prasa ruska o obchodzie grunwaldzkim," *Czas,* 1 July 1910, evening edition.

96. Reproductions sold by Kasper Wojnar at the Falcon jamboree bookstore on the Błonia field during the 1910 festivities proved very popular. ("Kronika," *Czas,* 16 July 1910, evening edition; "Kronika miesięczna," *Biblioteka Warszawska* no. 248 [December 1902]: 614–16.)

97. AUJ, S II 962, 500-rocznica chrztu Litwy 1996 r.

98. In many ways, as Timothy Snyder points out, the conversion of Lithuania was not from paganism but from eastern Orthodoxy. (Snyder, *Reconstruction of Nations,* 18.)

99. Bandurski's article appeared in a special addendum to *Czas* (supplement to *Czas,* 23 March 1910: W. Bandurski, "O najwyższy hołd Królowej Jadwidze," dated 1 January 1910) as well as in numerous commemorative volumes.

100. Kulczycki, *School Strikes,* 56; Fras, "Obchody," 83.

101. "Telegraficzne i telefoniczne wiadomości 'N. Reformy,'" *Nowa Reforma,* 8 July 1902.

102. "Kronika," *Nowa Reforma,* 9 July 1902.

103. "Z ostatniej chwili," *Głos Narodu,* 9 July 1902 and 10 July 1902.

104. See Wiktor Hahn, *Rok Słowackiego: Księga pamiątkowa obchodów urządzanych ku czci poety w roku 1909* (L'viv: Nakł. Komitetu Obchodu Setnej Rocznicy Urodzin Juliusza Słowackiego, 1911), 152–53. The history of the Słowacki translation, which was not resolved until 1927, deserves a monograph. A short piece has been written by Jerzy Piekarczyk, "Powrót Króla-Ducha," *Kraków* no. 4 (1986): 28–31.

105. According to *Słowo,* 4 July 1910, cited in Lisiak, *Paderewski,* 46.

106. Józef Buszko, *Dzieje ruchu robotniczego w Galicji Zachodniej, 1848–1918* (Kraków: Wydawnictwo Literackie, 1986), 356; Wic, "Stosunek PPSD," 173, 179; Emil Bobrowski, "Obchód 500-ej rocznicy Grunwaldu w Krakowie 1910 roku (Urywek z pamiętnika)," *Niepodległość* 14 (July–December 1936): 127–28.

107. The state of the Church in Russian Poland is discussed in Blobaum, *Rewolucja,* 234–59.

108. Władysław Wic, "Młodzi socjaliści galicyjscy wobec tradycji grunwaldzkiej," in *Tradycja grunwaldzka,* 4:83–92.

109. Buszko, *Społeczno-polityczne oblicze,* 40–41, 57. For more on the expulsion of students in the Kingdom of Poland, see Blobaum, *Rewolucja,* 177.

110. From a speech of Jan Baścik, cited in Wic, "Młodzi socjaliści," 93–94.

111. Ibid., 95.

112. M., "Dni grunwaldzkie w Galicyi," *Gazeta Warszawska,* 1 July 1910. For more on the attitude of the Archbishop Bilczewski and the Lwów archdiocese, see Jan Dzięgielewski, "Archidiecezja lwowska obrządku łacińskiego w obchodach pięcsetnej rocznicy zwycięstwa pod Grunwaldem," in *Tradycja grunwaldzka,* 2:188–204.

113. *Pomnik króla Jagiełły,* 16. Sermon published in *Księga pamiątkowa obchodu pięcsetnej rocznicy,* XVIII–XX.

114. Dzięgielewski, "Archidiecezja lwowska," 194.

115. Henryk Żaliński, "Grunwald i polityka niemiecka w krakowskich kalendarzach (1848–1914)," in *Tradycja grunwaldzka,* 2:53.

116. *Pomnik króla Jagiełły,* 18.

117. *Wieniec grunwaldzki,* 122–23.

118. Ferdinand Machay, *Moja droga do Polski* (memoir), 2d ed. (Kraków, 1938), 34–36, 47.

119. Roman Tomczyk, "Praojcom na chwałę braciom na otuchę," *Tygodnik Powszechny* 30, no. 37 (1976): 8. Bandurski's speech has been published in Wieniec grunwaldzki, 100–102; *Pomnik króla Jagiełły,* 17–18; and other commemorative publications.

120. *Pomnik króla Jagiełły,* 17.

121. *Echa Grunwaldzkie,* 26, 28.

122. Bobrowski, "Obchód 500-ej rocznicy," 127.

123. Ibid.

124. Words of Ferdinand Machay's younger brother, cited in Machay, *Moja droga do Polski,* 36.

125. See Andrzej W. Kaczorowski, "Tradycja grunwaldzka w działalności polskiego skautingu," in *Tradycja grunwaldzka,* 2:209. The scouts, incidentally, came under the leadership of the Falcons. (Ibid., 230–31 n. 7.) A history of the hymn/march has been written by Wawrzykowska-Wierciochowa, *Nie rzucim ziemi.* See also Andrzej W. Kaczorowski, "Związek Polskich Towarzystw Gimnastycznych 'Sokół' a tradycja grunwaldzka," in *Tradycja grunwaldzka,* 5:164–85. The song was even more important in a later period: Konopnicka's anti-German "Rota" would become the Polish "Marseillaise" during the Sile-

sian uprisings of 1919, 1920, and 1921. (Introduction to Stanisław Łempicki, *Słowo o Grunwaldzie* [n.p.: Czytelnik, 1945], 6.)

126. "Obchód grunwaldzki w Krakowie," *Czas,* 15 July 1910.

127. "Po obchodzie" and "Uczta dziennikarska," *Czas,* 18 July 1910.

128. This does not mean that nationalistic papers such as the Viennese *Deutsches Volksblatt* and Russian *Novoe Vremia* did not cast the event—and the Poles—in a less favorable light. See "Prasa obca o obchodzie," *Czas,* 19 July 1910.

129. "Uczta dziennikarska," *Czas,* 18 July 1910.

130. "Echa Grunwaldu," *Tygodnik Illustrowany* 51, no. 32 (6 August 1910): 652; in issue 3517, 1910, as reported in "Maurice Muret o Grunwaldzie," *Gazeta Warszawska,* 27 June 1910.

131. According to a Prussian pedagogical journal, cited in Kulczycki, *School Strikes,* 15.

132. "Grunwald," *Rzeczpospolita* 2, no. 36 (9 July 1910): 157.

133. Many publications still expressed their outrage at the past and present treatment at the hands of the Teutonic Knights–cum–Germans. See the new verses, containing elements of protest, by Kazimierz Gliński, Stanisław Rossowski, and Kazimierz Laskowski, cited in Wiktor Hahn, *Grunwald w poezyi polskiej: Szkic literacki* (Kraków: nakładem autora, 1910), 41–42.

7. POLES IN ARMS

1. Tadeusz Boy-Żeleński, *Znaszli ten kraj: Cyganeria krakowska* (Kraków: Czytelnik, 1945).

2. See, for example, APKR, DPKr 43, 515/pr 890.

3. For more on this conflict, see Victor Hugo Lane IV, "State Culture and National Identity in a Multi-ethnic Context: Lemberg, 1772–1914" (Ph.D. diss., University of Michigan, 1999); Dabrowski, "Reinventing Poland," 515–20.

4. *Drużyny Bartoszowe, 1908–1914* (L'viv: Wydawnictwo Zakładu Narodowego im. Ossolińskich, 1939), 5. (The entire statute can be read on pp. 8–13.) Dayczak called it the first Polish civic-military organization. (Wawrzyniec Dayczak, "Z dni wielkich przemian: Wspomnienia architekta," chaps. 7–10, Bibl PAN Kr, 7843, fol. 200.)

5. Bibl PAN Kr, 7843, fol. 189; Kyryło Trylowśkyj, "Moja znajomość z Józefem Piłsudskim," *Niepodległość* 8 (July–December 1933): 444. Dayczak admitted that his organization was modeled after the Sich: see W. Dayczak, "7 dni wielkich przemian," Ossolineum rkps 14093/II, vol. 1, p. 200, cited in Wolsza, *Narodowa Demokracja,* 281.

6. "Wojna," *Czas,* 21 October 1912; "Z chwili obecnej," *Czas,* 22 October 1912.

7. Although not an ideologue—that role would fall to Władysław Studnicki—Piłsudski provided the inspiration for the groups that put this new orientation on the map. (Jan Molenda, *Piłsudczycy a Narodowi Demokraci, 1908–1918* [Warsaw: "Książka i Wiedza," 1980], 8, 57.)

8. See Piłsudski's "Geografia militarna Królestwa Polskiego," published in Józef Piłsudski, *Pisma zbiorowe: Wydanie prac dotychczas drukiem ogłoszonych* (Warsaw: Instytut Józefa Piłsudskiego, 1937), 3:37–50.

9. Michał Sokolnicki, *Rok czternasty* (London: nakładem Gryf Publications, 1961), 22.

10. Andrzej Garlicki, *Józef Piłsudski, 1867–1935,* new abridged ed., ed. and trans. John Coutouvidis (Brookfield, Vt.: Scolar Press, 1995), 60–61; Marian Żychowski, *Polska myśl socjalistyczna XIX i XX wieku: do 1918 r.* (Warsaw: Państwowe Wydawnictwo Naukowe, 1976), 378; Sokolnicki, *Rok czternasty,* 23.

11. Bogusław (Kordjan) Kunc, "Od Związku Walki Czynnej do Strzelca (1909–1914)," *Niepodległość* 3 (October 1930–March 1931): 119. The Bartosz Squads were turned into a

military organization in 1912. On the Sich, see Trylowśkyj, "Moja znajomość," 444; I[van] V[asyl'ovych] Krups'kyi, *National'no-patriotychna zhurnalistyka Ukraïny (druha polovyna XIX–persha chvert' XX st.)* (L'viv: Vydavnytstvo "Svit," 1995), 83.

12. Piłsudski and Samuel Haecker were the only ones present mentioned by name. About thirty representatives of Polish student societies from within the country and abroad participated.

13. APKr, DPKr 79, 3537/pr/11.

14. The so-called congress of irredentists, held in Zakopane in the summer of 1912, is discussed in Andrzej Garlicki, *Geneza legionów: Zarys dziejów Komisji Tymczasowej Skonfederowanych Stronnictw Niepodległościowych* (Warsaw: Książka i Wiedza, 1964), 37ff. On donations, see Andrzej Garlicki, *Józef Piłsudski, 1867–1935* [Warsaw: Czytelnik, 1988], 153.

15. Cited in Marian Kukiel, *Wskrzeszenie wojska polskiego* (London: Instytut Historyczny im. Gen. Sikorskiego, 1959), 12.

16. Words of Henryk Kunzek, cited in Garlicki, *Geneza legionów,* 41.

17. Garlicki, *Piłsudski,* 62; Andrzej Chwalba, *Józef Piłsudski historyk wojskowości* (Kraków: Universitas, 1993), 17, 22.

18. These comments were made after his talk on the anniversary of the November Insurrection in 1912. ("Kronika: Wieczorek listopadowy," *Nowa Reforma,* 2 December 1912.)

19. Chwalba, *Piłsudski,* 55.

20. The next section is based on the text of the lectures, published in Piłsudski, *Pisma,* 3.

21. Cited in Chwalba, *Piłsudski,* 32.

22. The word "Provisional" was dropped from the title the next year.

23. Piłsudski, *Pisma,* 3:141.

24. "W 50-tą rocznicę powstania," *Ilustrowany Kuryer Codzienny,* 22 January 1913.

25. Perhaps this is why the commemoration is sometimes overlooked; for example, it is missing from the list of national celebrations in Christoph Freiherr Marschall von Bieberstein, *Freiheit in der Unfreiheit: Die nationale Autonomie der Polen in Galizien nach dem österreichisch-ungarischen Ausgleich von 1867; Ein konservativer Aufbruch im mitteleuropäischen Vergleich* (Wiesbaden: Harrassowitz, 1993), 315.

26. *Katalog Wystawy Pamiątek Powstania Styczniowego otwartej 3-go lutego 1918 r. w kamienicy ks. Mazowieckich,* prepared by Edward Chwalewik (Warsaw: tłocznia Wł. Łazarskiego, 1918), III–IV; APKr, IT 886, minutes of 30 December 1912 meeting of executive committee; Chwalba, *Piłsudski,* 72.

27. "Pięćdziesięciolecie powstania styczniowego," 15 July 1912 announcement of committee, *Straż Polska,* August and September 1912.

28. Ibid. Details of the Lwów program for the fiftieth anniversary of 1863 are provided in "Kronika lwowska," *Nowa Reforma,* 6 May 1912; "1863–1913," *Straż Polska,* May 1912; "Kronika," *Czas,* 4 May 1912, afternoon edition. By the beginning of this year, the link between the National League and Straż Polska had been publicly acknowledged. (See "Ze 'Straży,'" *Straż Polska,* January 1912.)

29. Letter of 1 August 1912 from Komitet 1863–1913 to the mayor of Cracow, APKr, R2.

30. The approbation of such distinguished figures did not prevent the archconservative Jerzy Moszyński from publishing a leaflet condemning the celebration. ("W wigilię styczniowego powstania," leaflet dated 2 February 1913 [Kraków: nakładem autora], BJ 224784 IV, I. V/2.)

31. APKr, IT 886, minutes of 21 October 1912 meeting of the executive committee.

32. For more on these organizations and endeavors, see Dabrowski, "Reinventing Poland," 542–43.

33. See "Odezwa do Polek," *Nowa Reforma,* 21 January 1913. Popular works by women included Marya Raczyńska, *Cienie* (L'viv: nakładem Związku teatrów i chórów włościańskich, 1914); Bogusławska's *Pamiątka powstania;* and Michalina Mossoczowa's *Krwawe dzieje, historya powstania styczniowego w 50-tą rocznicę opowiedziana* (L'viv: nakładem Macierzy Polskiej, 1913).

34. "Odezwa do Polek," *Nowa Reforma,* 21 January 1913.

35. Announcement of 2 January 1913, Komitet 1863–1913 and Obchód ku uczczeniu 50tej rocznicy powstania styczniowego, L. 2221-5772, APKr, IT 886. The citation comes from an announcement of the Tow. wzaj. pomocy uczestników powstania polskiego 1863/4 r. calling for Poles to purchase transparencies, in "Kronika," *Czas,* 17 January 1913, afternoon edition.

36. Stanisław S. Nicieja, *Cmentarz Łyczakowski we Lwowie w latach 1786–1986* (Wrocław, Warsaw, and Kraków: Zakład Narodowy im. Ossolińskich, 1988), 297, 301.

37. See, for example, "Obchód styczniowy we Lwowie (telefonem)," *Nowa Reforma,* 22 January 1913, morning edition.

38. Nicieja, *Cmentarz Łyczakowski,* 191.

39. Ibid., 192.

40. "Obchód styczniowy we Lwowie" (telefonem) Lwów 22 stycznia, *Nowa Reforma,* 22 January 1913, morning edition.

41. *Nowa Reforma,* 22 January 1913.

42. "Kronika lwowska," *Nowa Reforma,* 20 December 1912.

43. Stanisław Grabski, "1863," *Słowo Polskie,* 21 January 1913, afternoon edition.

44. Bohdan Urbankowski, *Filozofia czynu: Światopogląd Józefa Piłsudskiego* (Warsaw: Pelikan, 1988), 262; Józef Buszko, *Józef Piłsudski w Krakowie 1896–1935* (Kraków: Krajowa Agencja Wydawnicza, 1990), 27.

45. "Telegramy 'Czasu,'" *Czas,* 23 January 1913, morning edition.

46. "Zlot Sokoli we Lwowie," *Ilustrowany Kuryer Codzienny,* 8 July 1913; "'Zlot doraźny' we Lwowie," *Czas,* 7 July 1913, afternoon edition.

47. "Kronika," *Czas,* 24 January 1913, afternoon edition.

48. Minutes of the 21 October 1912 meeting of the executive committee, APKr, IT 886.

49. "50-lecie rocznicy powstania styczniowego," *Ilustrowany Kuryer Codzienny,* 19 January 1913.

50. "50-letnia rocznica styczniowa," *Ilustrowany Kuryer Codzienny,* 24 January 1913.

51. *Przyjaciel Ludu* no. 11 (1913): 8 9; *Zakopane* 6 (1914): 6–7.

52. Antoni Grabowski, chłop-ludowiec z Bocheńskiego, "Organizacja 'Związków strzeleckich': Pod jeden sztandar," *Przyjaciel Ludu,* 2 March 1913.

53. Garlicki, *Geneza Legionów,* 112.

54. Franciszek Ziejka, *Złota legenda chłopów polskich* (Warsaw: Państwowy Instytut Wydawniczy, 1984), has a chapter on Chochołów and writes about this celebration on pp. 288–90.

55. "Dni grunwaldzkie w Zakopanem," *Zakopane* 4, no. 20 (1911): 4.

56. The literature is a bit fuzzy on the beginnings of the paramilitary movement. Wątor claims that the initiative came at the third Podhale congress, 9–10 August 1913 (Wątor, *Działalność Stronnictwa,* 580). But the Zakopane press noted its formation as of 3 May 1913 (Józef Diehl, "Drużyny Podhalańskie," *Zakopane* 6, no. 28 [1913]: 2–3), as does Włodzimierz Wnuk, *Na góralską nutę* (Warsaw: Instytut Wydawniczy PAX, 1975), 10–17, esp. 15.

57. Józef Diehl, "Drużyny Podhalańskie," *Zakopane* 6, no. 28 (1913): 2–3.

58. From the printed announcement of the commemorative committee, BJ, Druki ulotne jubil. T. VI/1.

59. Józek z Dunajca, *Rebelja chochołowska w r. 1846* (Kraków: nakł. Wydawnictwa "Przyjaciela Ludu," 1912), 5. Ziejka (in *Złota legenda*) identifies the author (here, under a pseudonym) as Józef Kantor and discusses the work on p. 282.

60. Józek z Dunajca, *Rebelja*, 25–26. Part of this citation can be found in Ziejka, *Złota legenda*, 282.

61. Words of Wojciech Roj, one of the founders of Związek Górali and the Zakopane wójt, cited in Włodzimierz Wnuk, "Ruch regionalny," in *Zakopane: Czterysta lat dziejów*, ed. Renata Dutkowa (Kraków: Krajowa Agencja Wydawnicza, 1991), 1:720; part of this citation is also in Ziejka, *Złota legenda*, 290.

62. The growing sense of their Polishness led nearly two thousand highlanders to join the Polish Legions when war broke out in 1914. (Wnuk, *Na góralską nutę*, 17–18.)

63. "Kronika," *Czas,* 9 September 1913.

64. The Cracow commemorations machine was revved up in April 1913. ("Rada miasta Krakowa," *Czas,* 1 May 1913, morning edition.)

65. A good English-language introduction to this subject is chapter 2 of Piotr S. Wandycz, *Lands of Partitioned Poland, 1795–1918* (Seattle and London: University of Washington Press, 1974).

66. These are chronicled and analyzed in Wolfram Siemann, "Krieg und Frieden in historischen Gedenkfeiern des Jahres 1913," in *Öffentliche Festkultur,* 298–320.

67. Ibid., 304–306.

68. "Jubileusz wiarołomstwa," *Głos Narodu,* 19 October 1913.

69. See Krzysztof Karol Daszyk, "Szymona Askenazego neoromantyczna apoteoza czynu," *Studia Historyczne* 38, no. 2 (1995): 228 and elsewhere.

70. See his *Napoleon a Polska* (while the book did not appear until 1918–19, articles based upon his research were published in *Biblioteka Warszawska* in 1913), *Łukasiński* (1908), and *Książę Józef Poniatowski, 1763–1813* (first edition published in 1905).

71. Discussed in Daszyk, "Szymona Askenazego neoromantyczna apoteoza," 228.

72. Cited in Józef Dutkiewicz, *Szymon Askenazy i jego szkoła* (Warsaw: Państwowe Wydawnictwo Naukowe, 1958), 89.

73. Ibid., 17.

74. Szymon Askenazy, *Książę Józef Poniatowski, † 19 października 1813: Przemówienie w setną rocznicę zgonu na obchodzie w Starym Teatrze w Krakowie wygłosił . . .* (Kraków and Warsaw, 1913), 25.

75. Ibid., 26.

76. In a later foreword to *Łukasiński,* cited in Józef Dutkiewicz, *Szymon Askenazy i jego szkoła* (Warsaw: Państwowe Wydawnictwo Naukowe, 1958), 65.

77. "Książę Józef Poniatowski," *Czas,* 18 October 1913.

78. Sz. Askenazy, *Książę Józef Poniatowski, 1763–1813: Wydanie jubileuszowe ozdobione 152 rycinami* (Poznań: nakładem Karola Rzepeckiego w Poznaniu, 1913), n.p. (first page of foreword).

79. "Książę Józef Poniatowski," *Czas,* 18 October 1913.

80. Alfred Uznański, "Książę Józef a Targowica," *Głos Narodu,* 19 October 1913.

81. "Książę Józef Poniatowski," *Czas,* 18 October 1913; "1813–1913," *Czas,* 18 October 1913, afternoon edition.

82. "Uczczenie pamięci ks. Poniatowskiego," *Czas,* 19 October 1913, morning edition.

83. The description of the events of this day is based on "Rocznica zgonu Ks. Poniatowskiego," *Czas,* 20 October 1913.

84. "Uczczenie pamięci ks. Poniatowskiego," *Czas,* 19 October 1913, morning edition; "Obchód ku czci ks. Józefa," *Głos Narodu,* 19 October 1913.

85. "Wielkie święto narodowe, 1813–1913," *Ilustrowany Kuryer Codzienny,* 21 October 1913.

86. "Pamięci wielkiego bohatera," *Nowa Reforma,* 18 October 1913, afternoon edition.

87. "Uroczystości sokole ks. Poniatowskiego," *Czas,* 6 October 1913.

88. "Ku czci ks. Józefa Poniatowskiego," *Nowa Reforma,* 19 October 1913, morning edition.

89. Sokolnicki, *Rok czternasty,* 98–99.

90. Cited by Joanna Szarkowa, "Obchody rocznic narodowych w działalności propagandowej Naczelnego Komitetu Narodowego (1914–1917)," *Rocznik Biblioteki PAN w Krakowie* 39 (1994): 189.

91. Polacy! Announcement of 4 August 1914, Komenda Drużyn Podhalańskich, BJ, Druki ulotne.

92. Per minutes of the meeting, in part reproduced in Garlicki, *Geneza Legionów,* 239.

93. Leon Wasilewski, *Piłsudski jakim go znałem* (Warsaw: Towarzystwo Wydawnicze "Roj," 1935), 129–30.

94. This point has also been noted by Urbankowski, *Filozofia czynu,* 281.

95. A veteran of the First Brigade, Tadeusz Alf-Tarczyński, assumed that the timing of the foray into Russian Poland was no accident. (Tadeusz Alf-Tarczyński, *Wspomnienia oficera Pierwszej Brygady* [London: Nakładem Polskiej Fundacji Kulturalnej, 1979], 88.)

96. Sokolnicki, *Rok czternasty,* 183–84.

97. Ibid., 48.

98. Urbankowski, *Filozofia czynu,* 262–63.

99. Alina Kowalczykowa, *Piłsudski i tradycja* (Chotomów: Verba, 1991), 85–87; Piłsudski, *Pisma,* 5.

100. See the citations from Drobner's *Bezustanna walka* and Daszyński's memoirs in Buszko, *Piłsudski,* 35–36.

101. George L. Mosse, *Fallen Soldiers: Reshaping the Memory of the World Wars* (New York: Oxford University Press, 1990), 7 and elsewhere.

102. Feldman, *Dzieje polskiej myśli,* 353.

CONCLUSION

1. Dr. Ω, "Jubileusz literacki J. I. Kraszewskiego," *Przegląd Lwowski* 9, no. 18 (1879): 347–53.

2. Rousseau, *Government of Poland,* 12.

3. Cywiński, *Rodowody niepokornych.* I use Brian Porter's loose but apt rendition of the term into English. (Brian A. Porter, "The Construction and Deconstruction of Nineteenth-Century Polish Liberalism," in *Historical Reflections on Central Europe: Selected Papers from the Fifth World Congress of Central and East European Studies, Warsaw, 1995,* ed. Stanislav J. Kirschbaum [Houndmills, Basingstroke, Hampshire, and London: St. Martin's Press, 1999], 350.)

4. Topór, "Patryotyzm a obchody," *Straż Polska* 7, no. 10 (November 1913): 150.

5. Krawczak, "Kształtowanie świadomości," 150.

6. Anderson, *Imagined Communities;* William Isaac Thomas and Florian Znaniecki, *The Polish Peasant in Europe and America* (New York: Knopf, 1927).

7. Cressy, *Bonfires and Bells,* xiii. Such a calendar was published by Mieczysław Offmański [Orion, pseud.], *Historya Polaka w niewoli (1794–1894) rozłożona na dnie i miesiące* (Kraków: Nakładem i czcionkami drukarni Związkowej w Krakowie, 1894).

8. Urbankowski, *Filozofia czynu,* 263. Following Philippe Ariès, Stanisław Rosiek also emphasizes the way the living and dead, together, provided a "new picture of society." (*Zwłoki Mickiewicza,* 61.)

9. See the announcement of the Central Committee of the National League, dated Warsaw, 8 December 1899, in APKr, DPKr 55, 511/pr/901. Similar sentiments are found in Dmowski's "Po manifestacji 17 kwietnia," as cited in Wapiński, *Dmowski*, 66.

10. Stanisław Ossowski, "Analiza socjologiczna pojęcia ojczyzny," in idem, *Dzieła* (Warsaw: Państwowe Wydawnictwo Naukowe, 1967), 3:211, cited in Roman Wapiński, "Mit dawnej Rzeczypospolitej w epoce porozbiorowej," *Polskie mity polityczne XIX i XX wieku* (Wrocław: Wydawnictwo Uniwersytetu Wrocławskiego, 1994), 79.

11. Tarnowski, *Z doświadczeń*, 323.

12. Nora, "Between Memory and History," in *Realms of Memory*, 1:2.

13. Wilhelm Feldman, *Stronnictwa i programy polityczne w Galicyi, 1846–1906* (Kraków: Książka, 1907), 2:7.

14. Kieniewicz, *Sapieha*, 244.

15. Feldman, *Stronnictwa*, 2:14.

16. *Pamiętnik tajnych organizacyj*, 139.

17. Roman Dmowski, *Wybór pism Romana Dmowskiego* (New York: Instytut Romana Dmowskiego, 1988), 1:93.

18. While Wandycz emphasizes the nonethnic character of medieval "Crowns" in Poland, Bohemia, and Hungary, he claims that the Polish medieval state had been the least multi-ethnic. (Piotr S. Wandycz, *The Price of Freedom: A History of East Central Europe from the Middle Ages to the Present* [London and New York: Routledge, 1992], 23–25.)

19. Brock, "Polish Nationalism," 323.

20. This is a subtitle in Szporluk's article "Ukraine: From an Imperial Periphery to a Sovereign State," *Daedalus* (summer 1997): 92. Other ideas in this section also come from this article.

21. Brubaker, *Citizenship and Nationhood*, 5; chapter 6 is particularly illuminating in this regard.

22. Weeks, *Nation and State*, 194. Still, amazingly, some scholarship dealing with the "roads to nationalism" of Russia and Germany makes no mention of the Poles at all. An example of this is Liah Greenfeld, *Nationalism: Five Roads to Modernity* (Cambridge: Harvard University Press, 1992).

23. Szporluk, "Ukraine."

24. See Daniel Beauvois, "Rzeczpospolita polsko-litewska w XVII wieku i pięć narodów na jej obszarach w wieku XIX," in *Historia Europy Środkowo-Wschodniej* (Lublin: Instytut Europy Środkowo-Wschodniej, 2000), 1:244.

25. Roman Szporluk, "Polish-Ukrainian Relations in 1918: Notes for Discussion," in *The Reconstruction of Poland, 1914–23*, ed. Paul Latawski (London: Macmilllan, 1992), 42–43.

26. Tadeusz Boy-Żeleński, *Bronzownicy* (Warsaw: Towarzystwo Wydawnicze "Rój," 1930), 15.

27. Major events include the five hundredth anniversary (in 1882) of the arrival of the famous Marian icon in Częstochowa and its re-crowning in 1910. A recent work dealing with the Częstochowa sanctuary is Jabłoński, *Jasna Góra*. For an account of the 1882 festivities, see "Jubileusz pięciowiekowy obrazu Bogarodzicy w Częstochowie 1882," in *Józefa Czecha Kalendarz krakowski* (1883), 3–12. Still other events such as celebrations connected with the Blessed Virgin, Queen of Poland, have received mention elsewhere, for example, in Krawczak, "Udział chłopów galicyjskich," 25ff. Another celebration worthy of further investigation is the 1912 commemoration of the seventeenth-century Jesuit preacher Piotr Skarga. For more on the subject of this commemoration, which uneasily treads the border between religious and national, see Adam Galos, "Obchody ku czci Skargi w 1912 r.," *Sobótka* 47, nos. 1–2 (1992): 291–97.

28. The sense of Cracow as a site of both kinds of pilgrimages is nicely conveyed by Ziejka, "Krakowscy pątnicy," 9–35.

29. Bernard Lewis, *History—Remembered, Recovered, Invented* (Princeton: Princeton University Press, 1975), 3; Rożek, *Tradycja wiedeńska,* 7.

30. David Lowenthal, "Identity, Heritage, and History," in *Commemorations: The Politics of National Identity,* ed. John R. Gillis (Princeton: Princeton University Press, 1994), 46.

31. His statement of 14 August 1914, cited in Dariusz Radziwiłłowicz, "Rola tradycji grunwaldzkiej w działalności wychowawczej niektórych polskich organizacji zbrojnych w latach pierwszej wojny światowej," in *Tradycja grunwaldzka,* 5:188.

32. For more on this subject, see Janusz Tadeusz Nowak, "Pogrzeb Juliusza Słowackiego w Krakowie w 1927 r. (w 60-tną rocznicę sprowadzenia prochów wieszcza do kraju)," *Krzysztofory* 13 (1986): 117–30; Piekarczyk, "Powrót Króla-Ducha," 28–31.

33. Author's recollections. For more on some of these subjects, see Timothy Garton Ash, *The Polish Revolution: Solidarity* (New York: Scribner, 1984, and other editions); Jan Kubik, *The Power of Symbols against the Symbols of Power: The Rise of Solidarity and the Fall of State Socialism in Poland* (University Park, Pa.: Pennsylvania State University Press, 1994); and Roman Laba, *The Roots of Solidarity: A Political Sociology of Poland's Working-Class Democratization* (Princeton: Princeton University Press, 1991), esp. pp. 99–196.

34. Antoni Wrotnowski, *Porozbiorowe aspiracye polityczne narodu polskiego* (Kraków: G. Gebethner i spółka, 1898), 366.

BIBLIOGRAPHY

PRIMARY SOURCES

Archival Sources

Archiwum Akt Nowych (AAN)
  Archiwum I. J. Paderewskiego. Materiały polityczno-społeczne sprzed 1914.
Archiwum Główne Akt Dawnych (AGAD), Oddział II
  C. k. Ministerstwo Wyznań i Oświaty (K. k. Ministerium für Kultus und Unterricht)
    1848–1938
  C. k. Ministerstwo Spraw Wewnętrznych (K. k. Ministerium des Innern)
  Prokurator Warszawskiej Izby Sądowej
Archiwum PAN w Krakowie
  Protokoły posiedzeń Zarządu Akademii Umiejętności 1873–94
Archiwum Państwowe w Krakowie (APKr)
  Oddział I: Obchody i uroczystości krakowskie—zbiór szczątków akt komitetów. (I/4
    78) Temporary inventory (IT):
    IT 873: Setna rocznica Konstytucji 3-go Maja
    IT 874: Rocznica Powstania Styczniowego 1893
    IT 875: Opieka nad grobem J. Słowackiego 1893
    IT 876: Pogrzeb i budowa pomnika Adama Mickiewicza 1870–1913
    IT 878–79: Jubileusz Juliusza Słowackiego w Krakowie 1909
    IT 881–84: Obchód grunwaldzki w Krakowie 1910
    IT 886: 50-ta rocznica Powstania Styczniowego 1913–15
    IT 1022: Jubileusz Józefa Ignacego Kraszewskiego 1879
    IT 1067/1: Rocznica odsieczy wiedeńskiej 1883, 1933

  Also consulted were various other fascicles, listed on the same temporary inventory
  under the title "Varia w. XIX–XX" (IT 1023, 1024, 1029, 1068, 1325, 1326, 1612,
  1864). They were being reclassified in 1995–96. These may be listed in the book as #
  os, ins #, R #, the number sign representing the number of the file.

  This temporary inventory (IT) has been undergoing more systematic classification.
  Those interested in consulting the documents should contact the archive about their
  current status and location.

  Oddział II: Namiestnictwo we Lwowie
  Oddział II: C. k. Dyrekcja Policji w Krakowie (K. k. Polizei-Direktion in Krakau)
    (APKr DPKr)
Archiwum Państwowe w Łodzi (APŁ)
  Archiwum Juliana i Kazimierza Bartoszewiczów
Archiwum Uniwersytetu Jagiellońskiego (AUJ)

S II 962: Rocznice historyczne 1890–1939

S II 963: Wizyty dostojników państwowych austriackich i polskich w UJ 1851–1938

S II 964: Uroczystości pogrzebowe wybitnych postaci historycznych oraz współczesnych ze świata politycznego i naukowego 1869–1939

S II 965: Uroczystości religijne. Nabożeństwa okolicznościowe, żałobne, procesje 1850–1939

S II 784: Czytelnia Akademicka im. Adama Mickiewicza 1866–1923

Biblioteka Jagiellońska (BJ)

Manuscripts (BJ rkps, BJ przyb.):

In addition to miscellaneous materials related to the subject of the various anniversaries, these include relevant parts of the correspondence of Adam Asnyk, Józef Ignacy Kraszewski, Jan and Stanisław Tarnowski, Mikołaj Zyblikiewicz, and others; the typescript of Maciej Szarek, "Bieg mego życia" (przyb. 110/76); a collection of materials related to the location of the Mickiewicz monument in Cracow gathered by Walery Rzewuski (rkps 4955); and the papers of Michał Danielak (przyb. 189/90).

Also classified here, for the sake of convenience, are ephemeral publications (*druki ulotne*) held by the Jagiellonian Library:

Druki ulotne jubileuszowe z lat 1817–1938, T. I–XIV

Druki ulotne, Druki odnoszące się do Kraszewskiego i Jego jubileuszu z lat 1859–87

Biblioteka Polskiej Akademia Nauk, filial w Krakowie (Bibl PAN Kr)

Miscellaneous fascicles with materials related to the subject of the various anniversaries, celebrations, and monuments, including manuscripts of Stanisław Witkiewicz (rkps 2436); an article by Tadeusz Zaderecki entitled "Pomnik Mickiewicza znów staje w Krakowie" (The Mickiewicz monument stands again in Cracow) (rkps 3657); Lwów archbishop Seweryn Morawski's account of the 1891 celebration of the Third of May (rkps 5559); and the so-called Teka Zielińskiego, containing materials on the National Democrats (rkps 7785, 7791, 7797, 7801, 7809, 7811–12, 7817–18, 7829, 7843, 7846, 7855, and others).

Unpublished Theses and Manuscripts

Dabrowski, Patrice Marie. "Reinventing Poland: Commemorations and the Shaping of the Modern Nation." Ph.D. diss., Harvard University, 1999.

———. "The Uses of Poland's Past by Two Champions of Independence: Jozef Pilsudski and Roman Dmowski." Unpublished paper.

———. "Who to Lead the Slavs? Poles, Russians, and the 1910 Anniversary of the Battle of Grunwald." Unpublished paper.

Koropeckyj, Roman Robert. "Recreating the 'Wieszcz': Versions of the Life of Adam Mickiewicz, 1828–1897." Ph.D. diss., Harvard University, 1990.

Krawczak, Tadeusz. "Udział chłopów galicyjskich w ruchu niepodległościowym, 1912–1918." Master's thesis, Warsaw University, 1976.

Lane, Victor Hugo IV. "State Culture and National Identity in a Multi-ethnic Context: Lemberg, 1772–1914." Ph.D. diss., University of Michigan, 1999.

Lankosz, Izabella. "Wokół jubileuszu 50-lecia działalności literackiej Józefa Ignacego Kraszewskiego." Master's thesis, Jagiellonian University, 1995.

Oleszczuk, Joanna. "Wokół jubileuszu 200-lecia odsieczy wiedeńskiej w Krakowie." Master's thesis, Jagiellonian University, 1994–95.

Rehorowski, Andrzej. "Powszechna Wystawa Krajowa we Lwowie roku 1894 i siły produkcyjne kraju." Master's thesis, Jagiellonian University, 1995.

Unowsky, Daniel Louis. "The Pomp and Politics of Patriotism: Imperial Celebrations in Habsburg Austria, 1848–1916." Ph.D. diss., Columbia University, 2000.

Contemporary Newspapers and Periodical Literature Cited

Ateneum
Biblioteka Warszawska
Czas
Djabeł
Dziennik Polski
Gazeta Lwowska
Gazeta Narodowa
Gazeta Warszawska
Głos Narodu
Ilustrowany Kuryer Codzienny
Józefa Czecha Kalendarz Krakowski
Kłosy
Kurjer Krakowski
Kurjer Lwowski
Naprzód
Neue Freie Presse
Niepodległość
Przegląd Literacki i Artystyczny
Przegląd Polski
Przegląd Powszechny
Przyjaciel Ludu
Pszczółka (*Pszczółka Illustrowana*) (*Nowa Pszczółka*) (*Wieniec-Pszczółka*)
Reforma/Nowa Reforma
Rzeczpospolita (dwutygodnik polityczny—L'viv)
Słowo Polskie
Straż Polska
Świat
Świat Słowiański
Trybuna
Tygodnik Illustrowany
Wiek Młody
Wieniec (*Wieniec Polski*) (*Wieniec-Pszczółka*)
Z dzisiejszej doby
Zakopane
Die Zeit
Związek Chłopski

Contemporary Printed Sources

This is a list of works cited. The original orthography of the entries has been preserved, although they have been listed in accordance with American style requirements. The one major exception is the use of an ellipsis in title listings, Polish style, to indicate the presence of the author's name.

Alf-Tarczyński, Tadeusz. *Wspomnienia oficera Pierwszej Brygady.* London: nakładem Polskiej Fundacji Kulturalnej, 1979.

Archiwum polityczne Ignacego Paderewskiego. Edited by Halina Janowska et al. Vol. 1: 1890–1918. Wrocław, Warsaw, Kraków, and Gdańsk: Zakład Narodowy imienia Ossolińskich, 1973.

Askenazy, Szymon. *Książę Józef Poniatowski, † 19 października 1813: Przemówienie w setną rocznicę zgonu na obchodzie w Starym Teatrze w Krakowie wygłosił . . .* Kraków and Warsaw, 1913.

———. *Książę Józef Poniatowski, 1763–1813: Wydanie jubileuszowe ozdobione 152 rycinami.* Poznań: nakładem Karola Rzepeckiego w Poznaniu, 1913.

Bartoszewicz, K[azimierz]. "Z dziejów pomnika." *Przegląd Literacki* 3, no. 11 (1898): 1–7; nos. 12 and 13:1–6; nos. 14 and 15:6–10; nos. 16 and 17:6–11; nos. 18 and 19:1–5; 3, nos. 4 and 5 (1899): 6–9.

Bogusławska, Marya. *Pamiątka powstania 1863 roku w pięćdziesiątą jego rocznicę.* Kraków: nakładem Koła Pań Towarzystwa Szkoły Ludowej, 1913.

Boy-Żeleński, Tadeusz. *Bronzownicy.* Warsaw: Towarzystwo Wydawnicze "Rój," 1930. Later published as *Brązownicy i inne szkice o Mickiewiczu,* in *Pisma,* vol. 4. Warsaw, 1956.

———. *Słówka: 26–30 tysiąc.* Warsaw: Instytut Wydawniczy "Bibljoteka Polska," 1925.

———. *Znaszli ten kraj? Cyganeria krakowska.* Kraków: Czytelnik, 1945.

Chociszewski, Józef. *Sobieski pod Wiedniem dnia 12 września r. P. 1683: Na pamiątkę 22-letniego jubileuszu.* 4th ed. Poznań: nakładem Księgarni Katolickiej, 1883.

———. *Wspomnienie o życiu i pismach Adama Mickiewicza na pamiątkę przewiezienia jego popiołów do ojczystej ziemi w 1890 r.: Dla ludu polskiego i młodzieży skreślił . . .* Poznań: nakładem Karola Kozłowskiego, 1890.

Chromecki, Tadeusz. *Mowa miana w katedrze na Wawelu w setną rocznicę przysięgi Tadeusza Kościuszki przez ks. Tadeusza Chromeckiego dnia 31 marca 1894 r.* Kraków: nakładem autora, 1894.

———. *Mowa na obchód rocznicy konstytucyi dnia 3 Maja 1791 roku, miana w kościele OO. Bernardynów w Krakowie przez Ks. Tadeusza Chromeckiego, rektora II. Pijarów w Krakowie.* Kraków, 1890.

Dąbrowski, Józef [J. Grabiec, pseud.]. *Czerwona Warszawa przed ćwierć wiekiem: Moje wspomnienia z licznemi ilustracjami.* Poznań: Wielkopolska Księgarnia Nakładowa Karola Rzepeckiego, 1925.

———. *Dzieje porozbiorowe narodu polskiego.* Warsaw: Towarzystwo Wydawnicze, 1916.

Daszyński, Ignacy. *Pamiętniki.* 2 vols. Kraków: Z. R. S. S. "Proletarjat," 1925–26.

Dębicki, Zdzisław. *Grzechy młodości.* Warsaw: nakładem Trzaski, Everta i Michalskiego A. S., 1930. An expanded version of this autobiography can be found in Bibl PAN Kr.

Dmowski, Roman. *Pisma.* Vols. 3 and 4. Częstochowa: Antoni Gmachowski i S-ka, 1938.

———. *Wybór pism Romana Dmowskiego.* Vol. 1. New York: Instytut Romana Dmowskiego, 1988.

Drobner, Bolesław. "To już tak dawno." In *Kopiec wspomnień.* 2d ed. Kraków: Wydawnictwo Literackie, 1964.

Dubiecki, Marian Karol. "Rocznice Grunwaldu." In *Obrazy i studia historyczne.* Seria 3. Kiev, 1915. Originally written in 1901–02, published in *Czas.*

Echa Grunwaldzkie z 1910-go roku: Praojcom na chwałę 1410—Braciom na otuchę 1910: Wydawnictwo historyczne, pamiątkowe ilustrowane. Edited and published by Józef Paderewski. Kraków, 1910.

Estreicher, K[arol]. *Feniks polski.* Lviv: nakładem autora, 1887.

Feldman, Wilhelm. *Dzieje polskiej myśli politycznej, 1864–1914.* 2d ed. Edited by Józef Feldman. Warsaw: Instytut Badania Najnowszej Historji Polski, 1933.

————. *Stronnictwa i programy polityczne w Galicyi, 1846–1906.* 2 vols. Kraków: Książka, 1907.

Franko, Ivan. *Beiträge zur Geschichte und Kultur der Ukraine: Ausgewählte deutsche Schriften des Revolutionären Demokraten, 1882–1915.* Edited by E. Winter and P. Kirchner. Quellen und Studien zur Geschichte Osteuropas, Bd. 14. Berlin: Akademie-Verlag, 1963.

————. *Dokumenty y materialy, 1856–1965.* Kiev: Naukova Dumka, 1966.

————. "A Poet of Betrayal." Translated by Adam Hnidj. *Ukrainian Quarterly* 48, no. 1 (spring 1992): 49–57.

————. *Zibrannia tvoriv u p'iatdesiaty tomakh: Lysty (1895–1916).* Kiev: Vydavnytsvo "Naukova Dumka," 1986.

Górski, Konstanty M. *Polska sztuka współczesna 1887–1894 na Wystawie krajowej we Lwowie 1894 r. przez . . .* Kraków: drukarnia "Czasu" Fr. Kluczyckiego i sp., 1896.

Gorzkowski, Maryjan. *Jan Matejko: Epoka od r. 1861 do końca życia artysty z dziennika prowadzonego w ciągu lat siedemnastu.* Kraków: Towarzystwo Przyjaciół Sztuk Pięknych w Krakowie, 1993.

————. *Wskazówki do nowego obrazu J. Matejki "Sobieski pod Wiedniem" naszkicował . . .* [Kraków]: nakładem autora, Druk W. Korneckiego, [1883].

Goście krakowscy w Poznaniu: Jubileusz Kraszewskiego w Krakowie. Poznań: druk. W. Simona, 1881.

Hahn, Wiktor. *Grunwald w poezyi polskiej: Szkic literacki.* Kraków: nakładem autora, 1910.

————. *Rok Słowackiego: Księga pamiątkowa obchodów urządzanych ku czci poety w roku 1909.* Wydawnictwa Komitetu Obchodu Setnej Rocznicy Urodzin Juliusza Słowackiego we Lwowie, 3. Lwow: nakładem Komitetu Obchodu Setnej Rocznicy Urodzin Juliusza Słowackiego, 1911.

Hempel, Helena. *Wspomnienia z życia ś.p. ks. Stanisława Stojałowskiego.* Kraków: Związek Ludowo-Narodowy, 1921.

Hordyński, Zdzisław. "Sprowadzenia zwłok Adama Mickiewicza na Wawel." *Pamiętnik Towarzystwa Literackiego imienia Adama Mickiewicza* 4 (1890): 339–402.

Ivan Franko: Dokumenty y materialy, 1856–1965. Kiev: Naukova Dumka, 1966.

Jeziorowski, Kazimierz. *Wspomnienia z lat 1886–1924.* Siedlce: nakładem autora, 1933.

K. D. "Khronika. Pis'mo iz" Krakova: Iubilei Krashevskago, 3–5 oktiabria 1879." *Vestnik Evropy* 6 (November 1879): 401–27.

Kalinowski, Kazimierz. "Na Wawel: W 40 rocznicę pogrzebu Mickiewicza." In *Pamiętnik tajnych organizacyj niepodległościowych na terenie byłej Galicji w latach od roku 1880– 1897: Zebrał i ułożył . . . ,* edited by Wacław M. Borzemski. L'viv: wydany staraniem Komitetu Z. O. N., 1930.

Kantor, Józef [Józek z Dunajca, pseud.]. *Rebelja chochołowska w r. 1846 napisał . . .* Kraków: nakładem Wydawnictwa "Przyjaciela Ludu," 1912.

Katalog Wystawy Pamiątek Powstania Styczniowego otwartej 3-go lutego 1918 r. w kamienicy ks. Mazowieckich. Edited by Edward Chwalewik. Warsaw: tłocznia Wł. Łazarskiego, 1918.

Korta, Karol. *Gimnazjum św. Anny w Krakowie: Wspomnienia ucznia z lat 1888–96.* Biblioteka Krakowska, no. 97. Kraków: druk W. L. Anczyca i Spółki, 1938.

[Kostecki, Antoni]. *Wieniec wspomnień malujących charakter, przymioty, usposobienie i cnoty Tadeusza Kościuszki z różnych autorów zebrany w redakcyi "Kościuszki."* Kraków: nakładem zakładu introligatorskiego J. Gadowskiego na uczczenie stuletniej rocznicy, 1894.

Księga pamiątkowa jubileuszu J. I. Kraszewskiego 1879 roku. Kraków: nakładem komitetu wydawniczego, 1881.

Księga pamiątkowa obchodu pięćsetnej rocznicy zwycięstwa pod Grunwaldem w dniu 15, 16 i 17 lipca 1910 r. w Krakowie z dodaniem albumu literacko-artystycznego poświęconego wielkiej rocznicy dziejowej. Edited by Kazimierz Bartoszewicz. Kraków: nakładem Franciszka Terakowskiego, 1911.

Księga pamiątkowa setnej rocznicy ustanowienia Konstytucji 3 Maja zebrał i wydał Kazimierz Bartoszewicz. Vols. 1 and 2. Edited by Kazimierz Bartoszewicz. Kraków: nakładem K. Bartoszewicza, 1891.

Kulczycki, Ludwik [Mieczysław Mazowiecki, pseud.]. *Historya ruchu socyalistycznego w zaborze rosyjskim.* Kraków: Wydawnictwo "Proletaryatu," 1903.

Libański, Edmund. *1899–1901: Dwa lata pracy Uniwersytetu ludowego imienia Adama Mickiewicza.* L'viv: nakładem Uniw. lud. im. A. Mickiewicza, 1901.

Limanowski, Bolesław. *Pamiętniki.* Vol. 2. Warsaw: Książka i Wiedza, 1958.

Lorentowicz, Jan. *Spojrzenie wstecz.* Kraków: Wydawnictwo Literackie, 1957.

Machay, F[erdinand]. *Moja droga do Polski.* 2d ed. Kraków, 1938.

Magryś, Franciszek. *Żywot chłopa działacza.* Edited by Stefan Inglot. Warsaw: Ludowa Spółdzielnia Wydawnicza, 1987.

Mickiewicz, Adam. *Dzieła.* Vol. 5. Mikołów: nakładem Spółki Wydawn. K. Miarki, 1921.

Mickiewicz, Władysław. *Pamiętniki.* Vols. 1 and 3. Warsaw, Kraków, Łódź, Poznań, Wilno, and Zakopane: nakładem Gebethnera i Wolffa, 1933.

Miklaszewski, Juliusz. *Odczyt w stuletnią rocznicę Konstytucji 3 maja. Napisał . . .* Kraków: nakładem Ign. Żółtowskiego, 1891.

Mossoczowa, Michalina. *Krwawe dzieje, historya powstania styczniowego w 50-tą rocznicę opowiedziana.* L'viv: nakładem Macierzy Polskiej, 1913.

Nowolecki, A. *Uroczystości ku uczczeniu pamięci Jana III w dzielnicach polskich i za granicą: Na pamiątkę 200-letniej rocznicy odsieczy Wiednia 1683 r.* Kraków: staraniem "Wydawnictwa Czytelni Ludowej," 1883.

Objaśnienie do panoramy bitwy pod Racławicami. N.p., [1894].

[Odezwa do ludu polskiego przed obchodem złożenia prochów Adama Mickiewicza na Wawelu. Wyd. Stanisław Stojałowski.] Gródek, 1890.

Offmański, Mieczysław. [Orion, pseud.]. *Historya Polaka w niewoli (1794–1894) rozłożona na dnie i miesiące.* Kraków: nakładem i czcionkami drukarni Związkowej w Krakowie, 1894.

Paderewski, Ignace Jan, and Mary Lawton. *The Paderewski Memoirs.* New York: C. Scribner's Sons, 1938.

Pamiątka pielgrzymki ludowej do Krakowa urządzonej staraniem Redakcyi pism ludowych "Wieńca" i "Pszczółki" w wrześniu 1883 na uroczystość koronacyi cudownego obrazu N.P. Maryi na Piaskach i na uroczystość obchodu dwuchsetnej rocznicy zwycięstwa króla polskiego Jana III. pod Wiedniem. L'viv: z drukarni Towarzystwa imienia Szewczenki, 1883.

Pamiątka złożenia zwłok Adama Mickiewicza w katedrze na Wawelu w Krakowie dnia 4 lipca 1890 r. Kraków: nakładem księgarni J. K. Żupańskiego i K. J. Heumanna, 1890.

Pamiętnik tajnych organizacyj niepodległościowych na terenie byłej Galicji w latach od roku 1880–1897. Edited by Wacław M. Borzemski. L'viv: wydany staraniem Komitetu Z. O. N., 1930.

Pedagogika Mickiewiczowska: Książka pamiątkowa wydana przez Towarzystwo Pedagogiczne ku uczczeniu uroczystego złożenia zwłok Adama Mickiewicza na Wawelu. L'viv: nakładem Towarzystwa Pedagogicznego, 1890.

Pelczar, Józef. *Kazanie miane dnia 12 września 1883 r. jako w dwusetną rocznicę zwycięstwa pod Wiedniem, przez . . . rektora Uniw. Jag., kanonika katedr. krak.* Reprint from *Czas.* Kraków, 1883.

Peplowski, Stanisław Schnür. "Pomniki Mickiewicza." In *Na odsłonięcie pomnika Mickiewicza w Krakowie.* L'viv: "Słowo Polskie," 1898.

Perl, Feliks [Res, pseud.]. *Dzieje ruchu socjalistycznego w zaborze rosyjskim.* Vol. 1. Warsaw: nakładem Wydawnictwa "Życie," 1910.

Piekarski [T. J. Rola, pseud.]. *Józef Ignacy Kraszewski z powodu pięćdziesięcio-lecia pracy i zasługi jego dla społeczeństwa.* Warsaw: drukiem Józefa Ungra, 1878.

Pieśni narodowe, staraniem młodzieży na pamiątkę setnej rocznicy bohaterstwa ludu wydane. Wydawnictwo groszowe imienia Tadeusza Kościuszki. Rok 3. Serya 2. Książeczka 2. Kraków: nakładem dra Z. Kostkiewicza i K. Wojnara, 1894.

Pigoń, Stanisław. *Z Komborni w świat: Wspomnienia młodości.* Biblioteka dziejów i kultury wsi, 10. Kraków: Spółdzielnia wydawnicza "Wieś," 1946.

Piłsudski, Józef. *Pisma zbiorowe: Wydanie prac dotychczas drukiem ogłoszonych.* Vols. 1–8. Warsaw: Instytut Józefa Piłsudskiego, 1937; photo offset version published in Warsaw: Krajowa Agencja Wydawnicza, 1989.

Pisma iuzhnorussa po povodu iubileia Krashevskago (Izdanie redaktsii "Kievlianina"). Kiev: v universitetskoi tipografii (I. Zavadzkago), 1879.

"Polonia" obraz Jana Styki zakupiony dla gminy miasta Lwowa ku uczczeniu setnej rocznicy ogłoszenia konstytucji Trzeciego Maja 1791 (Objaśnienia drukowane w pismach lwowskich w czasie wystawy obrazu od 3. do 18. maja r. 1891). L'viv: nakładem i drukiem I. Związkowej drukarni, 1891.

Pomnik króla Jagiełły: Pamiątka uroczystości grunwaldzkich w Krakowie w dniach 15-go, 16-go i 17-go lipca 1910 r. Kraków: nakładem i czcionkami drukarni "Prawdy," 1910.

Program uroczystości jubileuszowych Adama Mickiewicza w Krakowie w dniach 26 i 27 czerwca 1898. Kraków: nakładem Fr. Pindora, 1898.

Raczyńska, Marya. *Cienie: Sceny dramatyczne z 1863 r.* Nagrodzone na konkursie jubileuszowym "1863–1913" we Lwowie. L'viv: nakładem Związku teatrów i chórów włościańskich, 1914.

Renan, Ernest. *Qu'est-ce qu'une nation?* (What is a nation?). Translated by Wanda Romer Taylor. Toronto: Tapir Press, 1996.

Rousseau, Jean-Jacques. *The Government of Poland.* Translated by Willmoore Kendall. Indianapolis and New York: Bobbs-Merrill, 1972.

Ruśkiewicz, T[omasz]. *Tajny związek młodzieży polskiej w latach 1887–1893: Na podstawie urzędowych dokumentów rosyjskich i własnych wspomnień skreślił . . .* Warsaw: Drukarnia Przemysłowa, 1926.

Rydel, Lucjan i Stanisław Wyspiański. *Epilog uroczystego przedstawienia w teatrze krakowskim w dniu 27-go czerwca 1898 na cześć Adama Mickiewicza.* Kraków: W. L. Anczyca i sp., 1898.

Rzewuski, Walery. *Gdzie postawić pomnik Mickiewicza?* Kraków: nakładem autora, 1883.

———. *Jeszcze kilka uwag i dokumentów w sprawie pomnika Mickiewicza.* N.p., 10 December 1883.

Siedlecki (Grzymała), Adam. *Niepospolici ludzie w dniu swoim powszednim.* Kraków: Wydawnictwo Literackie, 1961.

Sienkiewicz, Henryk. *Grunwald: Wydanie pamiątkowe (Wydano staraniem i nakładem lwowskiego komitetu dla wskrzeszenia obchodu pamiętnego pogromu Krzyżaków w r. 1410).* L'viv: druk. Sz. Bednarskiego, ze zezwoleniem k. wyd. dziełek ludowych we Lwowie, 1902.

———. *Listy.* Edited by Maria Bokszanin. Vols. 1 and 2. Warsaw: Państwowy Instytut Wydawniczy, 1977–96.

———. *Pisma zapomniane i niewydane.* L'viv: Wydawnictwo Zakładu Narodowego im. Ossolińskich, 1922.

Słomka, Jan. *Pamiętniki włościanina od pańszczyzny do dni dzisiejszych.* Kraków: Krakowska Drukarnia Nakładowa, 1929.

Śmiałowski, Eustachy. *Trzeci maj: Wspomnienie w stuletnią rocznicę, napisał . . .* Reprint from *Polski Lud* no. 5 (1891). Kraków: nakładem autora, druk W. Korneckiego, 1891.

Sokolnicki, Michał. *Rok czternasty.* London: nakładem Gryf Publications, 1961.

Stępowski, Maryan. *Towarzystwo Szkoły Ludowej: Jak powstało, co zrobiło i do czego dąży (1891–1911); w 20-tą rocznicę powstania Towarzystwa napisał dr . . .* Kraków: nakładem Tow. Szkoły Ludowej, 1911.

Styka, Jan, and Tadeusz Styka. *Grunwald w Rondlu Bramy Floriańskiej.* Kraków: nakładem Jana Styki, 1909.

Suchodolski, Karol [K. S., pseud.]. *Pamiątka podniesienia relikwij Adama Mickiewicza z dodatkiem najpiękniejszych wyjątków z jego Ksiąg Narodu Polskiego i Pielgrzymstwa Polskiego z 4-ma obrazkami.* Kraków: nakładem Karola Suchodolskiego, 1890.

Tajne dokumenty rządu rosyjskiego w sprawach polskich: Memoryał ks. Imeretyńskiego; Protokóły Komitetu Ministrów; Nota Kancelaryi Komitetu Ministrów. London: drukowane z polecenia Komitetu Centralnego Polskiej Partyi Socyalistycznej, 1898.

Tarnowski, St[anisław]. *Mowa przy odsłonięciu pomnika Mickiewicza w Krakowie dnia 26 czerwca 1898 roku.* Reprinted from *Przegląd Polski,* July 1898. Kraków: nakładem autora, w drukarni "Czasu" Fr. Kluczyckiego i spółki, 1898.

———. *Z doświadczeń i rozmyślań.* 2d ed. Kraków: Druk. "Czasu" Fr. Kluczyckiego, 1891.

1863 Jednodniówka. Drohobycz: staraniem Towarzystw polskich, 1913.

Twardowski, Bolesław [BT, pseud.]. *Historya Powstania Kościuszki 1794 r: Z dodaniem spisu osób, które brały udział w powstaniu, oraz dołączeniem życiorysów głównych przywódców.* 2d ed. Poznań: nakładem Księgarni Katolickiej, 1896.

Wasilewski, Leon. *Piłsudski, jakim go znałem.* Warsaw: Towarzystwo Wydawnicze "Roj," 1935.

Wasilewski, Zygmunt. *Pomnik Mickiewicza w Warszawie, 1897–1898.* Warsaw: nakładem Komitetu budowy pomnika, 1899.

Wiejscy działacze społeczni. Szkoła Główna Gospodarstwa Wiejskiego w Warszawie. Instytut Socjologii Wsi. Vol. 1. Warsaw: Kasa im. Mianowskiego, 1937.

Wieniec grunwaldzki z 1910-go roku: Wydawnictwo historyczne, pamiątkowe, ilustrowane; zbiór aktów i dokumentów historycznych z 1910 r.; ku uczczeniu 500 letniej rocznicy wiekopomnego zwycięztwa Polaków nad Krzyżakami. Edited by Józef Paderewski. Kraków: G. Gebethner i Spółka, [n.d.].

Windakiewicz, Stanisław. *Dzieje Wawelu.* Kraków: Krakowska Spółka Wydawnicza, 1925.

[Wisłocki, Władysław]. *Sobiesciana: Bibliografia jubileuszowego obchodu dwóchsetnej rocznicy potrzeby wiedeńskiej z r. 1683, z ryciną Apoteozy króla Jana III dłuta P. Welońskiego.* Lviv: nakładem centralnego komitetu jubileuszowego, 1884.

Witos, Wincenty. *Moje wspomnienia.* Vol. 1. Paris: Instytut Literacki, 1964.

Wrotnowski, Antoni. *Porozbiorowe aspiracye polityczne narodu polskiego.* Kraków: G. Gebethner i spółka, 1898.

Żeromski, Stefan. *Dzienniki.* 2d. rev. ed. Edited by Jerzy Kądziela. Vols. 2 and 6. Warsaw: Czytelnik, 1963–70.

———. *Dzienników tom odnaleziony.* Edited by Jerzy Kądziela. Warsaw: Czytelnik, 1973.

[Zetterbaum, M., and A. Niemojewski]. *Adam Mickiewicz, 1798–1898: Książka pamiątkowa dla polskiego ludu pracującego.* Lviv: nakładem Redakcyi "Naprzodu," "N. Robotnika," "Prawa ludu" i "Równości," drukiem Artura Goldmana we Lwowie, 1898.

Złożenie zwłok Adama Mickiewicza na Wawelu dnia 4-go lipca 1890 roku: Książka pamiątkowa z 22 ilustracyami. Kraków: nakładem i czcionkami Drukarni Związkowej, 1890.

SECONDARY SOURCES

Agulhon, Maurice. "Politics, Images, and Symbols in Post-Revolutionary France." In *Rites of Power: Symbolism, Ritual, and Politics since the Middle Ages,* edited by Sean Wilentz. Philadelphia: University of Pennsylvania Press, 1985.

Albin, Janusz, and Józef Ryszard Szaflik. "Listy Macieja Szarka z lat 1861–1904." *Ze skarbca kultury* 39 (1984): 65–160.

Anderson, Benedict. *Imagined Communities: Reflections on the Origin and Spread of Nationalism.* Rev. ed. London and New York: Verso, 1991.

Bąk-Koczarska, Celina. "Rada Miejska organizatorem obchodu 200-lecia Odsieczy Wiednia w Krakowie." *Zeszyty Naukowe Muzeum Historycznego Miasta Krakowa: Krzysztofory* 9 (1982): 38–55.

Beauvois, Daniel. "Rzeczpospolita polsko-litewska w XVII wieku i pięć narodów na jej obszarach w wieku XIX." In *Historia Europy Środkowo-Wschodniej,* edited by Jerzy Kłoczowski. Vol. 1. Lublin: Instytut Europy Środkowo-Wschodniej, 2000.

Bieńkowski, Wiesław. "Obchody 200-lecia Wiktorii Wiedeńskiej w Krakowie." *Zeszyty Naukowe Stowarzyszenia PAX.* Seria: Kultura, Oświata, Nauka. Zeszyt 6/7 (1983): 156–63.

———. "Rok 1883 w Krakowie (uroczystość 200-lecia odsieczy Wiednia)." *Rocznik Krakowski* 51 (1987): 97–118.

Blackbourn, David. "The Discreet Charm of the Bourgeoisie: Reappraising German History in the Nineteenth Century." In *The Peculiarities of German History: Bourgeois Society and Politics in Nineteenth-Century Germany,* by David Blackbourn and Geoff Eley. Oxford and New York: Oxford University Press, 1984.

Blobaum, Robert E. *Rewolucja: Russian Poland, 1904–1907.* Ithaca, N.Y., and London: Cornell University Press, 1995.

Borejsza, Jerzy W. *Sekretarz Adama Mickiewicza (Armand Lévy i jego czasy, 1827–1891).* 2d rev. ed. Wrocław, Warsaw, Kraków, and Gdańsk: Zakład Narodowy im. Ossolińskich, 1977.

Brix, Emil, and Hannes Stekl, eds. *Der Kampf um das Gedächtnis: Öffentliche Gedenktage in Mitteleuropa.* Vienna, Cologne, and Weimar: Böhlau Verlag, 1997.

Brock, Peter. "Polish Nationalism." In *Nationalism in Eastern Europe,* edited by Peter F. Sugar and Ivo John Lederer. Seattle and London: University of Washington Press, 1994.

Brodowska, Helena. *Chłopi o sobie i Polsce: Rozwój świadomości społeczno-narodowej.* Warsaw: Ludowa Spółdzielnia Wydawnicza, 1984.

Bromke, Adam. *Poland's Politics: Idealism vs. Realism.* Cambridge: Harvard University Press, 1967.

Brubaker, Rogers. *Citizenship and Nationhood in France and Germany.* Cambridge and London: Harvard University Press, 1992.

Bucur, Maria, and Nancy M. Wingfield, eds. *Staging the Past: The Politics of Commemoration in Habsburg Central Europe, 1848 to the Present.* West Lafayette, Ind.: Purdue University Press, 2001.

Burkot, Stanisław. "O jubileuszu J. I. Kraszewskiego." In *Dziesięciolecie Wyższej Szkoły Pedagogicznej w Krakowie.* Kraków: Państwowe Wydawnictwo Naukowe, 1957.

Bursztyńska, Halina. *Henryk Sienkiewicz w kręgu oddziaływania powieści historycznych Józefa Ignacego Kraszewskiego.* Katowice: Uniwersytet Śląski, 1977.

Buszko, Józef. *Dzieje ruchu robotniczego w Galicji Zachodniej, 1848–1918.* Kraków: Wydawnictwo Literackie, 1986.

———. *Polacy w parlamencie wiedeńskim, 1848–1918.* Warsaw: Wydawnictwo Sejmowe, 1996.

———. *Społeczno-polityczne oblicze Uniwersytetu Jagiellońskiego w dobie autonomii galicyjskiej (1869–1914).* Uniwersytet Jagielloński. Vol. 8, Wydawnictwa jubileuszowe. Kraków: Państwowe Wydawnictwo Naukowe, 1963.

———. *Uroczystości kazimierzowskie na Wawelu w roku 1869.* Państwowe Zbiory Sztuki na Wawelu. Biblioteka wawelska, 4. Kraków: Ministerstwo Kultury i Sztuki, Zarząd Muzeów i Ochrony Zabytków, 1970.

———. "Uroczystości patriotyczne na Wawel w latach Rzeczypospolitej Krakowskiej i w dobie autonomii galicyjskiej." *Annales Universitatis Mariae Curie-Skłodowska Lublin—Polonia,* vol. 51, 4, sectio F (1996): 31–41.

Cannadine, David. "The Context, Performance and Meaning of Ritual: The British Monarchy and the 'Invention of Tradition', c. 1820–1977." In *The Invention of Tradition,* edited by Eric Hobsbawm and Terence Ranger. Cambridge: Cambridge University Press, 1983.

Carrier, Peter. "Historical Traces of the Present: The Uses of Commemoration." *Historical Reflections* 22, no. 2 (1996): 431–45.

Chickering, Roger. *"We Men Who Feel Most German": A Cultural Study of the Pan-German League, 1886–1914.* Boston: Allen and Unwin, 1984.

Chruścicki, Tadeusz. Introduction to *The National Museum in Cracow: A Historical Outline and Selected Objects.* Translated by Elżbieta Chrzanowska. Warsaw: Arkady, 1987.

Chwalba, Andrzej. *Józef Piłsudski historyk wojskowości.* Kraków: Universitas, 1993.

Colley, Linda. *Britons: Forging the Nation, 1707–1837.* New Haven and London: Yale University Press, 1992.

Confino, Alon. *The Nation as a Local Metaphor: Württemberg, Imperial Germany, and National Memory, 1871–1918.* Chapel Hill and London: University of North Carolina Press, 1997.

Cottam, Kazimiera Janina. *Boleslaw Limanowski (1835–1935): A Study in Socialism and Nationalism.* Boulder, Colo.: East European Quarterly, 1978.

Cressy, David. *Bonfires and Balls: National Memory and the Protestant Calendar in Elizabethan and Stuart England.* London: Weidenfeld and Nicolson, 1989.

Cywiński, Bohdan. *Rodowody niepokornych.* 1971. Reprint, Warsaw: Świat Książki, 1996.

Czapliński, Czesław. *The Styka Family Saga; Saga rodu Styków.* New York: Bicentennial Publishing Corporation, 1988.

Czapliński, Marek. "Poczynania organicznikowskie a problem niepodległości Polski." In *Między irredentą, lojalnością a kolaboracją: O suwerenność państwową i niezależność narodową (1795–1989),* edited by Wojciech Wrzesiński. Polska myśl polityczna XIX i XX wieku. Vol. 11. Toruń: Wydawnictwo Adam Marszałek, 2001.

D'Abernon, [Edgar Vincent, First] Viscount. *The Eighteenth Decisive Battle of the World: Warsaw, 1920.* London: Hodder and Stoughton, 1931.

Dabrowski, Patrice M. "Folk, Faith and the Fatherland: Defining the Polish Nation in 1883." *Nationalities Papers* 28, no. 3 (2000): 387–416.

———. "What Kind of Modernity Did Poles Need? A Look at Nineteenth-Century Nation Making." Book review article. *Nationalities Papers* 29, no. 3 (September 2001): 509–23.

Danek, Wincenty. *Józef Ignacy Kraszewski: Zarys biograficzny.* Warsaw: Ludowa Spółdzielnia Wydawnicza, 1976.

———. "Setna rocznica Komisji Edukacji Narodowej w r. 1873 i udział w niej J. I. Kraszewskiego." *Sprawozdania z posiedzeń Komisji Naukowych PAN Oddz. w Krakowie* 17, no. 1 (1974): 30–31.

Daszyk, Krzysztof Karol. "Szymona Askenazego neoromantyczna apoteoza czynu." *Studia Historyczne* 38, no. 2 (1995): 225–42.

Dobrzanowski, S[tanisław]. *Restauracja diecezji krakowskiej w latach osiemdziesiątych XIX wieku.* Warsaw: Akademia Teologii Katolickiej, 1977.

Dolistowska, Małgorzata. "Panorama 'Bitwa pod Racławicami.'" In *W kręgu Panoramy Racławickiej,* edited by Bożena Steinborn. Wrocław: Zakład Narodowy im. Ossolińskich, 1985.

Drozdowski, Marian Marek. *Ignacy Jan Paderewski: A Political Biography in Outline.* Kraków: Interpress, 1979.

Drużyny Bartoszowe, 1908–1914. L'viv: Wydawnictwo Zakładu Narodowego im. Ossolińskich, 1939.

Dunin-Wąsowicz, Krzysztof. *Dzieje Stronnictwa Ludowego w Galicji.* Warsaw: Ludowa Spółdzielnia Wydawnicza, 1956.

Dutkiewicz, Józef. *Szymon Askenazy i jego szkoła.* Warsaw: Państwowe Wydawnictwo Naukowe, 1958.

Dużyk, Józef. *Henryk Siemiradzki, życie i twórczość.* Wrocław: Zakład Narodowy im. Ossolińskich, Wydawnictwo Polskiej Akademii Nauk, 1984.

Dzięgielewski, Jan. "Archidiecezja lwowska obrządku łacińskiego w obchodach pięcsetnej rocznicy zwycięstwa pod Grunwaldem." In *Tradycja grunwaldzka,* edited by Jerzy Maternicki. Vol. 2. Warsaw: Uniwersytet Warszawski, Zakład Historii Historiografii i Dydaktyki Historii, 1990.

Ekdahl, Sven. "Tannenberg/Grunwald—Ein politisches Symbol in Deutschland und Polen." *Journal of Baltic Studies* 22, no. 4 (1991): 271–324.

Eliade, Mircea. "Sacred Architecture and Symbolism." In *Symbolism, the Sacred and the Art,* edited by D. Apostolos-Cappadona. New York: Crossroad, 1986.

Estreicher, Stanisław. *Znaczenie Krakowa dla życia narodowego polskiego w ciągu XIX wieku: Odczyt wypowiedziany w "Klubie Społecznym" w dniu 21 października 1931 roku.* Kraków: W. L. Anczyca i spółki, 1931.

Florkowska-Frančić, Halina. "Emigracyjne obchody dwóchsetnej rocznicy wiktorii wiedeńskiej." *Przegląd Polonistyczny* 10, no. 4 (1984): 69–79.

Ford, Caroline. *Creating the Nation in Provincial France: Religion and Political Identity in Brittany.* Princeton: Princeton University Press, 1993.

Frančić, Mirosław. "Kopiec Kościuszki—Historia znaczeń." In *Kościuszce w hołdzie,* edited by Mieczysław Rokosz. Biblioteka Krakowska, no. 133. Kraków: Wydawnictwo i drukarnia "Secesja," 1994.

Fras, Z[bigniew]. "Obchody rocznicy bitwy pod Grunwaldem w 1902 roku wśród wychodźstwa polskiego w Niemczech i Austrii." In *Tradycja grunwaldzka,* edited by Jerzy Maternicki. Vol. 4. Warsaw: Uniwersytet Warszawski, Zakład Historii Historiografii i Dydaktyki Historii, 1990.

Galicja i jej dziedzictwo. 8 vols. Rzeszów: Wydawnictwo Wyższej Szkoły Pedagogicznej, 1994–96.

Galos, Adam. "Ewolucja tradycji trzeciomajowej w obchodach historycznych." In *Konstytucja 3 Maja z perspektywy dwusetnej rocznicy (1791–1991),* edited by Teresa Kulak. Acta Universitatis Wratislaviensis, 1502, Historia 110. Wrocław: Wydawnictwo Uniwersytetu Wrocławskiego, 1993.

———. "Obchody ku czci Skargi w 1912 r." *Śląski Kwartalnik Historyczny Sobótka* 47, nos. 1–2 (1992): 291–97.

———. "Obchody rocznicowe na prowincji zaboru austriackiego." In *Studia z dziejów prowincji galicyjskiej,* edited by Adam Galos. Acta Universitatis Wratislaviensis, no. 1532, Historia 111. Wrocław: Wydawnictwo Uniwersytetu Wrocławskiego, 1993.

———. "Obchody rocznicy odsieczy wiedeńskiej w Galicji w 1883 r." In *Z dziejów i tradycji srebrnego wieku,* edited by Jerry Pietrzak. *Acta Universitatis Wratislaviensis,* no. 1108, Historia 75. Wrocław: Wydawnictwo Uniwersytetu Wrocławskiego, 1990.

———. "Obchody rocznicy wiedeńskiej w XIX w." *Śląski Kwartalnik Historyczny Sobótka* 35 (1980): 437–39.

———. "Władze pruskie wobec rocznicy wiedeńskiej w 1883 r." *Śląski Kwartalnik Historyczny Sobótka* 36 (1981): 267–78.

———. "Wokół jubileuszu Kraszewskiego w 1879 r." In *Z przeszłości Europy Środkowowschodniej,* edited by Jadwiga Hoff, 61–75. Rzeszow: Wydawnictwo Uniwersytetu Rzeszowskiego, 2002.

———. "Z zagadnień roli rocznic historycznych w Polsce w XIX w." In [n.t.], edited by Adolf Juzwenko and Wojciech Wrzesiński. *Acta Universitatis Wratislaviensis,* no. 543, Historia 36. Wrocław: Wydawnictwo Uniwersytetu Wrocławskiego, 1981.

Galos, Adam, F. H. Gentzen, and W. Jakóbczyk. *Dzieje Hakaty.* Poznań: Instytut Zachodni, 1966. Also published in German under the title *Die Hakatisten: Der Deutsche Ostmarkenverein (1894–1934): Ein Beitrag zur Geschichte der Ostpolitik des deutschen Imperialismus.* Berlin: Deutscher Verlag der Wissenschaften, VEB, 1966.

Garlicki, Andrzej. *Geneza legionów: Zarys dziejów Komisji Tymczasowej Skonfederowanych Stronnictw Niepodległościowych.* Warsaw: Książka i Wiedza, 1964.

———. *Józef Piłsudski, 1867–1935.* Warsaw: Czytelnik, 1988.

———. *Józef Piłsudski, 1867–1935.* New abridged ed. Edited and translated by John Coutouvidis. Brookfield, Vt.: Scolar Press, 1995.

Garlicki, Andrzej, ed. *Pierwsze Maje.* Warsaw: Iskry, 1984.

Gellner, Ernest. *Nations and Nationalism.* Ithaca, N.Y., and London: Cornell University Press, 1983.

Giergielewicz, Mieczysław. *Henryk Sienkiewicz.* New York: Twayne, 1968.

Gillis, John R., ed. *Commemorations: The Politics of National Identity.* Princeton: Princeton University Press, 1994.

———. "Introduction. Memory and Identity: The History of a Relationship." In *Commemorations: The Politics of National Identity,* edited by John R. Gillis. Princeton: Princeton University Press, 1994.

Giza, Antoni. "Neoslawiści wobec obchodów grunwaldzich w Krakowie w 1910 r." In *Tradycja grunwaldzka,* edited by Jerzy Maternicki. Warsaw: Uniwersytet Warszawski, Zakład Historii Historiografii i Dydaktyki Historii, 1989.

———. *Neoslawizm i Polacy, 1906–1910.* Wyższa Szkoła Pedagogiczna w Szczecinie. Rozprawy i studia, vol. 61. Szczecin: Wydawnictwa naukowe Wyższej Szkoły Pedagogicznej w Szczecinie, 1984.

———. "Słowiański aspekt obchodów grunwaldzkich 1910 r. w Krakowie." *Studia Historyczne* 41, no. 1 (1998): 37–48.

———. "Tradycja grunwaldzka w opinii czeskiej, 1906–1910." In *Tradycja grunwaldzka,* edited by Jerzy Maternicki. Vol. 4. Warsaw: Uniwersytet Warszawski, Zakład Historii Historiografii i Dydaktyki Historii, 1990.

Godula, Róża, ed. *Klejnoty i sekrety Krakowa.* Kraków: Wydawnictwo Wawelskie, 1994.

Grabowicz, George C. "The History of Polish-Ukrainian Literary Relations: A Literary and Cultural Perspective." In *Poland and Ukraine: Past and Present,* edited by Peter J. Potichnyj. Edmonton and Toronto: Canadian Institute of Ukrainian Studies, 1980.

Grabski, Andrzej Feliks. "Program i symbol: 3 Maja w polskiej myśli politycznej." In *3 maja w tradycji i kulturze polskiej,* edited by Alina Barszczewska-Krupa. Vol. 2, edited by Alina Barszczewska-Krupa. Acta Universitatis Lodziensis, Folia Historica 41. Łódź: Wydawnictwo Uniwersytetu Łódźkiego, 1991.

———. *W kręgu kultu Naczelnika: Rapperswilskie inicjatywy kościuszkowskie (1894–1897).* Warsaw: Państwowy Instytut Wydawniczy, 1981.

Greenfeld, Liah. *Nationalism: Five Roads to Modernity.* Cambridge: Harvard University Press, 1992.

Grodziski, Stanisław. "Nationalfeiertage und öffentliche Gedenktage Polens im 19. und 20. Jahrhundert." In *Der Kampf um das Gedächtnis: Öffentliche Gedenktage in Mitteleuropa,* edited by Emil Brix and Hannes Stekl. Vienna, Cologne, and Weimar: Böhlau Verlag, 1997.

Grot, Zdzisław. *Dzieje pomnika Mickiewicza w Poznaniu, 1856–1939.* Poznańskie Towarzystwo Przyjaciół Nauk. Wydawnictwo popularno-naukowe z zakresu historii, no. 1. Poznań: Państwowe Wydawnictwo Naukowe, 1956.

————. "Dzieje pomnika Mickiewicza w Poznaniu (1859–1939)." *Przegląd Zachodni* 5, no. 11 (1949): 452–61.

Hagen, William W. *Germans, Poles, and Jews: The Nationality Conflict in the Prussian East, 1772–1914*. Chicago and London: University of Chicago Press, 1980.

Hansen, Wilhelm. *Nationaldenkmäler und Nationalfeste im 19. Jahrhundert*. Lüneburg: Niederdeutscher Verband fur Volks- und Altertumskunde, 1976.

Himka, John-Paul. *Religion and Nationality in Western Ukraine: The Greek Catholic Church and the Ruthenian National Movement in Galicia, 1867–1900*. Montreal: McGill-Queen's University Press, 1999.

————. *Socialism in Galicia: The Emergence of Polish Social Democracy and Ukrainian Radicalism (1869–1890)*. Cambridge: distributed by Harvard University Press for the Harvard Ukrainian Research Institute, 1983.

Historia Europy Środkowo-Wschodniej. Edited by Jerzy Kłoczowski. 2 vols. Lublin: Instytut Europy Środkowo-Wschodniej, 2000.

Hnidj, Adam. "Ivan Franko's 'A Poet of Betrayal': Causes and Consequences." *Ukrainian Quarterly* 48, no. 1 (spring 1992): 36–48.

Hobsbawm, Eric. "Introduction: Inventing Traditions." In *The Invention of Tradition*, edited by Eric Hobsbawm and Terence Ranger. Cambridge: Cambridge University Press, 1983.

————. "Mass-Producing Traditions: Europe, 1870–1914." In *The Invention of Tradition*, edited by Eric Hobsbawm and Terence Ranger. Cambridge: Cambridge University Press, 1983.

————. *Nations and Nationalism since 1780: Programme, Myth, Reality*. Cambridge, New York, Port Chester, Melbourne, and Sydney: Cambridge University Press, 1990; Canto edition, 1991.

Hobsbawm, Eric, and Terence Ranger, eds. *The Invention of Tradition*. Cambridge: Cambridge University Press, 1983.

Homola Dzikowska, Irena. *Mikołaj Zyblikiewicz (1823–1997)*. Polska Akademia Nauk. Oddział w Krakowie. Prace Komisji Nauk Historycznych, no. 10. Wrocław, Warsaw, and Kraków: Zakład Narodowy im. Ossolińskich, 1964.

————. *Kraków za prezydentury Mikołaja Zyblikiewicza (1874–1881)*. Kraków: Wydawnictwo Literackie, 1976.

Hosking, Geoffrey, and George Schöpflin, eds. *Myths and Nationhood*. London: Hurst and Company, 1997.

Hroch, Miroslav. *Social Preconditions of National Revival in Europe: A Comparative Analysis of the Social Composition of Patriotic Groups among the Smaller European Nations*. Translated by Ben Fowkes. Cambridge and New York: Cambridge University Press, 1985.

Hughes, Michael. *Nationalism and Society: Germany, 1800–1945*. London: Edward Arnold, 1988.

Hunt, Lynn. *Politics, Culture and Class in the French Revolution*. Berkeley and Los Angeles: University of California Press, 1984.

Irwin-Zarecka, Iwona. *Frames of Remembrance: The Dynamics of Collective Memory*. New Brunswick, N.J.: Transaction, 1994.

Jabłoński, Szczepan Zachariasz. *Jasna Góra: Ośrodek kultu maryjnego (1864–1914)*. Lublin: Redakcja wydawnictwa KUL, 1982.

James, Harold. *A German Identity, 1770–1990*. New York: Routledge, 1989.

Janion, Maria, and Maria Żmigrodzka. *Romantyzm i historia*. Warsaw: Państwowy Instytut Wydawniczy, 1978.

Jarnuszkiewiczowa, Jadwiga. *Pomnik Mickiewicza*. Warsaw: Państwowe Wydawnictwo Naukowe, 1975.

Jasiński, Janusz. "Polemika wokół Grunwaldu w 1902 roku." *Warmia i Mazury* 27, no. 2 (February 1981): 12–13.

Kącki, Franciszek. *Ks. Stanisław Stojałowski i jego działalność społeczno-polityczna.* Vol. 1, 1845–1890. Badania z Dziejów Społecznych i Gospodarczych, edited by Franciszek Bujak, no. 31. L'viv: Kasa im. Rektora J. Mianowskiego, 1937.

Kaczorowski, Andrzej W. "Tradycja grunwaldzka w działalności polskiego skauting." In *Tradycja grunwaldzka,* edited by Jerzy Maternicki. Vol. 2. Warsaw: Uniwersytet Warszawski, Zakład Historii Historiografii i Dydaktyki Historii, 1990.

———. "Związek Polskich Towarzystw Gimnastycznych 'Sokół' a tradycja grunwaldzka." In *Tradycja grunwaldzka,* edited by Jerzy Maternicki. Vol. 5. Warsaw: Uniwersytet Warszawski, Zakład Historii Historiografii i Dydaktyki Historii, 1990.

Kaminski, Ted. *Polish Publicists and Prussian Politics: The Polish Press in Poznan during the Neue Kurs of Chancellor Leo von Caprivi, 1890–1894.* Stuttgart: Franz Steiner Verlag Wiesbaden, 1988.

Kammen, Michael. *Mystic Chords of Memory: The Transformation of Tradition in American Culture.* New York: Alfred A. Knopf, 1991.

Kawyn, Stefan. *Ideologia stronnictw politycznych w Polsce wobec Mickiewicza, 1890–1898.* Badania literackie, 10. L'viv: nakładem Filomaty, 1937.

King, Jeremy. "The Nationalization of East Central Europe: Ethnicism, Ethnicity, and Beyond." In *Staging the Past: The Politics of Commemoration in Habsburg Central Europe, 1848 to the Present,* edited by Maria Bucur and Nancy M. Wingfield. West Lafayette, Ind.: Purdue University Press, 2001.

Kizwalter, Tomasz. *O nowoczesności narodu: Przypadek Polski.* Warsaw: Wydawnictwo naukowe Semper, 1999.

Kmiecik, Zenon. *Prasa warszawska w latach, 1886–1904.* Wrocław: Zakład Narodowy im. Ossolińskich, 1989.

Kochanowicz, Jacek. "Powstanie i chłopi: Cztery interpretacje." In *Kościuszko—powstanie 1794 r.—tradycja: Materiały z sesji naukowej w 200-lecie powstania kościuszkowskiego 15–16 kwietnia 1994 r.,* edited by Jerzy Kowecki. Warsaw: Biblioteka Narodowa, 1997.

Kolbuszewski, Jacek. "Rola literatury w kształtowaniu polskich mitów politycznych XIX i XX wieku." In *Polskie mity polityczne XIX i XX wieku.* Polska myśl polityczna XIX i XX wieku, edited by Wojciech Wrzesiński. Vol. 9. Wrocław: Wydawnictwo Uniwersytetu Wrocławskiego, 1994.

Kołodziejczyk, Arkadiusz. "Tradycje walki z naporem krzyżacko-pruskim i zwycięstwo grunwaldzkie na łamach warszawskiej 'Prawdy,' 1880–1915." In *Tradycja grunwaldzka,* edited by Jerzy Maternicki. Vol. 2. Warsaw: Uniwersytet Warszawski, Zakład Historii Historiografii i Dydaktyki Historii, 1990.

Konstytucja 3 Maja z perspektywy dwusetnej rocznicy (1791–1991). Edited by Teresa Kulak. Acta Universitatis Wratislaviensis no. 1502, Historia 110. Wrocław: Wydawnictwo Uniwersytetu Wrocławskiego, 1993.

Kościuszce w hołdzie. Edited by Mieczysław Rokosz. Biblioteka Krakowska, no. 133. Kraków: Wydawnictwo i Drukarnia "Secesja," 1994.

Kościuszko—powstanie 1794 r.—tradycja: Materiały z sesji naukowej w 200-lecie powstania kościuszkowskiego 15–16 kwietnia 1994 r. Edited by Jerzy Kowecki. Warsaw: Biblioteka Narodowa, 1997.

Kotkowska-Bareja, Hanna. *Pomnik Kopernika.* Warsaw: Państwowe Wydawnictwo Naukowe, 1973.

———. *Pomnik Poniatowskiego.* Warsaw: Państwowe Wydawnictwo Naukowe, 1971.

Kowalczykowa, Alina. *Piłsudski i tradycja.* Chotomów: Verba, 1991.

Kozicki, Stanisław. *Historia Ligi Narodowej: Okres, 1887–1907.* London: Myśl Polski, 1964.

Kraków Mickiewiczowi. Edited by Danuta Rederowa. Kraków: Wydawnictwo Literackie, 1956.

Krasa, Selma. "Das historische Ereignis und seine Rezeption: Zum Nachleben der Zweiten Türkenbelagerung Wiens in der österreichischen Kunst des 19. und 20. Jahrhunderts." In *Die Türken vor Wien: Europa und die Entscheidung an der Donau 1683.* Salzburg and Vienna: Residenz Verlag, 1982.

Krawczak, Tadeusz. "Kształtowanie świadomości narodowej chłopów polskich w Galicji w latach 1864–1914." *Przegląd Humanistyczny* 11 (1978): 135–50.

Krawczyk, Jarosław. *Matejko i historia.* Warsaw: Instytut Sztuki Polskiej Akademii Nauk, 1990.

Krukowski, Jan. "Komisja Edukacji Narodowej wobec setnej rocznicy zwycięstwa pod Wiedniem." *Studia Historyczne* 26, no. 4 (1983): 573–93.

Krups'kyi, I[van] V[asyl'ovych]. *Natsional'no-patriotychna zhurnalistyka Ukraïny (druha polovyna XIX–persha chvert' XX st.).* L'viv: Vydavnytstvo "Svit," 1995.

Krzyżanowski, Julian. *Dzieje literatury polskiej.* Warsaw: Państwowe Wydawnictwo Naukowe, 1879.

———. *Henryka Sienkiewicza żywot i sprawy.* Warsaw: Państwowy Instytut Wydawniczy, 1966.

———. *Henryk Sienkiewicz: Kalendarz życia i twórczości.* 2d rev. ed. Warsaw: Państwowy Instytut Wydawniczy, 1956.

Kuczała, Barbara. "Odsiecz wiedeńska w twórczości Jana Matejki." *Zeszyty Naukowe Muzeum Historycznego Miasta Krakowa: Krzysztofory* 9 (1982): 31–37.

Kukiel, Marian. *Wskrzeszenie wojska polskiego.* London: Instytut Historyczny im. Gen. Sikorskiego, 1959.

Kułakowski, Marian. *Roman Dmowski w świetle listów i wspomnień.* Vol. 1. Staraniem Instytutu Romana Dmowskiego w Ameryce. London: Gryf, 1968.

Kulczycki, John J. *School Strikes in Prussian Poland, 1901–1907: The Struggle over Bilateral Education.* East European Monographs, Boulder, Colo. New York: Columbia University Press, 1981.

Laqueur, Walter, and George L. Mosse, eds. *Historians in Politics.* London and Beverly Hills, Calif.: Sage Publications, 1974.

Łempicki, Stanisław. *Słowo o Grunwaldzie.* [N.p.]: Czytelnik, 1945.

Łepkowski, Tadeusz. *Polska—narodziny nowoczesnego narodu, 1764–1870.* Warsaw: Państwowe Wydawnictwo Naukowe, 1967.

Leśnodorska, Aleksandra, and Zofia Mleczkówna. "Pomnik Adama Mickiewicza w Krakowie." In *Kraków Mickiewiczowi,* edited by Danuta Rederowa. Kraków: Wydawnictwo Literackie, 1956.

Levi-Strauss, Claude. *Structural Anthropology.* Translated by Claire Jacobson and Brooke Grundest Schoepf. New York: Basic Books, 1963.

Levitt, Marcus C. *Russian Literary Politics and the Pushkin Celebration of 1880.* Ithaca, N.Y.: Cornell University Press, 1989.

Lewis, Bernard. *History—Remembered, Recovered, Invented.* Princeton: Princeton University Press, 1975.

Lichończak, Grażyna. "Pomnik króla Jana III Sobieskiego w Ogrodzie Strzeleckim w Krakowie." *Zeszyty Naukowe Muzeum Historycznego Miasta Krakowa: Krzysztofory* 9 (1982): 56–65.

Lisiak, Henryk. *Paderewski: Od Kuryłówki po Arlington.* Poznań: SAWW, 1992.

———. "Z dziejów walki o narodowe przetrwanie. Obchody pięćsetnej rocznicy bitwy pod Grunwaldem." *Życie i Myśl* 36, no. 12 (1988): 28–34.

Lowenthal, David. "Identity, Heritage, and History." In *Commemorations: The Politics of National Identity,* edited by John R. Gillis. Princeton: Princeton University Press, 1994.

Lukowski, Jerzy. *Liberty's Folly: The Polish-Lithuanian Commonwealth in the Eighteenth Century, 1697–1795.* London and New York: Routledge, 1991.

Maier, Charles S. *The Unmasterable Past: History, Holocaust, and German National Identity.* Cambridge: Harvard University Press, 1988.

Małaczyński, Aleksander. *Jan Styka (szkic biograficzny).* L'viv: Drukarnia Uniwersytecka, 1930.

Markiewicz, Henryk. "Rodowód i losy mitu trzech wieszczów." In *Badania nad krytyką literacką: Seria 2,* edited by M. Głowiński and K. Dybiak. Z Dziejów Form Artystycznych w Literaturze Polskiej, 65. Wrocław: Zakład Narodowy im. Ossolińskich, 1984.

Marschall von Bieberstein, Christoph Freiherr. *Freiheit in der Unfreiheit: Die nationale Autonomie der Polen in Galizien nach dem österreichisch-ungarischen Ausgleich von 1867; Ein konservativer Aufbruch im mitteleuropäischen Vergleich.* Wiesbaden: Harrassowitz Verlag, 1993.

Maurer, Jadwiga. "The Omission of Jewish Topics in Mickiewicz Scholarship." *Polin* 5 (1990): 184–92.

Mendelsohn, Ezra. "Jewish Assimilation in L'viv: The Case of Wilhelm Feldman." In *Nationbuilding and the Politics of Nationalism: Essays on Austrian Galicia,* edited by Andrei S. Markovits and Frank E. Sysyn. Cambridge: distributed by Harvard University Press for the Harvard Ukrainian Research Institute, 1982.

Micewski, Andrzej. *Roman Dmowski.* Warsaw: Wydawnictwo "Verum," 1971.

Micińska, Magdalena. *Gołąb i orzeł: Obchody rocznic kościuszkowskich w latach 1894 i 1917.* Warsaw: Wydawnictwo NERITON, Instytut Historii PAN, 1997.

Mirkiewicz, Marek. "Towarzystwo Gimnastyczne 'Sokół': Mit a rzeczywistość." In *Galicja i jej dziedzictwo,* edited by Andrzej Meissner and Jerzy Wyrozumski. Vol. 3. Rzeszów: Wydawnictwo Wyższej Szkoły Pedagogicznej, 1995.

Molenda, Jan. *Chłopi, naród, niepodległość: Kształtowanie się postaw narodowych i obywatelskich chłopów w Galicji i Królestwie Polskim w przededniu odrodzenia Polski.* Warsaw: Wydawnictwo NERITON, 1999.

———. *Piłsudczycy a Narodowi Demokraci, 1908–1918.* Warsaw: Książka i Wiedza, 1980.

Mosse, George L. *Fallen Soldiers: Reshaping the Memory of the World Wars.* New York: Oxford University Press, 1990.

———. "Mass Politics and the Political Liturgy of Nationalism." In *Nationalism: The Nature and Evolution of an Ideal,* edited by Eugene Kamenka. Canberra: Australian National University Press, 1974.

———. *The Nationalization of the Masses: Political Symbolism and Mass Movements in Germany from the Napoleonic Wars through the Third Reich.* New York: Howard Fertig, 1975.

Mroczko, Marian. *Ziemie dzielnicy pruskiej w polskich koncepcjach i działalności politycznej, 1864–1939.* Gdańsk: Wydawnictwo "Marpress," 1994.

Myśliński, Jerzy. *Grupy polityczne Królestwa Polskiego w zachodniej Galicji, 1895–1904.* Warsaw: Książka i Wiedza, 1967.

Narkiewicz, Olga A. *The Green Flag: Polish Populist Politics, 1867–1970.* London and Totowa, N.J.: Croom Helm and Rowman and Littlefield, 1976.

Nenasheva, Z. S. "Slavianskii s"ezd 1908 g. v Prage i ego mesto v formirovanii ideologii i programmy neoslavisma." In *Slavianskie s"ezdy XIX–XX vv.,* edited by E. P. Aksenova, A. N. Goriatnov, and M. Iu. Dostal'. Moscow: Rossiiskaia akademiia nauk Institut slavianovedeniia i balkanistiki, Nauchnyi tsentr obshcheslavianskikh issledovanii, Mezhdunarodnyi fond iugoslavianskikh issledovanii i sotrudnichestva "Slavianskaia letopis'," 1994.

Nicieja, Stanisław Sławomir. *Cmentarz Łyczakowski we Lwowie w latach 1786–1986.* Wrocław, Warsaw, and Kraków: Zakład Narodowy im. Ossolińskich, 1988.

Nipperdey, Thomas. "Nationalidee und Nationdenkmal in Deutschland in 19. Jahrhundert." *Historische Zeitschrift* (June 1968): 529–85.

Nolte, Claire E. *The Sokol in the Czech Lands to 1914: Training for the Nation.* New York: Palmgrave Macmillan, 2002.

Noltenius, Rainer. "Schiller als Führer und Heiland: Das Schillerfest 1859 als nationaler Traum von der Geburt des zweiten deutschen Kaiserreichs." In *Öffentliche Festkultur: Politische Feste in Deutschland von der Aufklärung bis zum Ersten Weltkrieg,* edited by Dieter Düding, Peter Friedemann, and Paul Munch. Reinbek bei Hamburg: Rowohlt, 1988.

Nora, Pierre. "Between Memory and History." In *Realms of Memory: Rethinking the French Past,* edited by Pierre Nora. Vol. 1. Translated by Arthur Goldhammer. New York: Columbia University Press, 1996.

Nora, Pierre, ed. *Realms of Memory: Rethinking the French Past.* 3 vols. Translated by Arthur Goldhammer. New York: Columbia University Press, 1996.

Nowak, Janusz Tadeusz. "Pogrzeb Juliusza Słowackiego w Krakowie w 1927 r. (w 60-tną rocznicę sprowadzenia prochów wieszcza do kraju)." *Zeszyty Naukowe Muzeum Historycznego Miasta Krakowa: Krzysztofory* 13 (1986): 117–30.

Nowakowska, Wanda. "3 Maja w malarskiej legendzie." In *Konstytucja 3 maja w tradycji i kulturze polskiej,* edited by Alina Barszczewska-Krupa. Łódź: Wydawnictwo Łódzkie, 1991.

Odsiecz wiedeńska 1683: Wystawa jubileuszowa w Zamku Królewskim na Wawelu w trzechsetlecie bitwy. Edited by Jerzy T. Petrus and Magdalena Piwocka. Vol. 1, *Historical Background and Archival Materials.* Kraków: Państwowe zbiory sztuki na Wawelu, 1990.

Oettermann, Stephan. *Das Panorama: Die Geschichte eines Massenmediums.* Frankfurt: Syndikat, 1980.

Öffentliche Festkultur: Politische Feste in Deutschland von der Aufklärung bis zum Ersten Weltkrieg. Edited by Dieter Düding, Peter Friedemann, and Paul Munch. Reinbek bei Hamburg: Rowohlt, 1988.

Ozouf, Mona. *Festivals and the French Revolution.* Translated by Alan Sheridan. Cambridge: Harvard University Press, 1988.

Pastuszka, Stefan J., Józef R. Szaflik, and R. Turkowski. "Chłopi i ruch ludowy w obchodach grunwaldzkich przed 1914 r." In *Tradycja grunwaldzka,* edited by Jerzy Maternicki. Vol. 5. Warsaw: Uniwersytet Warszawski, Zakład Historii Historiografii i Dydaktyki Historii, 1990.

Piekarczyk, Jerzy. "Miejsce dla wieszcza." *Kraków* no. 1 (1986): 33–36.

———. "Powrót Króla-Ducha." *Kraków* no. 4 (1986): 28–31.

———. "Veto prezydenta." *Kraków* no. 3 (1985): 15–18.

Pietrzak, Jerzy. "Podarowanie obrazu 'Sobieski pod Wiedniem' Papieżowi Leonowi XIII: Prawda i mity." In *Z dziejów i tradycji srebrnego wieku,* edited by Jerzy Pietrzak, 156–59. Acta Universitatis Wratislaviensis, no. 1108, Historia 70. Wrocław: Wydawnictwo Uniwersytetu Wrocławskiego, 1990.

———. "Świątynia Opatrzności Bożej." In *Konstytucja 3 Maja z perspektywy dwusetnej rocznicy (1791–1991),* edited by Teresa Kulak. Acta Universitatis Wratislaviensis, no. 1502, Historia 110. Wrocław: Wydawnictwo Uniwersytetu Wrocławskiego, 1993.

Pipes, Richard. *Russia under the Old Regime.* New York: Charles Scribner's Sons, 1974.

Pływawko, Danuta. *"Prusy i Polska": Ankieta Henryka Sienkiewicza (1907–1909).* Poznań: Wielkopolska Agencja Wydawnicza, 1994.

Pobóg-Malinowski, Władysław. *Najnowsza historia polityczna Polski.* 2d ed. Vol. 1, *1864–1914.* London: B. Świderski, 1963.

Pogodin, A. L. *Glavnyia techeniia pol'skoi politicheskoi mysli, 1863–1907 gg.* Sankt-Peterburg: Prosvieshchenie [190–?].

Polski Słownik Biograficzny. Edited by Władysław Konopczyński et al. 40 vols. (to date). Kraków: Gebethner i Wolff, 1935–.

Polskie mity polityczne XIX i XX wieku. Polska myśl polityczna XIX i XX wieku. Edited by Wojciech Wrzesiński. Vol. 9. Wrocław: Wydawnictwo Uniwersytetu Wrocławskiego, 1994.

Poniatowski, Jan. *Panorama racławicka: Przewodnik.* Wrocław: Krajowa Agencja Wydawnicza, 1987.

Porter, Brian A. "The Construction and Deconstruction of Nineteenth-Century Polish Liberalism." In *Historical Reflections on Central Europe: Selected Papers from the Fifth World Congress of Central and East European Studies, Warsaw, 1995,* edited by Stanislav J. Kirschbaum. Houndmills, Basingstoke, Hampshire, and London: St. Martin's Press, 1999.

———. *When Nationalism Began to Hate: Imagining Modern Politics in Nineteenth-Century Poland.* New York and Oxford: Oxford University Press, 2000.

Purchla, Jacek. *Matecznik polski: Pozaekonomiczne czynniki rozwoju Krakowa w okresie autonomii galicyjskiej.* Kraków: Wydawnictwo Znak, 1992.

———. "W stulecie powszechnej wystawy krajowej we Lwowie 1894 roku." *Cracovia Leopolis* 2 (1995): 6–7.

Radziwiłłowicz, Dariusz. "Rola tradycji grunwaldzkiej w działalności wychowawczej niektórych polskich organizacji zbrojnych w latach pierwszej wojny światowej." In *Tradycja grunwaldzka,* edited by Jerzy Maternicki. Vol. 5. Warsaw: Uniwersytet Warszawski, Zakład Historii Historiografii i Dydaktyki Historii, 1990.

Rearick, Charles. "Festivals and Politics: The Michelet Centennial of 1898." In *Historians in Politics,* edited by Walter Laqueur and George L. Mosse. London and Beverly Hills, Calif.: Sage Publications, 1974.

———. "Festivals in Modern France: The Experience of the Third Republic." *Journal of Contemporary History* 12 (1977): 435–60.

Rodkiewicz, Witold. *Russian Nationality Policy in the Western Provinces of the Empire (1863–1905).* Lublin: Scientific Society of Lublin, 1998.

Rolnik, Dariusz. "Obchody setnej rocznicy insurekcji kościuszkowskiej w Galicji." In *200 rocznica powstania kościuszkowskiego,* edited by Henryk Kocój. Prace Naukowe Uniwersytetu Śląskiego w Katowicach, no. 1407. Katowice: Wydawnictwo Uniwersytetu Śląskiego, 1994.

Rosiek, Stanisław. *Zwłoki Mickiewicza: Próba nekrografii poety.* Gdańsk: Słowo/Obraz Terytoria, 1997.

Rousso, Henry. *The Vichy Syndrome: History and Memory in France since 1944.* Translated by Arthur Goldhammer. Cambridge: Harvard University Press, 1991.

Rożek, Michał. *Królewska katedra na Wawelu.* Warsaw: Wydawnictwo Interpress, 1981.

———. *Tradycja wiedeńska w Krakowie.* Kraków: Krajowa Agencja Wydawnicza, 1983.

Ruble, Blair. *Second Metropolis: Pragmatic Pluralism in Gilded Age Chicago, Silver Age Moscow, and Meiji Osaka.* Washington, D.C., New York, and Cambridge: Woodrow Wilson Center Press and Cambridge University Press, 2001.

Sahlins, Peter. *Boundaries: The Making of France and Spain in the Pyrenees.* Berkeley and Los Angeles: University of California Press, 1989.

Sawicka, Franciszka. "Setna rocznica Konstytucji 3 Maja w świetle wydawnictw pamiątkowych." In *Konstytucja 3 Maja z perspektywy dwusetnej rocznicy (1791–1991),* edited by Teresa Kulak. Acta Universitatis Wratislaviensis, no. 1502, Historia 110. Wrocław: Wydawnictwo Uniwersytetu Wrocławskiego, 1993.

Sheehan, James. "What Is German History? Reflections on the Role of the *Nation* in German History and Historiography." *Journal of Modern History* 53 (March 1981): 1–23.

Siemann, Wolfram. "Krieg und Frieden in historischen Gedenkfeiern des Jahres 1913." In *Öffentliche Festkultur: Politische Feste in Deutschland von der Aufklärung bis zum Ersten Weltkrieg,* edited by Dieter Düding, Peter Friedemann, and Paul Munch. Reinbek bei Hamburg: Rowohlt, 1988.

Sierżęga, Paweł. "Centralny komitet jubileuszowy w przygotowaniach obchodów 200. rocznicy odsieczy wiedeńskiej w Galicji." In *Z przeszłości Europy Środkowowschodniej,* edited by Jadwiga Hoff, 76–99. Rzeszów: Wydawnictwo Uniwersytetu Rzeszowskiego, 2002.

Snyder, Timothy. *The Reconstruction of Nations: Poland, Ukraine, Lithuania, Belarus, 1569–1999.* New Haven: Yale University Press, 2002.

Solak, Zbigniew. "Obchody grunwaldzkie w listach Mariana Zdziechowskiego." *Studia Historyczne* 36, no. 3 (1993): 353–70.

Sperber, Jonathan. "Festivals of National Unity in the German Revolution of 1848/49." *Past and Present* 136 (1992): 114–38.

Śreniowska, Krystyna. *Kościuszko bohater narodowy: Opinie współczesnych i potomnych, 1794–1946.* Warsaw: Państwowe Wydawnictwo Naukowe, 1973.

Stachowska, Krystyna. "Materiały." In *Kraków Mickiewiczowi,* edited by Danuta Rederowa. Kraków: Wydawnictwo Literackie, 1956.

Stauter-Halsted, Keely. *The Nation in the Village: The Genesis of Peasant National Identity in Austrian Poland, 1848–1914.* Ithaca, N.Y.: Cornell University Press, 2001.

———. "Patriotic Celebrations in Austrian Poland: The Kościuszko Centennial and the Formation of Peasant Nationalism." *Austrian History Yearbook* 25 (1994): 79–95.

———. "Rural Myth and the Modern Nation: Peasant Commemorations of Polish National Holidays, 1879–1910." In *Staging the Past: The Politics of Commemoration in Habsburg Central Europe, 1848 to the Present,* edited by Maria Bucur and Nancy M. Wingfield. West Lafayette, Ind.: Purdue University Press, 2001.

Stekl, Hannes. "Öffentliche Gedenktage und gesellschaftliche Identitäten." In *Der Kampf um das Gedächtnis: Öffentliche Gedenktage in Mitteleuropa,* edited by Emil Brix and Hannes Stekl. Vienna, Cologne, and Weimar: Böhlau Verlag, 1997.

Świątecka, Maria. "Sprowadzenie zwłok Adama Mickiewicza do kraju." In *Kraków Mickiewiczowi,* edited by Danuta Rederowa. Kraków: Wydawnictwo Literackie, 1956.

Szablowski, J. "Obchody jubileuszowe zwycięstwa pod Wiedniem w 1683 roku w ciągu trzech stuleci." In *Odsiecz Wiedeńska 1683: Wystawa jubileuszowa w Zamku Królewskim na Wawelu w trzechsetlecie bitwy,* edited by Jerzy T. Petrus and Magdalena Piwocka. Vol. 1. Kraków: Państwowe zbiory sztuki na Wawelu, 1990.

Szacki, Jerzy. *Ojczyzna, naród, rewolucja: Problematyka narodowa w polskiej myśli szlacheckorewolucyjnej.* Warsaw: Państwowy Instytut Wydawniczy, 1962.

Szaflik, Józef Ryszard. "Czynniki kształtujące świadomość narodową chłopa polskiego w końcu XIX i w początkach XX wieku." *Przegląd Humanistyczny* 26, no. 12 (1982): 1–15, and 27, no. 4 (1983): 43–82.

———. *O rząd chłopskich dusz.* Warsaw: Ludowa Spółdzielnia Wydawnicza, 1976.

Szarkowa, Joanna. "Obchody rocznic narodowych w działalności propagandowej Naczelnego Komitetu Narodowego (1914–1917)." *Rocznik Biblioteki PAN w Krakowie* 39 (1994): 181–95.

Szporluk, Roman. "Polish-Ukrainian Relations in 1918: Notes for Discussion." In *The Reconstruction of Poland, 1914–23,* edited by Paul Latawski. London: Macmillan, in association with the School of Slavonic and East European Studies, University of London, 1992.

———. "Ukraine: From an Imperial Periphery to a Sovereign State." *Daedalus* (summer 1997): 85–119.

Szubert, Piotr. "Pomnik Adama Mickiewicza w Wilnie." *Blok-notes Muzeum A. Mickiewicza w Warszawie* 9 (1988): 195–236.

Terlecki, Ryszard. *Oświata dorosłych i popularyzacja nauki w Galicji w okresie autonomii.* Wrocław: Zakład Narodowy im. Ossolińskich, 1990.

Thomas, William I., and Florian Znaniecki. *The Polish Peasant in Europe and America.* 2 vols. New York: A. A. Knopf, 1927.

Tomczyk, Roman. "Praojcom na chwałę braciom na otuchę." *Tygodnik Powszechny* 30, no. 37 (1976): 8, 6.

Tradycja grunwaldzka. Edited by Jerzy Maternicki. 5 vols. Warsaw: Uniwersytet Warszawski, Zakład Historii Historiografii i Dydaktyki Historii, 1989–90.

Treiderowa, Anna. *Obchody Grunwaldzkie w Krakowie (1410–1910)*. Kraków Dawniej i Dziś 13. Kraków: nakładem Towarzystwa Miłośników Historii i Zabytków Krakowa, 1961.

Trzeciakowski, Lech. *Pod pruskim zaborem, 1850–1918*. Warsaw: Wiedza Powszechna, 1973.

Unowsky, Daniel. "Reasserting Empire: Habsburg Imperial Celebrations after the Revolutions of 1848–1849." In *Staging the Past: The Politics of Commemoration in Habsburg Central Europe, 1848 to the Present*, edited by Maria Bucur and Nancy M. Wingfield. West Lafayette, Ind.: Purdue University Press, 2001.

Urbańczyk, Andrzej. "To było w 1910 roku. Kto sfilmował?" *Kraków* no. 1 (1990): 15–17.

Urbankowski, Bohdan. *Filozofia czynu: Światopogląd Józefa Piłsudskiego*. Warsaw: Pelikan, 1988.

Vietig, Jürgen. "Die polnischen Grunwaldfeiern der Jahre 1902 und 1910." In *Germania Slavica II,* edited by Wolfgang H. Fritz. Berliner Historische Studien, Band 4. Berlin: Duncker and Humblot, 1981.

Vyšný, Paul. *Neo-Slavism and the Czechs, 1898–1914*. Cambridge, London, New York, and Melbourne: Cambridge University Press, 1977.

Walichnowski, Tadeusz. "Grunwald w świadomości współczesnych pokoleń Polaków." In Marian Biskup, Andrzej F. Grabski, Alfons Klafkowski, Henryk Samsonowicz, Tadeusz Walichnowski, *Grunwald w świadomości Polaków*. Warsaw and Łódź: Państwowe Wydawnictwo Naukowe, 1981.

Walicki, Andrzej. *Philosophy and Romantic Nationalism: The Case of Poland*. Oxford: Clarendon Press; New York: Oxford University Press, 1982.

———. *Poland between East and West: The Controversies Over Self-Definition and Modernization in Partitioned Poland*. Harvard Papers in Ukrainian Studies. Cambridge: Ukrainian Research Institute, Harvard University, 1994.

Wandycz, Piotr S. *The Lands of Partitioned Poland, 1795–1918*. A History of East Central Europe, edited by Peter F. Sugar and Donald W. Treadgold. Vol. 7. Seattle and London: University of Washington Press, 1974.

———. *The Price of Freedom: A History of East Central Europe from the Middle Ages to the Present*. London and New York: Routledge, 1992.

Wapiński, Roman. "Mit dawnej Rzeczypospolitej w epoce porozbiorowej." In *Polskie mity polityczne XIX i XX wieku,* edited by Wojciech Wrzesiński. Polska myśl polityczna XIX i XX wieku. Vol. 9. Wrocław: Wydawnictwo Uniwersytetu Wrocławskiego, 1994.

———. *Polska i małe ojczyzny Polaków: Z dziejów kształtowania się świadomości narodowej w XIX i XX wieku po wybuch II wojny światowej*. Wrocław, Warsaw, and Kraków: Zakład Narodowy imi. Ossolińskich, 1994.

———. *Roman Dmowski*. Lublin: Wydawnictwo Lubelskie, 1988.

Wątor, Adam. *Działalność Stronnictwa Demokratyczno-Narodowego w zaborze austriackim do roku 1914*. Uniwersytet Szczeciński. Rozprawy i studia, vol. (206) 132. Szczecin: Wydawnictwo Naukowe Uniwersytetu Szczecińskiego, 1993.

Wawrzykowska-Wierciochowa, Dioniza. *Nie rzucim ziemi, skąd nasz ród . . .* Warsaw: Wydawnictwo Ministerstwa Obrony Narodowej, 1988.

Weber, Eugen. *Peasants into Frenchmen: The Modernization of Rural France, 1870–1914*. Stanford, Calif.: Stanford University Press, 1976.

Weeks, Theodore R. "Monuments and Memory: Immortalizing Count M. N. Muraviev in Vilna, 1898." *Nationalities Papers* 27, no. 4 (1999): 551–64.

———. *Nation and State in Late Imperial Russia: Nationalism and Russification on the Western Frontier, 1863–1914*. DeKalb: Northern Illinois University Press, 1996.

Wereszycki, Henryk. "Międzynarodowe echa jubileuszu Kraszewskiego w 1879 roku." *Dzieje Najnowsze* 6, no. 3 (1974): 3–20.

Wic, Władysław. "Młodzi socjaliści galicyjscy wobec tradycji grunwaldzkiej." In *Tradycja grunwaldzka,* edited by Jerzy Maternicki. Vol. 4. Warsaw: Uniwersytet Warszawski, Zakład Historii Historiografii i Dydaktyki Historii, 1990.

———. "Stosunek Polskiej Partii Socjalno-Demokratycznej Galicji i Śląska do obchodów grunwaldzkich." In *Tradycja Grunwaldzka,* edited by Jerzy Maternicki. Vol. 2. Warsaw: Uniwersytet Warszawski, Zakład Historii Historiografii i Dydaktyki Historii, 1990.

Wielebska, Zofia. "Obchody 400-lecia śmierci Jana Długosza." In *Jan Długosz: W pięćset-ną rocznicę śmierci; materiały z sesji (Sandomierz 24–25 maja 1980 r.),* edited by F. Kiryk. Olsztyn: Polskie Tow. Historyczne, 1983.

Winnicka, Halina. "Socjaliści polscy wobec Adama Mickiewicza: Przewiezienie zwłok poety do kraju (1890 r.)." *Przegląd Humanistyczny* 21, no. 9 (1977): 53–63.

———. "Socjaliści wobec Adama Mickiewicza: Stulecie urodzin poety." *Przegląd Humanistyczny* 22, no. 1 (1978): 137–56.

Wnuk, Włodzimierz. *Na góralską nutę.* Warsaw: Instytut Wydawniczy PAX, 1975.

———. "Ruch regionalny." In *Zakopane: Czterysta lat dziejów,* edited by Renata Dutkowa. Vol. 1. Kraków: Krajowa Agencja Wydawnicza, 1991.

Wolff, Larry. *Inventing Eastern Europe: The Map of Civilization on the Mind of the Enlightenment.* Stanford, Calif.: Stanford University Press, 1994.

Wolsza, Tadeusz. *Narodowa Demokracja wobec chłopów w latach 1887–1914: Programy, polityka, działalność.* Warsaw: Ludowa Spółdzielnia Wydawnicza, 1992.

Wortman, Richard. "Moscow and Petersburg: The Problem of Political Center in Tsarist Russia, 1881–1914." In *Rites of Power: Symbolism, Ritual, and Politics since the Middle Ages,* edited by Sean Wilentz. Philadelphia: University of Pennsylvania Press, 1985.

———. *Scenarios of Power: Myth and Ceremony in Russian Monarchy.* 2 vols. Princeton: Princeton University Press, 1995–2000.

Wrzesiński, Wojciech, ed. *Polskie mity polityczne XIX i XX wieku.* Vol. 9, *Polska myśl polityczna XIX i XX wieku.* Wrocław: Wydawnictwo Uniwersytetu Wrocławskiego, 1994.

Żaliński, Henryk. "Grunwald i polityka niemiecka w krakowskich kalendarzach (1848–1914)." In *Tradycja grunwaldzka,* edited by Jerzy Maternicki. Vol. 2. Warsaw: Uniwersytet Warszawski, Zakład Historii Historiografii i Dydaktyki Historii, 1990.

Zerubavel, Yael. *Recovered Roots: Collective Memory and the Making of Israeli National Tradition.* Chicago: University of Chicago Press, 1994.

Ziejka, Franciszek. "Krakowscy pątnicy." In *Klejnoty i sekrety Krakowa,* edited by Róża Godula. Kraków: Wydawnictwo Wawelskie, 1994.

———. *Panorama racławicka.* Kraków: Krajowa Agencja Wydawnicza, 1984.

———. "Racławicka legenda." In *W kręgu Panoramy Racławickiej,* edited by Bożena Steinborn. Wrocław: Zakład Narodowy im. Ossolińskich, 1985.

———. *Złota legenda chłopów polskich.* Warsaw: Państwowy Instytut Wydawniczy, 1984.

Zlat, Mieczysław. "Wstęp." In *W kręgu Panoramy Racławickiej,* edited by Bożena Steinborn. Wrocław: Zakład Narodowy im. Ossolińskich, 1985.

Żmichrowska, Maria Jolanta. *Towarzystwo Szkoły Ludowej (1891–1939).* Olsztyn: Wyższa Szkoła Pedagogiczna w Olsztynie, 1992.

Żychowski, Marian. *Polska myśl socjalistyczna XIX i XX wieku: Do 1918 r.* Warsaw: Państwowe Wydawnictwo Naukowe, 1976.

INDEX

Page numbers in italics refer to illustrations.

Patrice M. Dabrowski is a historian of Central and Eastern Europe. She has degrees in Slavic languages and literature (Harvard/Radcliffe), international relations (the Fletcher School of Law and Diplomacy), and history (Harvard University) and has taught at Harvard and Brown. Dabrowski is currently a postdoctoral fellow at the Watson Institute for International Studies at Brown University, where she is working on an international and multidisciplinary research project entitled "Borderlands: Ethnicity, Identity, and Violence in the Shatter-Zone of Empires Since 1848."